Robert Grant Webster

The Trade of the World

Our Present System of Commerce Examined

Robert Grant Webster

The Trade of the World
Our Present System of Commerce Examined

ISBN/EAN: 9783744725965

Printed in Europe, USA, Canada, Australia, Japan

Cover: Foto ©ninafisch / pixelio.de

More available books at **www.hansebooks.com**

THE

TRADE OF THE WORLD.

OUR PRESENT SYSTEM OF COMMERCE

EXAMINED.

BY

ROBERT G WEBSTER, LL.B.,

Of the Inner Temple, Barrister-at-Law,

(Author of " The Amalgamation of the British Army," &c.)

LONDON:
DAVID BOGUE, 3, ST. MARTIN'S PLACE, TRAFALGAR SQUARE.
1880.

THE RIGHT OF TRANSLATION AND REPRODUCTION IS RESERVED.

PREFACE.

IN placing these pages before the British public I wish to state that they have not been written to support the views of any party. I am well aware that from this fact I necessarily lay myself doubly open to the attacks that anyone is sure to entail on himself who boldly and conscientiously utters the thought that is in him, who dares to emerge in the slightest degree from the accepted commonplace of this age.

In this work I have endeavoured to examine what have been the general conditions of our commercial relations with the world for the last few years, and our prospects for the future, without narrowly looking at any fortuitous circumstances which may cause it to be prosperous or the reverse during any given month or other comparatively short period of time. That our trade has been decreasing in amount for the last few years admits of no doubt. The present indications of its revival, if they have solid foundations, and are not ephemeral, cannot fail to be a matter of sincere congratulation for us all, in showing the existence of a natural demand for our products in spite of all barriers placed against their sale.

The great question to be solved, it appears to me, is not under what system are we most likely to have single years of prosperity followed by four or five years of stagnation ; but, how we can preserve a steady, continuous, and, if possible, an increasing commercial intercourse both with foreign nations and our own colonies.

Latterly, our thoughts have naturally been mainly turned to our armies in Africa and Afghanistan; in common with, I may say nearly every Englishman, I have eagerly scanned the telegrams from St. Vincent telling us how our brave soldiers were faring at the Cape, heartily regretted to see the news of a disaster, and scanned with deep pleasure the accounts of a success; e'en as I write these lines many an anxious heart at home must be with our armies near Cabul.

But it seems to me evident that sooner or later our trade relations with the rest of the world will have to engage our most earnest attention, and when that day arrives we shall have to meet that question as fearlessly as our soldiers have met their foes.

It has been my endeavour to discuss this question in a perfectly unbiassed manner, yet whilst freely admitting that Universal Free Trade is the great end and object to be aimed at, I possibly differ from many as to the most practical way of attaining it; since my study of political economy whilst at Cambridge failed to indoctrinate me with a dogma which would seem to be held by many at present, that an infallible system can be invented to attain this desired end, and to suit all countries in all ages. I should perhaps also apologize to those who apparently believe that political economy, like mechanics, is simply a theoretical science; for, making use of facts which have come under my own personal experience in various countries which it has been my fortune to reside in or visit; I humbly submit that a great question like this can only be studied in the actual world. And that it is still open to enquiry, when we examine our present commercial relations, and bear in mind the Protectionist import duties charged by America, Russia, Germany, Canada, Victoria, Spain (I trust I may not have soon to add France to this list), whether we have Free Trade or not, or whether we are only allowed to participate in the overflow of their commerce when it breaks over the barriers of their Protective systems.

In the following pages "this year" refers to 1879. I am glad to be able to take this opportunity of most cordially thanking both my personal friends and those foreign and colonial officials who have kindly given me information on the subjects herein referred to.

9, King's Bench Walk,
    Temple, E.C.,
        December 24th, 1879.

TABLE OF CONTENTS.

		PAGE
Chapter I.—	Introductory	1
Chapter II.—	Rise of our Present System of Commerce	32
Chapter III.—	On International Trade and Reciprocity	47
Chapter IV.--	General Survey of Our Trade with Foreign Nations	63
	(i) France	69
	(ii) Germany	87
	(iii) United States	96
	(iv) South American and Mexico	125
	(v) Italy	146
	(vi) Norway and Sweden	150
	(vii) Spain and Portugal	151
	(viii) Holland	156
	(ix) Denmark	161
	(x) Austro-Hungary	162
	(xi) Belgium	172
	(xii) Russia	178
	(xiii) Turkey and Egypt	193
Chapter V.—	Interchange with the Colonies	200
Chapter VI.—	Canada	206

CONTENTS.

		PAGE
Chapter VII.— Australia and New Zealand		226
(i) New South Wales		229
(ii) Victoria		241
(iii) New Zealand		254
(iv) Queensland		261
(v) South Australia		264
(vi) West Australia		265
(vii) Tasmania		266
Chapter VIII.—South Africa and her Colonies		269
Chapter IX.— British India		279
Chapter X.— Straits Settlements		309
Hong Kong		316
China		317
Japan		335
Chapter XI.— Our External Food Supply		357
Chapter XII.— A Free Trade Zollverein		377

APPENDICES.

I.— German Tariff (Past and Present)	425
II.— Canadian Tariff (Past and Present)	431
III.— British Export Trade to Australia and New Zealand	432
IV.— Sources of our Food Supply; and British and American Grain Crops	433
V.— Treaties of Commerce and Navigation between Great Britain and Foreign Powers	438
VI.— Provisional Commercial Agreement between the British and French Governments	440
VII.— The Opium Trade to China	441
VIII.—British Board of Trade Returns	444

THE TRADE OF THE WORLD.

CHAPTER I.

INTRODUCTORY.

To AN inquiring mind the present condition of this country cannot fail to be a subject of great interest. Many ask: Is the present depression of trade to be merely temporary, and will it soon pass away and trade revive, as it has done often and often before; or, on the other hand, are there causes at work which may prevent a thorough revival of prosperity in this country, and even cause us to gradually sink in the scale of mercantile nations, and become a second Holland?

It does not require one to travel far, or to take any particular line of railway, to see evidences—apparent to all—of the present depression in nearly every description of business. To quote an instance. I was myself passing through Sheffield not long ago, and, meeting a friend on the platform, remarked to him, 'How much clearer than I previously remember it your atmosphere seems to be.' 'Yes,' he said, 'and I'll tell you the reason of that. More than half our furnaces and smelting works are blown out.' This set me thinking, and I asked myself the question: Ought this at any time to be the condition of an important branch of industry in this hitherto, on the whole, prosperous country? I resolved to study the question, and in this small work I have endeavoured to describe truthfully—and I trust clearly—the present condition of our trade with our colonies and the rest of the world.

I am, however, met with a difficulty at the outset. In what spirit, it will be asked, are you about to inquire into and discuss our trade prospects? As a Free Trader or a Protectionist? For some leading authorities will not allow the large number of individuals who hold views in favour of reciprocity any title but that of 'Veiled Protectionists.' Indeed, the *Times* has gone so far as to state in a leading article, that any statesman adopting these views would be certain to entail on himself 'ridicule and failure.' In fact, Free Traders of the present day, unlike Adam Smith and John Stuart Mill, whose practice it was to prove their propositions by argument and logic, advance the monstrously absurd doctrine that all who dare to differ from them are fools.

I will, therefore, simply say that though I do not worship as a fetish that one-sided Free Trade we chance to possess, I most willingly admit that great evils might arise if we resorted to the old system known as Protection. The object of this work is simply to endeavour to ascertain what are the means best adapted to *preserve and increase* the trade of this country. Whoever solves that question — and I cannot help thinking that the question is worth inquiring into, even if it should be solved, as many hope, by a revival of trade after a certain number of years of depression—will certainly not deserve the ridicule, even if he does not earn the gratitude of thousands, including amongst others our iron-workers, whose pay in some districts, owing to the fact that so many were out of employment, averaged only twopence per day last November.

Cannot the question be asked now which Cobden asked in 1843, when he made one of his earliest speeches in favour of Free Trade: 'What do you now think of the condition of our trade, and the condition of our country? It is time to give up bandying the terms Whig and Tory, and engage in a serious inquiry into the condition of the country.'

Some of those engaged in the different industries in England at present not in a prosperous condition, such as the iron, coal, cotton, linen, silk, sugar, and other trades, may well say, now: 'Let us not bandy names, and call one another Free Traders or Protectionists, but let us freely and openly discuss the question, and see whether we can mend matters by any change in our system; or whether, on the other hand, our best policy will not be to let "well alone."' For it would seem to be within the power of any nation to either change or amend its system of trade, in the way which it considers would be in every respect most conducive to its own interests; though no change should, of course, be made without duly weighing all the probable consequences, both for the present and the future.

It would seem to be a view in favour of which there is a consensus of opinion in this country, that the best condition of things, not only for our own commerce but for that of the whole world, would be one in which every country should become an open market for the goods of all other nations. That such is not the case at present is evident. In fact, the open markets are rapidly becoming fewer than they were a few years back, and the only question that remains to be solved is: By what means, and in what way, is such a condition of things to be attained?

This is not a time in which we can afford to sit down

and fold our hands, and rely upon the fact that for several years past we have held almost undisputed supremacy in the commercial world. There can be no doubt that competition is now keener than it has hitherto been in all branches of industry, and that the tendency is to reduce all profits to a minimum; though whether this is a necessary result of the general increase of wealth throughout the world, as has been held by some political economists, appears to admit of much doubt.

Mr. Wakefield's explanation of the cause of the fall of profits seems to be not only clearly put, but the true one. It is, briefly, this: Production is limited, not only by the quantity of capital and labour, but also by the extent of the 'field of employment.' The field of employment for capital is two-fold—the land of the country, and the *capacity of foreign countries* to take its manufactured commodities. On a limited extent of land only a limited quantity of capital can find employment at a profit. As the quantity of capital approaches this limit, profit falls; when it is fuller attained, profit is annihilated, and can only be restored through an extension of the field of employment, either by the acquisition of fertile lands or by the opening of new markets in foreign countries, from which food and materials can be purchased with the products of domestic capital.

The fact remains: competition is greater now than it has ever been known to be before in all our branches of industry; nor can we shut our eyes to the fact that it is more likely to increase than to decrease. Nearly all the reports from our Embassies, Legations, and Consulates tell the same tale. All nations are seeking for new markets and 'fields of employment,' each striving to push its trade for its produce, and to secure a larger proportion of the commerce of the world.

As I shall have occasion to refer to this point again, I will now only quote one instance—America—and give an extract from a report from our Legation at Washington, made by Mr. Victor Drummond, May 17th, 1878 :—

'As to American competition in trade at the present time, if our employers and employed hold true to themselves, there is not much fear of any decrease in our trade, owing to many causes now existing here :—depression in trade in comparison with production and to what can be produced, caused by onerous taxes; endless failures; the unsettled state of the labour market; the withholding of capital, from the very uncertain results of the future of the silver bill and the resumption of specie payments; over-production; the dangers of the communistical, socialistical movement, probably receiving accession to its ranks from the number of people out of work, and caused, curiously enough, by a great abundance.' Mr. David Wells forcibly illustrates the position of a nation whose products cannot find a market :—'In the midst of our abundance there is no demand for our abundance, therefore labour and machinery employed in production *cease to find* employment;' whilst Mr. Drummond points out that there is possibly reason why American manufacturers can compete with ours in a small way at home; owing to our free-trade principle and the low shipping freight, part of the surplus stock *which cannot be disposed of* here is sent over and *sold to us at low rates*. He also adds :—' Thus there is little cause of anxiety for our carrying trade or commercial interests. This depends, however, on our labouring class accepting the reduced wages offered to them by their employers, until the latter have reduced their supplies. If they do this we have nothing to fear. But if, with our eyes wide open to what is going on around us, we give a loophole to competition in our cotton and woollen interests with the enterprizing manufacturers on this side the Atlantic, a great portion of the labouring class employed in our mills will discover that they will soon have to look for some other kind of employment. If the manufacturers here, who are suffering from a depression of trade, see their opportunity, and have a chance of putting on their machines and hands at full time, instead of half and three-quarters, they will be sure to do so. The working class must consent to the stern facts of the case, and remember that there is distress in nearly every country in the world just now, and that the conditions of trade prevent their employers giving the ordinary wages ; that if they did so, they would be paying out of their capital, and producing and selling at a loss, and one fine day they would find the mills closed, perhaps never to be opened again, and that then there would be no wages at all.

'It is very sad that it should be so, but such is the case. Economy is what must be carried out by all classes until this critical crisis we are rushing through is a thing of the past. At the same time we must consider and watch carefully the present, and look to brighter commercial prospects in the future. Whether we are still to hold British pre-eminence in our trade with other countries and our own possessions, or to succumb through our own fault, remains to be seen. *It depends entirely on our workmen*, who have been Britain's pride for years ; whose national character for *energy, honesty,* and *determination* for their just rights, mingles with an amount of common sense which makes them view matters conscientiously and with correct judgment, and saves them from many of the miseries their fellow-workmen in other countries often suffer from.'

He also adds the following extract from the *National Republic* of May 20th, 1878, which fully shows the smartness of the United States Consuls in England, as the information must have been sent by telegraph: —'The department of state has advices from London to the effect that the recent strikes of British operatives have had a beneficial effect to American producers in encouraging the manufacturers of this country.'

This shows plainly enough how clearly foreign nations see the result of the strife between capital and labour in this country, and how, whichever wins, the almost immediate result is the driving of some portion of the trade from our shores. English workmen should understand that, however hard it is to work for less wages than they formerly received during the most prosperous years, their lot is no harder than that of the workmen of every nation of the civilized world, and that since 1873 wages have decreased more or less everywhere.

'The reduction of wages mania,' as it has been called, is not peculiar to Lancashire or even to England, but is universal. To give an instance from our formidable competitor in the iron trade—Belgium. Wages of skilled labour stood in 1872 at 11 francs, in 1876 at five francs, and in 1877 at four francs, or only *three shillings and fourpence per day.*

Business can never flourish unless the masters can make a profit. This the Belgian workmen see; they do not strike, for they have to support themselves if they do, and are not supported in idleness on the rates levied upon the masters and the tradespeople whom the strike is ruining. Belgian ouvriers work twelve hours a day, six days a week. That is, they accept the inevitable, and work longer hours than Englishmen of the same class do. Due allowance being made for the oft-time quoted superior strength and skill of our artizans, it is a question if the greatest production is obtained by such heavy and grinding labour. Quite as much work would probably be done in the course of a year by a given number of men labouring for ten hours a day only, as by a like number working for twelve hours daily; the reason being that in the one case the strain upon their physical system would not be so great as in the other, and that they would not only accomplish more whilst they were actually employed, but would be less frequently absent through sickness. The fact, however, still remains, that whilst trade is depressed as it now is, the workmen must accept such terms as will leave the masters a profit, or they may drive English capital into Belgium or elsewhere.

Again, capital moves more easily than formerly, and will do so wherever it can find the cheapest raw materials and labour and the best markets, and where it can also find the security which we fortunately possess in this country, against the wrong-doing of the Government. Capitalists are, in fact, becoming more cosmopolitan, and have been known to accept smaller profits in changing their business, when by doing so they became less liable to be harassed by perpetual strikes. The following is an instance of this. In the north of England, a shipbuilder, who had for two years kept his shipyard working at a loss, hoping for better times, accepted a contract from a foreign government to build three vessels, binding himself down to have them finished by a certain time, as is usual in such cases—this fact being known to his workpeople; the result was, they at once struck for higher wages. He sent for them, and showing them his books, proved that even at their present wages, he had barely allowed himself any margin for profit, and had accepted the contract more to keep his works together and his workmen employed than for any other reason. They, however, persisted in their demand, saying that was his business, and that all they required was higher wages. Finding that the forfeit would entail a heavier loss than the rise in wages, he consented to give it, and built the ships, but immediately after their completion he withdrew his capital, and started a business in France, where he was less liable to the risks and the annoyance of constant strikes.

At one time in France disputes between workmen and masters were settled by a council called 'Prud'hommes,' and I believe the same friendly method is still in vogue in that country. We all know that great and permanent damage has been done to various trades in this country through the action of the workmen in allowing themselves to be led by certain unscrupulous agitators to attempt to wring from their masters higher terms than the state of the trade would warrant. Thus, the Thames shipbuilding trade was entirely destroyed by the action of trades unions. It is a well-known fact that shortly before the closing of several yards on the Thames they had offered to them, both from this country and abroad, large orders which they could not undertake unless the men moderated their demands for increased wages. This the men refused to do, and so the orders were declined and the trade transferred to the Clyde.

Mr. Bromley Davenport reminds us, in a letter published in January last, that the same thing, or nearly the same, has occurred in Warwickshire, in respect to the coal and iron trades. Those who are chiefly responsible for the privations and distress now so prevalent amongst us are such men as Mr. MacDonald. He advised them when there was a good chance of a resumption of work after a long strike to continue the strike, 'though they should turn Warwickshire into a desert for the next twenty years.'

During the strike which occurred last summer in the Durham district, the greatest coal-field in the world, it appears that at Elsworth, one of the largest mines at which the dispute has arisen, the men struck work and brought their gear out of the pit. The result of certain miners not 'standing by the union,' and respecting the right every Englishman has to sell his labour to whom he sees fit, is thus described by the *Times* of last April:—

On Monday, however, about 60 broke off from the union arrangement and went to work. This defection caused much discontent among the union men. As two hewers named James Ramshaw and Simon Crane were proceeding to the pit on Monday they were assailed by a mob of between 100 and 200 men and seriously ill-used. The following is a description of subsequent scenes which occurred at the same colliery on Monday night and Tuesday :—
About 9 o'clock on Monday night the cottages of those who had gone to work were visited by the strike hands, and the windows and doors were broken and smashed to pieces. There were only two policemen present, and it was with the greatest difficulty they made the crowd disperse. About 100 men all told returned to work on Tuesday morning. The rioting commenced about 11 o'clock, when Police-constables Carruthers and Brians were attacked with stones, &c. In the afternoon a meeting of the strike hands was held, and they seemed determined to resist the reduction. Shortly after the conclusion of the meeting, a party of young men visited the house of one of the men for the purpose of inducing him to remain out; but the man refused to listen to the 'deputation,' and told them to keep off, at the same time threatening to use a gun which he had in his hand. The party closed with the man, taking the gun from him, and fired it off. The gun was broken to pieces, and the windows and doors of the house smashed. Another house was entered, and the occupants seized the poker wherewith to defend themselves. A regular *mêlée*

ensued, and the furniture in the house was smashed. Stones were thrown into the houses of the men who had returned to work by the strike hands. About 3 o'clock Superintendent Woods and a number of men arrived on the scene, at which time the rioters seemed to have the upper hand. A bold front was put on by the officer and constables, and the rioters seemed to be cowed by their determination. Between 5 and 6 o'clock, as several men were leaving the pit, they were assailed with a shower of bricks and slag. A fireman was followed by the strike hands and very much ill-used.

The question how to *preserve* and increase, if possible, our trade affects not only iron-masters, cotton spinners, and manufacturing labourers, but every member of the community. Landlords who have their farms let on long leases, and who have not yet experienced the difficulty, as many *already have*, of obtaining new tenants at the same, or, in many instances, at any rent, must not say: 'Oh, this is no business of ours; you invented this system of Free Trade in Manchester, and you must make the best of it.' It is very much their interest to inquire into this question, and to acknowledge that land and trade are twins and have always been so, and always will wax and wane together. It cannot be ill with trade but land will fall; nor ill with land but trade will feel it. By that, I do not mean to go so far as Mr. Samuel Jones Lloyd, who is quoted as follows by Richard Cobden, in a speech delivered in London in 1843 :—

'As an Englishman, I may be proud of the town and trade of Manchester. [Again, the prosperity of Manchester is another expression for the well-being of England.] When that great town, and the immense population dependent on it, cease to advance in prosperity and wealth, the star of England has culminated. Failing trade will soon undermine the foundation on which every other interest rests. Our teeming population, deprived of employment, will soon convert this fair and happy land into a warren of paupers. Nor can the retrograde movement stop even at this stage. A dense population, maddened by disappointment and rendered desperate by undeniable want, will fall into a state from the contemplation of which one may well turn away.'

Had Mr. Lloyd lived to see how well England bore the great check to one branch of her industry, not only in Manchester, but over the greater part of Lancashire and Yorkshire, during the cotton famine, he would have seen that, although it would be a sad day for England should Manchester ever entirely cease to be prosperous and flourishing, still even then, if the general trade of the country remained in a good condition, the capital employed in Manchester would, in course of time, be diverted into other and more profitable channels. This country could well stand the loss of prosperity in one town, however important, or in one trade, however large, so long as other branches of the trade and other towns remained in a prosperous condition. England will only wane as a commercial nation when the trade of the country, taken as a whole, becomes permanently unprofitable. There is no disguising the fact that if our manufacturers can find no market for their goods, or only a restricted one, prices must inevitably fall, and in proportion as they fall—from the cause above stated—so, in the long run, must the value of labour. From experience we find that the condition of the working classes—who are the bone and sinew of the nation—is in the progressive state the happiest, that in the stationary their lot is only bearable, and that in the declining state it is miserable.

It would be well, here, to inquire what are the requisites to put labour into motion ? Firstly, tools to work with ; secondly, the raw material ; thirdly, the wages for the sake of which the labour is undertaken. Our manufacturers all over the country have at present no lack of the first ; in fact, as far as tools to work with are concerned, they possess them in the shape of idle mills and workshops in superabundance. The first class may be called fixed capital, and requires the two latter, or circulating capital, to set it in motion.

A short time ago some agricultural labourers from Kent appealed to the public compassion, and among other grounds of complaint dwelt on the injustice of decreasing their wages. They stated that their wages were not sufficient to supply their necessary wants, an assertion which, if correct, would entitle them to the sympathy of their fellow countrymen. But they were mistaken as to the cause which occasioned the lowering of their wages. They appeared to contend that the rate at which the land is let determined the price of the produce and the rate of wages ; whereas it is the average price which the farmer *anticipates to gain* on the produce that determines the rent of the land, and influences largely the rate of wages, although the price of produce is often highest in the countries in which the rent of the land is lowest ; because, in proportion to the fertility of the soil and the facility of the market, so is the rent of the land. A farmer who pays £4 an acre for his land may produce crops of such a superior description that he may be able to sell at a certain price, as, for example, 44s. per quarter for wheat ; whereas another farmer, who pays only 10s. an acre for his land, would have to sell at a loss to compete with him.*

---

* In the island of Jersey I was only this autumn informed that land was let as high as £10 and £12 an acre. But, owing to

We must not lose sight of the fact that the produce of all great manufactures for distant sale must depend not only on the price the goods can be made for in the country producing them, but also on the circumstances which affect the demand in the countries to which they are taken for disposal. One circumstance that would affect the demand, in a country which had previously been a market for goods, would be the levying of so heavy an import duty as virtually to prohibit importation. For instance, supposing that in 1864 we could afford to manufacture and sell in America razors at 1s. each; and that owing to cheapness in the material and improvement in machinery we could now sell them for 10d. each. The American Government, however, should place a fifty per cent. *ad valorem* duty on our exports, which obliges us to require 1s.3d. for them, and they themselves manufacture the same article for 1s. 2d., in order to undersell us. No doubt in the long run the Americans would lose more than we do, by having to pay more than they could purchase the razor for were their trade free, as the artizans manufacturing it might be employed in making goods which, from natural advantages, they could sell both to their own countrymen and the rest of the world at a larger profit. The greater price of the razor would, moreover, act as an indirect tax on the greater part of the community, including the artizan himself who made it; nor would that important functionary in America, the barber, fail to make his customers pay for the increased price the razors cost him. But still, at

the richness of the pasture land and the fertility of the arable land in that island, two, and in some instances three, crops a year are taken off the land. Besides which they are able, owing to the climate, to transmit large quantities of potatoes very early in the season to the English markets. Hence, notwithstanding the high rent, neither was farming unprofitable nor wages low.

the same time, we should lose a 'field of employment' for our labour.

In examining the trade of a country, one ought to enquire not whether *one particular branch* of trade is making small profits, but whether the greater proportion of the most important trades in the country are not suffering either from foreign competition, to which I have alluded previously, or from the check given to them by hostile tariffs, from over-production, or other equally important causes.

There is no doubt that competition must tend, in a measure, to reduce profits. One has heard lately, on all sides, complaints by the merchants of London, that the German merchants were underselling them and rivalling them in many branches of business. The reason of this is not difficult to find, for it is well known that, as a rule, their expenses are not so great, and that their style of living is less costly than that of English merchants. In Hong Kong, at one time, two or three large English houses had a virtual monopoly. Profits were of course very large, and all the clerks of the houses received very liberal salaries, which allowed them to indulge in every comfort, and even to enjoy the luxury of keeping race horses. The Germans arrived, competition ensued, salaries were reduced, and all had to be changed.

No country, least of all a country like England, which does not grow sufficient corn to feed its inhabitants, can afford to lose its export trade. Should we lose it, we should soon find all branches of trade overstocked, competition very close, and profits as low as possible. If, however, those profits became lower than the minimum our capitalists required, we should find them seeking in other countries for fresh fields for their capital. There is one complaint that the working classes urge with regard to capitalists, and that is this, when times are prosperous—that is, in most instances, when the supply does not equal the demand—we hear little or nothing about profits; but, as soon as times change for the worse, they urge their loss of profits as a cause for the reduction of wages. There is, no doubt, some truth in this, and in the statement that in prosperous times the master might pay higher wages than he does. As an offset against this, he sometimes has to pay more than he can afford in bad times, and it is evident that wages do rise considerably when trade is prospering. Witness the great rise in the wages of the iron and coal trades during the years 1870 to 1873. But any great rise in profits can only be temporary, for whenever any established trade or manufacture is believed to be yielding a greater profit than before, *almost immediately other competitors start up*, and soon force down prices even *below* the level from which they had previously risen. Therefore it is that trade does not resume its natural level until the supply once again equals, but does not exceed, the demand.

It is the general complaint that one of the principal causes of the stagnation of our trade has been over-production. In that respect we do not seem to differ from other nations of the world, all of which appear to have more produce than they *know how to dispose of*. The sudden inflation of trade, caused by a large demand after the termination of the Franco-Prussian war, caused new manufactories and works to be opened throughout the world; at length the demand ceased, whilst the manufacturers kept on producing at a loss. This is righting itself, and, except in one or two branches of trade, there does not appear to be much surplus stock in this country. Over-production might be the sole cause of the stagnation of trade for six months; but if that was the sole or principal cause, it would have cured itself in less than five years.

I have now touched on some of the causes which affect our trade—increased competition both with foreign nations and amongst ourselves; the former of which ought only to put us on the *qui vive* and increase our efforts to produce better and more cheaply, and the latter, though it may reduce the profit of the merchant or manufacturer, cannot fail to be an advantage to the country itself. Also, in the second instance referred to, the tendency of strikes amongst workmen to drive capital and trade from a country. In the next place, I have reviewed the question whether the protective tariffs adopted by foreign countries have a tendency to cramp our industry, and shut out fields of employment for our labour; and also maintained that over-production is not the sole cause of our trade being depressed.

A fifth circumstance which affects trade is want of confidence. One cause of this is adulteration—that is, goods not being what they are represented to be. As John Stuart Mill puts it, ' Conjoint action is possible just in proportion as human beings can rely on one another. There are nations whose commodities are looked shyly upon, because those dealing with them cannot depend on finding the quality of the article conformable to that of the sample. Such short-sighted frauds are far from unexampled even in English exports.'

I will not quote instances of this kind, which may be found in our recent law reports; as it would appear that, whilst one manufacturer is accused of selling goods of a different quality to that which they are represented to be, there are thousands who are not only not accused of doing so, but, as a matter of fact, keep up the name of this country for the general excellence of her manufactured goods. But I will refer to an instance, not by any means an uncommon one, of the result of confidence placed by one man in another—an incident naturally well known to fame from the position of the family to whom it relates. I allude to the great house of Rothschild, the founder of which—Meyer Anselm Rothschild, was born at Frankfort-on-Maine in 1743, and was placed by his father in a counting-house at Hanover. He showed a great aptitude for commercial pursuits. The Landgrave appointed him, in 1801, banker to himself and his court. Nor was this confidence misplaced, for during the sway of the great Napoleon in Germany the Landgrave entrusted Rothschild with his private fortune, which, by his devotedness, he contrived to save and restore to him. His name in the course of years has grown a tower of commercial strength over Central Europe. At his death he left his five sons not only the inheritance of his immense wealth, but the still more precious legacy of wise and prudent and *united counsels*. Has the British Empire at present united counsels for their commercial interests? I say decidedly not.

There is also another reason given, perhaps in particular instances with some truth, of a direct cause in a measure for the present depressed state of our trade, and that is, the system of ' bounties' offered by foreign Governments, notably the French, on certain articles, to cut out the manufacturers of other nations, and, as they imagine, foster and encourage their own. One of the grossest instances of this is the French ' bounty' on the export of their sugar. They object to the word 'bounty,' and urge they do not give one. Call it as they like, it is nothing more nor less than a ' veiled bribe,' and is practically a 'bounty' of 3s. 5d. per hundredweight on sugar exported. The cost of the 'system' to the French taxpayer by which a certain number of sugar refiners in France make their fortunes is estimated by some to be as high as nearly £1,000,000 yearly; the cost to this country is the gradual extinction of an important industry. The gain to this country appears to be that *at present* we buy, or ought to buy, our sugar a fraction of a farthing a pound cheaper; the French having for their ultimate object in paying this 'sugar bounty' at present the prospect that when they have run the other coaches off the road—when they have, in fact, destroyed the trade of their competitors in sugar refining, and have established a virtual monopoly—to take off the bounty and raise the prices. The mode by which the French sugar refiners gain their bounty is this, and, as Mr. Alex. Wilson remarks, it is extremely simple :—

All raw sugars are taxed according to a graduated scale, supposed to be in proportion to the amount of saccharine matter they contain, and the refiners merely contrive to have the raw French-grown beet sugar, which is entered in bond for refining, *classed lower* than its true saccharine nature. When this sugar is refined, if any of it is exported the refiners are entitled to get back the duty, and they accordingly demand a drawback equivalent to the full saccharine standard which the refined sugar shows, thus mulcting the state of the difference between the debit and the credit. By this means two very different objects appear to be accomplished : the refiner, under the pretext of the high duties, keeps up the prices of sugar at home and realises large profits; but abroad, by help of the excise drawback, he appears as a cheap seller, and in point of fact has within the last ten years almost driven English sugar refiners out of the market ; in short, the higher the duty, the bigger, as a rule, are his profits both ways ; for so long as his sugar is taken into bond by colour rather than by its true saccharine value, he obtains a larger profit on his drawback with every augmentation of duty, and rises into *more supreme command* of foreign markets at the expense of the tax-paying French public.

'The interest of these sugar refiners would, therefore, seem to be, to raise the duty on sugar as high as possible in France, to not only tax the French people to pay the bonus to them, but to tax them as high as possible indirectly on the price they pay for sugar.' When the French people awake to the fraud they may wipe away this scandal in their fiscal system and agitate for free trade in sugar and many other things besides ; meantime the refineries of Glasgow and Bristol are shut up, and the work-people cry aloud for a countervailing duty. The whole question with regard to the disadvantage under which our sugar refiners are suffering would appear to lie in a nut shell, and that is, does the drawback which the French, Austrians, Germans, Belgians, Russians, Dutch, and Americans allow on the exportation of refined sugar, represent the tax originally paid, or does it not ? For if the drawback is in excess, call it what they like, it is simply nothing less than a bounty paid to their refiners.

By the Sugar Convention of 1864 between Great Britain, France, Belgium, and the Netherlands, which had for its object the desire of regulating by common agreement the international questions relative to the laws affecting sugars, and especially to the drawback granted on the exportation of refined sugars, the present increased manufacture of beetroot sugar was not sufficiently foreseen, cane sugar having at that time a greater command of the market.

Cane sugar is composed of pure sugar and molasses; and, as pure sugar is white and molasses black, the mixture of the one with the other gives varying shades of colour, according to the proportion of the admixture. In this state of things, colour had been recognized and accepted as the indication of quality. *But colour does not adequately determine the quality of beetroot sugar*; and although there is variety in beetroot sugar with respect to its yield in the refinery, there is little of it which does not admit of crystallization. And so, apart from any possible discrepancies between the qualities and colours of cane sugar from different places of growth, colour, as applied to cane sugar, would not|be found to apply in the same manner to beetroot"sugar.

Sugar, cane or beetroot, it should be stated, undergoes the first process of manufacture in factories, and then, when the further process of refining is resorted to, is taken into refineries. It enters [into]consumption, or is exported, in a manufactured or purified condition. If exported, the right to 'drawback' the duty paid on the raw commodity is allowed by law, and hence, as the matter is well explained in a Report by Mr. Ogilvie, submitted to Her Majesty's Government in the course of the negotiation of the Convention of 1864, arises a question very difficult of solution. What amount, calculated according to the quantity of the sugar in its altered condition, will fairly represent the duty actually paid on the raw or unmanufactured material ? *

In 1872 the British sugar refiners made strong representations with respect to the Convention of 1864. They alleged that three departures from its principle were then in operation, 'the first of these arising from a defect inherent in a classified scale ; the

* Commercial Report, Sugar Industries (No. 22 , 1879).

second, from an incorrect classification of beetroot sugar; the third from appearance being not always an accurate test for the classification of such sugar.' They pointed out that a classified scale is only an approximation to accuracy, because each class will embrace sugars containing more or less actual sugar than the quantity on which the duty for that class is calculated. When the duty is low, and the steps between the classes therefore small, this circumstance is of little importance. But when the duty is high, this difference between the rates of duty becomes considerable, and the incompleteness of the system of a classified scale is clearly shown. In 1864 the rates of duty in the four countries were not dissimilar in amount, but in 1872 the English duty had been lowered and the French largely increased. This state of things enabled the French refiners, by adjusting the sugars used by them to the conditions thus produced, to obtain large bounties. A conference was held in London in 1872, by delegates of the four Powers—England, France, Belgium, and the Netherlands—in which the British delegates advocated the establishment of refining sugar in bond. A fresh Conference was held at Paris in April, 1873. Elaborate statements were made by the Commissioners of Belgium, France, and the Netherlands, and tests by saccharometry were strongly recommended by them. At the Conference on this sugar-refining question held at Brussels on the 11th of August, 1875, a draft Convention was signed but refused to be ratified by the Netherlands Parliament, and no settlement of this question has yet been arrived at.

I consider this French and other countries' bounty system has nothing to do either with "Free Trade" or

'Protection' in the general acceptation of those terms, and that it ought, in the interests of our own workpeople, to be viewed entirely on its own merits.

There are gentlemen who write the words 'Free Trade' in an article on any question connected with commerce, as if it were a talisman, not stopping to inquire if these two magic words have anything to do with the question or not; and when any question connected with our trade comes into discussion, they mostly content themselves with quoting some trite saying as to the advantages of Free Trade in the abstract, the truth of which few of us dispute. They rarely, if ever, condescend to consider whether under any altered circumstances any change in our present system might lead to good results.

I do not myself presume to decide whether such would or would not be the case, but submit it is a question open to inquiry, and that we should not overlook any circumstance (however small it may appear) in our vast and varied commercial transactions which may affect the course of our trade.

Some of our manufacturers allege that we are being undersold in some articles of commerce, because we are too confiding and generous in showing the whole world the mode of our manufactures at International Exhibitions and shows. That argument ought to cut both ways, as surely in many industries we have much to learn from the foreigner. Besides, if manufacturers have any secrets of their trade, no one forces them to divulge them at exhibitions, and the remedy lies with themselves.

There can be no doubt that our hap-hazard, puzzling, and 'unscientific' system, or, rather, want of system in our moneys and weights, may, now that our competitors more closely approach us, place us at some disadvantage, in comparison with nations like the French and Americans with the simplicity of their decimal system, and the ease with which calculations can be made by them; such systems, it has been calculated, save them at least 10 per cent in the number of clerks required to keep their accounts in their offices and counting houses. Besides which, as an English manufacturer, writing to the *Times* in the beginning of this year, complains, 'the French, owing to the difficulty of calculating decimals and paying them exactly in our money, now remit to him in francs, to his loss on the exchange.' After having touched upon the causes which may have affected the course of our trade, it would be as well to refer to the actual state of our imports from and exports to the various foreign countries and British possessions for the following three years :—

	1864	1872	1878
Imports.	274,952,000	354,693,000	368,770,000
Exports.	212,619,000	314,588,000	245,483,000

It will be seen, comparing 1864 with the year 1878, that in fifteen years, whilst our imports to this country increased in value by about ninety-four million pounds sterling, our exports increased by only about thirty-three millions. And again, comparing the year 1872, which was a period of general commercial prosperity, with last year, we find that whilst our imports to this country had augmented to the extent of fourteen million pounds sterling, our exports *had decreased by sixty-nine millions*, which, taking into account the increase of our population during the period of six years between these two dates, represents a considerable diminution in the value and volume of the manufactured and other goods we sell, and *consequently a large decrease in money circulating amongst every class of the community.*

INTRODUCTORY. 25

Throughout the whole of this work I purpose following as a rule the example set by the Statist, and usually adopted by many of the leading authorities who have dealt with any largeness of view on the question of the past and present position and future prospects of our trade, and omit the numerals below thousands.

I do so the more readily as, whilst acknowledging the great and infinite care with which the Returns published by our Board of Trade are prepared, and even allowing that which in most instances would be almost beyond the reach of possibility to believe—namely, that in all cases the thousands of merchants who supply the figures from which these returns are compiled take the trouble, even if they have the power, to give the exact value of their imports or exports with absolute accuracy—I omit them as they have no practical bearing on the general question of our trade relationships with the rest of the world.

Mr. Shaw Lefevre, at the opening meeting of the Statistical Society last November, pointed out that this is not by any means the first occasion in which complaints have been made of the general depression of trade of this country, and said, 'In the year 1868 there was a general stagnation of trade; large numbers of men were out of work, pauperism greatly increased, and manufacturing capital was fearfully depreciated. In the autumn of that year trade was so much complained of, that there occurred a revival of the old theories of protection under the disguise of a demand for reciprocity, of which we now hear a good deal. If I remember rightly, the Manchester Chamber of Commerce (Mr. Shaw Lefevre has since written to the *Times* a letter in which he allows his memory was slightly wrong in this particular) passed a resolution aiming at this; and many other Chambers of Commerce followed suit. In the session of 1870 these complaints of bad trade and increased pauperism had their expression in two motions in the House of Commons : one calling for state aid to emigration; the other, for a committee to investigate our commercial treaties, aiming at reciprocity.' He then proceeds to point out that, as probably the movers and seconders of these resolutions were not aware that trade was so soon to revive as it then did, so that anyone, at the present time, who advocates inquiry into the present causes of the depression of trade, may find trade revive before the inquiry can be completed. *No one but could wish such may be the case.* His argument amounts to this : as light always succeeds darkness, prosperity in the trade of this country has always succeeded depression. It is no use our attempting any artificial means of giving light ; the sun will soon blaze forth and put to shame any attempts we make to lighten the darkness of a depressed state of trade. As well might he argue that because rain usually falls and irrigates the rice fields of India, therefore there is no use in artificial irrigation : if rain does not come one year it will probably fall the next, and therefore irrigation works are useless.

In my opinion we ought to legislate so as to give the trade of this country a *steady* and *sure* basis—to legislate for, comparatively speaking, bad times as well as so-called good—very often the cause of these so-called prosperous times being the sudden demand for our manufactured articles after the termination of a war, such as the Franco-German, in which the producing classes in either country, being largely employed as soldiers, had to leave their productive avocations.

A form of investment which seems a very favourite one amongst our capitalists is Government securities. The words 'Government Loan' were at one time a sufficient bait to draw millions from our countrymen with the greatest ease. The sole security our capitalists seem to have had in investing their money in many of these foreign loans is, that if the borrowers refuse to pay the interest it would debar them from being able to procure further advances, or, what is denominated, float a fresh loan. No thought seems to have arisen as to whether the country which floated the loan was solvent or insolvent, and few seem to remember that a Government alone has the power to repudiate debts at a stroke of the pen, and that no Court, international or otherwise, can make them pay; so from the year 1867 to 1877, Mr. Hyde Clarke estimates that we have lent to foreign Governments £340,000,000, of which the interest of *one-third* is in default ; and Mr. Lefevre considers 'it is not unreasonable to suppose that at least as much has been invested in railways, mines, and other industrial enterprises abroad.' Mr. Thomas Brassey states, in an able article in the *Nineteenth Century* of last May, that '54 per cent. of the foreign loans issued in London are in default.'

It would seem, however, that the excess of our imports over our exports can be satisfactorily accounted for, *to some extent*, by the fact of our receiving large sums for interest on the capital we have invested in various foreign loans, and in foreign railways and other enterprises.

Mr. Shaw Lefevre, in his review of the present state of our trade, partly bases the condition of it on this fact, and comments on this subject thus: 'Upon this state of facts, then, the excess of our imports in ordinary times is easy of explanation. Foreign countries must pay us sixty-five millions before they begin to buy of us. In 1870-3 we were investing in foreign countries enormously, and reversed this balance of trade against us. In the last three years *we have invested comparatively little.* The magnitude of the indebtedness of foreign countries is, therefore, in a sense, an impediment to our export trade. When we cease to invest, they must pay us in money or goods; when we invest alone our export trade proportionately increases. In prosperous times the savings or profits of the country are so large that they cannot find adequate scope for investment at home; they spread over the whole world, fertilizing new fields of production, or supplying foreign Governments with the means of waste or war, and temporarily creating a fresh demand for British exports. Looking back, then, at the trade of the past ten years, there is no cause for alarm in this discrepancy between the value of our imports and our exports. There is equally no fear for our foreign trade from competition with others.'

I do not wish to take a less sanguine view of our trade than Mr. Lefevre does : but, having looked back to our trade returns for the last ten years, I confess they do not appear to me as satisfactory as he would have us believe.

In the year 1873 our imports exceeded our exports by about £60,000,000. Since that date, Mr. Lefevre acknowledges, 'we have invested comparatively little in foreign loans;' and though I am fully aware it is a difficult thing to ascertain with exactitude, I am told by those members of the Stock Exchange whom I have consulted, men who deal largely in foreign securities, that in their opinion we have sold in this country since 1873 more foreign securities than we have purchased. Yet we find our imports exceeded our total exports (including not only home but foreign and colonial produce and manufactures sent from these shores) last year (1878) by over £123,000,000, or more than double the excess they showed in the year 1873.

It would appear obvious to anyone that no nation can permanently retain the position of a leading commercial power unless it has 'natural advantages.' It may snatch them, as it were, temporarily, as we see Venice and Holland did, but can never hold the position nature has not accorded it in continuity.

I will, however, allow that there are other causes, besides the bullion which we receive from abroad as interest for our invested capital in Government loans and undertakings, that may account for some of the balance of import trade as against export. We have very large sums of money invested in our colonies in land and buildings. A large percentage of the proprietors of these properties, though exporting nothing, yet receive the rents, and expend the value of them in this country. In the same category one should also take into account the not inconsiderable amount paid by the Indian Government to retired Indian officials and officers as pensions, the greater portion of whom reside and spend their incomes in England. In fact, England has been called the Paradise of fixed annuitants (though Indian officials, since Bismarck decided to demonitize silver, have found their incomes depreciate with the value of that metal, and can hardly be fairly called 'fixed annuitants'). Some, however, have complained that, if we allow our export trade to be gradually taken from us, our wealth will decrease, and we shall soon have few ' fixed annuitants ' to enjoy the full advantages of a one-sided free trade.

In examining the natural advantages of England for

commerce, I do not think the record will be in any way unfavourable. We find that our island possesses an advantageous position for commercial purposes and a temperate climate suitable for manual labour. It has good harbours around its entire coast, and many navigable rivers. We have the two handmaidens of commerce at our door in the shape of productive iron and coal mines, easily worked, and comparatively near the surface.

Besides these natural advantages in our small island, we possess in the British Empire large and numerous dependencies, which give an outlet to our surplus population, where we ought to find lucrative employment for our capital, and markets for disposing of our products as well as for supplying our wants. To these natural advantages we can also add the fact that England is an old-established country, with a settled form of Government, and that its inhabitants are a strong, enterprising, and, as a rule, industrious race. We have also the advantage of having thoroughly developed communications, in the shape of railways, roads, canals, and bridges, nor do we lack capital. In fact, at present, the great difficulty is to find lucrative employment for our realized wealth.

This country ought, therefore, to be second to none in commercial prosperity. I do not except in this statement even that loosely-knit collection of peoples known as the United States of America. None amongst us deny that that country has before it a great future, and when the second centenary of the republic is celebrated, even Professor Huxley's estimate of the increase of the population, from 40,000,000 to 200,000,000, may prove to have been not over sanguine; nor ought we to lose sight of the fact that in proportion as the population increases so will the cultivation of the land not become such a profitable and ready outlet for those of the industrial classes who seek employment as at present. When America is fully peopled, wages for agricultural labourers will sink to the level of those paid by the other developed States of the world. It will also tend to equalize the price paid for labour by the British and American manufacturers ; and to the extent they are at present in favour of the British employer, so will one of the advantages he now holds against his American competitor be diminished.

But still it would seem to be the duty of Englishmen who call themselves statesmen not to fix their eyes in admiration on that Empire of the West, but *to look to the interests of their own country and the British Empire*, to encourage and increase her trade if possible, and to remember that they ought not to let easily or lightly pass out of their hands the commercial supremacy we now hold, not, however, with such an undisputed sway as we once did, and to remember that we gained and hold that supremacy, not because one man invented what he called, "a commercial system," or another man what he called "a free trade system;" but rather because in England we have perfect liberty, perfect security of property, and perfect administration of the laws.

CHAPTER II.

RISE OF OUR PRESENT SYSTEM OF COMMERCE.

THERE are few subjects more interesting than the gradual rise in different directions of the commerce of this country. We have not bounded suddenly to our present large commercial system, as has been the case, for instance, with America and Australia, but with us it has been the gradual growth of centuries. Sometimes even our trade has retrogressed, but always hitherto, and we hope such may be the case now, it has returned to us after a time, with an increased wave of prosperity. Without commerce what practical advantage would it be to us that an improved communication exists throughout the world, not only over the sea by steamers and sailing vessels, but over vast continents by means of railways, roads, and rivers, by which means we supply each other's wants; that we, for instance, can clothe ourselves in furs brought from the icy north, drink of the vineyards of France and Spain which we never planted, take our spices from India without feeling the scorching heat that brings them forth, and use the silks and other products of far-off China and Japan?

To arrive at a perfect commercial intercourse (will it ever be attained?) we must adopt a system that adds to and facilitates the production of wealth by enabling the inhabitants of each particular country to devote themselves in preference to those employments for the successful prosecution of which they may have some

COMMERCIAL SYSTEMS. 33

natural advantages. If the workman in each country acted on this principle he would have a great quantity of his own work to sell in excess of that required for his own wants, and every other workman, being placed in exactly the same position, would be enabled to change a great quantity of his own goods for a corresponding quantity of those of others, or, what comes to exactly the same thing, for the price of such quantity of their wares.

If no fine were imposed by either of two countries in the way of an import duty on the labour of the workmen in the other, *we should have perfect commercial intercourse, or Free Trade.* To call our present system Free Trade is a misnomer. It is not Free Trade with any foreign nation, or, in fact, with any of our colonies, except Hong Kong and the Straits Settlements, the Gold Coast, Sierra Leone, and New South Wales.

I know it was the hope of those who originally took off our protective duties, by showing the way, to induce other nations to follow their example, and to adopt Free Trade ; but, as a matter of fact, this result has not yet been attained, and although we still have import duties on spirits, wine, tea, tobacco, and a few other minor articles, none of our import duties are of a protective character, and so we may fairly call our present system '*Free Import Trade*,' by which term I shall in future allude to it in contradistinction to " Free Trade."

And now I must entirely traverse what one may call the creed of a certain class of writers who allude to the course of our present trade, as if it were 'our mission' to deal thus with other countries, and that no one must even give a thought to diverting our trade to other and possibly more profitable channels. It is not our 'mission' to buy corn from America, nor that of the natives of India to buy our cotton goods. Neither of us act from motives of bene-

D

volence, but simply because we consider it is our interest to do so; and if either of us saw a way in which we considered our interests would be better served by purchasing our corn or our cotton goods elsewhere, what should prevent us?

Commerce between nations is based on nothing more than self-interest, and herein lies the ground on which we maintain our present system of "Free Import Trade." We consider it 'our interest' to purchase foreign goods more cheaply; and that by enabling our labourers to purchase the necessaries of life at cheaper rates we can produce lower-priced goods for exportation. But if the foreigner places a higher protective import duty on our goods that more than counterbalances the advantage gained to our consumers in this country by our free import tariff, the advantage of this system is not so apparent.

Adam Smith's statement is beyond cavil, 'that the price a town or country really pays for the provisions and materials annually imported into it, is the quantity of manufactures and other goods annually exported from it; the dearer the latter are sold, the cheaper the former are bought.'

It may be not without interest to glance briefly at the origin of our different systems of trade in this country, and to note in what our wealth consisted. Originally the opinion was prevalent that wealth consisted solely in gold and silver. This was caused by the fact of these metals being the almost universal standard of exchange of wealth for wealth; and nearly every nation can find a decree in their early laws forbidding the exportation of gold and silver.

Thus exportation of bullion is said to have been interdicted by the law of England previous to the

Conquest, and numberless statutes were subsequently passed to the same effect, one as late as 1512 (3rd Henry VIII. cap. 1), which declared that all persons detected carrying over sea any coins, plate, jewels, &c., should forfeit double their value.

This cramping rule was first broken through by the East India Company, which, when it was first instituted in 1600, obtained permission to export £30,000 annually. This was only permitted, however, on the condition that they should import an equivalent in gold and silver six months after every voyage except the first. This privilege was opposed as *contrary to all principle*. The East India Company contended that the advantages of exportation of bullion to India lay in this, that the goods purchased in India with it were re-exported to other countries and sold for a greater amount of bullion, which returned to England; and a Mr. Thomas Mun, one of the ablest of the Company's advocates, compares the operations of a merchant conducting a trade by the exportation of gold and silver to the seed time and harvest of agriculture. 'If we only behold,' says he, 'the actions of the husbandman in the seed time, when he casteth away much good corn into the ground, we shall account him rather a madman than a husbandman; but when we consider his labours in the harvest, which is the end of his endeavours, we shall find the worth and plentiful increase of his actions.'

And so it was that those pushing adventurers were destined, not only to be the pioneers of an enterprise which should ultimately culminate in our holding the Empire of India, but also in giving an impetus to our future world-wide commerce. As I am treating of commercial matters, it may not be out of place to note the well-known fact that we owe our first great step towards the conquest of India, not to a professional soldier, but to the courage, determination, and skill of two men who began their career as clerks in the Company's employ—Clive and Warren Hastings. It is recorded that Clive took over a year in his journey to India, and it was an unusually tedious one even for that age. The origin of the six months' bills from India lay in the fact that then money took that time to be remitted, and the length of ordinary bills ought now to be considerably lessened since the journey can be accomplished in less than a month. The six months' bills seem only to encourage gambling, instead of honest trading transactions.* In 1607 we first commenced taking advantage of the discoveries in Queen Elizabeth's reign, and the first English settlement in America was made at Jamestown. From about this year also commenced the system of commerce known as the 'mercantile system,' by which the exportation of bullion was allowed, though at the same time it was enjoined that the commodities exported, or any portion of them, were to be afterwards sold for a greater sum in bullion than they had originally cost, or that an equal amount in value of native produce was to be exported in exchange for the foreign goods imported.

Our policy, then, was to encourage exportation as much as possible, and discourage importation of all products, except gold and silver, which we did not intend to re-export. And we held the famous doctrine of *The Balance of Trade*, that is, the excess of the exports over the imports was considered to be the sole criterion by which the relative position of the country as to wealth should be judged. And it was then held, that the excess

---

* Since this was written the banks have changed the usance of bills from the East from six to four months' bills.

of value of imports over exports could be balanced in no other way but by the importation of an equal value in gold and silver.

Mr. Mun, in fact, put it tersely thus, that if we wished to increase our wealth and treasure we must ever observe this rule, ' To sell more to strangers yearly than we consume of theirs in value.' There were other circumstances which tended to cramp the freedom of industry, amongst them the fact of Royal grants being made to the inhabitants of various cities and towns in this country of charters which gave them, amongst other things, the exclusive right to regulate matters connected with the trade of their respective cities. Such, for instance, was the power to prohibit the exportation of corn and other materials of manufacture, to enable the inhabitants, by keeping a close market, to buy their provisions at a less rate; or the authority to order that no manufactured articles should be imported from abroad, when heavy duties were placed on them, or, as in many cases, they were totally prohibited. To these may also be added the right granted to citizens of corporate towns to prevent anyone exercising any trade or calling until he had obtained leave from them. All these regulations were made with a view to' encourage home industries and manufactures, and were part and parcel of the then commercial system. During the Tudor reigns, and more particularly in Queen Elizabeth's time, patents were granted to individuals which gave them the sole right of making, buying, and selling particular commodities, and thus many people obtained lucrative monopolies. At length the abuse became so crying an evil, that the right of the Crown to grant monopolies was abrogated by an Act passed 1624 (21 Jac. 1., cap. 3). At last it was boldly maintained by many people, and amongst others by the advocates of the East India Company, that money was 'nothing but a commodity,' and that its exportation ought to be rendered as free as that of any other commodity, and in 1663 the statutes prohibiting the exportation of *foreign coins and bullion* were repealed.

About this period there appeared numerous tracts and works in which the germs of our modern system of commerce may be found. In 1668, Sir Josiah Child published his ' New Discourse of Trade,' which maintained that colonies do not depopulate the mother country, and clearly and forcibly argued in defence of the naturalization of the Jews, which plainly showed that he was in advance of his age. All writers of that period, however, advocated that all articles imported should be of a durable and not a perishable nature—except an anonymous writer, who, in a tract entitled ' England's Greatest Happiness; or, a Dialogue between Content and Complaint,' defends the French trade, then universally declaimed against. So strongly was it opposed, that, in 1678, it was prohibited for three years, and actually, in the reign of William III., the prohibition was made perpetual, the Legislature declaring the trade with France 'a nuisance!' The argument of those who then held more liberal views amounted to this, ' A, being a doctor, buys from B and C, butcher and carpenter, certain goods. It makes no difference to A if they do not employ him as their medical man as long as D does, and pays him enough to cover his payments to B and C.' This argument, one can see at a glance, is true as far as it goes; but if D does not employ A, or, if employing him, does not pay him *sufficient fees* to cover his payments to his butcher and carpenter, then A will have either to desist from purchasing goods from B and C, or endeavour to extend his practice to E, in order to gain sufficient to balance his payments to B and C.

In the year 1700, the East India Company, having gained their point about the exportation of bullion, a violent controversy arose with regard to the policy of permitting the importation of East India silks and cotton stuffs, which was strongly opposed on the ground that it would ruin our manufacturers, cause the exportation of coin, and impoverish the country. The merchants interested in the Indian trade stoutly maintained that it was for the interest of all to buy in the cheapest markets. Many publications supported their view, from one of which, entitled 'Considerations on the East India Trade,' and published in 1701, I make the following quotation, in reply to the objection that the manufactured goods imported from India deprive some of our own countrymen of employment:—

'The East India trade destroys no profitable English manufacture; it deprives the people of no employment which we should wish to have preserved. The foundation of this complaint is, that manufactures are procured from the East Indies by the labour of fewer people than are necessary to make the same in England: and this shall be admitted. Hence it follows, that to reject the Indian manufactures, that the like may be made by the labour of more hands in England, is to employ many to do the work which may be done as well by few, is to employ *all* more than is necessary to produce such things from the East Indies to do the work that may be as well done without them. A saw mill, with a pair or two of hands, will split as many boards as thirty men by manual labour. If, then, the use of this mill is rejected, that thirty men may do the work, eight and twenty are employed more than are necessary, or are employed to do the work that may be done as well without them. So if by any art, or trade, or engine, the labour of one can produce as much for our consumption as can otherwise be produced only by the labour of two or three, if this art, or trade, or engine shall be rejected, if three shall be employed to do the work of one, two are employed more than is necessary, or to the profit of the kingdom. For if the providence of God were to provide corn for England as manna heretofore for Israel, the people would not be well employed to plough, and sow, and reap, for no more corn than might be had without this labour. Wherefore, to employ more hands to manufacture things in England than are necessary to procure the like from India, is to employ so many to no profit that might otherwise be profitably employed. For there can be no want of profitable employment as long as England is not built, beautified, and improved to the utmost perfection, so long as we either have or can produce anything that others want, or that they have anything that we want. We are very fond of being restrained to the consumption of English manufactures, and therefore contrive laws, either directly or by high customs, to prohibit all that comes from foreign countries. By this time 'tis easy to see some of the natural consequences of this prohibition: 'Tis to oblige things to be provided by the labour of many which might as well be done by few: 'Tis to oblige many to labour to no purpose, to no profit of the kingdom; nay, to throw away labour which otherwise might be profitable. 'Tis to provide the conveniences of life at the dearest and most expensive rate, to labour for things which might be had without. 'Tis all one as to bid us refuse bread or clothes, though the providence of God or bounty of our neighbours should bestow them on us. 'Tis all one as to destroy an engine, or navigable river, that the work which is done by few may be done by many.'

Soon, however, after the publication of this work, an Act was passed prohibiting the importation of East India manufactured goods for home consumption. In reviewing the gradual growth of our present commercial system, we find published about the middle of the last century a work of considerable interest to us in the present day, if viewed only in the light of dealing with a subject to which the thoughts of many of us are turned at the present time. It is entitled, 'An Essay on the Causes of the Decline of Foreign Trade,' by Sir Matthew Becker, who proposed that all corporation privileges should be abolished, that all existing taxes should be repealed, and a single tax laid on all the consumers of luxuries proportionately to their incomes. He said, 'Trade cannot, will not, be forced. Let other nations prohibit by what severity they please, interest will prevail; they may embarrass their own trade, but cannot hurt a nation whose trade is free, as much as themselves.' Spain had at that time prohibited the importation of our woollens, but he held that we should not for that reason prohibit their commodities. 'Why hurt ourselves to hurt the Spaniards? If we would retaliate effectually upon them for their ill intent,' he continues, 'handsome premiums given to our plantations to raise the same growths as Spain might enable them to supply us cheaper than the Spaniards could do, and establish *a trade that would never return*. Premiums may gain trade, but prohibitions will destroy it.'

In 1776, Adam Smith published his 'Wealth of Nations.' This great work gradually produced a revolution in the minds of our statesmen; and the broadness and thoroughness of the way in which it indicates the true sources of wealth has never yet been approached. Some have doubtless been able to point out what they held were errors in his views; but the experience of 100 years has proved that the facts Adam Smith then stated, and the deductions he drew from them, were, in the main, right.

I will now refer to one or two points on which Adam Smith writes. It was Adam Smith who first pointed out to the world that labour was the only source of wealth; in fact, that human industry produces wealth by giving utility to matter already in existence, and that labour not only produced wealth when employed in cultivating the soil, but also when engaged in manufacture and commerce. He has most carefully pointed out the now well-known advantages which accrue to us from a division of labour, and sums up thus: 'This great increase in the quantity of work, which, in consequence of the division of labour, the same number of people are capable of performing, is owing to three different circumstances—First, to the increase of dexterity in each particular workman; secondly, to the saving of the time which is commonly lost in passing from one species of work to another; and, lastly, to the invention of a great number of machines which facilitate and abridge labour and enable one man to do the work of many.' And that it is the disposition 'to truck, barter, or exchange,' that allows each individual in our community to adopt a particular calling in which he may excel. That although one man may therefore be a philosopher, another a porter, they can mutually aid and assist one another in the production of wealth. The philosopher, for instance, might invent a crane which would allow the porter to lift a hundred-fold more goods than he could do by his unaided manual labour. If there was no exchange of commodities in this respect possible, and neither having the time to cultivate the science of mechanics, both being porters, they would be only able to lift weight of as 2 is to 100; and therefore the total gain, in this presumed case, in the production of wealth equals 98 in 100. It is said, at present, that although we export as much of our produce to foreigners as we did betwixt the years 1868 to 1873, yet the prices we receive are so much smaller, that the margin for profit is considerably reduced, and hence our merchants and manufacturers complain of the state of trade.

Some assert this to be solely due to a greater amount of produce being in the market than is required. On this subject Adam Smith complains that though prices gravitated up and down from the above cause, there was a 'natural' price of commodities, and that 'natural' price depended solely upon the cost of production, and that the market price rose above natural price, remained stationary, or fell below it, as goods offered for sale were below the demand, exactly equal to it, or in excess of the amount the purchasers required.

One of the most interesting chapters in this work is that on wages and profit in different employments, in which he points out the reasons why some callings are paid at a higher rate than others, and shows, in his clear, lucid style, that a calling which takes long in acquiring, or entails more risk, has the advantage of receiving as a rule larger emoluments than one that can be easily learnt, or that is not dangerous; so a carpenter is better paid than a labourer; a miner than a ploughman. He considered that 'capital may be employed in four different ways: either, first, in procuring the rude produce annually required for the use and consumption of society; or, secondly, in manufacturing and preparing that rude produce for immediate use and consumption; or, thirdly, in transporting either the rude or manufactured produce from places where they abound to those where they are wanted; or, lastly, in dividing particular portions of either into such small parcels as suit the occasional demands of those who want them.'

He then alludes to those who undertake the improvement of lands, mines, and fisheries, to manufacturers, to wholesale merchants, and to retail traders, and enunciates the Free Trade doctrine that the capital of all the individuals of a nation is likely to increase the fastest when it is employed in a way in which the natural advantages of the country give it the greatest advantage; and here occurs a passage which might almost lead one to believe that Adam Smith had foreseen the probable chance of a protective system being adopted in America.

'It has been the principal cause,' he writes, 'of the rapid progress of our American colonies towards wealth and greatness, that almost their whole capital has hitherto been employed in agriculture. They have no manufactures, those household and coarser manufactures excepted which necessarily accompany the progress of agriculture, and which are the work of the women and children in every private family.'

Having then shown that the greater part of the exportation and coasting trade of America, that the majority of their stores and warehouses, were carried on by and belonged to merchants residing in Great Britain, he goes on to say: 'Were the Americans, either by combination or by any other sort of violence, to put a stop to the importation of European manufactures, and by thus giving a monopoly to such of their own countrymen as would manufacture the like goods, divert any considerable part of their capital into this employment, they would retard, instead of accelerating, the further increase in the value of their annual produce, and would obstruct, instead of promote, the advancement of their country towards real wealth and greatness. This would be still more the case were they to attempt in the same manner to monopolize to themselves the whole export trade.'

Protectionists doubtless argue that had not the Americans protected their manufacturing interests they would never have risen to their present position. Whilst free traders contend, that had the original colonists to America determined by high protective tariffs to purchase from the first solely goods of home manufacture, two consequences would have resulted. First, less food would have been grown : and the fact of the inability in a new country to manufacture as well and cheaply as in an old one, would have caused manufactured articles to have been dearer and less serviceable than those which could have been imported. This would have retarded emigration to America, as both food and the produce of manufactures would have been dearer, and this increased dearness would have acted as an indirect tax on immigrants, and have retarded the growth and expansion of America ; and a large portion of the territory now occupied in the United States would either have remained still the hunting grounds of the Indians, or have been taken possession of by some race who had less restrictive views with regard to trade. Nor with Free Trade would the United States now be without manufactures, but would have, owing to all goods being cheaper, a much greater advantage in those manufactures for which she possesses a natural capacity.

Adam Smith points out that the power of a country to amass capital, and in consequence to advance in the

career of wealth, must be dependent and pretty nearly proportional to the respective rates of profit in each case, and that it is a great mistake to suppose that the utmost freedom of industry can ever attract capital to a comparatively unproductive employment. When one reads the following, it might almost seem that it was written but yesterday, instead of a hundred years ago :—
'The profits of foreign trade were greater than usual during the war, but especially towards the end of it ; this occasioned what it always occasions—a general over-trading in Great Britain: and this again occasioned the usual complaint of the scarcity of money which always follows over-trading.'

CHAPTER III.

ON INTERNATIONAL TRADE AND RECIPROCITY.

IN treating these two most important subjects, I intend to quote and examine some of the views of our leading writers and political economists, as I believe it is not only advisable in considering such topics to keep one's eyes fixed on facts and figures as one at present finds them, all important as such facts and figures are to many of us at present, but to see what previous inquirers have advocated under, in many cases, not very dissimilar circumstances. Adam Smith, in his 'Wealth of Nations,' maintained that if a foreign country could supply us with a commodity at a less rate than we were able to manufacture or make it, it was better for us to purchase it with the proceeds of our industry employed in a way in which we had some natural advantage; and whilst he condemned the theory of the Balance of Trade, he yet held the doctrine which modern political economists either entirely ignore or explain away in a sea of words and figures, viz., that 'There is another balance, indeed, which has already been explained, very different from the Balance of Trade, and which, accordingly as it happens to be favourable or unfavourable, necessarily occasions the prosperity or decay of every nation; this is the balance of the annual produce and consumption. If the exchangeable value of the annual produce' (and by this, I presume, he means every description of commerce—

the produce or interest of money lent to foreign nations, our receipts to those residing in this country from colonial and foreign possessions) 'exceeds that of the annual consumption, the capital of the society must annually increase in proportion to this excess. The society in this case lives within its revenue, and what is annually saved out of its revenue is ultimately added to its capital, and employed so as to increase still further the annual produce. *If the exchangeable value of the annual produce, on the contrary*, falls short of the annual consumption, the capital of the society must annually decay in proportion to the deficiency. The expense of the society in this case exceeds its revenue, and necessarily encroaches upon its capital, which, therefore, must necessarily decay, and together with it the exchangeable value of the annual produce of its industry.'

Although he maintained that it was for the general interest of all nations to abolish restraints on importation, still we find he held views which are, as far as I read them, nearly identical with those of our countrymen who advocate Reciprocity—with this exception, that those who now advocate ' Reciprocity ' in trade do not do so out of *revenge* or *retaliation* on the foreigner, but as a means to induce him to give their interests equal advantages and preserve their own trade. He puts it thus: 'The case in which it may sometimes be a matter of deliberation how far it is proper to continue the free importation of certain foreign goods, *is when some foreign nation restrains, by high duties or prohibitions, the importation of some of our manufactures into their country.* Revenge, in this case, naturally dictates retaliation, and that we should therefore impose *the like duties and prohibitions upon the importation on some or all of their manufactures into ours.*' And again he adds, 'There may be good policy in relations of this kind when there is *a probability* that they will procure *the repeal* of the high duties or prohibitions complained of.' On this point it may here be interesting to notice one of our earliest Treaties of Commerce. In 1703 a treaty was made with Portugal, by which we were permitted to sell our 'woollens' in that country in return for our allowing the Portuguese to import wine into England at one-third duty less than the French. History repeats itself—the Spaniards at the present time, by placing an almost prohibitory duty on our manufactured goods, are apparently trying to get from us more favourable terms on the importation of their wines, holding out as an inducement the reduction of their duties.

Those amongst us who advocate Reciprocity do not contend that putting import duties on any foreign goods would be for the advantage of the country *per se*, but simply that they are a means to an end, namely, to force protectionist nations to remit the higher duties they have placed on the goods we export to them.

Their opponents boldly assert that all protective duties are bad, for whatever reason they may be imposed, and also that we should simply injure ourselves without forcing the foreigner to give us a free market. It would, however, appear that there are several precedents which show that nations have been forced to take off a prohibitory duty, and substitute freedom of trade. Thus one instance occurs, in which we were forced by the Prussians to take off large port dues on their ships by their retaliating and placing heavy port dues on ours.

We made a treaty with the United States in 1815 that in future *equal charges* should be imposed on the ships of either country in the ports of the other, and that equal duties should be laid upon all articles—the produce of the one country imported into the other—whether such importation was effected in the ships of the one or the other. The principle of the Reciprocity system having been thus conceded in the case of the United States, it was not possible to refuse acting on the same principle in the case of such European countries as might choose to admit our ships into their ports on a footing of equality. The Prussians, finding this Free Trade arrangement between England and America injured their trade, and that whereas they let in our ships at a low rate of port dues, we charged a higher rate, then placed a discriminating duty on theirs. In 1822 they put on large additions to their port dues, with the view of injuring the trade of this country, in which endeavour they so far succeeded, that the British merchants and shipowners immediately applied to the Government for relief. Mr. Huskisson, the then Prime Minister, was appealed to from all quarters connected with the shipping and trade of the country against the heavy charges imposed upon British ships in the ports of Prussia. ' I had,' he said, in replying to a deputation of merchants, 'a conference with the Prussian Minister at this court, and I well recollect the substance of his reply to me. · You have,' he said, 'set us the example by your port and light charges and your discriminating duties on Prussian ships : and we have not gone beyond the limits of that example. Hitherto we have confined he increase of our port and tonnage charges to ships only: but it is the intention of the Government next year (and of this he showed me written proof) to imitate you still more closely, by imposing discriminating duties on the goods imported in your ships. Our object is a just protection to our own navigation ; and so long as the measure of our protection does not exceed that which is afforded in your ports to British ships, we cannot see with what reason you can complain,' &c., &c. Mr. Huskisson continued :—' In this state of things, more prudently, as I contend, we entered upon amicable negotiations with the Prussian Government upon the principles of our treaty with the United States : that of abolishing on both sides all discriminating duties on the ships and goods of the respective countries in the ports of the other.'

Similar conventions on the same reciprocal terms were soon after entered into with the Swedes and the Danes. In Mr. John Stuart Mill's work—' Political Economy,' he says — 'The only direct advantage of foreign commerce consists in the imports. A country obtains things which it either could not have produced at all, or which it must have produced *at a greater expense* of capital and labour than the cost of the things which it exports to pay for them.' He then proceeds to point out what will be the only result if we lose our export trade. 'If prevented,' from any reason, 'from exporting this surplus it would cease to produce it, and would no longer *import anything*, being unable to give an equivalent,' that is, we should lose what he calls our own only 'direct advantage'—our import trade. He proceeds to attempt to explain that this would be of no consequence to us, thus:—' But the labour and capital which had been employed in producing, with a view to exportation, would find employment in producing those desirable objects which were brought from abroad, or, if some of them could not be produced, in producing substitutes for them.' He omits to notice what would happen to a country physically unable to grow sufficient food for its inhabitants, and without resources to pay for the importation of such articles of food as corn and maize, or what substitutes a country in such a position could find for them. I will supply that deficiency. One substitute would be 'starvation,' the other, 'emigration.' He then goes on to remark thus, respecting 'these substituted articles' we are to make at home to replace those previously imported:—'These articles would, of course, be produced at a greater cost than that of the things with which they had been previously purchased from foreign countries. But the value and price of the articles would rise in proportion, and the capital would just as much be replaced with the ordinary profit from the returns as it was when employed in producing for the foreign market. *After the temporary inconvenience of the change, the only losers would be the consumers of the heretofore imported articles, who would be obliged either to do without them*, consuming in lieu of them something they did not like so well, *or to pay a higher price for them than before.*'

It is to be presumed that Mr. John Stuart Mill included, under the head of 'temporary inconvenience by the change,' the loss of our foreign trade, the ruin of a large number of manufacturers, merchants, shippers, and owners of manufactories, warehouses, and docks, besides owners of every description of house property (these latter being what I find he, in common with a certain class of economists, denominates 'the landed interest,' whose interests they always appear to imagine are dissevered from the rest of the nation); the throwing out of employment of a million or so of workmen; and the vast depreciation of every description of property in the kingdom. It would therefore appear that the loss of our export trade would, ultimately, result in the loss of our power to import the products we required. Thus we should be deprived of what he describes as 'the only direct advantage of our foreign trade.'

In my humble opinion the direct advantage of foreign or inter-colonial commerce does not depend on *impor alone*, but on *both the imports and the exports* of a country. It is equally a direct advantage to sell as well as to buy; for a nation, in disposing of its surplus produce, derives direct advantage from receiving commodities of an equal —and in many cases a greater—value in lieu of those exported. For, after all, is not the *mutual exchange of commodities* produced by the different nations of the world the direct advantage of commerce?

No one who has read Mr. John Stuart Mill's works on Political Economy can deny that he was a man thoroughly cognizant of the advantages that would accrue to a country in adopting free trade principles and therefore his views on the circumstances which might render it advantageous to a country to adopt reciprocity in defence of their export trade are entitled to some weight. He was strongly opposed to any import duty being imposed simply with the view of encouraging some particular branch of domestic industry, and maintained that such duty could only have a mischievous effect. But he appears to have held that an import duty was justified when imposed by one nation solely with a view of obtaining a fair and reciprocal tariff from another. 'If England,' he says, 'sought to obtain more than her natural share of the advantage of the trade with Germany, by imposing a duty on linen, Germany would only have to impose a tax on cloth, sufficient to diminish the demand for that article, about as much as the demand for linen had been diminished in England by that tax. It is evident, too, that considerations of reciprocity, which are quite unessential when the matter in debate is a protecting duty, are of material importance when the repeal of duties of the other description is discussed.' By the 'other description,' he referred to prohibitive duties laid on our goods by foreign nations.

We now come to a time when the majority of our protective import duties were either modified or abolished altogether. One of the greatest agitators in attaining this result was Richard Cobden, than whom no other man in this country did more in his day towards procuring the abolition of protective duties on food. Who can read his speeches without being struck with their fiery and impassioned eloquence? In one of the earliest of them, in 1843, in his agitation for the removal of the duty on corn, he attacked Sir Robert Peel, who had recently reduced the duties on 700 articles, for his having taken the duty off every unimportant article of consumption and still retained those on sugar and wheat. He roundly censured him for having reduced the duty on timber, when 10,000 houses were standing empty within a radius of 20 miles of Manchester. 'You reduced your timber duties,' he said, 'when there were no factories to build, and when there was no employment for ships.'

In examining this question of our commercial depression, we ought not to look at it from the narrow standpoint of whether it is the effect of a particular tariff in this country, or whether it can be temporarily removed by the action of some foreign 'ring' of railway speculators, but whether it is caused by a combination of events all over the world. It is needless here to recall to mind how Cobden spared neither time, money, nor talents in his agitation for the repeal of the corn laws— how he held meetings, made speeches, employed paid lecturers, distributed tracts, and advised one and all to qualify themselves as voters in order to vote for the abolition of the obnoxious Act. The original object proposed by the promoters 'of protection in the corn trade' was the provision of employment for the agricultural labourers of this country, but Mr. Cobden stated that the effect was one continual juggle played off on the farmers to enable the landlord to obtain artificial rents; the loss of capital falling on the farmer, whilst the landlords profited by it, owing to the competition for farms. One of his great arguments against protection in any shape was that it tended to increase rents solely, and that rents had doubled in this country in about fifty years after the year 1793. Have they not, it may be asked, equally doubled in the last thirty-six years?

He had a hard and uphill fight, and he would be a bold man now who would deny that the abolition of the tax on corn, situated as this country is, is not to our advantage, although many still maintain, and probably with some justice, that the taking off the 1s. per quarter registration duty on foreign wheat was a loss both]to]_the revenue and the agricultural interests of this country, without a compensating advantage to the consumer. As]I am touching on the abolition of the corn laws, it may not be uninteresting to refer shortly to the mode in which this great reform came about, for, strange though it may seem, the majority of us are absolutely more conversant with the facts connected with such landmarks in our political history as the signing of Magna Charta, and 'The Bill of Rights,' than with our great modern reforms, many of the chief promoters of which still live amongst us.

Sir Robert Peel was returned to Parliament in 1841, by the 'country party,' to maintain the corn laws, but he would seem never to have been at heart a thorough Protectionist, and in 1842 he refused to fetter the discretion of his party in dealing with the protection of home-grown grain. Mr. Disraeli also concurred in the views held by Sir Robert Peel; and about this period there was formed in this country what was then termed a 'Young England Party,' whose avowed object was to bring the country back to the times when all classes were more linked together by ties of friendship. Young noblemen vied with one another in joining in the out-door sports of their tenants, such as cricket and football; and 'doles' were given at their mansions to all who chose to ask for them. Of this party our present Premier was, as is well known, a prominent member. Year after year Mr. Villiers brought on a motion in the House of Commons for the repeal of the corn laws, and it was regularly defeated by large majorities — his chance of success seeming to be not much greater than that which the Bill to admit women to the franchise now has.

About this period there was started in London an Anti-Corn Law Association, which counted amongst its members no less than twenty members of Parliament. It, however, came to nothing. London, it may be observed, is not a place well calculated to start an agitation in. It is too vast, and lacks that social cohesion which in smaller places tends to encourage the development of fresh reforms. No proposal, however salutary, that does not meet the approval of 'influential noblemen' and 'wealthy citizens' residing in it, can count on more than a spasmodic existence. On the other hand, it is worth noting that nearly all our great reforms have originated in Lancashire. 'What Lancashire says to-day,

England will say to-morrow,' has passed into a proverb. Lancashire, too, had a large interest at stake in the question of the corn laws. Her mills were being closed, and her people were starving. At Bolton-le-Moors, in the year 1838, five thousand people were without means of subsistence, while thirty out of fifty of the manufactories were closed. The Manchester Chamber of Commerce adopted a petition to Parliament against the continuance of the corn laws—and the agitation commenced in earnest. The Anti-Corn Law League held their sittings in Newall's Buildings, Manchester, for years, till at length the present Free Trade Hall was built, the site of it being on the very ground where several citizens lost their lives during the Peterloo riots. The 'Proletariat' were, however, not in favour of the 'League,' and the Chartists were opposed to them, as they considered the abolition of the corn laws would cause a general reduction of wages.

As I have before remarked, however, their most prominent champion was Mr. Cobden, who was a man of great quickness and intelligence, and had a knack of gaining information from all he came in contact with. He had, during his life, visited more than once most countries of Europe, many parts of the East, and also the United States and Canada, and in each visit had examined with his clear perception all he saw or heard. Among others who strongly supported the Anti-Corn Law League was the famous Daniel O'Connell; and two of those statesmen who lent Mr. Cobden their powerful assistance in this agitation were Mr. John Bright and Mr. Milner Gibson. The Whigs at length admitted the advantage of 'free trade' in the abstract, though they held that it was unadvisable to abolish the corn laws, and proposed that there should be a moderate duty placed on corn instead of the 'sliding scale;' and even Lord Macaulay, who at that time seems to have believed it impossible that any measure of reform could be passed save by a Whig ministry, wrote to advise his constituents in Edinburgh to accept the 'fixed duty' on corn as the then most feasible mode of obtaining concessions. The progress of the movement was also helped by events in Ireland. The greater proportion of the Irish peasantry were at that time nearly entirely dependent for food on the potato crops. Whole generations of people lived and died in the south and west of Ireland without having ever tasted meat. In the autumn of 1845 there came a sudden blight on their 'staff of life.' Thousands of acres were devastated owing to the potato rot, and the whole of the country was threatened with the horrors of famine. Sir Robert Peel, on Nov. 25th, 1845, called a Cabinet Council to consult on this matter, and in the *Times* of Dec. 4th it was announced that on the assembling of Parliament the Duke of Wellington in the House of Lords and Sir Robert Peel in the House of Commons would propose the abolition of the corn laws. This news came like a thunderclap on the whole country. At first no one would believe it, and while many said that even if it were true the *Times* could not have received the information, it was indignantly denied by others. The *Times*, however, repeated its previous statement on Dec. 6th.* There was at the time a rumour amongst many that the blandishments of a gifted and beautiful lady, with a dash of political intrigue in her, had somehow extracted the secret from a young and handsome member of the cabinet, and that she had communicated it to the *Times*.

* From 'History of our own Times.'

Be that as it may, the result was as had been stated, and the Duke of Wellington proposed the abolition of the corn laws in the House of Lords, holding, as he did, the opinion 'that a good government to the country was of more importance than the corn or any other law.' Sir Robert Peel advocated the measure in the House of Commons, and it was triumphantly carried. As it is simply my intention to attempt to demonstrate the position of our present commercial relations, and whilst offering suggestions which I believe, if carried out, would be for their permanent advantage, I shall quote some of the powerful arguments used by Sir Robert Peel in 1849, when he advocated the present system of our trade in the House of Commons, and said, in the course of one of his speeches *—

'In bringing forward the present motion, the honourable gentleman the member for Buckinghamshire (Mr. Disraeli) was equally explicit. He observed, speaking of our recent legislation, "That we have established a new commercial system, which mistakes the principles upon which a profitable exchange can take place between nations; that we can only encounter the hostile tariffs of foreign countries by countervailing duties; that such a system occasions not scarcity and dearness, but cheapness and abundance. Hitherto," he said, " in expressing the principles upon which the theory of reciprocity of commerce depends, I have laboured under the disadvantage of appealing only to abstract reasoning; now, however, we have practical results before us in the suffering of our people, and in the decline of our wealth." Now, in opposition to these doctrines, I boldly maintain that the principle of protection to domestic industry, meaning thereby legislative encouragement for the purpose of protection, duties on imports imposed for that purpose, and not for revenue, is a vicious principle. I contest the honourable gentleman's assumption that you cannot fight hostile tariffs by free imports.

[* In order to decrease the bulk of this volume, I have had extracts of any length printed in smaller type.]

I so totally dissent from that assumption, that I maintain that the best way to compete with hostile tariffs is to encourage free imports. So far from thinking the principle of protection a salutary principle, I maintain that the more widely you extend it the greater the injury you inflict on the national wealth, and the more you cripple the national industry."'

Again he stated :—

'The principles which should govern the commercial intercourse of nations do not differ from those which regulate the dealings of private individuals. It is the same law which determines the planetary movements and the fall of the slightest particle of matter to the earth. It is the same law which determines the accumulation of wealth by the private trader and the powerful kingdom. We only obscure and mystify the truth by overlooking the principle which governs the dealing of every man of common sense.'

And again, in allusion to the petition presented in 1820 by Lord Ashburton (then Mr. Alexander Bains) from the citizens of London to the House of Commons, he remarked :—

'In that memorable petition it was observed :—'That although, as a matter of mere diplomacy, it may sometimes answer to hold out the removal of particular prohibitions or high duties, as depending upon corresponding concessions by other States in our favour, it does not follow that we should maintain our restriction in cases where the desired concessions on their part cannot be obtained; our restrictions would not be the less prejudicial to our own capital and industry, because other governments persisted in preserving impolitic regulations."'

He concluded his eloquent and powerful speech with the following passage :—

'No doubt it would be for the advantage of trade, for our own advantage, and for the advantage of the countries with which we deal—that hostile tariffs should be reduced. It is nothing but the private interest of powerful individuals that induces the Government of those countries, to the manifest injury of the great body of the people, to keep up those restrictive duties. Unquestionable as would be the benefit derived from their reduction, still, if that benefit cannot be obtained, I contend that by the attempt at retaliation you would aggravate your own loss. Let this also be borne in mind, that the retaliatory system, after it has been once abandoned, is infinitely more difficult than the continued adherence to it might have been. To re-establish duties upon the import of foreign produce, to be regulated by the principle of reciprocity, would be accompanied with insuperable difficulties. You have, in my opinion, no alternative but to maintain that degree of free trade which you have established, and gradually to extend it, so far as consideration of revenue will permit.

'These are the grounds upon which I join issue with the honourable gentleman, and upon which I earnestly deprecate the success of a motion which would displace the noble lord (Lord John Russell) and the advocates of commercial freedom, for the purpose of placing in power those who contend for countervailing duties, who would establish that which they call protection to domestic industry, but which, I believe, would be nothing but discouragement and detriment to that industry.'

Amongst the arguments, one which was not the least powerful and had great weight at the time was that the sole result of the corn laws was to increase the value of land, and that for the landlords' interest alone these laws did exist, and that it was principally owing to them that the value of land had increased. On the other hand, it was stoutly urged that the corn laws were established at a time of agricultural distress to encourage native industry, and give employment to farmers and farm-labourers, and that the increase in rents had nothing to do with protection, but was caused by the general increase of wealth in this country. Without further entering into the points raised during this discussion, it appears Richard Cobden advocated that 'all duties for protection should be removed, and free and unfettered intercourse established between all the nations of the earth—as was clearly the design of nature.'

It would not be worth while here to recount the

gradual reduction of all our import duties, nor to recall the circumstances which brought about our commercial treaty with France in 1860. This treaty, substantially, was renewed in 1873, and it remains to be seen whether it will or will not be renewed in 1880. It was in Great Britain that the rights and advantages of *unrestricted trade* were first developed by statesmen; it was by many hoped and anticipated that if we only set the example, it would be followed by every nation in the world, and that it would lead to universal Free Trade, and the undisturbed freedom of industry—by that, I mean the mutual advantage of reciprocal exchange of commodities, and the free intercourse of all the tribes and families of mankind. Has this been realized? I fear not.

CHAPTER IV.

GENERAL SURVEY OF OUR TRADE WITH FOREIGN NATIONS.

FOR the purpose of taking a brief survey of our export and import trade, both with certain of the principal foreign nations and also with our colonies, it has appeared advisable to me, in order to avoid the continual use of figures in the review of each separate State, to compare in a tabulated form the result of our trade for the three years 1864, 1874, and 1878. For it appears to me that the questions, "Which countries do we purchase most from?" and "Which nations give us the most favourable markets for our manufactured and other goods?" will be best answered by comparing the general state of our import and export trades in each of the three years above indicated. For a similar reason I propose to compare the amount of ad valorem duty each nation now charges on six of the principal products which we export.

The total value of the British produce, it appears, exported to foreign countries and British possessions in 1878 was £192,848,000. Of this amount we exported about £123,000,000 in six different classes of British manufacture and produce, which included, firstly, cotton goods and cotton yarn; secondly, iron, steel, and machinery; thirdly, woollen and worsted manufactures; fourthly, coal; fifthly, linens and linen yarn; sixthly, silk. I am aware that we also exported largely apparel, alkali, arms and ammunition, beer, chemical products or preparations, haberdashery, hardware and cutlery, leather goods, copper and brass, oil seed, painters' colours, paper, vinegar and pickles and salt, besides lesser quantities of many other products. But for a basis of comparison the six classes of goods I have quoted above, which form nearly two-thirds of our export trade, will offer a fair criterion by which to judge the terms on which our goods are received by our foreign and also our colonial purchasers. On none of these six classes of goods do we charge any import duty. It has been a task of some slight difficulty to find out the exact duty charged, and also to strike a fair average amidst the manifold taxes levied on different species of the same class of goods; and I am in a measure indebted to a return, asked for in the House of Commons by Mr. Fawcet in 1877, " of the estimated average ad valorem rate of import duty levied in the principal European countries and in the United States on the following articles of British produce or manufacture, so far as the same can be given.*" Whilst acknowledging the impossibility of striking an exact average, owing to the circumstance of having to deal with so many tariffs, framed under totally different systems, I may, I believe, claim that the average ad valorem duty given approximates so closely to being exact, as to offer a fair basis of comparison of the duties at present charged, and to give a fair means of judging how near each country approaches, as far as our interests are

* In several countries the import duty has been raised since this return was published.

concerned, towards Free Trade or Protection. By a reference to this table, the general amount of our trade can also be seen, and an idea formed as to which countries are our best customers, and which our worst, and also of the relative proportion of products we draw from each external source.

Table giving the total value of imports to, and exports from, the Principal Foreign Countries for the years 1864, 1874, and 1878; with a column showing the average ad valorem duties on six of our principal export trades, viz., cotton, iron and steel, woollen, coal, linen, and silk.*

(In this table '000 are omitted.)

	Ad valorem Duty charged on British Exports.	1864.	1874.	1878		
Belgium......Impts.	5 %	6·410	15·048	12·386	Impts.	Belgium
,, ...Expts.		5 979	12 653	11·355	Expts.	
Holland......Impts.	Free.	11·660	14·464	21 405	Impts.	Holland
,, ...Expts.		14·053	21·289	14 676	Expts.	
Swed'n&N'way Impts. (including the Dutchies)	4½ c/°	5·099	11 393	9 127	Impts.	Swed'n & N'way (including the Dutchies)
,, ...Expts.		2·248	7 057	4·324	Expts.	
Denmark ...... Impts.	6¼ c/°	1 728	3·890	4 584	Impts.	Denmark
,, ...Expts.		1·458	2 873	1·900	Expts.	
Turkey ......Impts.	10½ o/°	5·924	5·842	4·779	Impts.	Turkey
,, ...Expts.		7·702	7·490	8 301	Expts.	
Italy ......Impts.	7 7/12 o/°	2·693	3·634	3 252	Impts.	Italy
,, ...Expts.		6 937	7·763	6 444	Expts.	
Germany † ......Impts.		15 149	19·047	23 570	Impts.	Germany
,, ...Expts.		24·823	35·127	29 169	Expts.	
France ......Impts.	Return incomplete.	25·640	46·518	41·378	Impts.	France
,, ...Expts.		23·825	29·389	26·595	Expts.	
Austria ......Impts.	10¾ c/°	·369	·799	1·665	Impts.	Austria
,, ...Expts.		1·060	1 435	1·089	Expts.	
Portugal ......Impts.	27¾ c/°	2·202	4 265	3·319	Impts.	Portugal
,, ...Expts.		2 475	3·128	2 614	Exps.	
Spain......Impts.	31½ c/°	5·879	8 641	9 115	Impts.	Spain
,, ...Expts.		3·845	5·030	3 794	Expts	
Russia (N'thern Ports) Impts.	21¾ %	11·437	15 094	12·352	Impts.	Russia (N'thern Ports)
,, ...Expts.		5 713	9·548	7 974	Expts.	
United States ...Impts.	54¾ %	17·923	73·897	89 146	Impts.	United States
,, ...Expts.		20·183	32·238	17·531	Expts.	

* It may be objected that silk is hardly *at present* one of the principal export trades of this country. I am aware of it, but I believe that this is in a great measure owing to the protective tariffs imposed on our manufactured silk.

† The German Import tariff is in a transition state. See Appendix (1).

F

It will be seen from the above, that since 1864 our imports from the various countries have increased in much greater proportion than our exports to them; and also that, whereas in 1864 we exported more than we imported from Holland, Italy, Turkey, Germany, Austria, Portugal, and America, in 1878 we find this was the case only with Germany, Italy, and Turkey. It appears that Holland alone of all these countries gives us what we may term Free Trade. Another fact to be noted is, that whereas in 1878 we purchased from the United States goods valued at £71,000,000 more than in 1864; we exported to them last year goods valued at actually less by £2,600,000 than we sent them in 1864.

In the remarks now offered to the reader relative to our trade with the principal foreign nations, with whom we have the largest interchange of commodities, I would say that I propose simply to consider whether their import tariffs are to our advantage or disadvantage, and also in what way either country would be benefited by absolute free trade. I thereby shall have to touch on a question of *vital importance* to ourselves at the present time, more so indeed than many of our Statesmen seem to think. This is, I well know, but one branch, though by no means an infinitesimal one, of the large group of subjects relating to the trade of the several countries to be referred to; but that branch, small or great, is one on which perhaps the future prosperity of England largely depends. I know well that in looking at the question from an English standpoint, one may be accused by stern modern political economists, of not being sufficiently cosmopolitan, of being narrow-minded, and of not looking at the question in its broadest and most sublime bearing. I maintain, however, that the standpoint I look at the question from, and the views I have endeavoured to enunciate in my last chapter, are those which would seem to be ultimately for the benefit not only of England, but of the world at large. It is the custom of the present age to look more to the interests of the foreigner than to our own. Nor do we seem to be thoroughly roused to the fact that, the great markets of Europe being practically, if not absolutely, closed against them, or at any rate greatly restricted by these hostile tariffs, our manufacturers find their best markets at present, not amongst the nations to whom had we "free trade" we should dispose of our manufactures year by year in greatly increased quantities, but in a great measure at the "ends of the earth," China, for instance, Brazil, or the Argentine Confederation.

Whilst it cannot be doubted that our trade relations with no civilized State in the world can fail to be of importance to us, or that the general course of our trade with each country is not influenced both by its local requirements, as well as by its political and social institutions; yet the general bearings of our relations with each State have so much in common, that in order to avoid my going needlessly over the same ground, I shall confine myself principally to the considerations affecting our trade relations with France, Germany. Holland, Belgium, and the United States; countries with which the changed conditions of our trade have latterly been most marked. M. Felix Hare, in a paper he recently read before the Bristol Chamber of Commerce, pointed out that whilst in 1872 our exports to the five countries above mentioned amounted to £154,786,733, and our imports from them to

£142,018,782, showing a balance in our favour of an excess of imports over exports of £12,767,951, in the year 1877, only 5 years later, our exports to these countries had decreased to £102,292,321, and our imports from them had increased to £182,669,318. Mr. Bright and others may affect to despise these figures, but they cannot but be aware of their importance to the prosperity of this country. The statistics quoted by Mr. Bright in his speech at Birmingham last April* were calculated to give, to my mind, a wrong impression of facts. He stated that our exports to India on *the average of the last six years* amounted to 24 millions sterling, and compared them with the United States, which he said amounted to 30 *millions a year.*

Now if we examine *the bearings of this average*, it will appear, according to the Statistical Abstract, that in 1873 we exported to British India (exclusive of the Straits Settlements and Ceylon) goods to the value of £22,313,988, and that in 1878 this *had increased* to £24,659,167, whilst to the United States of America in 1873 our exports were estimated at £36,698,424, and in 1878 *had decreased* to the value of £17,531,904 out of Mr. Bright's *thirty millions*. He also told us that Russia '*has a very small tariff.*' This is hardly borne out by the fact that it averages over 21 per cent. on our six principal articles of export, and our merchants have to pay all their duties in gold.

But to revert to my previous enquiry—cannot we examine this question of interest to ourselves in some degree as Englishmen? To me it appears that a question of such interest to this country would be approached in a better spirit if we looked at it as the late Lord Macaulay did,

*Vide *The Times* April 17th, 1879.

when, in a speech on the sugar duties delivered in the House of Commons, he said, "A man would not be justified in subjecting his wife and children to disagreeable privations in order to save, even from utter ruin, some foreigner whom he never saw. If a man were so absurd and perverse as to starve his own family in order to relieve strangers with whom he had no acquaintance, there can be little doubt that this crazy charity would produce much more misery than happiness. It is the same with nations. No statesman ought to injure other countries in order to benefit his own country. No statesman ought to lose any fair opportunity of rendering to foreign nations such good offices as he can render, without a breach of the duty which he owes to the society of which he is a member. But, after all, our country is our country, and has the first claim on our attention. There is nothing, I conceive, of narrow-mindedness in this patriotism."

FRANCE.

Whether considered from a geographical point of view, or with reference to the products of each country, having regard also to natural causes, such as the variety of climate, the productiveness of the soil, or to mineral resources, it may be said that there can be no two countries better fitted for the freest possible interchange of commodities with one another than are England and France. And there can be no doubt that the freer you can make the trade between two such countries, the more prosperous they would both become. As well as on account of natural causes, as from the acquired bent of the industry of the inhabitants of either country, they need fear, were trade between them absolutely free, no rivalry, except the rivalry of supplying each other's wants. We can supply them with the solid utilities of commerce, the motive power of progress—coal—besides the products of our smelting furnaces and engine shops, and the useful manufactures of our power looms ; whilst they can give us in return the produce of their vineyards, as well as those countless objects of art and luxury in which they excel our workmen in taste and skill ; and it is therefore to be hoped that the day may arrive when we shall have reciprocal free trade with France.

France would have "peaceful" revenge upon Germany for her losses in the late war (whether she ever have a warlike one, or not), if she could divert a large portion of England's trade with Germany to her own shores. At present our total trade with France exceeds in value £67,000,000, and is now nearly one-fourth more than that with the Empire of Germany. The volume of our export trade to Germany will, in consequence of their new tariff, decline, and may cause some of our merchants now resident in Germany to migrate to France, if the latter country is not closed to us by higher and more protective duties imposed on our products. By diverting our trade to her shores France would thus gain a peaceful victory and deprive her rival of some of the sinews of war. Trade is more easily diverted than some people imagine ; and the trade, either import or export, with this country is one no nation, however rich, can afford to despise.

One of the greatest marvels of modern times has been the comparative ease with which France has paid Germany the enormous war indemnity, amounting, together with the local fines she had to pay for the maintenance of the German troops in the northern provinces held in pledge, to the sum of £240,000,000. Some maintain that the ease with which the indemnity was raised is not a true sign of its well-being, and that the enormous sums the French have to pay in interest and amortization of their debt, amounting to about £48,000,000 in 1874, cannot but have a detrimental effect on the permanent prosperity of the country. One thing, however, tends to make the immense burden which the French "rentes" must undoubtedly be to the country less heavily felt, and that is, that the interest that accrues from these securities is disbursed so widely through the French nation. The number of French holders of their own "rentes" being 3,380,933, or one-tenth of their total population, which importaat "interest" must indirectly include almost the whole nation, this also adds to the value of the French rentes as a security, for it would appear difficult to believe from the above named fact that the French nation would ever permit any of their diverse forms of Government to repudiate their National Debt of honour (which, after all, a National Debt really is.)

The French National Debt is a creation almost entirely of modern days, and has increased from about two hundred million pounds sterling in 1851 to over nine hundred millions in 1874; and it is curious to note that during the years 1800 to 1814, a period of fourteen years, during which the French nation was almost constantly at war, and during which we were subsidizing half Europe to fight the Great Napoleon, that he can then fairly be said to have actually done what is reported to have been a great maxim of his,—" made war support itself." He only increased the French

National Debt by less than six million pounds sterling, a sum we should not think unreasonable for one of our small wars! Whereas we, during a period of seven years anterior and three years later, namely, from 1793 to 1817, increased our National Debt by over six hundred and one million pounds sterling.

There is, as is apparent to all, another cause which has a detrimental effect upon France as a commercial nation, besides the drain on her resources in paying so large a sum as nearly thirty millions a year for her National Debt; and that is the large sum she annually expends in what has been justly called a "Blood tax." I allude to the maintenance of the large army distributed throughout her territories. This army and Gendarmerie consists, permanently, of no less than nearly 500,000 men, and 124,000 horses. It abstracts from her working power, and it must be owned that it is at best a heavy, very heavy, premium to pay for the security of her territories, when it is considered that the estimates, as it appears for the army alone, were 538,326,499 francs in 1878. Her debt and her army cost France very nearly half the annual revenue she has to raise; that revenue has assumed gigantic proportions, and was nearly one hundred and twelve million pounds sterling in 1878, or about thirty-two million pounds more than our own.

For some reason or other, direct taxes seem very unpopular amongst the French nation, and her rulers have therefore increased the indirect taxes, not only on nearly every article imported into France, but also on some of their own exports, and have since 1870 diverged almost yearly more and more from the paths of free trade. Her policy, it would seem on looking at the tariff, has not been so much to extract large sums from a few important articles of trade, but to tax one and all; to get here a little, and there a little, and not to let any imported article, if possible, escape paying duty.

The result to our own country has been, that whilst the exports from France have increased since 1873, our imports to that country have steadily declined. We seem to have become much larger purchasers of their leather manufactures, such as gloves, boots and shoes; and also of their woollen manufactures, having purchased more by one million sterling last year than in 1874, whilst again in comparing these two years we find that our sale of woollens to the French on the other hand fell off, as did also in a marked degree the value of the coals and raw silk we have exported to them. The French prohibit the importation of tobacco, both raw and manufactured, and also matches. When we remember the dislike felt last year to a small increase of duty on the former article in this country, and the outcry Mr. Lowe raised when he proposed some years back to place an import duty on the latter, we can see how apparently different our views and those of the French are on the subject of taxation.

In glancing, however, at the French import duties which principally affect the trade of this country, it will be seen that they are in many instances unduly high ones, and, although not in a marked degree affecting one branch of our trade, press upon all. To begin with, our coals are charged by them an ad valorem duty of ten per cent. As I before remarked, the value of coals, exported to them by us, had decreased from 1874 to 1878; not owing to the diminution in quantity but to a large fall in price. The reduced price of coals has, therefore, been the sole reason of the apparent decrease of trade in that respect. It appears, however, that our coals, even with the import duty, can undersell the French at the present price; and the result is that coal mining in France has become unprofitable, and several mines have been closed.

Comparing the same two years as before, we exported less of cotton goods in the latter year than the former; it appears that we have lost the sale not so much of our high-priced cotton goods, but of the cheaper descriptions. Their import tariff on cotton goods is very high, the lowest duty charged being 20 shillings per hundredweight; and the scale advancing to upwards of six pounds per hundredweight, which is the duty on fine cloth containing forty-five threads and upwards to the five square millimetres. These high duties originated when Alsace was French territory, in which department there were over 2,000,000 spindles, and were imposed to protect the interests of the cotton manufacturers who had their mills there. But why they should be imposed now, when the cotton manufacturing interest in France is comparatively unimportant, it is difficult to imagine; it cannot be alleged that it is to protect any interest, and as it increases the cost of the clothes of the French labouring classes it is a most injurious tax to the prosperity of the whole country. One effect of it is doubtless to put into the hands of certain French manufacturers large profits, whilst it offers little inducement to them to cheapen their manufacture of cotton goods by the use of improved machinery and in other ways; in fact, it bolsters up this industry at the expense of the whole French nation. From a statement made by Mr. Hugh Mason in a letter to the *Times* of March 11th, 1877, it would seem that French cotton manufacturers did not require these high import duties to enable them to compete with us. For he points out that the French factory hands work sixty-six hours, whereas the English work only fifty-six hours a week; and he maintains that the French get off as much work per hour as the English. Besides which, wages are considerably less in France than in England. In the following statement of wages the French rates* are kindly given me by Mr. Bernal, British Consul at Havre, whilst those in England have been furnished by a large master manufacturer in Lancashire, and are those paid since the late reduction.

	France.	England.
WEEKLY WAGES.	£ s. d.	£ s. d.
Men in cotton room	0 12 9	1 0 0
Grinders and strippers	0 18 8	1 0 0
Head carders	1 11 9	2 5 0
Can tenters	,, ,, ,,	0 13 0
Flying frame tenters	0 14 8	,, ,, ,,
Drawing frame tenters	0 11 6	0 14 0
Self actor minders	1 4 0	1 10 0
Roller coverers	,, ,, ,,	1 6 0

In the price of coals, the English have doubtless some advantage, although it is often asserted that the French are more economical in their consumption of that article than we are, and are able to maintain the same pressure of steam with a less expenditure of coals. However that may once have

* The rates here given are those paid in the department of the Seine Inférieure. Can tenters are rarely employed in France. It is difficult to give an average for Roller coverers; the system of remuneration varying in the different mills.

been, I feel confident that, at present, with the close prices our manufacturers have to content themselves with, they will not be behind the French in economy of fuel. Doubtless the English can purchase machinery at a slightly lower rate than the French. But if the French manufacturer has to pay somewhat higher than certain of his competitors for such machinery as he imports from England and Belgium, in having to pay carriage, commission, and last and not least, the duty charged on its importation, which I find is ten francs for every hundred kilos, the English manufacturer has on the other hand to pay the cost of transit of all goods that he finds a market for in France, which has been estimated to amount to about fifteen per cent. This, with a perfectly free trade, ought to more than compensate the French manufacturer for any advantages we may possess.

The tax levied on the importation of iron and steel goods into France varies from an ad valorem duty of twenty-seven per cent. in the case of railway metals, including steel rails, to an ad valorem duty of from thirty-five to fifty per cent. With the exception of the duties charged by the United States, Russia, and Spain on these commodities, this is the highest tariff one finds imposed against this branch, of one of the staple trades of this country; and were France well supplied with coal and iron within her own boundaries might prevent us exporting these metals to her ports. The highest duty charged is on fire arms; next in order comes needles,—small things seem to strike the great minds of the French legislators. The importation of military stores, gunpowder and projectiles for obvious reasons are absolutely prohibited. The importation of all metals from this country into France has increased in quantity since the year 1874; but for none, except copper, have we received as much bullion in the case of any of our mineral products, wrought or unwrought, imported into France last year as in the former year referred to.

On our woollens the rate of duty charged appears to be about ten per cent. ad valorem. Our linen, hemp, and jute goods are also highly taxed on importation—fine cloths as high as 8f. 3c. per hundredweight. The coarser descriptions are, however, admitted into France at considerably lower rates. Silk is less heavily taxed, in fact some manufactures of it are admitted duty free. There has been a large diminution in both our imports to and our exports from France, in this material since 1874. In no other country in Europe is locomotion so heavily taxed. This tax alone was estimated to pay 3,700,000f. in 1876—one-eleventh of the total receipts of the railways—and must press very heavily on the commercial industry of the country. France appears to have every prospect of being thoroughly opened up, as far as railway communication is concerned, in the year 1888; for by a law passed in the Chamber of Deputies in 1878, no less than 10,000 English miles will then have been added to her railway system, to provide for the cost of which the Chamber granted a credit of 120,000,000f.

Should the French ever change their present short-sighted system of taxation, and reduce, if they do not absolutely abolish, a large number of their hampering and irritating customs, excise, stamp, and octroi duties, and the trade with this country be made a free one, I believe the result would be, not only to reduce the price of all commodities in their country

workers after church hours into the public house. The steadiness of the French workmen cannot fail to be a gain to her manufacturers, and I cannot omit to add that they possess an additional advantage in the comparative freedom from strikes enjoyed by France (there were only 21 in 1878 as against 277 in England), whilst any attempt at intimidation or "rattening" would be quickly stamped out. The machinery, moreover, used by the French manufacturers cannot be justly said to be inferior to our own ; and all these considerations, together with the fact that the French hands work longer hours at their mills than ours, may make it a matter of great difficulty for our manufacturers to contend against them, should they increase their tariffs.

The French know all this as well as we do ; and as an English merchant residing in France and a member of a French Chamber of Commerce said to me, " Nothing will prevent their placing hostile tariffs against the English manufacturers but the fear that if they did so we should retaliate by placing reciprocity duties on articles of luxury, such as wine, brandy, silks, velvets, and ribbons. If they thought that there would probably be far less agitation for Protection in France."

Mr. Halford Thomson gave a clear *resumé* of facts connected with our trade with France in *Fraser's Magazine* for last February. " The following table," he writes, " shows the amount of our manufactures exported to France and the amount of manufactures of a similar kind imported into this country from France, and thereby coming into direct competition with our home market."

FRANCE. 81

Nature of Manufactures	Exports to France.	Imports from France.
	£	£
Brass and bronze	nil.	42,479
Chemicals	211,476	269,843
China and earthenware	80,325	175,399
Clocks	*	314,325
Cotton manufactures (including yarn)	1,958,822	766,831
Glass manufactures	*	291,771
Hides (tanned)	nil.	316,224
Iron and steel manufactures	870,354	76,131
Lace	nil.	439,255
Leather manufactures	12,467	527,657
Linen do.	444,139	124,264
Machinery and implements	583,012	nil.
Oilseed cake	nil.	148,613
Paper	nil.	213,036
Silk manufactures	345,971	8,401,028
Sugar (refined)	nil.	3,464,915
Watches	nil.	16,636
Woollen manufactures (including yarn)	3,244,197	3,719,950
Unenumerated articles of manufactured goods.	1,079,079	1,152,011
Total	8,829,842	20,460,368

* The quantities of these articles exported is too trifling to be mentioned in the list of exports published by our Board of Trade, but they are included in the 'unenumerated articles' in this table.

If we examine this table carefully we find that in 1877 we imported from France over 20 million pounds worth of manufactured goods, *each* and *all* of which competed with precisely similar manufactures here, while during the same period we only exported to France nearly nine million pounds worth. "What then," he asks, "would be the result if French manufactured goods were excluded by import duties from this country, and in retaliation our manufactures entirely excluded from France?" The answer, in my opinion, is plain; it would be difficult to exclude our manufactures more than they are at present; and on the other hand, we should manufacture in England a large percentage of the goods we now import from France. Nor, as I previously remarked, would that be an

G

unimportant loss to their trade when one remembers that whereas our imports from them in 1860 were, including food supplies, horses, raw materials of industry, wines, spirits, and luxuries, such as artificial flowers, ornamental feathers and gloves, only £17,774,031 in value, this sum had risen to £45,823,324 in 1877. Were our manufactures only placed on fair and equal terms, and were we allowed to supply the French nation with our produce as favourably as those on which we allow them to supply us, I believe the balance would not be so heavily against us as it now appears. Their present system being to undersell our home traders, by sending goods to England aided by bounties as in the sugar trade; or by selling us surplus goods at a minimum of profit to compete at an unfair advantage with our English manufactures. This is especially the case with regard to such articles as lace, ribbons, gloves, ladies' boots, &c.; their object being to gain a monopoly of these goods in our market and to be able ultimately to charge whatever they choose for them.

We are told by "Free Import Traders" that their system alone has given us all the advantages we possess in the decreased price in any description of goods or material. May I ask them to consider how utterly they are carried away by their "one idea"? As a proof let me ask them this question—presuming England 100 years ago had had the same free import trade which she now possesses, how, in the name of all that is sensible, would she have imported the same ratio of eggs in proportion to the number of the population then living in this country that she now does? The means by which we now import eggs to the value of one million six hundred thousand pounds from France are simply increased facility in transport, and increased speed in transit. I may add that this source of income appears not to be sufficiently appreciated or taken advantage of by the farmers or cottagers of Great Britain.

Certainly the Great Cobden Treaty with France has not ended in our purchasing much raw produce from that country; and we only appear to have gained by the Free Trade (?) treaty the advantage of purchasing, as previously noticed, large quantities of ribbons, feathers, fans, artificial flowers, fancy boots, and French gloves.

In a work recently published by Professor Fawcett on Free Trade and Protection one of his arguments in favour of the present system is this :—" Before the last Franco-German war, when Alsace and Lorraine belonged to France, it was never even hinted that there ought not to be the most perfect freedom of trade between these provinces and the rest of France. Unless the annexation of Alsace and Lorraine to Germany has changed the character of the industries carried on in these provinces, how can it possibly be less advantageous for the people of France to trade with Alsace and Lorraine than it was before the annexation took place ?"

This is a specious enough argument on the face of it; but let us examine the facts as they stand. When Alsace and Lorraine were French territory there was perfect freedom of trade between those provinces and the rest of France, as Professor Fawcett states. Had there been protection in Alsace and Lorraine against the goods of the manufacturers of the rest of France at that time, does Professor Fawcett imagine that the manufacturers of the other French Provinces would have allowed their trade to be jeopardized by a large influx of goods from Alsace and Lorraine, whilst they, owing to a prohibitive tariff, were debarred from selling their goods in these two districts? This is a parallel case to the present position of our trade in manufactured goods to France, and not the one we are invited to contemplate in the above quotation.

Before leaving this slight sketch of some of the incidents of our trade with France, it may not be considered out of place to refer briefly to some of the facts connected with the sugar bounty question; and here I will make an extract from the report of Mr. Adams as to the system in France by which these premiums accrue to the French manufacturer and refiner.

" Raw sugars, as has been seen, are divided into classes, and a certain yield of refined sugar is assigned to each class. This, which is called the legal yield, is the average between a minimum and a maximum of saccharimetric richness. For instance, the class of sugars from No. 7 to No. 9 comprises all the sugars from 76 degrees to 85 degrees, and the legal yield of this class is 80 refined per 100 raw. That is, the State allows that 100 kilog. of raw sugar of the class in question should yield to the refiner 0 kilog. of refined sugar, the rest being counted as waste. Hence, when the refiner exports 80 kilog. of refined sugar, the State gives him back the duty he has paid on 100 kilog. of raw sugar.

" If, then, the refiner extracts *more than* 80 *kilog.* of refined sugar from 100 kilog. of raw, he will have, over and above the legal yield, a certain quantity of refined sugar which escapes taxation. This is called the *excédant indemne*, and the refiner can sell it in the home market at a price which includes the amount of leviable duty, which, however, is not in fact paid by him; and thus he will make a clear profit, corresponding with the amount of such duty.

"Hence it follows: (1) *that it is the refiner's interest that the duty on raw sugar* should be as high as possible, inasmuch as the extent of his profit on the *excédants indemnes is in exact proportion to the rate of that duty*; (2) that it is the refiner's interest that the native or Colonial trade should only supply him with inferior sugar, inasmuch as the worse the quality, the lower will be the legal yield, and, consequently, the *excédants indemnes* resulting from skilful manipulations may become considerable."

Now, the question of course arises, What does this premium amount to? what advantage does it give to the French over the English manufacturer and refiner in our home market? It is difficult to estimate the exact bounty which has been calculated at the enormous sum of £2,400,000, whilst M. Léon Say stated to a deputation of British sugar operatives at Paris, in July, 1878, that it did not exceed £94,000. He, however, I was informed in France, is largely interested, in sugar manufactories, and can therefore be hardly called a good witness. The sum at which most authorities set down the bounty is between £800,000 and £1,000,000 a year. Such, therefore, is stated to be the price the French nation pay to carry out the idea first started by Napoleon I. to encourage the cultivation of beetroot, as one of the many plans he conceived to destroy the commerce of England. This system appears to have had in this instance the desired effect; for whereas in 1864 there were thirty sugar refiners in Great Britain, there is now only one. It has been necessary for the French refiner hitherto because without this bounty he could not have beaten his English rival; but when he has compelled all the English refiners to discontinue their works he will raise the price of sugar and make the English consumer pay a higher price, instead of exacting the bounty from the French taxpayer. As a writer in an article in the "Saturday Review" of last September, says:—" It may be said that as soon as prices reach a level which will enable the English producer to compete with the French producer, the need for a bounty will again arise; but in the meantime the English producer will have been ruined or will have withdrawn his capital from the trade, and he will have no inclination to invest capital again in a trade from which he can at any moment be driven by the re-imposition of the bounty. Thus the British consumer is only a temporary gainer by the low prices caused by the rivalry which the existence of a bounty has rendered possible and successful. In the end he will find prices once more raised with little chance of their being again reduced."

After the International Convention of 1864 and Cologne experiments, the scale of bounties and drawbacks on sugar in France was fixed by a graduated scale of yields from 67 to 94 per 100 kilog. according to quality; by the law of December 30th, 1875, now in force, it was altered to a graduated scale of yields from less than 76° to 98° and above.

The duties charged on sugar in France since 1871 are as follows, and appear to have gradually increased :—

Laws of July 8 and 11, 1871.		Law of January 22, 1872.		Law of December 30, 1873.	
	Fr. c.		Fr. c.		Fr. c.
Raw sugar—		Raw Sugar—		Raw sugar	....65 52
Below No. 13....	54 60	Below No. 13	63 00	Below No. 13	..
From No. 13 to		From No. 13 to		From No. 13 to	
No. 20	52 00	No. 20	66 00	No. 20	68 64
Above No. 20....	58 50	Above No. 20....	67 50	Above No. 20....	70 20
Refined	61 10	Refined	70 50	Refined	73 32

We ought not, however, to lose sight of the fact that, whilst the sugar refining interest complain of the unfair working of this system of drawbacks allowed to their French competitors, these latter in turn complain of the same thing as regards the Austrian and Russian refiners, who are said to be far bigger culprits in this respect. France has, as every nation of the world, suffered from the general depression in trade and commerce, yet undoubtedly to a less extent than many other countries. She is not as hampered as we are by the fetters and shackles imposed on our manufactures by trades unions. She has already risen superior to many of the effects of her late war, and there would appear to be no nation in the world that has more to gain by an increased and closer intercourse of both mercantile and friendly relations with Great Britain than France.

GERMANY.

An extreme depression of trade has been so universal during the last three years in all the States of Europe, nay, I think it would not be beyond the mark to say in all the States of the world, that it has latterly been difficult to take up a trade report from any of our legations or Consuls without finding that it contained that almost stereotyped phrase, "There has been great depression of trade." From which state of things I am glad to note a re-action has already set in. Has this increment to trade, however, altogether a sound foundation?

Germany has been no exception to this rule; the conqueror has suffered as well as the vanquished, and the land which gained the five milliards has not been flowing with milk and honey. Besides the check to commercial prosperity caused by wars and rumours of wars throughout the world, nothing has contributed more to retard her progress than the ever increasing exigencies of military service, the removal of tens of thousands of the class which a nation relies on to increase its wealth ; and the subjection of young and able hands to the unproductive employment of a soldier's life ; a life, it may be added, which does not consist in moving from one end of the world to the other, in seeing new countries, and in gaining new ideas, as is the case with the English soldier, who not unfrequently becomes a colonist on leaving the army ; but in Germany means idling away existence for two or three years in some second-rate German town, in the dull routine of a monotonous garrison life.

Germany has certainly lately been passing through a time of trade depression. But was it not inevitable, when we take into consideration the period of feverish mania for speculation influencing all classes throughout the whole country, which followed the termination of the war with France in 1870 ? The country, which had always been a poor one in comparison with England or France, made haste to become rich. Railways were constructed to open out districts without due consideration as to whether they would pay or not. Joint Stock Companies were started, for the two succeeding years, at the rate of one a day. The demand for iron and the prices offered for it became enormous. New mines were started and smelting furnaces opened by the score of which now seventy per cent. lie idle. But although the immediate result of the employment of the capital handed over by France to Germany has not been to turn a poor country into an El Dorado, Germany will reap the fruits hereafter of the large sums expended by her in opening out her national resources by the construction of new railways. Whether these railways were laid down, as in some cases, for strategic reasons, or as in others, for the purposes of trade, and of establishing the inter-communication of districts, they cannot fail to increase the wealth of the country and to aid her in her efforts to become a leading commercial as well as a leading military nation.

A large amount of the indemnity paid by France was devoted to purchasing railways, to the invalid fund, and to the completion of the German fortresses, while portions of it were also devoted to the expenses of the navy and to those occasioned by remanning the fortresses. All the sums thus paid out of the five milliards were either returned directly to the German nation in the shape of wages to the labourers employed on the works and in the factories, or indirectly by giving its territories additional security without obliging the Imperial Government to levy fresh taxes or to increase the National Debt; and it may be noted whilst referring to the National Debt of Germany, that there is, fortunately for that Empire, no nation in Europe which has, comparatively speaking, so light a one. The kingdom of Prussia owes, exclusive of railway loans, the sum of about 25 millions sterling, or very nearly £1 per head of the population of the kingdom; while the total burden of the National Debt of France amounts to £20 12s. per head of the population. Saxony, Bavaria and Hamburgh, have also small national debts the slight amount of interest to be paid on which can be hardly felt; and Germany has, therefore, no inducement, on the score of a heavy debt, to tax, by heavy import duties, either clothing, implements of labour, or any other articles that the German nation find they can purchase more cheaply than they can make.

Our trade with Germany has hitherto been based on the soundest and most advantageous principles for both countries concerned, and has mainly consisted in our purchasing largely from them articles of food, such as live stock, grain, and sugar, besides wines and spirits and numberless descriptions of "middle class goods" which, either from the cheapness of their labour or from other causes, we find they can produce and sell to us at a cheaper rate than we can purchase the same articles in England, while they receive from us principally coals, iron, woollen and cotton goods, tea and sugar.

In 1878 we exported (including foreign and colonial produce) goods to the value of about £6,400,000 more than we bought from the Germans. The above figures, however, though they give a fair general idea of our trade with Germany, do not give at all an exact one. It is indeed impossible to speak with accuracy on the subject, for the amounts we find in the Government returns are only those which are registered in England for exportation direct to German ports, and are quite irrespective of all iron destined for Germany shipped to Dutch or other ports, or, on the other hand, of those goods sent through Germany to other countries. In the case of some articles the consideration of this fact is of importance; for instance, the large increase in the import of English rails, especially in the port of Königsberg, was known to be attributable to the supplies intended for Russia and Roumania. Since 1874 we have to notice, however, an increase of over four millions sterling in our imports from Germany, and a falling off of six millions from the value of our exports to that country.

Notwithstanding the fact that a large number of smelting furnaces have been closed, there is an undoubted increase in the export of iron, steel, and machinery from Germany. Prices, however, in the iron trade had materially fallen there, as elsewhere, from which fall there is at present a certain reaction, though this did not seem to affect the amount of metal produced. Not to multiply examples, I may mention, that the Dusseldorf Iron Works produced and yielded more iron and steel, and more iron and steel goods in 1877 than in 1876 by 200 tons. Until recently it was the policy of the German Government not to put any tax on several classes, and on others only a light one, on the importation of iron or steel goods, and that policy may have been dictated by the fact that the Government itself had large requirements as to both those metals, and did not care to pay a superior price at home for an article which it could obtain elsewhere at a less rate. What an argument against the German and other Protectionists! The Government, requiring large quantities of a certain article, ordains it shall be subject to no import duty, and be absolutely free. Let it, however, only be required by the nation at large, and a tax is imposed without any great compunction. The German iron works were suffering from the same cause as the English and Belgian, and for this simple reason, there was less demand for iron than in 1872. Not one twentieth part of the amount of railways laid down seven years ago are now added to the railway system of the world, and those recently constructed or in progress have their lines almost invariably laid with steel rails. Nor are as many steel rails sold for repairing the lines as iron ones previously were, owing to the fact that the former last nearly three times as long; so that the yearly amount of rails of this description required to keep a given hundred miles of railway in order will only be about one-third the amount it once was.

It would be needless to enumerate the hundred and one ways in which the general depression in trade has affected the iron trade. Those workmen who were retained in the iron works were receiving less pay in 1877 than they received in 1873, although considerable relief has been afforded to the labour market in Germany by the return of foreign workmen to their homes, and agricultural labourers to agriculture. Germany appears to be by no means backward in pushing her trade in iron, steel, and machinery, and seems not only to retain for her own manufactories the making of steel rails for her railways. Consul-General Crowe reports from Dusseldorf that German corporate bodies are instructed to foster the patriotic tendency to give preference to home produce, even though it should be dearer than the same article imported from abroad, and quotes the following instance. Last autumn, one of the principal railway companies in the neighbourhood advertised a contract for 7,000 tons of steel rails, and accepted the tender of a Rhenish company, *though higher by* 15s. *a ton* than that of a foreign company. The excuse given was that Rhenish railways are carriers for the Rhenish iron works, and have an interest in their welfare; and a case was cited where a company of ironmasters at

Hörde which paid £74,000 for railway freight in 1872, so reduced its production in 1878 that it only paid £42,000 in that year. Whether the answer will satisfy free traders or even the shareholders of the railway in question is uncertain. But it would appear that railways hardly require to pay this regard to iron companies, seeing that last year, in a period of unexampled depression, their traffic receipts were much higher than they had been in 1877. The German ironmasters are exporting not only locomotives but railway plant to both Russia and Austria, as an illustration of which I will quote from Mr. Dering's report, dated Berlin (Embassy and Legation, Part I., 1877), in which he points out the aims of Germany in respect to her trade in iron.

"The Berlin-Stettin Railway Company lately gave the contract for their annual supply of steel rails to native firms, at the price of 170 marks a ton (£8 10s.), delivered free at Stettin. In 1876 the contract for steel rails, of the same quality and dimensions, was taken at 162 marks per ton. The tenders from England in these cases, it is true, were mostly lower; but the railway company declared they accepted the German tenders on account of their experience of the superior lasting quality of the steel."

Russia is one of the largest customers for locomotives and railway plant, which she orders largely from Germany and the Continent. The bulk is made by German firms, who deliver their locomotives at the Russian frontier at £2,250 apiece. The Americans cannot deliver them under £2,500. Russian firms, who accept Government contracts, order the several component parts to be made separately in Germany, and have nothing to do but to put them together.

We have as yet by no means seen the last of the uses to which steel will eventually be applied. It is in the bounds of possibility that the day may not be very far distant when an iron man-of-war will be as much out of date as any of our "wooden walls" now lying up in Portsmouth harbour.

The coal trade between Germany and England is perfectly free; yet we are selling the Germans 10 per cent. less coals than we did in 1874, which reduced quantity has not realized half the amount we then received; or, to quote the figures, £1,626,000 in 1874, as against £812,000 in 1878. Not only, however, are they purchasing less from us, but they are making the most strenuous efforts to extend the sale of Westphalian coals, and to take the place of English merchants in their trade with Holland, Belgium, and Sweden, an endeavour in which they are not altogether unsuccessful. The German Admiralty authorities, after scientifically conducted experiments, claim that there are several kinds of the Westphalian article which are equal in quality to the best British coals, and as a practical result of these experiments the German navy on home stations is now almost exclusively supplied with German coal.

No very flourishing account has reached us latterly of their trade in textile fabrics, including cotton, linen, and woollen goods, either in the districts of Dusseldorf and Studgardt or in Southern Germany. As a set off against this fact, however, there has been a large increase in the importation of raw material both in the wool and flax industries, which, in the case of jute, has amounted to no less than ninety-five per cent. It seems, however, that whilst we appear to be able to beat the German manufacturers in the higher class of goods, they excel us both in quality and price in the coarser fabrics; indeed, their former tariff by no means seemed to have prevented these trades from holding their own not only as regards their supplying the wants of their own countrymen, but also with respect to their sales to foreign merchants.

Two reasons appear to have urged the Germans to a Protectionist policy. One is the fact that many of their larger manufacturers, finding that their trade and profits have considerably diminished in the last few years, imagined that the simplest way of again making large profits and to obtain the means of securing a higher price for their goods, was to prevent foreign competition by the imposition of high protective duties. This class being wealthy and powerful, have naturally strong interests, and have for the present, notwithstanding strong opposition in Bremen and other towns, gained their point. Another reason which carried weight was the annoyance and inconvenience the German merchants experienced from the heavy import duties placed on their goods by the French, Belgians, Austrians, * and Russians. If the Germans had decided to place retaliatory duties on these protectionist nations, and had granted free trade to nations with a free import tariff, there would have been at any rate some consistency in such a course of action, and the German Government might have induced certain protective nations to reform their tariffs and have given them reciprocal advantages in trade. They might have urged, that they taught the English, at present the greatest of free traders, that it was to their self-interest to

* This was written ere the conjoin and harmonious working of the Prussian and Austrian commercial systems now rumoured was spoken of.

reduce their tariffs by threatening a retaliatory tariff in 1822 ; and therefore that they had reason to believe that the same line of action if adopted now would have had the same result with other nations. A perfectly free trade between England and Germany would simply tend to make each country strive to produce such articles as it could make better and cheaper than the other. A competition of this description would tend to equalize prices, and at the same time it would be an incentive to economy in manufacture ; and whilst furnishing a motive to enterprise in invention, would add to the comforts and wealth of the inhabitants of both States.*

UNITED STATES.

It is a somewhat rapid transition to pass to a review of the trade position of the above country after a consideration of that of Germany; to leave one of the oldest of the nations and go to one of the newest ; to leave a country with which we have exchanged, at any rate till this summer, the mutual benefits of a comparatively speaking free trade, and to go to one which at present is certainly one of the most protectionist nations in the world, a State in which we have to pay an almost prohibitory import duty, which averages over 54½ per cent. ad valorem on our six principal exports. These high duties were chiefly imposed or at least greatly increased after the late American war, about the year 1868, and were supposed by those responsible for their imposition to fulfil two objects : firstly, to make foreigners pay the interest of the enormous debt contracted during that war ; and

* See Appendix I., the German Tariff.

secondly, to protect, foster, and encourage home manufacturing industry; to make America, as it were, a self-contained country, able to supply its own wants in every direction. It has also been the policy of the Americans to encourage and foster as much as possible their export trade, and in consequence the total result last year was as follows: we bought from them over eighty-nine million pounds in value of their produce and manufactures, and only sold them seventeen and a half million pounds worth of ours; whereas during the decennial period from 1868 to 1877, our exports from them increased at the rate of eighty-five per cent., the imports of our home produce into the United States, though never during that period above half the value of their exports, decreased at the rate of twenty-five per cent.

The general course that our commercial relations with America will apparently take, if their present tariff is maintained, is that the flow of our exports will gradually diminish (except during short-lived periods of inflation) and during the time of their gradual diminution the natural course of our trade will gradually lead us to purchase less and less from the Americans, and to ascertain from which other States we can have reciprocal dealings in order that our ships may have a full cargo both ways, and avoid making their outward voyages in ballast. Such will be the natural, the inevitable course of our trade; and the Americans will find that they will gradually lose the market in this country. We are at present their best customers, taking 43·13 per cent. of the total American exports in 1878, whilst of the imports to the United States 24·55 per cent. consisted of imports from the United Kingdom. Of what does our vast imports from them mostly

H

consist? Of cotton, corn, and cattle, in which latter class I include the alimentary substances derived from them, such as bacon, butter, cheese, preserved meat, &c.

It appears that during the year ended June 30, 1878, the value both of cotton and of bread stuffs exported to the United Kingdom exceeded the value of the total imports of merchandise from the United Kingdom into the United States. Breadstuffs, cotton, and provisions together constituted 85 per cent. of United States exports of domestic merchandise to this country during the fiscal year 1878. A consideration of these facts will show the important point at issue between ourselves and the Americans.

The whole question lies in this, Can England, a great agricultural country, afford to find herself gradually becoming more and more dependent for food on foreign lands? Can she do so unless she have compensating advantage in having a steady and continuous outlet for her manufactured produce in foreign markets? The American can afford to look at home for his markets; not so the Englishman, who must look abroad. Thus in 1876, 93 per cent. of the products of the spindles in the United States were used at home, and about 7 per cent. exported; while of the cotton fabrics of Great Britain only 15 per cent. were used in this country, and 85 per cent. were sent to foreign nations.

As I previously said, there can be no doubt but that for the last two or three years we have been purchasing from the Americans, by selling them back their bonds, of which I O U's it is calculated they have already purchased nearly 1,000,000,000 dollars formerly held abroad, 200,000,000 dollars only being mentioned as the amount still owned by foreigners; and it ought, therefore, to be the duty of our statesmen to inquire (presuming that the Americans do not greatly change their present tariff) whether our colonies cannot grow more corn and cotton for our home market, and make the British Empire more self-supporting, at the same time taking great care that that important individual "the consumer" does not have to pay an iota more; and that whilst we are supplied with these necessaries, I may almost say of our national existence, by the Colonies, we may at the same time find a sure field of employment for our home labour in supplying their wants. Political economists must, however, remember, that the English workman cannot become "a consumer" unless he receives some wages to pay for what his wants demand. He must pay for that which he wishes to "consume;" and it is idle to talk transparent fallacies to an unemployed and destitute man for instance, and say to him :—" By ' Free Import Trade' I am aware your industry has been depreciated in value, and the surplus, Belgian and American produce, disposed of in many instances below its true value, has, to some extent deprived you of manufacturing for the home market; whilst the foreigner prevents you from selling to him by protective tariffs. But then think of the great advantage the country gains in being able to buy such articles as fire-irons under cost price!"

Before proceeding to touch on the present position of our principal exports to and imports from the United States, it would be as well to examine their import tariff, although it is hardly a pleasant document for perusal, since it is one which cannot fail to have a most detrimental effect upon our manufacturing interests, framed as it is by a nation which our late Premier assures us in his work entitled "Kin beyond Sea" published last autumn) is destined to wrest from us our commercial supremacy. If this dictum be true, whether any " murmur " or not is immaterial, but I mistake my countrymen if this be accomplished without a desperate struggle on their parts to prevent it.

Mr. Gladstone says :—"I do not speak of the vast contributions which from year to year through the operations of a colossal trade, each makes to the comfort and wealth of the other, nor of the friendly controversy which in its own place it might be right to raise between the leanings of America to Protectionism and the more daring reliance of the old country upon free and unrestricted intercourse with all the world, nor of the menace which in the prospective development of her resources America offers to the commercial supremacy of England. On this subject I will only say that it is she alone who at a coming time can and probably will wrest from us our commercial primacy. *We have no title, I have no inclination to murmur at the prospect.* If she acquires it she will make the acquisition by the *right* of the strongest and the best. . . . *We have no more title against her* than Venice or Genoa or Holland has had against us."

But to revert to this American tariff, one can hardly help smiling at some of the items of our home manufacture, which the Americans (*the future greatest commercial nation in the world*) have considered in their wisdom to be fit objects for protection.

The general tendency of the tariff is, that the foreigner must be fined in order that native manufacture may prosper; and therefore all our staple English trades, such as the iron, cotton, linen, wool, &c., are treated with great severity.

To begin with the iron trade, the duties range from

forty-two per cent. ad valorem to one hundred per cent. The duties charged are of the most complicated character, and must make the task of finding out the amount the English manufacturer has to pay on any given article a task of a tedious and probably also uncertain nature. Iron wire, for instance, bright, coppered, or tinned, drawn and finished, has not only to pay an ad valorem duty of fifteen per cent., but also a duty, varying from 9s. 4d. to 18s. 8d. per hundredweight, according to the gauge. Handsaws and backsaws are similarly taxed, first having to pay an ad valorem duty of thirty per cent., and then a duty varying from 3s. 1½d. to 4s. 2d. according to their length. Needles and pens are also inflicted with these complicated double duties, the former having to pay twenty-five to thirty-five per cent. ad valorem, besides again paying a graduated tax per thousand, and the latter twenty-five per cent. ad valorem, as well as a tax per hundredweight. The duties on cotton goods vary from fifty to eight-five per cent. on their declared value; and in numerous, I may say in the majority, of instances they are subjected to this double duty. Linen and woollen goods are similarly taxed, both to the amount of from about thirty-five to forty per cent. ad valorem, the latter being also charged high specific duties. Nothing appears too small, nothing too trifling to be placed under the guardianship of these prohibitive tariffs; and I will instance here a few protected articles out of the hundreds enumerated, which may serve to show that the result of these duties is, that though numbers of them do not pay for the trouble of collection, the price of goods must be increased to the American purchaser. One can easily understand the cause of this from the following list. The tariff comprises amongst other commodities, accordions, apple sauce, asthma cigarettes, bees and bees-wax, bodkins, bog oak, chatelains, catsup, cauliflowers, celery seed, billiard chalk, chestnuts, children's rattles (!), chip bonnets, cold cream, comfits, comforters, court plaisters, crackers, crochet needles, dolls, dominoes, elastic garters, feeding bottles, fiddles and (" in the name of the prophet ") figs! grand marbles as toys, mits, masks, mousetraps, needle-cases, orange peel, nutmegs ("wooden" or otherwise doubtless) parasols, paving stones, pills, pincushions, putty, quill tooth-picks (!), guava jelly, guitars, hairpins, hair restoratives, magnesia, hobby horses, hour-glasses, hyacinth bulbs, lavender water, liquorice, and marmalade. Then come three articles which, whilst they are about it, it seems a pity they did not prohibit the use of altogether, namely, rouge, ringlets, and shirt fronts! and I will close this list of protected articles with snuffers, soap and soy, truffles, twine, tooth-paste, and tea-pots.

It would be difficult to imagine the scene in our House of Commons if our Chancellor of the Exchequer was to come into the House and gravely propose to put a prohibitive duty on the above named list of articles. Though, however, granting that the principle has in this case been carried to absurd lengths, I must still maintain that a nation is justified in imposing import duties which it has fair grounds for believing *may cause other countries to remove* thoroughly protective tariffs.

Till I read through the American tariff, the great care, and the immense amount of inspection of every hole and corner of one's trunks that is displayed at an American Custom House seemed strange to me, and it brought to my recollection the occasion when I had to go through that ordeal on landing with several friends at San Francisco from Japan. We had made our passage, by the way, in one of the American Pacific Company's steamers — called the "Japan," a huge vessel constructed with deck above deck and "walking beam" engines, which was, I afterwards noticed, burnt at sea. On this occasion our worst adventure was "colliding" with two vessels at the mouth of San Francisco harbour, when, as fortunately for us, we were near the shore, tugs came out to our assistance and the passengers were landed in one of them, whilst two others towed the "Japan" in a sinking condition to a dry dock in the harbour. Next morning we went down to claim our baggage. I was travelling with but little luggage and had nothing to declare, so, although a way was pointed out to me that might expedite matters, as I was in no particular hurry, I let the proceedings take their own course, and patiently watched the Custom House officials make the most minute examination of everything, even to looking down the barrels of my guns for contraband goods, which, as I possessed none, I need hardly say they failed to discover. My objections to their tariff, it is scarcely necessary to add, is not the result of this trifling incident; for nothing has more conduced to make me like and admire the Americans as a nation than the great kindness and hospitality I everywhere experienced in their country; and I trust that whether or no we ever have "reciprocity" in trade, we shall always have reciprocity in the above-named friendly relations.

But to resume after this digression. Of course, the American Custom House officials, with their high tariff, have to keep a sharp look out to protect the revenue; Many may remember reading accounts in the "Times" about four years ago, of prosecutions brought against leading American merchants of New York for falsifying invoices for the purpose of defrauding the revenue. To prevent this, importers from this or any other nations have to go through a rather troublesome formula with the American Consuls residing in their several countries, which, whether it prevents smuggling or not, must act to some extent as a block to the channels of international trade.

Mr. Trendells, who wrote the tariff appendix to the Catalogue of the Philadelphia Exhibition, describes it to be in substance as follows. A British merchant having goods to export to the United States, must make three invoices, each stating the weight, measure and number of his goods. He must have the accuracy of the invoices sworn to before the Consul or his agent, and the Consul then signs a warrant endorsing the merchant's declaration, when the latter has to pay fees amounting in all to 12s. 10d., on each consignment of goods to the value of £20. One of these invoices the Consul retains, the second is sent to the Collector of Customs at the port of destination, and the third is retained by the shippers, who can send it to the consignee.

The Consul has also the power, if not satisfied with the true value as given, of placing his own estimate on the invoice, and thus leaving to the consignee the onus of proving the exact value to the Customs authorities when the goods arrive. He can also retain invoices for a reasonable time for inquiry if he is not satisfied, or demand samples of the merchandise to be left at his office. Doubtless under their present tariff, these regulations are needful, but, whether they are so or not, they cannot fail, as previously remarked, to have a deterrent effect on trade, and, whilst it is to be acknowledged that the interests of a nation are more to be considered than the sentiments of the foreigner, looking at them from an English standpoint, they must also be onerous in more respects than merely the merchants' pockets, since no class of individuals probably dislikes, more than do the latter, what is known as "red tape."

Everyone is aware that our two greatest staple imports from the United States are cotton and grain; these fluctuate largely in amount year by year, as the crops are either large or small in the one country, and the demand is great or otherwise in the other. Last year we imported over seventy-five million dollars in value of bread stuffs from the United States, and nearly forty-seven million dollars in provisions, not including sugar and molasses, and over one hundred and seventeen million dollars in value of raw cotton. Notwithstanding all the bolstering up of their manufacturing industry, our imports from their workshops were comparatively speaking small; and even those goods brought over were said to be mostly surplus stock, sold here at low prices.

But at the same time we must not lose sight of the fact that in examining the last decade of the American trade returns she appears to be gradually purchasing less manufactured goods from abroad, and is doing her utmost to compete with us, not altogether unsuccessfully, in China, British India, South America, Africa, Canada, Australia, Japan, and the Mediterranean ports; and at present it is stated that the Americans can produce the coarser qualities of cotton cloths at a price almost the same as we can, whilst we still hold our own in that respect in the manufacture of the finer descriptions.

Amongst other trades in which we have lately heard that the United States artizans have made marked progress is that of cutlery. In 1834 all the table cutlery used in that country was imported from England. To-day we export to them only 8 per cent. of their table cutlery. It is said that the Americans endeavour in their manufactures to combine strength with lightness, whilst we only appear to aim at the former; and some point out as instances of this their locomotives and cars, and their implements and tools, which have beautiful finish and lightness, and are more convenient than ours. If American be compared with English scythes it is stated that the former will be found to weigh only a little over 2lbs., and to have a good curve and polish under the surface, and that they are handier, lighter, and cut more easily and closely than the latter, which weigh nearly 5lbs., and are broad, straight, and rough, just as the hammer leaves them.*

It would almost seem worth while to have this statement thoroughly sifted; for I confess at the various Exhibitions at which I have seen English and American goods displayed side by side, I have failed to see this alleged superiority. But if it does exist in the case of some few small articles, our manufacturers ought to lose no time in regaining their pristine superiority with regard to them.

* Commercial Report, No. 14, 1879.

The high price of labour in America destroys competition in razors, as there is no machinery by which a razor can be ground fine enough, and therefore the cheapness with which we can command manual labour gives us the advantage. The Americans also appear to do a large trade in machine-made boots and shoes, in sole leather, and in tramway cars, but in heavy machinery they cannot successfully compete with us. In fact, to quote the words of Mr. Victor Drummond in his report from the British Legation, Washington:—

"We have the advantage in England in our existing extensive mills and machinery, in the cheapness of living for our workmen, who can accept a smaller wage than here; and particularly are we fortunate in the immense number of our skilled hands for manual labour, but perhaps unfortunate in having too many unskilled. If our manufacturers can reduce the cost and expenses of production, look to superiority in the quality of their goods and wares, be satisfied with small returns, show a desire to make the welfare and happiness of the workmen their own, and they mutually work with energy, I feel sure we shall see happy times again in our manufacturing population."

In estimating the volume of the United States debt, we must not only look at the amount of the Government "Five-Twenties," but also remember that each State has its own debt, and that, including the railway debt, the whole has been estimated at £400,000,000, a certain proportion of which is still held abroad.

It is, therefore, a matter of great importance for the Americans to maintain the present high position of their agricultural interests, and to make their country *par excellence* the granary of the world. They are not, however, it would seem, going the right way to retain that position, since in their attempt to make the foreigner pay their war bill by their import tariffs they are really handicapping their own farmers.

If the foreign merchant finds that owing to their high protective tariff he cannot sell his goods at a profit he will leave off sending them; the absence of foreign competition will tend to increase their price in the United States, and this enhanced value of goods will affect not only the artizan class, but also the bulk of the inhabitants, namely, the agriculturists. Hence, as the prices for the many necessaries, not only of the artizan but of the farmer, rise, the latter must demand a higher price in order to make a profit on his crops which would cause him to be undersold in the markets of the world by a corn-producing State which adopted a free trade policy.

Notwithstanding the artificial barriers erected, and the inflation in prices and the demand for manufactured goods, caused by the immense volume of money poured into the United States in the shape of loans, the manufacturing interest of America seems to have recently been unable to hold its position for the last ten years, nor has it prospered to the same extent as has the agricultural interest. To quote a letter written by a correspondent of the New York " Bullionist, " September 16th, 1876 :—" Depend upon it from the way in which the agricultural interest here has been extending as compared with the manufacturing we shall still need to import a very liberal amount of foreign manufactures. Within the last three years most of our manufacturers have been crippled, many of them, with inferior advantages, have been ruined, and their comparatively worthless machinery will be little used again; thousands of our factory hands will be driven to other employments. The vast army of workmen employed before the panic in railway construction are now working in the fields, and the constant increase of traffic of the western roads shows that our expansion is principally westward."

This fact may have no detrimental effect either on the prosperity of America or of the world at large; and I think this extract from an article in the American paper " The Nation " of last October as to "the restoration of equilibrium between industrial and agricultural labour" entitled to serious consideration. The writer says :—

"The present distress points in one direction, over-production in certain great fields of industry, and notably in cotton and iron manufacture, coal-mining, and ship-building. The condition of England disposes of the tariff theory, and of the soft money theory. The condition of Germany disposes of the losses of war theory. The condition of France disposes of the heavy taxation theory. The key of the problem is the enormous industrial activity of the past twenty-five years. This has led to a glut of certain things, as, in railroads here, more than is needed for people or freight. More cotton than people will wear, as in France and England. More houses than required, as in the United States, France, and Germany. Production has run ahead of the requirements of the population. As Mr. Morley puts it, no matter how cheap shirts are, a man will not wear two at a time. High wages did not bring comfort to coal-miners in 1866-1873, for they spent it in expensive wines and food, instead of dress, furniture, and dwellings. Steam transportation, again, has run away with capital uselessly, as it turns out, for look at the millions of tons of shipping lying idle. There has also been a glut of population to the large manufacturing cities and towns. Steam and the telegraph have been agents to bring matters to a speculative point, not in one spot, but all over the world." The article continues: "*The process of recovery is not going to be very rapid. For this purpose there must be a restoration of the equilibrium between industrial and agricultural labour. The artizan and mill-hand must go to the plough and the hoe, there will have to be a great comparative increase in the world's stock of raw material, of the products of Mother Earth as distinguished from the products of human dexterity before steam can have full swing in manufactories and transportation.*"

The writer concludes that the working classes have not kept up their culture with the growth of invention, that they have had things showered on them which they do not know how to use, and thus make no market for; to quote as an illustration of this, take for example microscopes, which, however cheaply they can now be constructed, are to the average working man an absolute non-essential; and he states that the problem is, how to raise him as a consumer by easy and healthful processes to require those comforts, asked for by the minister, lawyer, and doctor, whose earnings are not greater than his own.

It is one of the greatest advantages which a young and immense country such as America can possess, that no congestion in her labour market can last long. The inhabitants can change their districts or their employment as suits their interest, with greater facility than they can in an older and more settled country. Thus we see that Texas has increased her inhabitants in the last five years by one million, a large proportion of whom have emigrated from other parts of the United States. In the same way, the State of Kansas has increased by half a million; and Nebraska, Colorado and Minnesota have also largely increased their population by emigration from the manufacturing districts. The State of Texas, in size 60,000 square miles, could be made one of the most productive in the Union, both for growing corn and cotton; and Americans maintain that if fully colonized and properly developed, it could, besides supplying the wants of its own population, have a surplus for foreign trade equivalent to the present total exportation of these two products from the United [Sates, namely, five million bales of cotton, and four hundred million bushels of wheat. However that may be, it seems to be regretted that a country with such undeveloped wealth should turn its attention in a direction in which it appears its industry can only be maintained by artificial means.

The increase of the railway system of America has been very rapid of late years. In 1830, the extent of railways in operation was, I find in the "Statesman's Year Book," but 23 miles; the mileage increased to 9,021 in 1850, and to 53,399 in 1870; and on January 1st, 1878, there were 80,853 miles of railway open for traffic. It is, however, a startling fact, that during the past three years one-seventh of the present railway mileage of the country, representing considerably over one-seventh of the reputed total capital invested, has passed through the final stages of bankruptcy: and there appears to be little doubt that the recent orders for English steel rails have been in a great measure given by the purchasers of these bankrupt lines in order to develope their properties. In 1878 the total number of mercantile failures in the United States was 10,478, an increase of 1,606 more failures than in 1877. That fact is accounted for that during the last year there were "circumstances peculiarly influential in encouraging casualties of that character." The Government have given large grants of land to the different railways which have opened out the Far West; and amongst others the Central Pacific Railway Company received a grant of 11,722,000 acres to assist it in constructing its line. Up to 1870 the company had sold 127,626 acres of this at an average of 10s. an acre. The Government would seem to have alienated their land with a lavish hand. The whole of the public domain is surveyed and divided by parallel lines into townships of six miles square, or thirty-six square miles, and these again are divided by parallel lines exactly one mile apart. The smaller squares are called sections, and contain 640 acres, which are again divided into half or quarter sections, and then into eighths. These plots of land are offered for sale at the several land offices in the districts, to be sold, the price being fixed at one dollar and a quarter per acre. The purchaser comes to the assignee of the United States, and receives a patent from the President. There are some fifty different land offices, and from two to three million acres are sold annually.

It is provided by law that two sections of 640 acres of land in each township are reserved for common schools, so that the spread of education may go together with colonization.

A large proportion of the public land suitable for farm purposes has, however, been allotted, particularly those portions which have " water privilege," land without such privilege being, comparatively speaking, of little value. In many instances large tracts have been taken by gigantic capitalists and companies, and the opportunities for a working emigrant to select a good lot, and rapidly make a fortune or even a good living, are not so great as they once were. A man has doubtless still many facilities in the States for raising himself to a station far above that which he held in the old world; but these advantages are not now by any means so available as in former times.

I found the permanent way of the railways in America to be not so solidly built as we find them in England. Amongst other things, however, which must strike a traveller is the immense advantage enjoyed by the Americans of being able to run their lines in most instances direct from point to point.

Who can look at the magnificent cities of Chicago, Omaha and San Francisco, and reflect that 30 years ago none of them existed, without being convinced that the Western States of America, great as they now are, have a still greater future before them?

There has been, as I previously remarked, a considerable falling off in our exports to the United States, of which the following table will give a clear idea:—

EXPORTS FROM UNITED KINGDOM TO THE UNITED STATES.

Commodities.	Year ended June 30—		Decrease.
	1872.	1878.	
	Dollars.	Dollars	Dollars.
Wool, and manufactures of..	50,845,273	17,840,303	33,004,970
Flax, ,, ,, ..	21,047,713	13,615,083	7,432,630
Tin, ,, ,, ..	13,675,757	10,864,503	2,811,254
Cotton, ,, ,, ..	27,335,811	10,674,729	16,661,082
Iron and steel, ,, ..	46,746,171	6,704,865	40,041,306
Silk, ,, ,, ..	18,759,085	3,323,561	15,435,524
Earthen, stone, & china ware	4,151,150	3,082,355	1,068,795
Chemicals, drugs, dyes, &c...	4,676,413	2,732,738	1,943,675
Total	187,237,373	68,838,137	118,399,236

When one reads these figures, it is not difficult to understand one cause, at all events, of the depression of the trade of this country.

It is difficult to understand how so practical a nation as the United States permit their Navigation laws to remain in force. Their bearing will be clearly shown by a consideration of the substance of some of their provisions. An idea may be formed of their general tenure when I state, though it may seem almost incredible, that these laws are founded on, and are almost identically the same as, those which the Americans as colonists found so oppressive as to constitute one of the causes of their rebellion from the mother country. They date back from 1789, 1792, and

I

1817. Some of their most essential enactments are the following:—" No American is allowed to import a foreign-built vessel by purchase, to acquire a registry or title to, or of using her as his property." "An American vessel once sold to a foreigner can never again become American property. An American vessel ceases to be such if owned in the smallest degree by any person naturalized in the United States who may subsequently reside for one year in his native country or more than two years in a foreign country." " Merchandise, the produce of countries east of the Cape of Good Hope, when imported from countries west of the Cape, are subject to a duty of ten per cent. in addition to the duties imposed on such articles imported directly."

Of a similar character are the clauses enjoining that foreign vessels losing their gear and arriving in distress in the United States shall not import others to replace them without paying a tax on the same; and that a foreign vessel with a party of pleasure on board is liable to a tonnage tax, &c.

Such is the spirit of these laws, the result of which has been to prevent the Americans, since their civil war, from getting back the carrying trade they once had. It is, doubtless, partly owing to these laws, that whereas in 1857 the value of the foreign trade carried from all American ports in American bottoms was 102,000,000*l*., and the total in foreign bottoms, 42,600,000*l*., in 1877, foreign ships carried 171,600,000*l*., American only 63,000,000*l*. The gradual decline of their mercantile navy has also been occasioned by the high cost of shipbuilding in America, caused by their protective tariff, which has raised the price of shipbuilding materials so high that it would not pay the Americans to run their vessels against the more cheaply constructed British ships. Last year of the tonnage entered in American ports from various foreign countries over 42 per cent. was from the United Kingdom. We must not close our eyes to the fact that the Americans have lately been striving their utmost not only to recover some portion of the carrying trade which they have lost, but also to drive the British merchant out of several of his most important markets. To begin with, they have cast somewhat envious glances upon the large trade which the United Kingdom carries on with Brazil in comparison with their own, the exports to which country from the States were two years ago little above the value of seven million dollars.

A large American shipbuilder, Mr. John Roach, noting the fact that there was not even a single line of steam ships between the United States and Brazil, succeeded in obtaining from the Brazilian Government a subsidy of 100,000 dollars a year for ten years commencing May, 1878, and has opened a line of steamers between New York and Rio de Janeiro.

Mr. Roach, who seems to be a man of great enterprise, urged his countrymen to assist him in a similar manner with a subsidy; but in this he was not successful. He contended that, as in the United States there had been a large over-production of manufactured goods, and they were in fact making more goods than their people could consume, they would be obliged either to close up some of their factories or extend the field they were intended to supply. He told them that during the Centennial Exhibition he had made himself acquainted with the representatives of the leading South American nations, and found that they were very much interested in their labour-saving machinery, and were desirous of exchanging their agricultural products for the manufactures of the United States. He pointed out that no other country presented such an inviting field as Brazil. With a territory of 4,000,000 square miles larger than their own country before the annexation of Alaska—"she produces in abundance many things," he said, "that we require, such as coffee, rubber, valuable hard woods, dye woods, &c., while she is anxious to get in exchange agricultural implements, and many other kinds of our manufactured articles."

With regard to this statement I may note that there can be no doubt that not only the Americans but also the Germans are striving to secure a larger share of the South American trade into their own hands. Many believe that at present we hold our position as the principal importers to these States mainly through the fact that our splendid steam mercantile marine offers greater facilities to our merchants than those of other countries possess for carrying on trade with them. That we may find our supremacy as respects the transmission of goods more keenly contested in these regions ere long I do not doubt, nor is it unlikely that in the future our Australian Colonies may divert some share of this trade to their own shores. Whilst on the subject of the competition our trade may have to face it may be well to note that our Consul at New York reports that:—

"There is at present in this country *a delegate from the Chambers of Commerce* in France for the purpose of collecting statistics, and ascertaining the feeling of the country in regard *to a reciprocal interchange* of commerce. A deputation of representative commercial men of this and other cities of the United States is also now in

Mexico endeavouring to develope the trade between Mexico and the United States;" and he asks, " Might it not be in the interests of British manufacturers to send over here a similar deputation to ascertain for themselves the true position of manufacturing industries in the United States? Useful and important information would doubtless be derived from such a visit, and the knowledge so gained *might be applied to good account in connection with future trade.*" *

These are not times to sit idly by and let things take their chance. The American farmer has already the advantage of the Englishman in respect of having to till the virgin soil at, comparatively speaking, no rent, and he gains also in this respect, that whereas in England when there is a bad season the farmer loses the fruit of his labour *plus* his rent, the American practically only loses slightly over the amount it cost him to till his land. Nor does the Englishman have the compensating advantage that he formerly had from the heavy rate of carriage his American competitor once had to pay, for that has been greatly reduced. To give an example. During the year 1866 the average rate for the carriage of wheat from Chicago to New York by Lake and Erie Canal, was a little over 27 cents per bushel; but during the year 1878, by the same route, the average rate was 7¼ cents, and by all rail 12 cents. During the present year the average cost of transporting wheat from the region of the Red River of the North, in the northern part of the State of Minnesota, to the city of New York, has been only 26 cents per bushel. This is a marvel of cheapness of freight, and enables the

* Since this was written, the British Agricultural Commission has despatched two of its members to America to collect evidence.

The joiner's work is *dazzlingly beautiful*! the style is white walnut, the panels are Hungarian ash and French walnut with Honduras mahogany mouldings, &c., &c. Another item worthy of mention is the grand stairway, composed of highly polished woods, at the bottom of which in the main saloon are two elegant Memel posts, finished to match, and surmounting each is a handsome bronze figure supporting a lamp. This stairway, which leads to the social hall, or ladies' saloon, is of rare beauty."

Then follow minute descriptions of the furnishing of the "social hall" and "state rooms." One may smile at these high-flown descriptions, but if the day ever came that we had in reality again to compete in ocean steamers with the Americans, we should not only have to keep up our prestige in the most important point in steam navigation, namely "security," by having our passenger boats well found, officered, and manned, but should also be obliged to have them made to look as a rule a little less dreary, and also to see that the cooking on board should be "second to none." These may seem minor points on which to write, but they are nevertheless not altogether unimportant. A merchant is often a traveller, and may bring a great deal of business to a line upon which he is made comfortable.

Mr. Roach's motive for having advocated the building of these ocean steamers is commented on in the "San Francisco Chronicle" of the 15th April, 1877, and as Mr. Drummond, writing from the British Legation in New York, reports, "We find there an article on this subject from the pen of a man who is not only master of the subject, but one capable of expressing his views in a very unpleasant way concerning this subsidized Chester shipbuilder." At the close of his article the writer makes some remarks which clearly show the price the Americans have to pay for their steamers in consequence of their protective tariff and navigation laws and which I shall therefore quote here. He says :—

" Mr. Roach must have some other and better reason for his anxious, unselfish, and patriotic defence of the prohibitory registry law, which his well-known modesty forbids him to disclose to the President and Congress. We shall endeavour to relieve him from his dilemma, and make his patriotism and disinterestedness so clear that they shall be understood and appreciated by all men. The price which Mr. Roach names as the cost of a British-built steam-ship of the first-class is the price at which the ship is delivered to the ship-owner, and includes the builder's profit. The price which he gives as the cost of a first-class steam-ship built at Roach's yard is exclusive of Mr. Roach's profit. What those profits amount to is shown by the following figures :—The *City of Peking* and *City of Tokio*, 5,060 tons each, cost as stated by Mr. Roach (for the information of the President and Congress), 632,500 dollars each. The *City of San Francisco*, *City of New York*, and *City of Sydney*, 3,010 tons each, cost, on the same authority, 376,200 dollars each. Total cost of the five steamers, 2,393,600 dollars. Turning to the construction account of the Pacific Mail Steam-ship Company, as printed in their official report of April 30, 1876, we find that the Company paid Mr. Roach for the *City of Peking*, 1,264,404 dol. 69 c. ; for the *City of Tokio*, 1,275,102 dol. 44 c. ; for the *City of San Francisco*, 744,960 dol. 42 c. ; *City of New York*, 757,539 dol. 46 c. ; *City of Sydney*, 744,331 dol. 51 c., making a total of 4,786,338 dol. 52 c., and leaving honest John Roach a profit, by his own showing, of 2,392,738 dollars (just 100 per cent.) on the five steamers. The price paid for the *Peking* and the *Tokio* is exclusive of the 300,000 dollars expended on them in San Francisco. With this explanation of Mr. Roach's methods for ' reviving American commerce and striving for the mastery of the ocean,' it is useless to follow his plea for ocean subsidies. He says we cannot establish and keep up steam lines to foreign ports without liberal subsidies for long terms. Of course we cannot do without subsidies if our ship-owners and steam-ship companies are to start with paying a toll equal to 100 per cent. on the cost of their steamers, and compete with foreign ship-owners.

" *If the Pacific Mail Company could have brought their five steamers named above upon the Clyde, the Company would have saved* 2,600,000 *dollars on their first cost, and* 300,000 *dollars in repairs, besides several months' detention to the two large steamers.* Allowing 20 per cent. per annum on this sum for interest, insurance, and depreciation, the saving would be equal to a subsidy of 520,000 dollars per annum, plus the money expended every winter at Washington in efforts to extract a subsidy from the taxpayers of the country through their representatives in Congress. Such subsidies when obtained do not benefit the stockholders of the Pacific Mail, as the experience of the past ten years and the present financial status of the Company abundantly prove. It is obvious that such part of the endowment as escapes the clutches of the managers *pro tem.* goes to swell the already colossal fortune and extravagant profits of ' the great American ship-builder' and patriotic defender of our prohibitory ship registry law. Hence his desire for a general system of ocean subsidies, all of which he proposes to absorb afte- his manner of absorption of the late subsidy and profits of the Pacific Mail, and hence his opposition to a relaxation of the ship registry law, which would relieve ship-owners, and force Mr. Roach to be contented with a fair and moderate profit on the work turned out from his ship-yard."

The United States apparently do not only intend to enter into competition with us in South America, where, among other plans adopted by her, she is having a large American Trade Directory published in the Portuguese language in Brazil, which will be distributed gratuituously through Government means, but are also striving to extend their own trade with every country with which they have commercial relations, and apparently leave no way untried in order to succeed in this object. They have recently entered into a contract for a mail ship service to Portugal, and even propose a scheme for sending a surveying party from Siberia to South Africa, with a view, *aided* by coloured colonists from the United States, of opening out trade in that direction, while they are also striving to increase their commercial intercourse with some of our Colonies in Australia and New Zealand. Whilst on this subject, I may note the fact that already the Australian Colonies are making representations to the United States Government, and pointing out to the latter that whilst they are importing, year by year, increased quantities of the products and manufactures of the United States, they find that, owing to the protective tariffs in the States, they are unable to increase their exports to that country.

One fact connected with the late commercial proceedings of the United States cannot, however, fail to have a satisfactory result both on her internal and external commerce,* and that is the resumption of specie payment, for no one can doubt that the statement

* I annex the following clear resumé given by Lord Cottesloe in a letter to "The Times," April 6, 1879, of the increase of our exports to, and the decrease of our imports from, America in the year 1877, in comparison with what they were in 1873 :—
Total Trade of the United Kingdom, 1877.—Imports had increased from £371,287.372 in 1873 to £394,491,612 in 1877; but our exports (British) had fallen from £255,164,603 in 1873 to £198,893,065 in 1877, showing a falling-off of one-fifth; while, comparing the total imports for the year 1877 with the exports for the same year, the difference amounts to £142,073,602, being in the proportion of 8 to 5. Total imports,£394,419,682 : total exports (British and colonial),£252,346,020; loss on the year, £142,073,662.

Trade with America, 1877.—The imports have increased from £71,471,403 in 1873 to £77,825,973 in 1877—above one-twelfth; while our exports have decreased (British produce) from £33,574,664 in 1873 to £16,376,814 in 1877 ; or, including foreign produce, from £36,698,424 to £19,885,893—nearly one-half in five years.

The Annual Statement of Trade for 1877, p. 207, enumerates 39 articles of export from the United Kingdom to America ; on all these, with three exceptions only, there is a decrease, e.g. :—

	Decrease.	1873.	1877.
Alkali, by value	1-3	£1,392,138	£938,055
Apparel and haberdashery	3/4	1,471,279	318,823
Books, printed..	1-3	271,486	192,912
Cotton goods ..	2-5	2,715,601	1,318,948
Do., at value	—	1,553,924	1,225,429
Glass ..	3/4	325,377	76,607
Hardware	1/2	797,145	322,843
Iron	2-3	8,002,526	2,685,881
Paper of all sorts	5-6	161,104	27,082
Salt	1/2	248,933	144,305
Silk manufactures	Nearly 2-3	322,056	124,881
Woollens	2-3	5,990,036	1,655,594

Three articles of increase :—
1. Rags and materials for making paper from £280,810 in 1873 to £370,083 in 1877. But then paper exported of all sorts was reduced, as stated above, from £161,104 to £27,082, so that they took the raw material instead of the paper manufactured.
2. Sugar (refined) shows an increased export, but the imports were much larger.
3. Wool shows an increase from £62,281 to £236,587. [But,

which the President was able to make last December in his Annual Message, could not fail sooner or later to have a beneficial effect on American trade relations. "Resumption of specie payments has passed off quite quietly; and the Treasury continues to be the gainer rather than the loser of gold in consequence. The paper money, which was depreciated to less than half the value of coin, is now practically at par." Another reason which has assisted the United States to live through these times of trade depression has been, that American workmen have accepted the inevitable, and, unlike the British, have not made bad worse by striking for terms which the masters have been unable to

But, turning to imports from the United States, the table contains 63 articles, of which 18 are the products of agriculture:—

	1873.	1877.
Total increase has been..	£71,471,493	£77,825,973
Animals—		
Bulls, oxen, sheep ..	340	11,523
Bacon and hams, cwt. ..	2,626,876	2,506,513
But by value..	£5,191,901	£5,916,077
Beef, fresh, cwt. ..	nil.	443,042
Showing an increase in value ..	—	£1,203,997
Beef, salted, cwt...	196,596	204,007
Butter ,, ..	43,406	118,491
Or in value ..	£199,639	£920,561
Cheese, cwt.	790,238	1,082,844
Value ..	£2,353,181	£3,129,829
Wheat, cwt.	19,796,414	21,386,980
Value ..	£12,938,848	£13,583,543
Maize, or Indian corn, cwt.	10,762,353	25,577,778
Value ..	£3,814,125	£8,225,437
Meal and flour, cwt.	1,582,957	1,765,620
Value ..	£1,382,304	£1,543,793
Hops, cwt...	13,076	116,880
Value ..	£46,740	£557,650
Meat, preserved otherwise than by salting, cwt...	6,289	256,339
Value ..	£16,398	£794,856

Seven other articles of agricultural produce might be extracted.

give, but have either accepted lower wages, or elected to choose that which has been called the labourer's safety valve, namely emigration.

There appears to be no doubt that the United States would renew her prosperity and wealth if she decided to reduce her tariff sufficiently, and thus lower the price of her manufactured goods and give her money more purchasing power. This would render the States doubly attractive to colonists who would not only cultivate large districts now unsettled, and thus add to the wealth of the nation; but also by their wants encourage her manufacturing industry, and take large quantities of the cotton, woollen, and iron goods manufactured at home as well as purchasing a certain quantity from Europe. No difficulty would then be experienced in finding abundant "fields of employment" for both labour and capital.

Freights would naturally be reduced if shipowners found they could load their ships with produce not only on returning from but on going to the United States which would be a gain both to the farmers and manufacturers in their competition in foreign markets with the products of other nations. When she lets trade take its " natural course " her prosperity will increase, not the least *by adding to the wealth of those nations who are the largest purchasers of her raw produce*; and she will become again, as formerly, the most progressive State in the world's history.

SOUTH AMERICA AND MEXICO.

When an average Englishman reads in the newspapers respecting South America it is usually only to learn that some Republic has just gone through a Revolution, or has engaged in a war with another State; that one government is trying to float a loan to regenerate its country, or that another has repudiated its debt; and the usual impression conveyed is, that the nature of the majority of these governments may be well described by the phrase "anarchy tempered by revolution;" and that South America, except for an Englishman engaged in business in such towns as Rio de Janeiro, Monte Video, Buenos Ayres, or Santiago, is about the most unsuitable portion of the world to emigrate to. Such is the general impression; and I fear that in the main it is not an entirely incorrect one, for, with the exception of Brazil, and perhaps Chili, the remaining States are, as the Irishman said, "about the finest countries in the world not to live in." There are those who may attempt to refute this somewhat general statement by pointing to the vast and wealthy regions in these countries, which are only waiting to be tilled, and the unbounded mineral wealth in them which at present remains unworked; but they overlook the fact, that this undeveloped wealth is in the majority of cases useless on account of the absence of any efficient means of sending it to a market, and that the guarantees as to the security for life and property are at present so very slight as to offer a serious obstacle to the accumulation of riches of any kind.

I purpose here touching briefly on the trade with the United Kingdom of several of the States of South America, including Brazil, the Argentine Confederation, Chili, and Peru, whilst making some reference to their physical characteristics and interior government. Probably there are scarcely any territories in the world at present of much greater importance to our manufacturing interest, and at the same time few of which we as a rule know less.

The Empire of Brazil is, perhaps, at present the most settled and prosperous State in South America, though one must not expect to find exactly the same amount of what I may call settled prosperity that one finds in countries more fortunately situated. Brazil lacks in the first place a sufficiently large population to develope her resources, and moreover the population she has, besides being composed of several races, is not by any means of the most industrious character. Her planters, mostly of Portuguese extraction, form a sort of nobility. There are besides mulattoes, the offspring of Europeans and negroes, also large numbers of negroes and Creoles, in addition to a native Indian population. The Aborigines are of a bright yellow copper colour, short, robust, and well made. They are in an extremely low state of civilization; their sole occupations being in most instances fishing, hunting, and the culture of manioc and bananas. In some tribes clothes are not worn, in others the women wear only a scanty covering round the middle, and in others again both sexes are partially clothed. It is extremely doubtful whether some of the more barbarous tribes have any idea of a Supreme Being, but almost all of them believe in the existence of a malignant demon, whom they are anxious to conciliate. I found a similar idea with regard to "devil worship" in existence in the Kulu valley in the Himalayas in 1871, and was informed that the priests of these "devils" were subsidized by our Indian Government, nor did there seem at the time I refer to apparently any chance of this form of worship

being "disestablished." There are besides in Brazil a large number of respectable and useful emigrants from Europe and the other States of America; and one also finds in her territories,—though where indeed does one not?—a certain number of those individuals, who, to quote from the note book of a celebrated personage, "having no money but much brains," are not too particular in the way they use the latter to acquire the former.

The climate of Brazil is well described by M. von Landsdorff, formerly Russian Consul at Rio:—" Winter in this country resembles summer in the North of Europe; summer appears one continuous spring, while spring and autumn are unconsciously lost in winter and summer,"—a description he could hardly have written with accuracy as regards England had he been Consul for the last twelve months at one of the ports of this island.

In size Brazil is equal nearly to the whole of Europe. Among its rivers is the Amazon, probably the largest river in the world; and the country is intersected by several large and important chains of mountains, the chief of which is the range of the Serrai do Mar which runs north and south on the East side of Brazil, at varying distances from the Atlantic, being in some places as near as 16 miles and in others as far as 160 miles from the ocean, and averaging about 3,000 feet in height. On crossing the Serrai do Mar, we meet with a barren table land called Campos Gareas, where there are few traces of cultivation; and although I am aware it would be impossible to overrate the extraordinary fertility of those vast tracts of country of which Para and Rio de Janeiro are the capital cities, yet the often repeated story of the superior abundant wealth of the soil in every part of the Empire is decidedly erroneous. Mr. Consul Cowper, in a report to the British Government, alludes to this, as follows:—" I believe the fertility of the soil of Brazil to be absurdly exaggerated. I have heard much but seen little of its extraordinary powers of production. I have travelled a great deal in this empire, and as a general rule have found along the coast a sandy unproductive soil, covered with cocoa-nut trees and mangoes, varied occasionally near the embouchement of rivers by alluvial deposits hard as a rock in summer, and impassable mud in the winter, further inland undrained valleys forming muddy lakes in winter and very precarious cane fields in summer, the produce of the hills in common with that of the whole country being a prey to that great destroyer the Formiga de Roca, or red ant, and in the very interior sterile mountains, and vast pasture lands, which are subject to droughts, that not only cattle, but hundreds of the population fall victims to."

All over this vast country, however, one finds great and varied natural resources; and probably the forests of Brazil are unsurpassed for the variety of the useful and ornamental woods they contain. In addition to this there are many iron mines, although as yet not nearly enough iron is produced to supply the wants of the country, and it must also be added that the diamond mines of Brazil were at one time of very considerable value.

No one can help being struck with the spirit with which Brazil has endeavoured to develope its resources, nor has she been unaided in this by our own enterprise and capital. On her mighty river, the Amazon, ply the vessels of an English steam ship
K

and tug company, a fact which does much to foster and encourage the trade of the districts. At the beginning of 1877 no less than 1,438 English miles of railway were open for traffic, and it is to be regretted that a country, as in this instance, should have to learn by experience, that railways do not always bring wealth, but that, in certain cases, until the country is sufficiently developed and populated to make them pay, they are a heavy drain on its resources. The railways of Brazil as a rule have not paid.

One of the most unfair pieces of recent legislation has been the imposition of a duty on goods imported for the use of the foreign corporations who had sunk their capital in developing the resources of the country, on the understanding that they should be allowed to import certain goods duty free; as is also the decree by which French railway iron is given a preference over English.

The National Debt of Brazil is large, and including the paper currency and Treasury bills amounted to about £76,000,000 in 1876 ; whilst the taxation of the country, considering the wealth of the inhabitants, is correspondingly heavy.

The returns I have been able to get of the actual revenue and expenditure of Brazil are not so recent as those of many other countries. They date back as far as 1874 and 1875, at which time the expenditure was over £12,000,000 and the revenue over £10,000,000, showing a deficit of about £2,000,000. More than one half of the revenue is raised by Customs duties which are levied on exports as well as imports. Those on exports must prevent the Brazilian merchants competing favourably in foreign markets with the products of those countries in which a similar class of duties is not imposed.

The trade of Brazil with the United Kingdom, although it has decreased nearly one third since 1874, is still of considerable importance, our imports being valued at over four and a half million pounds sterling, whilst the merchandise from her shores is estimated to amount to over six million pounds. Last year we purchased barely one-fourth the quantity of raw cotton that we did five years before; in neither coffee nor raw sugar do we appear to have imported less.

I understand that the United States Government employ their Consuls in the various countries of the world in the most matter-of-fact way. Amongst their other duties they have to send written reports of the products and the probable demands of the markets of each country in which they reside. At Washington such reports are constantly being received from their Consuls in Brazil.

It seems strange that the Brazilians, although exporting large quantities of raw sugar, do not find it pay to refine it on the spot. Our principal exports to them are cotton goods, hardware, wrought metals and woollens, and, as before stated, were nearly £6,000,000, or more than one third the value of our outward trade to the United States in 1878. Brazil has greatly increased her import tariff of late years; but even now it is not nearly so high as that of the United States, and appears to average about 25 per cent. ad valorem. To quote a few items—

Coverlets of certain descriptions .... 25 per cent. ad val.
Cotton tissues .... 25 per cent. ad val.
Towels and napkins .... 30 per cent. ad val.
Sheets, quilts, &c. .... 30 per cent. ad val.
Ready made clothing .... 20 per cent. ad val.

Should the Empire of Brazil ever reduce her expenditure, spend less on a large standing army and fleet, do away with her annual "extraordinary credits," and attract more suitable colonists to her shores, she ought not only to recover a large share of the sale of raw cotton in the English market, but also obtain a greater demand for her produce all over the world. Should her commerce increase, Brazil ought to be able to afford to reduce that which is a heavy indirect tax on her inhabitants—namely, her high tariffs; and the sooner she is enabled by reduced expenditure or by some other mode of taxation to do this, the sooner will she become as a nation a competitor in commerce whom even the enterprising "Yankee" will be unable to afford to despise. With regard to colonists, it may be noted that notwithstanding the beauty of the climate it is a question whether it suits the Anglo-Saxon race, and whether an English labourer in Brazil would not be enervated by the climate, and be more of a burden to the State than a benefit to it.

Of the South American States, the next in importance after Brazil, both in point of size and also as a trading community, is the Argentine Confederation; and although our trade with that State has considerably diminished since 1873 it is still of some magnitude. In 1878 we purchased from the Republic goods to the value of over one million pounds, whilst we sold them two million three hundred thousand pounds worth of our merchandise. This country is nearly six times larger than the United Kingdom, but it is placed in one respect in a somewhat difficult position; for while on the one hand it requires railways to open out its vast territories inland; on the other, judging from the average experience of its 1,409 miles of line open at the end of 1877, they do not appear to have been, any more than in those of the neighbouring territories of Brazil, a form of lucrative investment.

A sensible man would hardly choose to live in the Argentine States in preference to any other country, for he would there find himself highly taxed, and would also have to pay an export duty on the products he raised or the goods he manufactured; and would also discover that, except perhaps in the immediate vicinity of Buenos Ayres, the Government did not take overmuch care of his life or property; nor could he be expected to feel unmingled respect for the individuals whose tenure of office only dated from the "last revolution," and who usually, feeling their lease of power to be uncertain, appear to have personally few scruples of "making hay while the sun shines;" he might even have to complain of the Argentine Congress voting themselves increased salaries at a time of the greatest embarrassment in the finances of their country. Then, too, like many more civilized communities, this Republic has a debt that must be pronounced very heavy, amounting in all to about twenty-five millions sterling, and this has to be borne by less than two million people, consisting, like the inhabitants of Brazil, of mixed races of European, Creoles, half castes, and Mulattoes.

It does not, however, appear that all the rulers of the South American States, by whatever titles they may be known, whether Emperor or President, are such arch-fiends as they are described by some English critics. I cannot believe they are such fools as to voluntarily wish to destroy the prosperity of their own countries. But by some accounts they can do no right, and remind me of the story of the late Emperor Napoleon III., which was adapted in the play of "Rabagas." If the Emperor was seen driving on the boulevards his traducers said, "Look at that man, who ought to be attending to the business of the nation, driving about and amusing himself;" or if he was not seen out driving for several days they said, "Ah! the traitor is afraid to show himself before his incensed people, but is lurking at home plotting fresh conspiracies against the liberties of France!" So when these South American potentates have railways built to open out the interior of their country, because these lines do not pay (if I remember rightly the majority of our English lines did not pay up till the year 1848; and, in fact, some do not even now), they are accused of having constructed them out of sheer malice. Indeed, Mr. J. W. Wilson would even appear to complain, in his article in *Fraser's Magazine* on the South American States, that the object of these Argentine rulers in having a line made through a sparsely-populated district was to place it in communication with the capital, and thus render control more easy. It would seem that no better reason could be urged in its favour; for nothing more conduces to attract and keep population in a district, to encourage trade, and to make a railway ultimately pay, than the fact of its helping the Government of a newly-settled State to exercise proper "control" over the inhabitants. It also acts as an inducement for capitalists to settle in a country; for, as has been justly said, capital is timid, and flies from anarchy and disorder.

Two of the staple trades of this Republic are wool and hides. There can be no doubt that the enormous flocks the farmers and cattle graziers of Buenos Ayres possess ought to form an increasing source of wealth.

The species of sheep are, however, of a somewhat inferior description. Their import tariff is a high one, higher even than that of Brazil. Our principal exports are cotton goods, machinery, iron, and woollen fabrics; and a consideration of the returns extending over the last several years, in each of these branches, tends to show that our commerce with them appears to be in a sound condition.

In no part of the southern portion of America does an Englishman find himself more at home or stand a better chance of getting on than in Chili. The independence of that country was nobly striven for by Lord Cochrane; and his deeds still live in the memories of the inhabitants, hence the *prestige* which clings to the English name in that region.

The natural features of this country have in some measure been of great advantage, as they have rendered almost impossible the constant revolutions and "pronunciatos" to which the other States in South America have been subjected. Chili extends in a long narrow slip along the western shores of South America, and in no part does the breadth of this State much exceed 120 miles, whilst on the east it is bounded by the great Cordillera of the Andes. Whether it is owing to the fact that its Government has been always able by means of the sea to communicate with facility with every part of the country, or to other reasons, it has certainly kept singularly free from internal strife.

In Southern Chili the great mountain range abovenamed rises to a mean elevation above the sea of about 13,000 feet, although many peaks are of a considerably greater height. Many of these peaks are volcanic, and shocks are felt in the country almost daily. These, of course, are usually very slight, but there have been earthquakes of such violence in Chili that their recollection will not yet have faded from the minds of many of the inhabitants. In 1819 the town of Copiapo was utterly destroyed, whilst in 1835 Concepcion and the towns on the coast in the middle provinces were nearly ruined by an earthquake.

The country is particularly rich in mineral products, the principal of which is copper, and which is one of her chief exports; the price of this product has somewhat decreased in the last two years, but many imagine only temporarily. Chili exported last year of this mineral to the United Kingdom £1,448,000, out of a total exportation of £2,199,000 worth of her goods to our shores.

The South of Chili is the most fertile portion of the country. At Concepcion the eye is delighted with the richest and most luxuriant foliage ; whereas at Valparaiso, about 150 miles further north, the hills are poorly clad with a stunted foliage and little grass. It is, taken as a whole, in a good year a large cornproducing country; but she, however, only sent us last year slightly over fifty thousand hundredweights of wheat, a large falling-off from 1874, when we purchased over one million nine hundred thousand hundred-weights, the reason of this being that there was a failure in the crops of Chili last year, and she was even obliged to import grain for her own consumption—from among other countries, Uruguay. The demand for Chilian cereals in the markets of Europe is not as great as it was just after the Franco-Prussian war, at which time large fortunes were made by the planters of that State. Still, if these planters cannot make as rapid fortunes as they then did, and have now to contend against the rival produce of their former customers, the Australians, they still retained till recently a large share of the export trade in grain to Peru, and also found markets for their cereals with Bolivia and the Argentine Republic.

Chili appears now to have been *dragged* into a war with these two States with whom she formerly had commercial relations, namely, Bolivia and Peru. Dragged is the only word which would appear properly to explain the position of affairs, for, however the contest may end (and those that are in the right, unfortunately, do not always win), Chili would appear to have had no other course left open to her, if she wished to preserve her national existence, than to resent the injury which these two confederates have attempted to inflict on her. The history of the events which have led up to the war may be shortly stated as follows:— There is a strip of utterly worthless land between Chili and Bolivia, for the possession of which, though each State claimed it, neither in the least cared. But when, in 1866, guano was found on the shores of this dreary waste, an agreement was made that whilst Bolivia should administer the government of the territory, one-half of the revenue collected from it should be paid over to Chili. Further explorations brought to light not only deposits of nitrate, but the great silver mine of Caracoles, situate in the interior ; and the Chilians commenced working these discoveries with the greatest enterprise. It was agreed by a treaty between the Chilian and the Bolivian Governments in 1874 that on the renunciation by the Chilian Government of its half share of the revenues, Bolivia should guarantee that no duties beyond those existing at the time would be imposed on Chilians working the minerals in this territory, and this treaty should continue in force 25 years. This undertaking the Bolivians kept to until the beginning of last year, when they levied, without giving any warning to Chili, an alarmingly high export duty on nitrate, which they had pledged should be duty free. The Chilian Government remonstrated with Bolivia for this breach of faith, but the latter absolutely ignored their complaint; and knowing that she would be backed up by Peru, and believing that there was no chance of Chili's going to war, proceeded to publish a further decree confiscating all the property of the Chilian Company for their own use. The incitement to Peru in this matter was the fact that having forced all the proprietors of the nitrate deposits in her territory to sell their rights to the Government, she wished to secure the monopoly in them to Bolivia and herself, in order to force up their price to an exorbitant rate, and then probably be enabled to borrow more money on the security of this nitrate. Chili has hitherto maintained a high character for honesty and straightforward dealings; she has a courageous and determined local militia, and a fleet superior in strength of ironclads to the Peruvians, the former having recently, as we are aware, augmented her strength by the capture of the "Huascar," and though it may be a severe drain on her resources, we now hope that the contest may ultimately turn out to her advantage. But, alas! who can gauge the chances of war?

Notwithstanding this war, they are said to still find an outlet and markets for their surplus minerals, coffee, cattle, horses, timber, and wool. Amongst the inhabitants of this country are a fair proportion of either Englishmen or men of English extraction, and it is needless to add that these conduce greatly by their energy to the prosperity of the country. The public debt is about £10,300,000, three-fourths of which was incurred in making railways and in other public works.

Santiago, the capital of the country, appears to attract the larger proportion of the wealthy inhabitants as residents. There the rich planters settle, leaving their stewards to look after their estates in the country. That this is certainly an evil must be admitted, and I will quote what Mr. Rumbolds says on the subject :—" A first visit to the city of Santiago cannot but be a matter of agreeable surprise to an intelligent European, but after a more lengthened stay the ambitious growth and luxury of the town will probably seem to him out of due proportion with the power and resources of the country of which it is the capital. One is, indeed, scarcely prepared to find ninety miles inland at the foot of the Andes a city of some 160,000 inhabitants, with such handsome public buildings, stately dwelling-houses, and exceptionally fine promenades. What, perhaps, strikes the stranger most, next to the marvellously beautiful situation of the town, is the atmosphere of aristocratic ease and exclusiveness pervading it. Unfortunately, it is an absorbing place, drawing to itself too much of the wealth of the country. The dream of the provincial Chileno is to make enough money to build or buy a house at Santiago and there live at ease. It has thus become an idle, expensive, and, so to express it, an artificial capital of a busy, thrifty country. It is also a place of ugly contrasts, for cheek-by-jowl with palatial structures the most dismal hovels are to be seen, poverty flaunting its rags at every step in the bright sunshine, instead of being relegated to remote suburbs as in European great cities. It is termed by its inhabitants 'The Paris of South America,' but is more like slices of Paris dropped down here and there in the middle of a huge straggling Indian village."

The climate of this country is equable and healthy, epidemic diseases being rare, and the new silver mines recently opened out at Florida will add to the wealth of the country and give her probably more opportunities for developing her other natural resources Chili ought, before many years are over, to take a more important position in the " trade of the world " than she now does.

Our trade with Bolivia is small and did not amount to half a million in 1876; and until that country can either find some further outlets for its undoubted resources in raw produce, either down the Amazon, or by Chili or Peru, there will be no great prospect of its being increased.

Before leaving South America, I must speak briefly with regard to the course of our commerce with Peru.

Peru, as most of us know, has been a large borrower, but a bad payer. One of the latest schemes which she has embarked in has been the Oroya Railway. It is reported to be badly constructed, though the cost is said to be £4,500,000; and it is to be feared that not even the high elevation of about sixteen thousand feet above the sea level, at which this line has been made, will console those Peruvians and others who have taken shares in this line for the present loss they sustain. The course of our trade with Peru is simply told. We buy from them large quantities of their guano and nitrate of soda, a smaller amount of their excellent wool from the Peruvian Llama, and in 1878 we purchased £1,400,000 worth of their guano, the other principal imports from

Peru being nitre and sugar each to the value of slightly over £1,200,000, cotton and woollen goods and iron, less by about two hundred thousand pounds than in the former year.

They purchased from us goods to the amount of £1,369,000 last year, which amount was a slight increase in our outward trade of 1877, our total imports being to the value of £5,232,000, which show an increase of about seven hundred thousand pounds since 1874.

Peru may be of some importance to this country's commerce both as an importing and exporting nation, but there certainly seems to be other States in South America with equal natural advantages, (I will not say with greater, for few States in the world can boast of a greater reserve power for fertilization in the shape of guano and nitrate of soda than can this) which may rival, and eventually, even leave Peru behind in more surely developing the wealth and solidity of their countries.

VALUE OF GREAT BRITAIN'S TOTAL IMPORTS FROM AND EXPORTS TO		Increase or Decrease of Exports.
	1874	1878.
Central America	Imports from......1,120, Exports to 175,	968, 766, Increase.
New Grenada. United States of Columbia	Imports from ...... 995, Exports to 2,592,	932, 1,048, Decrease.
Venezuela	Imports from ...... 50, Exports to 528,	98, 483, Decrease
Ecuador	Imports from ...... 297, Exports to 67,	299, 210, Increase.
Uruguay	Imports from ......1,437, Exports to 1,304,	644, 1,035, Decrease

Thousands (000) omitted in this table.

Before concluding my reference to the state of our trade prospects with the Southern States of the American Continent, I will add the above table, which shows the present value of our exports from and imports to the remainder of these States, many of which are of equal importance to our commerce as those South American countries already named; in this table it will also be easily seen whether our exports have increased or decreased since 1874.

In one and nearly all these States the import tariff appears to be a high one; most of them have also been large borrowers from ourselves and the other European nations; and naturally were we to again subscribe to their loans we should temporarily increase our exports to them. Whether we should receive interest for our capital if we again invested in their bonds, is a totally different question.

They possess a vast amount of raw produce which we require in the shape of cotton, guano, sugar, tobacco, grain, hides, wood, &c., whilst they have a large demand for the manufactured products of the United Kingdom. Therefore, our trade with them rests on a sound and legitimate basis, and ought to increase and prosper; most of these countries, however, labour under the disadvantages incident to the instability of their governments. In many, the security to life and property is, comparatively speaking, slight. They nearly, all lack capital and enterprise to develope their resources, and it would be well if they could, one and all, follow the example set by the United States, and do without the, comparatively speaking, large standing armies which they at present employ.

MEXICO.

A few words will suffice respecting our trade with Mexico, reference to which country nearly always brings to my mind the sad fate of the Emperor Maximilian, the man who stuck to his post from a firm sense of duty, and refused to leave his adopted country with his French allies. The return of the French troops from Mexico, and the tragic end of Maximilian was the first great blow to the prestige of Napoleon III.—a blow which culminated in the disaster of Sedan. The import tariff of Mexico may be justly described as high, in fact in many classes of goods, actually more onerous than that of the United States. Why the Mexican Government have placed such a prohibitive duty it would be difficult to understand, as they have no manufactures to foster and protect. It, however, defeats its own object, and the Government does not gain by these high import dues; indeed, Mr. A. J. Wilson asserts that "the Customs officials at the various ports simply strike a bargain for themselves with importing merchants, and pocket what they please."

The Central Government of Mexico can scarcely be said to have any control over its loosely knit provinces; and the adjoining territories of the United States such as Texas have been much exposed to the depredations of lawless bands invading their lands, lifting their cattle, burning their homesteads, and oftentimes not stopping short of the crime of murder. These bands escaping back to Mexico find there a safe asylum. Justice is denied the American citizens through the professed inability of the Mexican Government to stop their depredations, and it is computed that of the vast herds of cattle that had covered the plains adjacent to the Mexican border in 1866 only 10 per cent. remained. The American Government have been, however, taking active means to put a stop to this state of affairs. Amongst the other favourite ways of plundering foreign merchants in Mexico are "forced loans." These are a regular Mexican "institution," and they have been thus graphically described :—" The ordinary mode of raising funds during times of revolution is by 'forced loans,' *and there is no escape, for these are levied by the two contending parties.* The merchants having ready money are generally the sufferers, but as trade is to a great extent in the hands of foreign merchants the contributions fall principally upon them, who have not, as a rule, any connections or friends in power, and are held legitimate prey."

As revolutions are by no means unfrequent in Mexico, besides which even in ordinary times these forced loans are sometimes levied, it is fortunate for English merchants that by a special clause in a treaty they are exempt from them, which arrangement one can only hope for their sakes is strictly carried out. Another rather peculiar Mexican "institution" is the sale of Custom house certificates at large discounts. This system is in the form of an anticipation of revenue, as the wealthy merchants receive, for the money exacted from them, Custom-house certificates at large discounts; thus results the anomalous condition that while commerce, as a rule, thrives in peace and shrinks before war and lawlessness, some of the rich merchants who understand the management of the system, and make themselves useful to all parties, profit by continuous revolutions and favour them, as they make the discounting of their Customs duties at low rates a regular business, which gives them an advantage in trade over those who have less money and influence. The few thus gain while the many lose.

Our imports from and exports to Mexico are comparatively speaking insignificant in amount, the former only being about half a million sterling, and the latter slightly exceeding seven hundred thousand pounds; by the last Mexican returns available of 1873, however, we appear to have had the largest share of their commerce, the United States coming next. The Mexicans appear to be rather jealous of the United States, and dread that which would appear to one almost their inevitable fate, namely, annexation by that country. When, however, that takes place it cannot fail to have for one of its effects the development of the resources of this by nature highly favoured country. The Americans have already succeeded in getting lines of steamers subsidized by the Mexicans between the Gulf ports and Vera Cruz to New Orleans and New York, and between the Mexican Pacific ports to San Francisco and Panama. On this subject, namely, the subsidizing of American steamers, a committee appointed in the States to enquire into the affairs of Mexico have decided "that the Mexicans deserve all praise."

Mexico is a country that, in one respect, resembles our own as it was fifty years ago, that is, in hostility to machinery; for though the Mexican tariff admits machinery duty free, their importation is very small, the reasons for this being that the Mexicans are not a progressive nation, and that there is a prejudice against improved implements, their use not being understood, and the labouring classes destroying them whenever they get the opportunity, as they appear to consider that by so doing they will avoid being deprived of their employment by the substitution of machinery for manual labour.

Some of the inhabitants contend that with thorough development this country might compete with Cuba in the production of sugar, coffee, &c.; be that as it may, notwithstanding the richness of the soil and the wealth of their silver and copper mines, one finds, quoting the words of a former Mexican Minister of Foreign Affairs, "Chronic anarchy here produces the phenomena of humiliating poverty in the midst of elementary riches." What is the cause of this? To put it briefly, one word will explain it, and that word is "Revolution."

ITALY.

Our trade with Italy is of great importance to this country, and appears to be increasing. Who could have believed that a people who were struck down in their attempts to gain their liberties in 1848, and that a country that was once sarcastically described as but a 'geographical expression,' should now have developed into a nation such as we find the Italy of to-day?

I know I should be treading on treacherous ground were I to descant on the advantages of her present over her old régime. I will therefore simply point out her position as a commercial nation.

Italy appears destined to be always a great maritime and agricultural power, though to take a position as a manufacturing country does not seem her rôle. She possesses a mercantile marine of about 951,000 tons, and from her position in Europe she is already gaining a very large share of the trade of the Mediterranean ports, and the day may come when she will bring Indian cotton through the Suez Canal, and when raw cotton instead of being imported to Austria and Hungary viâ England may be sent through the Italian ports of Venice, Naples, Genoa or Leghorn. Her naval force is of considerable relative strength to the other navies of the world, and large sums have been lately spent in its equipment and armament. The possibility of hostile relations ever arising between England and Italy would seem at present out of the question; we may, as I before noticed, however, expect year by year to have a more peaceful rivalry between Italian merchantmen and those conducting our carrying trade to the East.

A large proportion of the inhabitants are employed in agriculture, and although the holdings are small, and the soil is not cultivated to the high standard which it probably might be, still Italy exports to England a vast amount of her agricultural products, the chief of which are corn, oranges and lemons, olive oil, and wine—though it may be observed, with regard to the latter article, that, from imperfect cultivation or manufacture, or from the nature of the soil, the produce of her vineyards is not so much esteemed in this country as is that of France and Germany.

The present tariff differs considerably from the free trade tariff framed by Count Cavour. It is now very heavy, duties being levied not only on imports, but also on nearly all the goods exported. One of the most striking instances of folly in this tariff is shown in the high protective duties placed on iron and steel, since in this class of goods there is nothing really worth speaking about to protect. Pig iron is imported free, rails 7 per cent. ad valorem, and bar iron from 27 to 67 per cent. ad valorem. Italy also (though the fact naturally does not affect our export trade) has actually placed a 5 per cent. duty on silk. Surely her manufacturers should be able to protect their own interests in this industry. If they are unable to do so they will find that our Australian colonies, China and Japan, will beat them in the English as well as in the other markets of the world.

The British Consul at Venice mentions the following with regard to one of our exports to that port:—

"A great quantity of English earthenware is imported here, it being cheap and suitable to the market. British exporters, however, complain that besides the freight and other expenses connected with the transit of the ware, which amount to from 35 to 45 per cent. on its value, the duty is levied on the gross weight of the packages without any tare being allowed; the weight of the package without the ware being on an average one-third of the gross weight. Continental competitors enjoying railway communications pay little more duty than on the net weight of the ware, owing to the fact that they can pack their goods in trucks."

He also mentions that there is a great stagnation of trade in this city, once known as the "Queen of the Adriatic," caused by the suspension of merchant shipbuilding, and of hydraulic works in the Lagoons, that there is sad distress amongst a great number of the workmen, who are unable to find employment in any branch of trade.

On the other hand, one hears from Genoa very satisfactory accounts of one branch of their industry, namely, the refining of sugar, on which product, by the way, there is a proposal to enormously increase the duty; and as the report seems to be of interest to us for more reasons than one I will quote it here.

"An establishment that has made an enormous stride, and has attained proportions deserving of special notice, is the Ligure Lombarda Sugar Refinery, in the suburb of Sampierdarena. This establishment gives employment to about 600 hands, and produced in 1878 no less than 35,000 tons of refined sugar. In going over the works of the Ligure Lombarda, and the distillery annexed to it *I was sorry to notice nothing English about the place.* The two very fine driving engines were from the United States, and all the rest of the valuable plant was from Prague and from Vienna—nothing British but the coal and the jute from Dundee for making the bags (some 400,000 a year); and I heard that even this sacking is, in future, to be made at Voltri, from jute imported direct for the purpose."

Italy also places an ad valorem duty varying from 5 to 13 per cent. on another of our staple manufactures, namely, cotton. With regard to that industry, I here append a table, from which it will be seen that our export trade in it not only to Italy but also to other States of the world has certainly declined since 1875. Export trade of the United Kingdom in cotton goods:—

	1875 Million Yards.		1878. Million Yards.
Holland	57	......	47
France	87	......	63
Portugal	71	......	65
Italy	87	......	71
Austria	14	......	12
United States	80	......	48

From the above table it will be seen that while in the former year we exported to both France and Italy the same number of yards of cottons in 1878, the former took to a diminished extent by *twenty-four million* yards from our mills, and the latter *sixteen millions* less.

It appears to admit of no doubt that our trade with Italy would increase, were there only in that country a well organized and classified import tariff, which the one that came in force in June of last year can be hardly said to be.

Although the volume of our exports to Italy has decreased since 1874, we still send them nearly five and a half million worth of our products, and the merchant shipping under the British flag in Italian ports has shown a marked increase of late years.

NORWAY AND SWEDEN.

In looking to the north of Europe, to the lands of the hardy race from whence came our Norman ancestors, that sturdy stock from whom so many Englishmen of to-day are sprung, we find that our trade has temporarily receded in the last few years, with Sweden and Norway, whilst its total value in 1874 was £18,000,000, it decreased to £16,500,000 in 1877, and last year to £13,400,000; in fact, these kingdoms, like most other European countries, have felt the effect of the Russo-Turkish war in a reduced demand for their products, arising from a diversion to military purposes of an unusually large proportion of the revenue of some of their best customers. So far the capitalists have apparently suffered most, but it is expected that when the accounts are made up for the current year, a serious reduction under the head of exports will have to be recorded.

Our principal imports are various kinds of timber; those ranking next in importance are oats and iron. The mines of Sweden being of great importance to that country, although at present many of them do not pay for the working, their import tariffs are, comparatively speaking, light, and do not appear to have a deterrent effect with respect to our trade to these countries. About 40 per cent. of their total commerce is transacted with the United Kingdom, our greatest rival to these countries in that respect being the Empire of Germany. Most of the trade between the United Kingdom and Norway and Sweden comes to the Port of Hull; and we probably owe, in a great measure, to the energy and enterprise of our merchants and shipowners in that port that we have so large a share of the commercial interchange of these two countries.

SPAIN AND PORTUGAL.

Any one having carefully compared the past history of Spain and Portugal, a history fraught with interest whether looked at from a military point of view or from the solid commercial gain they seemed to have acquired by the conquest of their once vast and wide world possessions, and then travelling in them, and seeing their present position in material prosperity, would feel that they were two countries which were once great, and though still in a measure prosperous, both now (partly from loss of the majority of their vast colonies) by no means relatively of the importance in the scale of nations that they once were. With neither of them is our trade large. With the former in 1878 it slightly exceeded £12,800,000, and with the latter £5,900,000. In the case of Spain this is a considerable decrease since 1877, when our trade in all amounted to £15,000,000.

Mr. Phibbs, writing from the British Embassy, Madrid, states: " The disorganization of the administration during late years, owing to the rapid changes in the forms of the Government which have succeeded one another, has rendered the publication of statistics so irregular that the compilation of any report presenting a fair picture of the financial condition of Spain has hitherto been rendered a matter of considerable difficulty." Of late there has been a great deal of complaint in England owing to the fact that the Spaniards placed our traders at a disadvantage by giving some of our competitors a less onerous import tariff, whilst we were left out in the cold. One of the causes alleged by the Spaniards for acting thus was, they considered, the scale of our wine duties prejudicial to their interests. The duty we levy is one shilling a gallon on wines below 26 per cent. proof, and two shillings and sixpence per gallon on all above proof. Their wines being stronger than the minimum tax allowed, were taxed on the higher scale, and they maintained that they thus found themselves at a disadvantage with the lighter wines of France. It, however, appears that we are now taking into consideration the question of our present scale of wine duties; and a Committee of the House of Commons has been appointed this Session to report concerning them. Should this vexed point be settled as the Spaniards desire, it is not improbable that the prohibitory duties placed on our imports to Spain will be removed. That their trade is not large I am aware ; still, large or small, it is to our advantage not to lose it, and it does not appear we should be, so to speak, permitted to retain our share of it had we nothing to offer the Spaniards in exchange; for, as Professor Fawcett allows, "A Protectionist country is obviously in a much better position to negotiate a commercial treaty than one that has adopted a complete free trade policy." He says, in fact, that in no single instance (I presume he excludes this country from this sweeping assertion) has a protective duty, when once imposed, been voluntarily relinquished, that is to say, without a *quid pro quo*. For reasons connected with our revenue we have not adopted with regard to the importation of wine what he calls a "Free trade system," and what I call a "Free import trade one;" and therefore to aid us in removing prohibitory duties placed on our exports by the Spaniards we have in this instance something more to offer than "the good example" which we have been told was to be an open sesame to the portals of a Protectionist State.

Presuming, therefore, our export trade to Spain was ten times what it is, and was relatively of great importance to a large district in this country, and that we had had no duty on wine, and therefore no other lever to act upon their self-interest, by what means, may I ask, should we induce them to relax their *preventive* import dues on our commerce?

English capital and enterprise have been opening out the immense mineral wealth of Spain in the mines around Bilboa, with such effect that before the opening of the Carlist war there was a large and prosperous mining company at work in that district, and a considerable amount of iron ore is still imported from Bilboa for the manufacture of steel.

Now that the Cuban insurrection is at an end (in which contest from 1870 to 1876 Spain expended immense treasure, besides having lost, it is computed, 90,000 soldiers) and Cuba can once more peaceably become a happy hunting ground, out of which country the Government officers can squeeze " loot."

With regard to taxes in Spain I may point out that there is one levied on salaries which has been greatly increased of late years. On salaries not exceeding £60 it is fifteen per cent.; on those from £60 to £400, twenty per cent.; and on those exceeding £400, and on all pensions whatever their amount, and on ecclesiastical salaries it is twenty-five per cent. In Spain, perhaps more than in most countries, those in power are generally disposed to reward themselves and their immediate dependents more than they are justly entitled to, when we take into consideration the mode of living prevalent and its cost; they can therefore well afford to be taxed. Spain has now once more settled down for a time, and the present Government has become the paramount power, and has virtually repudiated two thirds of its debt, by the simple process of only arranging to pay £1 per cent. interest on their loan, instead of £3. Spanish finance ministers are the most sanguine description of statesmen to be found in the world, if one may judge from their flattering estimates of revenue, which are, unfortunately, not even approximately realized. It, however, would appear that, although the country will have great difficulty in meeting even the modified engagements now acknowledged, considerable energy has been shown in enforcing the payment of taxes; and we must wait to see whether energy will also be shown in reducing expenditure.

It was not until the year 1877 that our imports to Portugal were placed on an equality with those of

France, but their tariff from the latest returns obtainable appears however still very heavy, as will be seen from the following list of ad valorem duties:—Linen, 18 to 42; and woollens 47 per cent. Iron is, however, only charged at the rate of five per cent., and coals are free. The two great internal resources of Portugal appear to be port wine, and banks, and the two principal exports are, as might be expected, port wine, and demands for "loans." Whereas twenty-five years ago, there was scarcely a bank in Portugal, she has now no fewer than forty; and when one remembers that Oporto and Lisbon are the only considerable towns, that number would appear to be almost more than the necessities of business can require. The principal occupation of many of these banks is in fact to bolster up each other, and to finance one another's affairs. With respect to the subject of finance it may be remarked that each year Portugal exceeds its revenue by its expenditure, though the deficit in 1876 was somewhat less than it had previously been, and amounted to about £600,000. The income of the country has greatly increased since 1870 and 1871, and has arisen from £2,000,000 to £5,500,000. There are exceptional causes at work which account for this large increment; the principal of which is the amount of revenue that has been drawn from duties charged on imported iron and other goods in carrying out the very large public works which have been latterly in course of construction. Portugal too, has been largely assisted by the inflation of business which occurred in her old dependency Brazil, in a great measure caused in that colony by the amount of capital expended in constructing railways during the last ten years.

HOLLAND.

Of all the nations in Europe Holland gives us the nearest approach to absolutely free trade. She admits cotton, linen, silk, woollen, jute, iron, copper, leather, alkali, and coals free, and charges a five per cent. ad valorem duty on jute and paper. Naturally, our trade, however free, cannot be very large with a country the size of Holland ; although our exports, including foreign and colonial produce, alone amounted to £14,676,000, and it was in 1878 in the aggregate six times that of our trade to the country I have just referred, namely, Portugal. A certain proportion of the business we transact with Holland is viâ her ports of Rotterdam and Amsterdam, and is simply a transit trade to Germany. The shipping interest of Holland is being hard pressed by competition with England and Germany; she does not possess the materials to build modern vessels, and has to buy most of them on the Clyde, (though there are a number of ships constructed both at Rotterdam and Amsterdam), some of her competitors may gain a slight advantage in this respect. The energy of the Dutch is, however, well-known to be great, and it will not be the first time they have succeeded even when " natural advantages " were against them. There is, perhaps, no region in which nature has done so little and man so much as in the Netherlands. The works in the country which demand the greatest admiration are the stupendous " dykes," the construction and repair of which are placed under the control of a special department of the Government, a corps of engineers being expressly appointed for the service. The expense of making and repairing these dykes is met by a tax on the surrounding lands. The expenditure in labour is very great, but is even exceeded by that in willows and other timber. The former are grown in extensive plantations near the places where they are used.

As the fact of the fearful inundations this year at Szegedin, Hungary, is still fresh in our minds, and also as the security of life and property are acknowledged to be very important factors in connection with the commercial position of a country, it will not be altogether a digression from the consideration of our trade prospects with this country if I briefly point out some of the steps the Dutch take to secure the entirety and safety of their land, which is the following. Should there be a danger of inundation, the population, on a signal being given, at once repair *en masse* to the spot. There is no backwardness on these occasions, every one being fully aware, not only that their public interests are at stake, but also that perhaps each man's life, besides that of his family and friends, would be in extreme peril should the water break through the dykes. Hence the most strenuous efforts are made to ward off the impending danger, and everything that forethought or skill can devise is done to strengthen the dyke, and to prevent the threatened inroad or to mitigate its consequences. In spite, however, of all precautions, Holland has suffered extreme injury from inundations on numerous occasions. The greatest danger exists when the "debacle" or "breaking up of the ice" takes place, as is sometimes the case, on the upper part of a river before it has begun nearer the sea when the risk of inundation is extreme. Cheap communication, as all are aware, is very thoroughly provided throughout the entire country, not only by railways and roads, but by one immense network of canals, the larger number of which are appropriated to the drainage of the land, though many of them are navigable by large vessels. The principal canal in Holland is the Helder, between Amsterdam and the fine harbour of Nieuwediep. This noble work, the greatest of its kind in Europe, is 50½ miles long, 125 feet broad, and 20ft. 9in. in depth, and was constructed between 1819 and 1825 at the expense of £950,000. Perhaps one of the greatest monuments of Dutch science and enterprise is a series of locks or sluices, of enormous size and strength, constructed in 1809 at the mouth of the branch of the Rhine on which Leyden is situated.

Holland's decline from the position of one of the first commercial nations in Europe was occasioned principally by the natural growth of trade and navigation in other countries as well as by the heavy taxes which had to be levied on her inhabitants owing to the numerous contests in which the republic was engaged.

The export trade of this country to the United Kingdom is a large one, and in nearly every description of the very numerous articles that Holland exports to us do we see an increase since 1873-4, in fact the total increase from that date to last year was from fourteen to twenty-one million pounds sterling. In looking through the Board of Trade returns it will be seen that our importation of butter increased from about one and a half million pounds sterling in 1873 to two and a half millions in 1878, the amount of grain we take from this country is increasing but is still inconsiderable—a fact that can be accounted for; since in South Holland the proportion of pasture to arable land is two to one, and she cannot be reckoned as a large corn-producing country.

In nothing has the rise in value of our imports from Holland been more marked than in manufactured silk. It is, on the other hand, unsatisfactory to note that there has been a marked decrease since the former year mentioned in our exports to Holland, which have decreased about five million three hundred thousand pounds. There can be no doubt that the chief danger that the commerce of Holland has to contend against lies in the anxiety of the newly re-constituted great Empire of Germany to increase her trading interests throughout the world. The ports of Bremen and Hamburg are already contending for the commercial mastery with Amsterdam and Rotterdam. The severity of the new German tariff will, however, greatly aid the Dutch ports in this contest, though at present, however, the North German Lloyd steamers seem to have outstripped the Dutch and American in the struggle with freights in the last few years of close competition and small profits. When, however, trade thoroughly revives there will be ample space for them both to prosper in the trade between the north of Europe and America; nor is it to be apprehended that the one will interfere with the prosperity of the other. The greatest colonial possession of the Dutch, Java, has been always looked on by them in the most matter-of-fact and commercial spirit. They simply said, " We have this colony; it is a rich one, and we will make it pay us ;" and so for several years after they obtained complete mastery of the island they obtained from it a revenue of from two to three million pounds towards their home exchequer.

A consensus of opinion in this country would rightly decide that this principle was a wrong one, and that there were other "missions" and duties appertaining to the rulers of a colony besides the extraction of revenue. A Dutchman might plausibly reply, "It is my theory, and I find it answers as well in practice as yours. I certainly do not try to improve and civilize my colony as you do your dependencies, with the Bible in one hand and the bayonet in the other; nor do I hand over to it the entire management of its own internal affairs as you do your colonies, whom you even now leave the power (as in the case of Canada) to impose hostile tariffs against you, and to give more favourable terms should they see fit· to favour other nations; notwithstanding you appear to have slight power of preventing yourself being dragged into wars on their account, where you have to spend your blood and treasure and enrich their contractors, for which service you barely seem to receive their thanks."

Holland, however, seems to have made a step in the direction of free trade in her colony of Java. There are rather conflicting reports about the reality of this change, which, moreover, has not as yet had an altogether satisfactory result as far as our merchants are concerned, since it led them immediately to consign goods to Java without considering the requirements of the settlement, and thus to completely glut the market with unsaleable goods which they were obliged to sell at ruinous prices, and indeed, in many instances we are now told the purchasers have omitted the formality of paying our merchants for the consignments of our products and manufactures sent to them.

DENMARK.

In turning our eyes to the neighbouring kingdom of Denmark, we find our trade is less in volume than that to Holland, and yet it appears to have resembled it in this respect, namely, that since 1874 our exports have diminished by nearly a million sterling, whilst our imports have increased by about the same amount. Since the annexation of Schleswig-Holstein by Prussia, which seizure we had told the world through the voice of the late Earl Russell, we would not permit, and having thus in a great measure encouraged the Danes to fight the combined armies of Prussia and Austria, we left them in the lurch.

Since then, naturally, our prestige as a nation in Denmark has not been considerable, nor are we received with open arms by the inhabitants of Copenhagen should we chance to reside in that capital. This was not always the case; the time was when an Englishman would be not only received for his own sake but for that of his country. But what has this to do with trade, the reader may enquire? A great deal, I contend. The affinity of feeling that brings races together has an indirect influence in establishing and encouraging commercial transactions, and is *one* of the reasons, I opine, that has led, although we are not placed by nature in such close proximity to Belgium as France is, to the large commercial interchange we have with that kingdom.

Our trade with Denmark could naturally never be a large one, and is of course reduced since the diminution of their territory, which now is only 694 square miles.

M

Of this 25·1 per cent. are uncultivated soil, as heath, &c., 31·1 per cent. was under cultivation for the production of cereals, garden, &c.; 38·9 per cent. pasture land; 4·3 per cent. forests. The climate of Denmark is humid, and in its principal features it approaches pretty closely to that of Scotland, the transition from one season to the other being, however, more abrupt. Her import tariff is not a heavy one. In calculating some of the duties charged at an ad valorem rate per cent., we find cotton yarns are charged 5 to 9, whilst linen is somewhat less heavily taxed from 3 to 6, silk, and woollen and worsted yarns at 3, and iron at 9. There does not seem any prospect at present on the one hand of the diminution of our trade with Denmark, or, on the other hand, of an increase.

AUSTRO HUNGARY.

There are always two methods of regarding the question of our present position, and the probable future of our trade prospects with the several nations of the world: the one is to consider the prospects of our own commerce to and from their shores, the other to enquire whether they are likely to be our successful competitors in other markets of the world. Now, under the first head in the case of Austro Hungary our trade is insignificant, and can never be of vital importance to us. True it is, that in 1870 and in 1871 our exports to Austria were nearly double that which they now appear to be, when *they barely reach two-thirds* the value of our exports to Peru, as will be seen from the following facts, that whereas in 1878 our total exports to Austria were £1,089,000, to Peru they were £1,591,000, our exports to Austria were in fact less than we sent to Chili, and about equal to the value of the merchandise sent from this country to New Granada or Uruguay. Our large outward trade at one period to Austria, of which fact I have previously referred, was due to a number of transitory causes. In 1867 and 1868 she was fortunate enough to have excellent harvests, whilst in other countries the crops had failed; hence a considerable balance was paid under this head by foreigners, and never previously had this Empire so much ready money. Besides which her political difficulties appeared to have been smoothed over by the Treaty with Germany and the cession of Venice to the Italians. Austria, although not a rich country, then set to work to develope her resources with prodigious haste and without reference to her requirements or trade. In four years 12,000 miles of railways were constructed, joint-stock companies were formed who explored mines, manufactured iron, and purchased for these works in the meantime machinery of every description from foreigners. The whole of Austria seemed, in short, thoroughly determined to carry out in practice Mr. J. Stuart Mill's theory that the only direct advantage a nation gains by commerce is her import trade.

At length there came a relapse—a doubt in the direct advantage of this system being evident. The artificial and exorbitant prices charged for iron dropped, and the market became inundated with shares of the various companies, till affairs culminated in the crisis of 1873, after which time the working of numerous mines was stopped, important machinery lay for many years standing idle, men were dismissed, and furnaces extinguished.

Though Austria and Hungary are nominally united, race-antipathies and divergent interests make the joint political action often difficult. Of this we have had evidence only lately during the present settlement of the Eastern Question, when, as a rule, the German population of Austria sympathized in the struggle with the foes of Turkey, whilst their influence was counteracted by the ruling race in Hungary, who had Turkophile tendencies, and there is said to be at the present moment no inconsiderable difficulty in the arrangement of a tariff to suit the divergent views and interests of each of the races of the Empire.

The Austrian tariff is by no means a light one, and taking the six classes of goods together will be seen to average about 10·6 per cent. Still it is much lighter than that which we should have had placed on our goods, had not the commercial treaty, held up the beginning of 1877, been renewed. Had not this been the case the duties charged on our imports to Austria would have been almost prohibitive, and would have entirely put an end to the little export trade we transact with the Austrian Dominions; and as it would have been contrary to our "principle" to have retaliated in any way, it would have afforded another instance of the power we have handed over to other Governments of the world of checking if not destroying the industry of our own manufacturing population.

Our imports from Austria, which consist chiefly of corn and flour, have considerably decreased since 1869. The tillage of the farms in Hungary would not appear to be of a very scientific or at any rate of a very successful nature, for their grain crops only yield an average per acre of eight or nine bushels, as against twenty-eight in Great Britain and twelve in the United States. So that our own "Landlord-ridden country," as it is sometimes called, does not seem to be so very badly cultivated after all. In an article in "Macmillan's Magazine" on "Remedy for the Present Industrial Distress," the writer (Mr. A. J. Wilson) seems to attribute a great part of trade depression of the last few years to those wicked landlords; and one is almost astonished to find that the gradual diminution of the exportation of our manufactures has not been ascribed to the system of our tenure of land. Our landowners, he writes, "have not merely burdened the land with their game preserves, they have tied it up and actively conspired to prevent its cultivation. Instead of rising to the true necessities of the case, they cling to their game, make penal enactments about it, and thus augment the intensity of the evil which it is to the people, as if the very existence of the country depended upon hares and rabbits." And unless all this is changed he states the result will be a revolution, the whole distress of the country has been caused by hares and rabbits,—hares and rabbits have deprived us of markets for our cotton and iron, have driven our sugar refiners from Glasgow and Bristol, and destroyed the silk trade of Coventry! Lord Derby is said some years ago to have given currency to the assertion that, " with proper tillage the yield of the soil of England could be doubled," and Mr. Wilson adds that "those who know anything of agriculture are not disposed to question the estimate."

I suppose he will allow that the farmers of this country could not raise very greatly increased crops off the greater part of the land at present under cultivation without permanently exhausting the soil. Then how is it to be done? By growing crops, he explains, on the lands which the landlords have turned into "gardens of pleasure." Mr. Wilson states his case against the landlords still more explicitly in another passage. "They have enlarged their vermin preserves, their deer parks, their grouse moors, and fox-hunting districts, and set more store by the life of a rabbit (most destructive of land pests) than on human life." Inhuman monsters!

In the first place, this assertion is incorrect with regard to the increase of vermin preserves, since hundreds, I may say thousands, of landowners in the country have utterly destroyed the beforetime cause of dispute betwixt them and their tenants, and have not a single "cony" on their estates. There are tracts of land in this kingdom, I am well aware, which are devoted to rabbit warrens, and where these "destructive pests" are bred by the thousand. For instance, the sandy soil around Thetford, in Norfolk, is, and has been so for many years, let to a contractor as a rabbit warren. Any evening the traveller along the road there may see thousands of black rabbits feeding on the sparse vegetation of the land, which I can hardly dignify by the name of grass. These rabbits do not afford "sport" to the wicked landlords; on the contrary, when required for market, are caught in a most prosaic manner by the contractor's men in pits dug as traps for the purpose. Every portion of these "destructive pests" is utilized; the skin is tanned, and the black hair is used extensively in the manufacture of hats; the ears are boiled down and used as glue, and the bodies are then sold, and are largely used as cheap food amongst the poor of Birmingham.

Presuming that half this land was reclaimed and taken away from these "pests" by the person I shall designate

Farmer A, whilst the remainder was left to the present occupier, Contractor B, Farmer A having fertilized the land, and having imported guano from Peru and bone manure from France, would find that his endeavours to add to the wealth of the country would not result in his growing crops one-half either the weight in human food or one-third in value of that which his neighbour, Contractor B, was rearing in animal food; and whilst the farmer would speedily be ruined, the latter would be making a fair profit.

It is not fair to look at statistics and say, There are so many acres of land in the kingdom; every acre must grow corn. That description of argument does well enough for platform oratory, but in practice is found impossible. No one can suppose that every acre of land on the Grampians would be benefited by attempting to grow crops, since the land is entirely unsuited by nature for any other use than the feeding of sheep or grouse. Even the Duke of Sutherland, backed as he is by his great experience in the reclamation of moor land on his property, aided by his vast wealth, which enables him to command the most skilful engineers and the most approved machinery, knows well that there are vast tracts amidst the mountains of Sutherlandshire on which no crops *could* ever be raised; and even in the flat districts he is reclaiming near Bonar Bridge, it will be years before he receives any interest on his expenditure, and problematical even then if it will ever pay. He is, doubtless, causing the reclamation to be effected with a view to adding to the ultimate wealth of his family and the corn-producing power of this country; but a small proprietor in Scotland with similar aspirations could scarcely be expected to possess the resources to carry them out. How "fox-hunting" can be dragged in as a cause of "the present industrial distress" it is difficult to imagine. For in the first place, it keeps the landlords in their own country amidst those who are engaged in tilling the land, thus preventing in a measure the evils of "absenteeism" and the withdrawal of the money received as rent from the district in which it is received to be spent in large cities—an evil which is greatly felt in France (for it is a popular error to imagine that there are no landlords in that country), which evil is with us thus in a great measure avoided. Not only do the fox-hunters purchase horses from the farmers, but the friendly feeling between all classes in the country districts, partly caused by their meeting in the hunting-field, makes all the more improbable Mr. Wilson's "revolution," which if it ever occurs will be caused by ill-feeling between the *manufacturer and his employés*. To give another sample of the ills which this writer states the landowners have brought on the State, which rather reads as if he had been annoyed during the work of composition by hearing a piano played in the adjoining house: "To his exclusive privileges and over-mastering claims we owe it that our modern cities are built well nigh as insecurely as the 'paper houses' of Japan, so that three-fourths of modern London may have to be rebuilt within thirty years." The facts of this case being that where the landlords have invested capital in constructing houses on their own land in London, they are as a rule well built, as it is their direct interest to build them substantially, and as where they have let the lands to others for building purposes it is usually on a lease of ninety-nine years, it appears evident that if any of the houses in London are only constructed to last thirty years, it is the fault of the speculators who constructed them, and not of the landlords.

Besides grain we also import olive oil and timber and paper from Austria. The former varies very considerably from year to year, according to the abundance or otherwise of the crop, and amounted in value to over two thousand pounds in 1873, to over eighty-six thousand pounds in 1875, and over fifty-seven thousand pounds in 1877, in last year it had sunk to about five thousand pounds. In our exports to Austria iron has considerably decreased since 1874, this product being charged an ad valorem duty of from 17 to 35 per cent. This can also be easily accounted for, since the Austrians have reduced their demand for iron very considerably since 1873, for the simple reason they could not afford to pay for more. It will give a clear idea of the extent to which their own mining industry has decreased when I state that in 1873 11,028 persons were engaged in the Austrian iron ore mines, and in 1876 only 5,671; whilst wages have decreased for miners about 20 per cent. The proprietors of the mines and furnaces in Austria take a great interest in the welfare of their steady workmen, and make provision for their habitations, for the accommodation of their sick, and for the education of their children. In fact, by erecting them cottages (with fields and gardens attached), by building hospitals, schools, and provision stores, they are making large outlays to improve the condition of the workmen. Nor does it yet appear that the workmen have attempted to ruin their masters by unnecessarily "going on strike" when they clearly saw that, in consequence of the fall in prices, wages must inevitably be reduced. By law each proprietor of mines is obliged to establish a friendly society on his property. This is a very old German custom : there has of late been an attempt made to amalgamate all these societies together in a general " Union," for the purpose of increasing their strength, and for enabling a workman to quit one mine for another without forfeiting his previous contributions. This project has, however, hitherto failed, the older and richer societies objecting to a union with the smaller ones. Should they ever be united, one result to be feared is probably they would soon get in the hands of some paid agitator (we have had several instances of the kind in this country), who for his own selfish ends, and to give some *raison d'être* for his existence, would do his utmost to destroy the friendly relations between master and workman in Austria.

Amongst other systems legalised in Austrian mining is that of "free diggings," which Mr. French, writing from the Embassy at Vienna in 1877, reports opens a large field for wild speculation.

There appear few indications that Austrian purchases from us will not be much increased at present, one reason for this being that the bulk of her circulating medium is silver, which has at present a more depreciated value relatively in paying for the external products of the world than for those of home manufacture. This depreciation in the value of silver may increase the exportation of goods from Austria, goods being a more profitable medium of exchange with the Austrians than silver at its present price. I have good authority for stating that in neither of the great silver-holding countries, Austria or India, does silver apparently appear less valuable in the purchase of *internal commodities*. And it appears to me that one of the principal causes of what has been termed the "depressed condition of our trade" between India, China, and the United Kingdom has arisen from the anxiety of our merchants to send goods to England—cotton, silk, and tea, for instance—regardless of the absolute requirements of the English market, in preference to remitting in exchange for our exports the depreciated silver currency. In this way they have frequently overstocked the English market, and have consequently been obliged to sell their goods at a loss.

Some maintain that even allowing for the large output of silver ore in America this depreciation in silver is merely temporary, and that when the Empire of Germany has sold the remainder of the surplus of silver it holds, which it is estimated will be in about two years, the price will again rise.

Not only do the heavily-taxed Austrian iron-masters at present demand more protection, and find it hard to compete with our manufactured iron, notwithstanding our having to pay freight and import duties, but the cotton and woollen manufacturers of Austria are also putting forward their greatest influence to obtain the same.

To turn now to the second point to be considered, and with which these comments on Austrian trade commenced, namely, In which markets of the world is she likely to become our successful competitor? The answer to that question seems to be, In Turkey and Roumania, and in the Levant trade generally. For she not only possesses great facilities for commerce in these directions through that great river the Danube, but also, by the extension of her boundaries on recently assuming the protectorate over Bosnia and Herzegovina, is brought into nearer relations with the Eastern market, and will probably have in future larger trade transactions with these countries than even at present, which is not inconsiderable when we recollect that her export trade to Turkey alone has averaged in value five million pounds for the last few years, and her imports from that country have been about three millions sterling annually.

BELGIUM.

Belgium is often held up as an example of a comparatively speaking small unimportant State which has prospered solely on account of her free trade tariff. Her tariff is liberal, but it is by no means "free trade," in the original meaning of the word. I will here give the import duty charged on the several articles enumerated ; on none of these, I need scarcely remind my readers, have we any import duty :—

ESTIMATED IMPORT DUTY AD VAL.

Cotton Yarns, undyed........4 to 19 per cent.
Linen Yarns ....Free.
Silk........................Free.
Woollen goods.............2 to 4 per cent.
Glass (Manufactured).......10 per cent
Jute (Manufactured) ....10 per cent.
Iron ....5 to 7 per cent.
Copper ....Free.
Tanned Leather ....3 to 4 per cent.
Alkali ....Free.
Paper ....3 per cent.
Seed oils..................Free.
Coals ....Free.
Herrings...................Free.
Sugar, refined ....59 to 63 per cent.

It will thus be seen that being a country a large portion of whose trade consists in the transit of goods, they put a small duty on such merchandise as they wish to have sent through Belgium, whilst imposing one high enough to protect their manufactures in any product they consider a foreigner can compete with them in their own country. Such are the duties which are placed on iron and cotton manufactures, which cannot fail to check the importation of English goods, and the duty on sugar against the competition of the French refiners.

The articles of British manufacture exported to Belgium are comparatively speaking few, and consist chiefly of oil for manufactures, copper, chemicals (chiefly soda), woollens, pig iron, and rough salt. The spirit of the Commercial Treaty of 1862, which contemplated a maximum import duty of 10 per cent., does not seem to have been carried out in its entirety, for the charge on printed calicoes, coarse quiltings, and dimities is 18 per cent. ad valorem while the specific duties on the lower qualities of unbleached cotton cloths are equivalent to 20 per cent. of their value.

The rise in the trade of Belgium has been one of the most marked in the European system. The average aggregate imports and exports from 1831 to 1840 reached £14,000,000; from 1841 to 1850, £24,000,000; and from 1861 to 1871, £103,000,000. This is a most satisfactory increase of trade. The only particular in which Belgium seems to have of late years failed to hold her own has been with regard to her mercantile navy, which appears to grow yearly "small by degrees, and beautifully less." England transacts the greater portion of this branch of industry at the Belgian ports, and, to quote figures, the tonnage of British vessels cleared in 1876 was 1,849,895 tons, out of a total of 2,858,657 tons.

When considering the Belgian commerce our thoughts turn naturally to their alleged competition with our iron trade. I will not weary my readers by recapitulating the reasons of the prosperity of the Belgians in this industry up to the year 1873, or those of its subsequent decline; nor will I detail the reasons of the iron market losing the power it might have possessed of recovery by the improved processes invented for the manufacture of steel by Bessemer and Siemens; neither will I dilate on the loss the rolling mills experienced in consequence of the substitution of steel for iron rails, which deprived them of one of their principal sources of revenue—subjects which have already been fully dealt with in regard to Austria and other countries. I must, however, mention the fact that Belgium appears to have found this branch of her trade in a very embarrassed condition in 1875 and 1876, partly owing to an accumulation of unsaleable stock, which has in a measure been attributed to the factories being largely turned into joint stock companies (*sociétés anonymes*). These were managed by directors, who, naturally, had not the same personal incentive to economy as a proprietor would have had, but who, on the contrary, had a direct pecuniary interest in increasing the output, as their salaries were regulated in proportion to its actual amount.

The Belgians, however, temporarily checked the quantity of their production of iron, for out of seventy-three furnaces, only thirty were in blast at the end of 1876.

I may mention that iron can by no means be fairly termed a natural product of this country, as only a small proportion of the ore consumed therein is found in the country; and though the iron mines of Luxemburg are not far from the Belgian works, the charge for freight on ore counterbalances the advantage they thus gain, and is as high as for the carriage of pig iron. The province of Namur produces nearly all the native ore, but even there the output has considerably fallen off. As, however, the profits are small on iron ore, it is not a great subject for congratulation if this country has still to supply Belgium with a large amount of it. One thing slightly in favour of the Belgian manufacturer is that he receives an indirect bonus on iron, as he has to pay a duty on the pig iron imported; and if, as *sometimes occurs*, it turns out from this iron he produces more finished goods than he was originally charged for, he gains by the amount of rebate he receives for such iron on exportation.

After having carefully examined the returns of our trade with Belgium for the last ten years, I was somewhat struck by the following passage in Professor Fawcett's work on " Free Trade or Protection :"—" With regard to Belgian iron competing successfully against English iron in our own market, so little reason is there to suppose that our trade can be thus injured that the quantity of iron and steel imported from Belgium into England is so trifling that it is not *enumerated* in her articles of export, whereas iron is mentioned as one of the chief articles which Belgium imports from England."

This appears to me scarcely compatible with the facts; for whilst " the chief article of British exports "— iron, wrought and unwrought—was sent from this country to Belgium to the value of £966,000 in 1874, it decreased to £443,000 in 1878, even including any iron sent in transit through Belgium ; whilst, on the other hand, we imported from Belgium of this produce (not worthy of being " enumerated"), namely, *manufactured and wrought iron and steel goods*, in 1874, to the value of £634,000, and in 1878 it had slightly increased to £679,000, or about £236,000 more than we exported.

The principal trade to this country of Belgian iron

appears to be in rolled joists and flitch plates, and they also import to us large quantities of angle and T iron for girder work. Their Legislature last year appointed a commission to inquire into the question of the substitution of iron instead of wood in various ways, such as the sleepers on railways ; but judging from the experience of the London and North-Western Railway in this country, when they tried stone sleepers, which having no elasticity in them, shook the carriages to pieces, they were therefore very soon discarded. I should imagine that the report will not be favourable on the use of iron railway sleepers.

Their railway companies give the Belgian merchants every advantage for their export trade in low freights. The carriage from Antwerp to London is only 6s. a ton, so that, if anything, they have to pay less in that respect than our manufacturers have in sending their goods from Staffordshire to London. As might be expected, the coal trade of Belgium has suffered equally with the iron, and one learns that from their principal coal-mining province, Hainault, there was a large diminution in the output. It appears that their coal miners regulate the amount of their output according to whether the demand of the trade is large or the contrary. Should it be the former, they are not afraid to work their best, knowing that however great the output may be, it will not have the effect of diminishing their wages, whilst as they see the demand diminish they endeavour to decrease their productive powers in the same ratio. The average profit on coals per ton in Belgium in 1876 was only 26c., or $2\frac{1}{2}$d. The quantities of fruit, meat, eggs, and potatoes we import from Belgium are very large—of the latter no less than fifty thousand tons in 1877.

There is another of the principal exports of Belgium to

this country in respect of which we have barely the mutual advantage of reciprocity. I allude to glass, which we admit duty free, whilst they charge us a ten per cent. *ad valorem* on all manufactured glass except bottles, which are charged 1fr. per 100 kilos, they at the same time taking good care to admit broken glass (as it can be remelted and worked up in their own glass works) free. The result is that whilst in 1876 we purchased their glass to the large value of 16,329,000 francs, not one shilling's worth of our glass was exported by us to Belgium. I confess I can see no reason except their import tariff to cause this result. We have equal, if not greater, facilities for purchasing the raw materials used in the manufacture of glass that the Belgians have. No manufacture—except, perhaps, the smelting of iron—probably requires more coals; in thát respect we have the advantage both in quality and cheapness. I have visited several glass manufactories both in England and Belgium, and examined the work, if with unskilled, at any rate with an unbiassed eye. It struck me that the English work seemed to be equally well finished, and to compare with the Belgian in most instances favourably in point of price. And yet the Belgians beat our manufacturers and undersell us in the cheaper description of window and other glass, though unable to do so in plate and other superior descriptions. The reason assigned is this—The Belgian manufacturer ships off to England all his inferior and commonest glass, taking care just to undersell our manufacturers. In case he loses in this transaction he can recoup himself in the price he can charge in his own country, where, he need fear no competition. This he can do the more easily as to manufacture 15 cwt. of the best glass, the manufacturer has to produce 85 cwt. of inferior glass.

The Belgians have not, it will be seen, followed our good example of free trade in glass, and by reason of their ten per cent. import duty apparently not only retain the monopoly to their countrymen at home, but also can afford to flood our markets with their surplus stock of this manufacture. The value of our exports to Belgium in 1877 amounted to eleven million three hundred thousand pounds, and our imports from them were to the greater value of about one million sterling. Comparing the year 1877 with 1876, whilst our imports from Belgium increased 15 per cent., our exports to them decreased in the same proportion.*

RUSSIA.

The Empire of Russia contains many institutions entirely differing from any we find elsewhere in Europe—amongst which none is more marked than their com-

---

* During a course of study of the commercial reports from the British Embassies and Legations abroad, I must admit that a more clearly stated and ably written body of reports it has never been my lot to read. Occasionally one comes across a passage which requires reading twice to comprehend, such as the following, which in a recent report follows a statement of the population of Bruxelles, and of some adjoining communes:—
'The city of Bruxelles covers an area of 893·52 hectares (2,207 acres), and contains a population of 161.816 souls, in both respects largely exceeding the area and population of London, which are set down at 667 acres and 74,844 souls. The whole agglomeration covers 6,590 hectares (16,277 acres), and contains, according to the last census, 369,030 souls. The administration is now divided amongst ten different municipalities, united by no bond, and often conflicting with each other. The inconvenience of this state of things is more apparent than the remedy. It is felt that a single commune formed of the whole agglomeration would be dangerously large.'
I chanced to read this at first sight strange statistical statement respecting the relative populations of London and Bruxelles whilst sailing down Channel in a yacht, and I confess I had to pace up and down the deck once before I grasped the idea that the writer had apparently left out the words 'city of' before 'London.' What an 'agglomeration' may be I leave my readers to decide, suggesting it may be some Foreign Office expression for a 'collection of units.'

munal and agrarian systems. Russia extends over a vast extent of territory, occupying an area more than forty times the size of France, sparsely inhabited by a population of eighty millions of people, she is still pushing her conquests eastward to Kashgar and in a southerly direction towards Merv and Herat; and though there ought to be room for the Russians, ourselves, and the Chinese to share the vast territories of Asia, there would appear one thing certain, that when the Russian Cossack arrives in a district, *from that district the British merchant has to depart*. And there can be no doubt that if the Russian rule is not as equitable, or, according to our lights, as beneficial, to the races it governs in Asia as our own, it at any rate appears able to make each conquered race become more an integral part of the Empire than our own. Let us hope that the day is not far distant when Great Britain will unite her Asiatic subjects by making them feel our interests are in common, and so weld them into a firmer bond of union with ourselves.

The Russians have a dash of Asiatic blood in their veins, and mingle more with the races they conquer than we do. Probably no stroke of policy on our part was better conceived than bringing our Asiatic troops to Europe, to let them feel that they were equally esteemed and valued with the Queen's European soldiers, and that they were not treated or thought of only as local troops, but as being part of the general forces of the British Empire.

We have lately heard a great deal respecting Russia, not only regarding her military, but financial and commercial position. Some have pointed out the great reforms she has made since the reign of the late Emperor Nicholas —the emancipation of the Serfs, the increased freedom of the press, the vast number of railways which have been constructed to open out her manufacturing, mining, and agricultural resources, to weld that empire together, and increase her power as a nation. Attention has also been called to the fact that her export trade has doubled in the last ten years. Others, on the other hand, have pointed out the great strain that is laid on the resources of the country by the debt, estimated to be no less than £500,000,000, of which sum about £240,000,000 is interest bearing debt held by England, France, Holland, and Germany—this estimate includes paper roubles, interest-bearing treasury bonds, internal debt, foreign debt, railway and land bank bonds; and also notice the great depreciation in the value of her paper roubles.

During the continuance of this war the increase of paper roubles issued was simply immense. A curious fact in connection with this extra paper money is that the value of the rouble did not fall in proportion to the increase of the number of notes put into circulation. On the contrary, the rise or fall of the exchange seemed to be governed far more by political events than by any consideration of the steady increase of the issue. For instance, the exchange on London, which, before the war had become inevitable, stood at 30d., fell to nearly 22d. while the Russian army was lying before Plevna. At that time the issue of extra paper did not much exceed 200,000,000 of roubles. At the time of the armistice, when the extra paper had been increased to over 300,000,000 of roubles, the exchange rose to over 26½d., to fall again in April to 22½d., when it was again supposed that war was inevitable. The conclusion of the Treaty of Berlin (by which time more than 450,000,000 roubles of extra paper had been engraved) put up the exchange again to over 25¾d.; but the refusal of the Ameer of Afghanistan to receive the British Envoy drove it down to 24*d*. The late Russo-Turkish war has caused the expenditure, it has been estimated, of £130,000,000. One well may ask, What have they gained by the immense loss of life and money this war has cost them? The increased expenditure was said this summer not to have entirely ceased, such as the payment for stores purchased during the war, though it was naturally not at as high a rate as last winter. This war has naturally led to a large increase in the National Debt. A comparative table of the increase of annual interest paid for the various items of the National Debt of Russia may be worth the attention of the Russian bondholders in this country:—

			Roubles.
1872	Audited expenditure	..	95,435,937
1873	” ”	..	100,583,395
1874	” ”	..	100,813,719
1875	” ”	..	107,478,064
1876	” ”	..	109,344,815
1877	Estimated expenditure	..	108,264,871
1878	” ”	..	133,676,719

And the estimate just published, and which seems to be semi-official, places it for—

| 1879 | Estimated expenditure | .. | 145,000,000 |

The railway system in Russia has hitherto proved a heavy drain, as hardly any of the railways have paid sufficiently well to cover the Government guarantee, the large deficiency, amounting in 1875 to £1,500,000, having to be paid out of the public purse. Some deprecated the action of the Government in attempting to keep up the price of the paper rouble by exporting large sums of gold to draw against, which plan they have now discontinued, and at present others urge that the increased volume of Russian exports is no sign of prosperity, the country being simply forced to export largely to pay her indebtedness. They also cite the large export of timber from Russia, no care being taken to plant young trees, as a sure way of exhausting one of the most valuable resources of the country. A very large source of Russian revenue, the taxes on imports, has been diminishing, partly owing to the foreign merchant finding himself unable to import goods with the high tariff now imposed on them by the Government. Those duties are now not only very heavy, but their actual amount is uncertain. The cause of this is that the Russian Government, in order to draw gold into the country, makes the importer pay his duties in that coin, thus making the duty on any particular article fluctuate. According to the rates of exchange current during the late war, the increase in all duties was about 50 per cent. It would seem of great importance to Russia that her revenue from import dues did not decrease, as it seems to be a general conviction, in well-informed circles, that there is no prospect of any economies being even attempted. So far, indeed, from such a hope being entertained, it is universally believed that, even if all dangers of further complications were averted to-morrow, the expenditure, more especially in the War and Navy Departments, would be increased instead of diminished.

The necessity of renewing the "matériel," which is inevitable after every war, of replacing with newer inventions the rifles, &c., which have been found defective, will entail an immense outlay of money, and there is no doubt that, at whatever sacrifice, money for such a purpose must be procured. Not only have imports been discouraged by this increased tax, but also *by obliging all Russian railways to purchase half their steel rails of home manufacturers*. In order to encourage this manufacture, a decree has been issued that for a period of twelve years a premium will be allowed by the Government on all steel rails made, or old rails remade, in Russia, and during the three years a premium will also be granted on all pig iron produced, besides which premium the manufacturer, if he desires, can receive one-half the amount of one year's supply of rails in advance, giving his works as a guarantee, which guarantee, however, is in no case to exceed 75 per cent. of the estimated value; and further, all future concessions to railway companies are to contain a clause obliging them to accept a certain quantity of rails manufactured by order of the Government. The Minister of Finance and the Minister of Ways and Communications are now preparing a reduced tariff for the internal transport of rails, iron ore, fuel, &c. Our export of iron, wrought and unwrought, to the northern ports of Russia amounted to the value of £2,485,000 in 1874, and decreased to £976,000 in 1878, whilst British exports generally to her northern ports have decreased by about a million and a half pounds in value since 1874.*

But in comparing 1878 with the previous year we find

---

* On importation of goods from England, I append as examples a few of the duties charged in Russia, in nearly all of which the duty is higher if imported by sea :—

COTTON GOODS—
(a) Close-woven Tissues, imported by sea, per cwt. £8 13 5
    Do., do. imported by land...... „ 7 11 9
(b) Light Cotton Textures, printed........ „ 30 6 10
(e) Cotton Stuffs, with applications of straw „ 43 7 0
(f) Lace and Tulle of Cotton .... „ 86 13 11
Linen and Hempen Tissues, pure or mixed
  with Cotton................By sea.. „ 27½ ad val.
                   By land. „ 25½ ad val.
Woollen Tissues, per cwt......from £2 3 4 to £86 13 11
Iron and Steel, unmanufactured, per cwt. from
                              0 0 6½ to 0 16 3
Iron, wrought, per cwt..........from 0 0 6 to 0 12 0

that there was an increase of £2,380,000, of which
£1,570,000 is credited to the northern and £810,000
to the Black Sea ports. The increase to the exports to
the northern ports is mainly caused by larger
quantities of alkali, cotton yarn, and piece goods,
copper, linen, woollen and worsted goods; and to the
southern ports larger quantities of coal, wrought iron,
machinery, mill work, and cotton yarn was shipped.
Russia, since the duty was taken off the importation of
corn, has, excepting during the years of the Crimean War,
been one of the countries to whom we have looked for
a supply of grain to feed our population; and although the
quantity of this product we receive from her is not equal
to that which we obtain from the United States—owing
partly, it is alleged, to her primitive and, consequently,
less productive system of farming—still the amount we
received in 1878 was considerable, being over eleven
million cwts. of different descriptions of corn, a falling-
off, however, from the previous year.

Whilst mentioning the subject of our importation of
grain from Russia, it may seem pertinent to notice the
fact that it has been calculated that fifteen millions of
the inhabitants of these isles are dependent on foreign
sources for the supply of wheat from which the
bread they purchase is made. This is a very im—
portant, and to my mind rather a serious fact. Some state
that the monopoly of the soil of the United Kingdom is
one of the causes of its not producing more food, and it
is alleged that the withholding of it from the people
is one of the darkest features in our social economy
and one of the greatest causes of the depression in our
agricultural interest at present. It may not be without
use to us to examine the Russian system of distributing
the land amongst the 'Mir,' or village community, by

which system land is not only not 'held back from the people,' but they are forced to take it *nolens volens*, and to cultivate it partly for their own benefit and partly for the benefit of the 'village community,' of whom each resident is obliged to become an integral part, not only in our sense of the word as a resident and probably a taxpayer, but as having a more direct interest in the common weal. The result of this system in Russia may be briefly told. The land is not one-half so well cultivated nor so productive as in this country. Mr. Mackenzie Wallace, in his graphic work on Russia, written after nearly six years' residence in and study of that country, thus describes this system:—
'According, then, to theory, all male peasants in every part of the Empire are inscribed in census lists, which form the basis of direct taxation. These lists are revised at regular intervals, and all males alive at the time of the revision, from the new-born babe to the centenarian, are duly inscribed. Each commune has a list of this kind, and pays to the Government an annual sum proportionate to the number of names which the list contains. During the interval between the revisions, the financial authorities take no notice of the births and deaths. A commune which has a hundred male members at the time of the revision may have in a few years considerably more or considerably less than that number, but it has to pay taxes for a hundred members all the same, until a new revision is made for the whole Empire.'

He then goes on to explain that the payment of taxes is inseparably connected with the possession of the land, whilst at the same time they are neither paid as the rent of the land nor as a land tax—for in Russia the members of one commune may possess six acres and of a neighbouring one seven, and yet the taxes may be identically the same—the fact being the taxes are simply personal, and are calculated according to the number of 'souls' inscribed in the communal lists at the time of the revision.

Each commune has the power to distribute the land as it sees fit, and as a rule allots the land in the number of shares corresponding to the number of individuals in each family; and as the receiving a share makes it obligatory to pay the tax in many communes, the shares are allotted and re-allotted in accordance with the number of able-bodied adults there are in each family; for in Russia the possession of a share of communal land is often not a privilege, but a burden. Naturally, owing to deaths and a variety of other reasons, the working powers of the several families in the village commune change; hence there are often independent re-allotments of the land made by the commune itself, besides the general Government revision, which occurs on the average once in about fifteen years. This village commune is governed, as we should term it, by local self-government of a most democratic character. The elder merely represents the executive power, whilst all real authority resides in the assembly, of which all the heads of households are members. They assemble to transact business at any open space near the village, the discussion, though at times animated, being rarely marred by long speeches. If any one, young or old, attempts to 'indulge in oratory he is sure to be interrupted, as they have never any sympathy with fine talking.' Sometimes the discussions become warm, and the noise deafening, but the disputants never indulge in such 'striking' arguments as are commonly used by village politicians in Great Britain, especially in the sister isle.

The elder, as a rule, takes no greater part in the discussion than any other householder, and only comes forward prominently when it is necessary to take the sense of the meeting. On such occasions he may stand back a little from the crowd, and say, 'Well, orthodox, have you decided so?' and the crowd will probably shout, 'Ladno! Ladno!' that is to say, agreed, agreed.

Communal measures are generally carried in this way by acclamation, but it sometimes happens that there is such a decided diversity of opinion that it is difficult to tell which of the two parties is in the majority. In these cases the elder requests the one party to stand to the right, and the other to the left. The two groups are then counted, and the minority submits, for no one ever dreams of openly opposing the will of the 'Mir.'

The 'Mir' grants permission for a villager to go to another village or town whilst, as a rule, still exacting from him his share of the taxes, and has the power to recall him to the village commune should it be considered that his services are required.

Nearly all the artizan class in Russia leave their wives and families at their village commune, whilst they work in the towns; thus they do not look on the towns as their homes, and at harvest time mostly leave the manufactories to assist in getting in their crops. The lot assigned to the members of one family may amount to as much as 20 acres or more, but the position of it is decided by lot. The chances are it is scattered in different patches all over the communal land. The 'Mir' decides the earliest date the crops shall be taken in, and also, should the redistribution not be decided by lot, which plots of land each family shall take. In the instance of a family having highly cultivated their land, the fact of this lot standing a chance of being apportioned to others at the redistribution is of course to some extent a hardship; but it appears the Russian peasant looks at it philosophically, and is content as long as it is owned by another member of his 'Mir.' Such is this communal system of holding the soil. Whether it will last, and whether it is a system conducive to the welfare and improvement of the Russian peasant, I leave to the future to decide.

For different reasons, which I shall subsequently enter into, Russia has in comparison to her size fewer towns than any other European State. Excluding Finland, the Baltic Provinces, Lithunia, Poland, and the Caucasus, which, although they are a part of the Russian Empire, do not form socially part of Russia proper, there are only 127 towns, and of these only 25 contain more than 25,000, and only 11 more than 50,000 inhabitants, and this notwithstanding the fact that both their Emperor Peter the Great and the Empress Catherine II. did all in their power to encourage the establishment of towns throughout the Empire, and to create a *bourgeoisie* in their dominions. In this they failed, partly because the inhabitants of the towns found that they were more heavily taxed in comparison than they had been in their native communes, and also because the rapid extension of the Russian dominions gave to the inhabitants an early and, comparatively speaking, lucrative employment in agricultural industry. There are residing in these towns the nobility, clergy, and officials, besides which are three groups of those whom we describe more particularly as townsmen, namely, the merchants, shopkeepers and artizans, who do not inherit their social standing from their fathers, as is the case with the Russian nobles and clergy, but acquire them by the payment of certain dues; and a man can change from one class to another by paying the higher dues levied on the respective grades of mercantile life. So a man can rise from the position of a retail trader to being styled a merchant if he sees fit to pay the additional tax assessed on the latter class. Each of the above-mentioned classes forms itself into a distinct corporation, and assumes official rights and privileges of its own.

The merchants, many of whom are very wealthy, are naturally the most important of these groups. They are very 'smart' men of business, so that the foreigner dealing with them has, to use a sailor's expression, 'to keep his weather eye open' lest he should get the worst of the bargain. But in this respect they are surpassed by the wily Greek and Armenian merchants, and the children of Israel who are traders in Russia. Be the reason what it may, it is an acknowledged fact that many of the Russian manufacturers are now much more prosperous than they have been for many years past.

There can be no doubt that the immense loans advanced to Russia by England and other countries (although the interest of them may now hang like a millstone round her neck) have in a measure helped this Empire to recover from the disastrous effects of the Crimean War.

The increase of the railways in Russia has been very rapid, and out of the 13,500 miles open at the end of 1878, about 6,630 were constructed since 1870. It, however, remains to be seen whether the great expense of keeping several of them up, may not for many years, till the country is more thickly populated, be more than they are worth; and whether those two great arteries of trade in Russia, the Rivers Dneiper and Volga, aided by good ordinary roads, would not have answered for the transit of merchandise in a great part of the empire equally well for the next twenty years. We would appear to have been losing ground in our trade with the Caucasus, Persia, and Turkestan; but should the Turkish rule in Asia Minor enjoy the advantage of peace, and that race show the world they can rule as a firm but just Government; in a few years, English merchants will find that not only will the inhabitants of Asia Minor be benefited, but that their own trade will revive both there and in the neighbouring territories where a Russian prohibitive tariff does not interpose to prohibit our trade. No one can doubt that it is the mutual interest of Russia and England to remain at peace with each other.

It is curious to observe that the trade of Russia by sea has either declined or remained stationary, whereas that by land has increased. Both St. Petersburg and Odessa have lost ground latterly as trading ports, whereas Moscow has increased its receipts very largely, as has Warsaw. The explanation of this is, that Russia is becoming more dependent on the railways and shipping of Germany for communication with the outer world.

We have latterly seen our newspapers and periodicals inundated with descriptions of Russian policy, Russian finance, or military organisation and strategy. Mr. E. T. Reed has certainly not lately frightened us by describing to us the immensely destructive power of those unwieldly Russian men-of-war called 'Popoffkas.' Perhaps it might be not uninteresting to look for a moment on the other side of the picture, and to think over a Russian view of our commercial prospects, one in which, I need hardly say, I do not agree. Still, to quote Robert Burns—

'Oh, wad some power the giftie gie us
To see oursels as ithers see us!'

Mr. John Bright has lately told us, in language more remarkable for its abusive character than for any attempt at either argument or logic, how he "sees" anyone who presumes even to inquire into the question of our trade prospects (and does not take his dictum respecting them as Gospel), and who ventures to ask whether the protective tariffs placed against our industries by the whole continent of America, from the Arctic regions to Cape Horn, and by three-fourths of the inhabitants of Europe, Asia, and Africa, cannot by some means or other be modified.

Now, to glance at our present trade prospects from a Russian's point of view. 'In England you have no longer a peasantry in the proper sense of the term, and unless some thorough measures be very soon adopted, you will never be able to create such a class, for men who have been long exposed to the unwholesome influences of town life are physically and morally incapable of becoming agriculturists. Hitherto England has enjoyed, in consequence of her geographical position, her political freedom, and her deposits of coal and iron, a wholly exceptional position in the industrial world. Fearing no competition, she has proclaimed the principles of Free Trade and has inundated the world with her manufactures, using unscrupulously her powerful navy, and all the other forces at her command, for breaking down every barrier tending to check the flood sent forth from Manchester and Birmingham. In that way her hungry proletariat has been fed. But the industrial supremacy of England is drawing to a close. The nations have discovered the perfidious fallacy of Free Trade principles, and are now learning to manufacture for their own wants, instead of paying England enormous sums to manufacture for them. Very soon English goods will no longer find foreign markets, and how will the hungry proletariat then be fed ? Already the grain production of England is far from being sufficient for the wants of the population, so that, even when the harvest is exceptionally abundant, enormous quantities of wheat are imported from all quarters of the globe. Hitherto this grain has been paid for by the manufactured goods annually exported, but how will it be procured when these goods are no longer wanted for foreign consumers, and what then will the hungry proletariat do ?'

There is no greater dissimilarity in any respect between this country and Russia than the incidence of our respective systems of taxation. Whereas in this country it is mostly levied on the monied classes, in Russia it falls most heavily on the peasantry and lower orders; and also, whilst here the cost of collection of taxes is reduced to a minimum, in Russia not only is the cost greater in proportion to the amount collected, but in diverse ways there is a vast amount of 'waste,' and the sum paid into the exchequer in Russia is considerably smaller than the sum actually collected.

The revenue coming in from tobacco barely amounts to twelve million five hundred thousand roubles ; that appears very little when we recollect the Russians are great smokers, and it is expected that the Government will sell this tax to a company (in the same way as was done in Italy in 1868), and will receive by doing so a revenue of about 25,000,000 roubles. The tax on spirits and the direct taxes in Russia amount to three-fifths of the whole ordinary income of the Empire. To make the income of Russia approach more closely the expenditure which even in 1876, according to the 'Statesman's Year-book,' exceeded £81,000,000, it has been proposed to add 10 per cent. to these two taxes. This would seem almost impossible, as at present they press too heavily on the peasantry and working classes, and the necessity would appear very pressing to lighten the burden on the peasantry and get at the larger proprietors. Mr. Plunkett refers to this in his report, and remarks :—' As an illustration of the unjust manner in which large properties are spared, at the expense of the peasant, under the present mode of collecting the direct taxes, I will mention that on an estate of about 8,000 English acres, of which 1,200 acres were classed as "best" land, the Government and local taxes of all kinds amounted a couple of years ago to only 167 roubles for the year, while the peasantry in the same district were paying 9 roubles per annum on their holdings of about fourteen acres, besides a further sum of 9 roubles which they have to pay in redemption of the lot of ground in question.' This may be one of the causes of the present agitation in that country.

TURKEY AND EGYPT.

One finds Turkey much less protective in its import tariff than Russia. The Turk is not anxious to become a manufacturer; his bias, as we all know, inclines him more to military pursuits. The Russians found, in the unfortunate province of Bulgaria, the farming to be of such a description that it would compare favourably with their own corn-growing districts. However anxious the Turk may be to purchase our cotton and other goods, he will not be able to do so to the same amount as in the past, unless the financial position of his country improves. The only means by which that can be effected is the development of its internal resources. No one can expect that foreign capitalists

o

will again consent to lend money to be expended in building palaces and the purchase of arms and ironclads and extravagance at the Court.

There would seem to be no chance whatever of the Turk ever resuming payment of his bonds, so that it would be simply wasting one's trouble in calculating how much they nominally were, how much commission the bankers and others who floated them made, and to what amount the English public are affected by loss of nterest and capital.

The Berlin Treaty left the Sultan ruler over diminished though still considerable territories—indeed, much of that which he has recently lost had only hitherto proved a source of weakness to him. All agree that it is the interest of the Turks to appear now before Europe as a well-organised and well-governed race; but not until a year or two have passed shall we have any opportunity of judging whether that will ever be the case. That Turkey is very much impoverished since the late war seems evident. A correspondent of the *Times*, writing in April last, says, 'The absolute necessity of procuring money somewhere is pre-occupying not only the Sultan, but the higher officials generally. One of them, who has special opportunities of knowing the real state of affairs, stated that unless something extraordinary occurred the Treasury would be empty in about ten days, and no large sum would be expected till the month of May.'

The Turkish soldier and official will serve on uncomplainingly for months without pay, but they cannot serve without food; and in their distress the Turks have asked our Government to send out Commissioners to assist in getting their customs and indirect taxes into order. Whether the British Government will comply with the request remains to be seen ; though the manner in which Mr. Wilson has recently been treated by the ex-Khedive of Egypt is not calculated to encourage them to do so.

The value of the produce and manufactures of the United Kingdom we exported to Turkey in 1878, including both the European and Asiatic Dominions, was £7,748,000, or an increase of over two million pounds from the previous year, this increment being most marked in cotton and woollen goods ; and this is only another instance of how export trade to a country usually increases just after the termination of a war. Another instance of this is Roumania. We sent her goods in 1878 to the amount of £887,000, being an increase of £690,000, which consisted principally of larger quantities of cotton and woollen goods and iron and steel; in fact, the only foreign countries that show any conspicuous increase in the value of goods exported from the United Kingdom are those which were engaged in the late war, and the class of their imports is indicative of the subtraction from industrial pursuits of the inhabitants of the combatant countries. Our imports from Turkey have, on the other hand, decreased, and were about one million sterling less in 1878 than they were in 1877 ; the falling-off being largest in grain, goat's hair, and tobacco.

Turning to Turkey's overgrown dependency, Egypt, no one can for a moment doubt that she cannot continue permanently to pay her debt in full, and appears to be absolutely incapable of bearing the weight of it laid on her shoulders by the ex-Khedive, the sole effect of which debt to Egypt has been to add to the wealth of the financial harpies who surrounded the palace to their own personal aggrandisement. Their loans have in no way added to the prosperity of the country, and have been a great burden on the unfortunate inhabitants.

Whilst our exports to Egypt last year—although they show a falling-off since 1874—are about the same as they were in 1877, or to the value of slightly over two million pounds, our imports show a very marked decline since 1877, when they amounted to over eleven million pounds' worth of their goods instead of only exceeding six millions pounds sterling. This falling-off can be accounted for, as the drought in Egypt caused a serious diminution in their crops, so that they were able to send us hardly any corn, and barely half their usual supply of raw cotton. These are their two great articles of importation to this country, but all our principal commercial interests connected with Egypt are really centred in the Suez Canal, in its being kept an open highway for our ships going to and from India and the East. Still, I cannot help remembering that when the Suez Canal was opened with what a flourish of trumpets it was announced that not only was it to give additional facilities to the trade of the East with Europe, but also to open out and develop the vast resources of Egypt, to make it once more not only an important depôt, but one of the chief granaries of the world. When I think of all the marvellous advantages which it was proclaimed that Egypt would derive from the Canal, and remember how the late Khedive was congratulated by his guests on the great future that was then opened out to his country—when I recall the prophecies delivered not only in enthusiastic after-dinner speeches, but in the columns of the whole European press—I am reminded of the inauguration of our Crystal Palace at Sydenham, which was opened, if I mistake not, 'for the benefit of art and science,' but now endeavours to fill its coffers by bicycle races, canary and cat shows. How lavish was the expenditure in those halcyon days at the time of the opening of the Suez Canal through Egypt, when the whole country was inundated with French 'invités,' living at the expense of the Khedive Ismail Fasha, when an opera-house had been raised by his order in three months, and, amongst other opera singers, 'Schneider' was imported from Europe regardless of expense! It was a strange though somewhat a sad sight to see in Cairo the most lavish expenditure in the costly modern luxuries of the west within a stone's throw of the most abject penury and misery of the East.

Whilst on the subject of the fêtes given at the opening of the Canal, I may be allowed to give a not altogether uninteresting personal reminiscence of being at a ball given by the then Khedive at the opening of the Suez Canal, at the Schumla Palace, and seeing the Empress of the French and the Crown Prince of Prussia dancing in a quadrille as partners, only six months before the Emperor of the French surrendered his sword to the King of Prussia.

Whilst in Egypt I went down to Port Said, and had a look at the Canal, then just opened. In appearance it resembled any other canal; and it is only when one remembers its vastness and the dreary desert through which it runs, that one is able to appreciate this great work, for which the world has chiefly to thank Napoleon III., the ex-Khedive of Egypt, and M. Lesseps. It was, I understood, in width about 100 feet at the surface, shelving down towards the centre of the channel, which is about 70 feet wide at its base: the extreme depth is 27 feet. At first no ship was allowed through drawing more than 25 feet, and several even drawing less water than that managed to get their keels fast embedded in different parts of the Canal, amongst others an English man-of-war, which it was no easy matter to tug off; now, owing to the pilots being more experienced, vessels only occasionally come to grief. There was at one time a theory that there was a different height in the Mediterranean and Red Seas. The only variation is caused by the tides, the spring tides varying the height at the Mediterranean end by 7 inches, and at the Red Sea end about 7 or 8 feet. Steam dredging machines are constantly at work at each end clearing away sand which is drifted up by the in-flowing tides. The traffic is worked on the block system, each vessel going from port to port about six miles apart; and no two vessels are allowed to meet one another in the channel of the Canal itself, one having to remain in a siding whilst the other passes.*

* A Blue Book has been issued presenting an official report of this great enterprise up to the end of last year. This shows, as was to be expected from the then condition of trade, a slight diminution of the receipts from the Canal in 1878 as compared with 1877. And it may not be uninteresting to quote the volume of tonnage passing through this link between the East and the West, useful to all nations, and not entirely dependent on the special fortunes of any one country, although the unsettled state of the Eastern question has doubtless had a detrimental effect on the Suez Canal, as on other industries connected with the East. In 1870 the tonnage passing through from sea to sea was 436,000; in 1871 it increased nearly 75 per cent. and became 761,000; in 1872 the increase became nearly 90 per cent., the total reaching 1,439,000; but in 1873, although the actual increase was nearly the same, so that the whole tonnage passing through was 2,085,000, the relative increase barely exceeded 45 per cent. Still a large increment was annually registered until 1876, which barely held its own; and, although 1877 showed a considerable recovery, last year, for the first time of its history, the Canal returns showed an absolute diminution. The tonnage passing through the Canal was 3,291,500, as against 3,419,000 in the previous year, and the diminution would have been greater but for the fact that the convoys bearing the Indian troops to and from the Mediterranean passed twice through the Canal in the course of the twelvemonth. There was thus, in 1878, a perceptible decline in tonnage and in the corresponding receipts, but it is already believed that this experience is transitory.

Although we have hitherto enjoyed the position of sending the largest preponderance of the traffic through the Canal, we must not lose sight of the fact that the French are naturally anxious to make

Unless Egypt very much changes for the better-
it can never be of the first commercial importance
to this country, and probably the less we have to
do politically with its internal affairs the better. Supposing that other European nations who consider
they have a direct interest in Egypt do not propose that panacea for all Eastern evils, 'a mixed occupation,' our interference can only end in our having to
take over the government, not only of Egypt itself, but
with it the major part of Central Africa ; and at present
we seem to have sufficient responsibilities in the south
of that continent.

In speaking of our commercial relations, I have avoided
as far as possible giving figures in regard to our trade
with either Turkey or Egypt, as under existing conditions they cannot give a definite idea of our future
prospects; and we have yet to see whether Turkey will
carry out the reforms she promised in Asia Minor, in
her Convention with this country, whether her own self-
interest will prevail over the old suicidal policy of delay.

---

a greater use of this great monument to French perseverance and
genius ; whilst the Dutch have taken already great advantage of
this route in their trade to their Eastern colonies ; the Austrian
Lloyd and an Italian company, the Rubattino, have now set on
foot regular lines of steamers through the Canal. The bonds we purchased from the Khedive are a valuable property in remainder. For
the next 27 years the interest is to be paid to us on the guarantee
of the Egyptian Government, after that date from the actual
receipts of the Suez Canal Company. The sum decided to be
annually expended for the next 27 years on the improvement of the
canal, £40,000, seems a moderate amount.

CHAPTER V.

INTERCHANGE WITH THE COLONIES.

I NOW propose to turn aside from the aspect of our trade with foreign countries and look more fixedly on our 'interchange' with our own colonies and dependencies' with the exception of a few remarks respecting our commerce with China and Japan, which I find more convenient to touch on in this part. The trade of these countries is likely to affect the prosperity of our Indian Empire, and also be of future greater relative importance in the world's commercial system than it is at present.

It is difficult to cast one's eyes over the vast and varied possessions of our Queen without wishing to see one day realised, both for Imperial defence and offence, both for weal or woe, that unity of Greater Britain which theorists have dreamed of.

When Her Majesty first began to reign, the Colonial Empire consisted of twenty-four colonies and settlements, having amongst them a population of only four millions. Their exports and imports were about thirty millions sterling, and their revenue was about two and a-half millions. Now, their aggregate trade is more than sixfold what it then was, and amounts to two hundred millions sterling, and their revenue is twenty-seven millions sterling, eleven times greater than in 1837. This is a very large increment, and these colonies hold a vastly different position in the world's system than even they did twenty years since, and one which we at present seem only to dimly realize.

At one period in the present century we appear to have entertained the idea that they were a heavy drain upon our resources, both military and financial, and that the less we were mixed up with their affairs the better for ourselves. So we gave them our blessing, and, to a certain extent, an imitation of our form of Government, withdrew all the officials and military we chanced to have on their shores, except the 'Governor' and his staff, and perhaps a 'Judge,' and congratulated ourselves on having considerably reduced both our obligations and expenses.

Remembering that the nominal cause that our colonies in America first revolted was a grievance in connection with our fiscal arrangements, we left them each to settle their tariffs as they saw fit; and although we were thoroughly satisfied of the great advantages that would accrue to all were free trade universal, we made no attempt even to offer any suggestions on that subject, much less to make their acceptation of a free trade tariff like our own a condition of their remaining, as most of them now are, 'detached British nationalities.' Perhaps, in a sense, Sir William Molesworth and Mr. Charles Buller, to whose efforts the settlement of the constitutions of the colonies were mainly due, were right in neglecting such an opportunity, as they seem to have acted as though they believed that it was simply a matter of time as to when each respective colony would secede, and, therefore, that it was most advisable to make their secession a matter of total indifference. If this was not a heroic policy, it has, perhaps, tided us over many a difficulty. We have lived in hopes our colonies might follow our example and be free traders.

But the fact at present stands that in no colony proper have we free trade, except in the case of New South Wales, and with certain trading or military settlements, such as Hong Kong, the Straits of Gibraltar, or Malta and Ceylon, over which we have retained direct authority.

Varied are the ways in which we became possessed of these colonies. Some were acquired by naval explorers taking them from the aborigines, as in the case of Australia and New Zealand; others from France, such as Canada, Nova Scotia, Newfoundland, Louisiana, Mauritius, and the small settlements of Dominica, Grenada, St. Lucia, Tobago, and St. Vincent. From the Spaniards we have 'annexed' Jamaica, Trinidad, Honduras, and Gibraltar. Holland gave us the Cape of Good Hope in exchange for Java, and we captured from them Ceylon and Guiana. How countless are the native rulers we have dispossessed in India in forming our great Empire there! Our acquisition of Hong Kong, the Gold Coast, the Fiji Islands, Cyprus, and the Transvaal, belongs to history of comparatively speaking recent date, and one also full of curious interest. On each of these colonies, both large and small volumes have been written, and yet many of them are still, comparatively speaking, unknown to the inhabitants of these isles.

Here space will only permit me touching on some of the leading features of our commercial interchange with the Empire of India; three of our largest colonies—Canada, Australia, and the Cape; and two military or trading settlements—Hong Kong and the Straits Settlements. It will be my endeavour to briefly show how the populations of these various regions live, in what their trade consists with the world at large, and also with the United Kingdom, and touch on what are their present and their future prospects of material prosperity. These matters must form most important factors in the future of the world, and are also well worthy of notice as affecting the mere trade prosperity of Great Britain. Neither the present nor the next century may be destined to see Macaulay's New Zealander philosophizing over the ruins of our metropolis, but within this period our Antipodean brethren will probably have caught up with us in the race of civilization and commercial prosperity. We must not lose sight of the fact that our colonies are growing apace, and it is just within the range of possibility they may prove to be sturdy scions of a sturdy oak; in fact, to become great and prosperous nations, with more abundant wealth and a larger population than the land from which they sprang can boast.

Our colonies, like ourselves, have felt the effects of the present prolonged depression, which has been, in my opinion, aggravated by the lack of real community of commercial interests apparent betweeen them and ourselves; and, probably as I write these lines, many of the sons of the very men who helped Cobden and Bright to pass the abolition of the Corn Laws in this country are legislating against the very principles their fathers professed in Australia and Canada.

I have seen it written, 'It is towards the States, however, that all eyes are directed at the present time. In their capacity for feeding us cheaply we may be said as a manufacturing nation to depend for our very existence.' Whilst we fix our eyes on one granary (a large one, I grant), are we not possibly forgetting to look at others that we ourselves could equally largely store?

There is an absence of mutuality in the present relations between ourselves and our colonies; but it does not inevitably follow that *that* should always be the case.

I append a table for reference, showing the volume of our trade to and from their shores, and also, for the purpose of comparison, the relative *ad valorem* duty charged on our six principal exports, as far as the same can be given:—

VALUE of TOTAL IMPORTS from and EXPORTS to the United Kingdom and the British Possessions, and average Duty charged on six of our principal exports :—

Note.—In this table the thousands are omitted. Thus, 69 stands for 69,000.

		Average *ad val.* duty charged.	1864.	1874.	1878.
		per cent.	£	£	£
Channel Islands-	Imp.	- -	836	650	726
	Exp.		1 208	982	733
Gibraltar - - -	Imp.	Free -	117	82	334
	Exp.		1,333	1,234	778
Malta - - - -	Imp.	Free -	128	285	176
	Exp.		870	997	1,371
North American	Imp.	See	6,850	11,858	9,530
Colonies - - -	Exp.	note (a)	6,269	10,210	7,033
West India Islands	Imp.	See	11,073	6,188	6,149
and Guiana - -	Exp.	note (b)	4,611	3,593	2,944
British Honduras -	Imp.	12	372	196	182
	Exp.		210	160	122
Australia - - -	Imp.	See	10,039	18,547	20,855
	Exp.	note (c)	12,926	20,668	21,525
British India - -	Imp.	2 5-12	52,295	31,198	27 470
	Exp.		20,753	25,434	24,659
The Straits Settle-	Imp.	Free -	2,069	2,604	2,536
ment - - - -	Exp.		1,230	2,808	1,882
Ceylon - - - -	Imp.	4	3,173	3,600	2,922
	Exp.		883	1,239	850
Hong Kong - - -	Imp.	Free -	2,881	747	1,174
	Exp.		1,769	3,909	3,041
Mauritius - - -	Imp.	5⅜	1,589	1,044	887
	Exp.		674	615	431
Cape of Good Hope	Imp.	8	1,975	4,297	4,381
	Exp.		2,382	4,702	5,458
The Gold Coast- -	Imp.	Free -	198	468	492
	Exp.		134	512	557

COLONIAL TRADE AND TARIFFS.

(*a*).—Extracts from the new Canadian tariff, which came in force on the 15th of last March, by which the duties have been much increased, will be found in Appendix 2.

(*b*).—The import tariffs charged in these Islands are of such a varied description that no average, to give a definite idea of the relative protectiveness of their systems, can be drawn. Our largest trade is with the Islands of Jamaica, Barbadoes, and Trinidad, and the former levies an average duty of 12½ per cent. *ad valorem* on our textile manufactures, Barbadoes one of 4 per cent., and Trinidad one of from 3¾ to 10 per cent. *ad valorem*.

(*c*).—In Australia the various Governments each have their independent tariff. In New South Wales the six classes of goods enumerated are all free, except a duty on a certain class of iron goods varying from 20s. to 60s. per ton. The other Governments of Victoria, South Australia, Western Australia, Tasmania, New Zealand, and Queensland, all have protective duties, varying from —in the case of Queensland—about 5 per cent. to the highest import duty charged in any colony; that of Victoria, which averages 15 per cent. *ad valorem* on the six principal classes of our export trade.

CHAPTER VI.

CANADA.

CANADA is the oldest and largest of England's colonies, and, excepting the dreary waste of Newfoundland, is the nearest to the mother country. I have not space to recount the incidents of our original conquest of it from the French, nor the many wars in which the 'provincials,' as the first settlers in the northern provinces were called, fought shoulder to shoulder— aye, right gallantly—in support of our own regular troops; and though we have only a small aboriginal population, numbering about one hundred thousand souls, in Canada at present, it is satisfactory to note that we have, as a rule, always lived on terms of friendship with these native races, a result the United States people have apparently been unable to manage with the neighbouring tribes, nor have we succeeded in every part of the world to win the friendship of all the aboriginal races our wide rule brings us in contact with. Perhaps the address sent to the Queen by the chiefs of the Six Nations, assembled at their council fire during the Crimean War, has not faded from the memory of all in England. 'Great mother,' they wrote, 'your children of the Six Nations have always been faithful and active allies of your Crown, and the ancestors of your red children never failed to assist in the battles of your ancestors.'

The confederation of the provinces of Ontario, Quebec, Nova Scotia, and New Brunswick, was decided on in 1867, and the Dominion of Canada established upon a model of the British constitution. British Columbia afterwards joined the confederation in 1871, and Prince Edward Island in 1873. The Governor-General represents the Crown, life senators and an elective legislative assembly fill the same positions as our Lords and Commons, and a responsible Ministry is entrusted with the executive power.

The body thus constituted was clothed with powers by the Imperial Parliament of Great Britain tantamount in nearly all respects relating to Canada to those our Parliament exercises over the affairs of this country, such as laws in relation to public debt and property, trade and commerce, indirect taxation, borrowing on the public credit, postal service, militia and defence, and generally to provide for the peace and good government of the Dominion. Ottawa was finally settled on as the seat of Government, if rumour speaks correctly, as a compromise to settle the rival claims for it set up by Quebec and Montreal. As I have previously remarked, nothing conduces more to the prospects of commercial advancement in a country than its security from the effects of foreign invasion and internal riot, when this is done without subtracting more than is absolutely needful from the productive labour of the inhabitants; and in no way has Canada taken the lead in a greater degree, not only over all the other colonies of the Queen, but even the mother country itself, than in the carefully drawn and considered 'Militia and Defence Act' of 1868. That Act has remained unchanged to the present day, and at once provided for the obligation thrown on Canada to guard in ordinary circumstances her own borders on the withdrawal of the main bulk of the British troops from her shores. She adopted principles of organization which are obligatory on all her citizens. I must refer my readers on this subject to the able lecture delivered by Captain Columb, R.M.A., on the Naval and Military Forces of the Colonies, which will be found in the journal of the Royal United Service Institution, and content myself with mentioning here that the Militia of Canada is divided into three classes: —

1st class—Men from 18 to 30 years who are unmarried, or widowers without children.

2nd class—Men from 30 to 45 who are married, or widowers with children.

3rd class—Men from 45 to 60.

These forces are divided into active and reserve, the former consisting of the volunteer, regular, and marine militia. The country itself is divided into twelve military districts; these are subdivided into brigade and regimental divisions, and again into company divisions.

It may be well to turn aside and enquire what are the physical and other characteristics of the Canadian territories, which cannot fail to be of great importance in considering the prospects of our future imports from and exports to her shores. In looking over a map, one cannot fail to notice the immense extent of territory of which this country consists; it is, in fact, larger than the United States, if we except Alaska, although large useless regions in the dreary North can never add in any way to its productive powers or prosperity.

But still there remains, out of a total area of 3,346,701 square miles, two millions of timbered and agricultural lands, and in the remainder, which as yet has been only partially explored, there is known to be valuable minerals, fur-bearing animals, and productive fisheries.

There is, however, one feature which has hitherto been antagonistic to the rapid development of Canada, and that is, the line of frontier between it and the

United States at present prevents easy communication between one part of the Dominion and the other without crossing into the United States territory. This was in a great measure caused by the large extent of territory our commissioners surrendered in 1842, who, without warrant, and apparently without necessity, gave up to the United States not only perhaps as fine territory as any in the world, including parts of what are now Ohio, Indiana, Michigan, and Illinois, but also, so to speak, in a measure cut off one part of Canada from the other, and isolated British Columbia from Montreal and Quebec. It is idle to speculate on the value of the territory we then flung away, or how much a larger and better knit-together confederation Canada would now be had we not given away a large part of her most valuable corn-producing districts. This blunder, for it was a blunder, may be partly rectified when the Canadian Pacific Railway is laid; and if Canada can never have a 'scientific frontier' in a commercial sense, one must trust these commissioners decided on a satisfactory frontier in other respects, and that it is as defensible as its great length will admit.

But when on the subject of facility of transit between one part of the Dominion and the other, it may be as well to point out that during the long Canadian winters, so far from traffic being stopped by the snow, it is, as a rule, facilitated. Over the hard, frost-bound snowy tract the heaviest loads can be drawn with ease even across swamps and streams which are at other times impassable, and it greatly assists in one of the Canadian national industries, 'lumbering,' which can only be carried out effectually by its powerful co-operation. In fact, the whole country derives great benefit from this splendid means of internal communication. The greatest incon-

P

venience is of course occasioned during the winter, when thaws occur which break up the roads and arrest the flow of business. Still, one must remember that if frost pulverises the ground, and snow acts as a valuable covering as a manure, the former often kills the young wheat, and the whole real work of the farm has to be done in six or seven months, instead of, as in this country, in ten or eleven; and naturally during this long Canadian winter, horses, cattle, and other farm stock require a proportionately larger supply of fodder for their keep. It is, however, said that winters are milder in Canada than they were. Be that as it may, a Canadian will tell you that although the average winter temperature of Ontario is unquestionably much lower than that of Britain, yet, owing to the comparative dryness of the Canadian atmosphere, it is just as easy to bear as the cold of the winter here. And it is a fact which few of us perhaps realize, that the cold of Canada is not caused by its high northern latitude, as one would be led to imagine; for the south of the province of Ontario extends to about the same latitude as Rome, whilst its most northern settlers are five degrees nearer the equator than the most southern inhabitants of England.

There can be no doubt that the resources of Canada have not as yet been fully developed, and that the day is probably not so far in the future when a five-fold increased quantity of cereals will be grown than there are now. There are immense tracts in her corn-growing zone, the whole of which, cultivated and uncultivated, is estimated at one million square miles, and doubtless when the agricultural population of Canada increases will produce millions of cwts. more grain than are at present. I am assured by a Canadian gentleman of large experience that the province of Manitoba has tens of thousands of acres of the richest and most suitable land for corn-growing in the world, and that there are boundless prairies of this 'virgin soil' entirely unencumbered with trees. This district simply awaits the time when the Pacific Railway or some other line opens it out. When that day arrives, it will doubtless attract farmers as settlers on its soil, and materially aid Canada in becoming a formidable competitor with the United States in the corn markets of the world.

Canada has always been a favourite resort for that canny race, the small Scotch farmers, who are not men to follow one another to a country unless they understand the chance of their success is considerable. It is not to be imagined that men without either a small capital or without any technical knowledge of farming are likely to succeed. The best men to emigrate are our small tenant farmers, who are finding it an uphill task to compete at home with both foreign produce and the more economically working improved plant on the farms of their richer rivals in England. The best settler in a new country is a man who goes there after deliberation and the full assurance, with the facts before him, that he has the qualities requisite in the selected field.

It has been often asserted that the most healthy climate in North America is Quebec; and that the soil is rich and susceptible of the highest cultivation, and that cereals, hay, and green crops, grow everywhere in abundance. Under a moderately good system of farming, about 25 bushels of wheat is considered a fair average—under a higher class of farming the crops would be much heavier; in fact, this province is a great corn-producing district. Mr. O'Neill, the agent for this

province of Quebec, reports that in that district 242,726,
acres produced — Wheat, 2,068,000 cwts. ; barley,
1,668,208 cwts ; besides large crops of oats, rye, peas,
beans, and buckwheat. A total of 128,185 acres produced 18,068,563 bushels of potatoes, of turnips 812,073,
and of other root crops, 597,160 bushels, whilst on
1,211,953 acres there were grown 1,224,640 tons of hay
and grass, besides clover. The melon and tomato
grow and fully ripen in the open air. Indian corn,
hemp and flax, and tobacco, are grown, and yield good
returns. The extent of the farms is generally 100 acres ;
these farms in the older settlements are worth from
2,000 to 4,000 dollars, whilst in the new a partially
cleared farm may be purchased for about 200 dols. The
settler can also purchase the Crown lands at a cost of
between 30 or 40 cents (1s. 3d. to 2s.) per acre, or have
a free grant along one of the colonisation roads.

There are five main centres of colonisation—the Valley of
the Saguenay, the Valley of the St. Maurice, the Valley of
the Ottawa. Besides the Eastern townships and Gache,
the Crown offers for sale a large quantity of land on the
south shore of the Lower St. Lawrence. The lands
taken from the Crown, whether for purchase or as a
free grant, are subject to easy conditions of payment on
settlement. Cattle-breeding is becoming quite an occupation in Quebec, and the province has sent back
to England a class of cattle unsurpassed by her own
best breeds. The lands in the Eastern townships and
north of the Ottawa for pasturage are of special excellence

To conclude these remarks on some of the agricultural
prospects of the Dominion, I should not omit to notice
that the province of Ontario has long been celebrated for
the superior quality of its wheat. Canada exported to
this country in 1878 over two and a half million hundred-

weight of wheat, over two million eight hundred thousand hundredweight of Indian corn, besides over two million hundredweight of other cereals, including oats, wheatmeal, and other alimentary substances. A large proportion of our imports from Canada consisted last year, as is usually the case, in timber, though there is a falling-off in this import as compared with the year 1877. Canada possesses extensive forests, probably as fine as any in the world. In Ontario and other parts of the Dominion there are magnificent forests, which constitute one of the principal sources of her revenue.

In the aggregate there can be no doubt that at present building operations have been overdone amongst us in England; and partly from that reason, and also because the cost of carriage is less, we obtain our chief supplies from Norway, Sweden, ahd Russia. The forests of South America are also being gradually opened out to our traders, and Australia may become a keen competitor for a share of our timber trade; but, when trade revives, the ring of the woodman's axe will again resound as often as before in the Canadian forests. Soon, the districts around their towns will, naturally, become largely denuded of trees, even where that is not the case already. Their mode of transmitting the timber to the depôts on the coast is by dragging them during the winter to the river's bank over the snow bound tract, and floating them down the rivers in the spring.

It must be acknowledged that whilst there has been no lack of enterprise displayed or money spent in the construction of railways in Canada (no inconsiderable portion of which was advanced by our capitalists), that financially they have barely been a success. In fact, taking one with another, the five thousand five hundred miles of Canadian railway at present working do not pay more than one per cent. on the average: However, one cannot wonder that they do not pay good dividends when one remembers that the total population of Canada at present is only four millions, or little over that of London. Her general produce, too, is of such bulky descriptions that it will not pay a heavy land carriage; and the principal province in Canada that produces minerals (Nova Scotia) is favoured by nature with excellent water carriage. No doubt, although Canada might have jogged along for many years to come with her water carriage, even although a great portion of this is practically available little more than eight months in the year, and although her railways are said to be a great drain on her present resources, still they have increased the population by encouraging settlement and thus opened out vast regions that would be now unexplored. I look on the opening out of railways in a new country in very much the same way as a Zulu commander seems to look on the first few ranks of his men in making an attack. He says 'Let them be killed; those behind will reap the advantage of the attack they have made on our enemies.' So, in the same way, if a few thousand investors lose their money in making railways in a new country, one cannot help commiserating them as individuals, and at the same time seeing that the fact of their unwittingly sacrificing their money has encouraged the development, and thus added to the ultimate prosperity of the country.

One great advantage that the opening of railways must have been to Canada is the increased facilities afforded for transporting cattle and other live stock from out-of-the-way districts; and the importation of them to this country has greatly increased in the last few years. In 1874 we only took from the Canadians to the number of two hundred and seventy-three under the head of animals, including cattle, sheep, and horses; whilst in 1878 the number had increased to nearly fifty-nine thousand. They appear to have some very good stock in Canada, and a farmer in that country who invests his capital in either grazing or cattle breeding will have no difficulty in finding animals of the purest blood to select from; in fact, some of our most noted stock breeders are said to have been glad to give enormous prices for cattle bred in Canada.

Mr. Wells, the well-known American statesman, thus writes concerning the cattle of Ontario, in the "North American Review:"—

"North of Lakes Erie and Ontario and the River St. Lawrence, east of Lake Huron, south of the 45th parallel, and included mainly within the present dominion province of Ontario, there is as fair a country as exists on the North American continent, nearly as large in area as New York, Pennsylvania, and Ohio combined, and equal, if not superior, to these States in its agricultural capacity. *It is the natural habitat on this continent of the combing wool sheep,* without a full, cheap, and reliable supply of the wool of which species the great worsted manufacturing interest of the country cannot prosper, or, we should rather say, exist. It is the land where grows the finest barley, which the brewing interest of the United States must have if it ever expects to rival Great Britain in its present annual export of over 11,000,000 dols. of malt products. It raises and grazes the finest of cattle, with qualities especially desirable to make good the deterioration of stock in other sections, and its climatic conditions, created by an almost encirclement of the great lakes, specially fit it to grow men."

When the Dominion of Canada was formed, the Central Government undertook the debt of the various States, in all about 35 millions sterling. This debt, thought not *per se* a heavy one, must be heavily felt by a country in which the realized wealth is of necessity less than that of an old-established *progressive* nation. It is a matter of satisfaction to note the increase in the last few years in the Canadian mercantile marine, which exceeds that of France, Spain, or Germany, and ranks fifth in importance amidst the nations of the world, increasing yearly at the rate of 50,000 tons.

Before reviewing the general bearings of our export trade to Canada, I purpose making two or three remarks on the new tariff, which came into effect on the 15th of last March, and cannot fail to hinder our commercial relations with the 'Dominion.' In the first place, it would seem to be mistaken policy to attempt to nurse the manufacturing interests of Canada, to encourage a small class of manufacturers to spring up, and to thereby divert capital and labour from what would appear Canada's true field of development at present, namely, the opening out of vast tracts of untouched agricultural territories, thereby becoming one of the chief granaries and markets for the sale of food to nations partly dependent on an external supply, such as Great Britain.

This fact has been seen by some of the Canadians, and already those interested in the importation of raw and refined sugars, who have been greatly affected by the increased tariff, have petitioned on the subject, and contended that the old rate of duties was equitable to the consumer, and left ample room of profit to the refiner, and pointed out that Canada imported over twenty-five thousand tons of sugar from Great Britain during the year ending June 28th, 1878. This trade, they urged, is of great importance to Canadian shipping, as it supplies freight to vessels seeking the St. Lawrence, thereby encouraging cheap outward freight for the products of Canada, and enabling her to compete successfully with the agricultural products of the United States in external markets through this cheapness in freight. Governor-General the Marquis of Lorne states in his report respecting the customs tariff—

'That the present Government were returned by a large majority in September, 1878, the issue at the general elections being revenue *versus* a protection tariff.

' A protection tariff, in order to encourage the industries of the Dominion, was advocated by the leaders of the then Opposition; and the Government they have since formed do not desire to avail themselves of direct taxation. They also desire to point to the very hostile action of the American Government towards the Dominion of Canada in all matters relating to tariffs; and to the fact that manufacturers in the United States have established combinations under such perfect organisation, that should any special industry arise in Canada the Canadian market is at once flooded with a corresponding article of American produce sold below value; the effect of such combination being equal to that which is produced by a Government bounty.'

The deficits which have appeared in the annual income since 1875, although additional taxation had been resorted to by Mr. Mackenzie's Government, have perhaps had some weight in turning the scale of Canadian public opinion, and may have been partly the means of inducing them to establish a protective tariff, in order to increase their annual receipts from their indirect taxes.

The Canadian Finance Minister, the Hon. T. L. Tilley, in bringing in the Tariff Bill, urged that 'the large balance of trade against us is one of the difficulties with which we have to contend;' And in a memoranda to a despatch sent last April in respect to the incidence of this tariff, he stated that 'the general effect must certainly be to decrease importations from the United States and to re-establish commercial relations between Canada and the West Indies, while if it materially alters the measure of trade with Great Britain, he maintains it must be on the side of increase, and in several branches this will certainly be the case. Fostering and promoting Canadian industries, and especially manufactures, will not lessen the necessity for large imports of various commodities which are now largely supplied to Canada by Great Britain; but if the result should prove the means of restoring prosperity, the effect upon British mercantile and manufacturing interests must be most favourable.'

I will not enter into all his arguments in detail; suffice to say that he states the result of the duty of fifty cents per ton on coals will have a more unfavourable result to the United States than to this country, and even maintains that the increased duty on iron, and our manufactured cotton goods, will not materially affect our export of them to Canada, as he states that 'the smallest increase of duty is that which applies to British manufactures, or goods chiefly imported from Great Britain, while the heavier rates of duty will fall upon goods now imported from the United States, but which can and will be produced in Canada.' He also tells us that reprints of British copyright works are to be taxed twelve and a-half per cent. in addition to the duty of six cents per pound, and that this tax has been assessed for the benefit of the proprietors of these copyrights. I will quote in full his remarks with regard to the increased duty on sugar, as it indicates the manner the Canadians have met the bounty allowed by several Governments on the exportation of sugar :—

'Sugar, as will be seen by reference to the table given,* of the higher qualities is nominally raised from 25 to 35 per cent. *ad valorem* duty, while the specific duty of 1 cent per pound remains unaltered. This *ad valorem* duty, however, will now be levied on the net cost of sugars imported direct from the place of growth and production, without any addition for the cost of packages and expenses, and hence it is not really much more than 30 per cent., or 5 per cent. increase instead of 10 per cent. A provision of law is also made whereby the duty on refined sugars, imported *from any country allowing drawbacks on sugar exported, will be collected on its full market price when sold for home consumption.* This provision makes the duty on sugars from Great Britain considerably less than that on the same classes of sugar from the United States, the drawback in the latter country being on an average of 2½ cents per pound, on which the *ad valorem* duty will be collected.'†

Whilst on the subject of this tariff, I may remark that although I am aware one must not, as a rule, attribute much weight to the falling-off or increase of exports or imports in any one month, but look more generally to their incidence in a course of years, still I think this fact—

*For table of certain duties which affect our industries in the Canadian market, see Appendix (2.)

† Mr. James Duncan, Chairman of the British Sugar Refiners' Committee, remarks in a letter to the *Times* of Nov. 4th, 1879, that "I believe that sugar refineries are now being erected by Americans in Canada in the hope of reaping, like their European and American brethren, the benefit of an export bounty. No time should be lost in representing to the Government of Canada the danger which thus threatens their revenue."

noticed by the "Statist," which happened concurrently with their increase of tariff—worthy of notice, that our exports to British America were as follows:—

In the two following tables ooo omitted, thus, 54 stands for 54,000.

		In March, 1879.	In March, 1878.	Decrease.
Cotton piece goods,	yards	2,220	3,889	1,660
Linen	,,	460	992	532
Seed oil	galls.	21	75	54
Ribbons (silk)	£	—	£3	3
Spirits, British	galls.	12	20	8
Sugar, refined	cwts.	9	21	12
Woollen cloths	lb.	213	300	87
Worsted stuffs	yards	550	1,535	985
Carpets	,,	146	190	44

This Table below will give an idea of the decrease in 1878 of some of the principal articles we exported to British North America:—

QUANTITIES.

		1877.	1878.	Increase or Decrease per cent.
Cotton piece goods -	Yds.	43,650	38,891	—10·9
Linen piece goods -	,,	6,493	6,264	— 9·8
Metals:—				
Iron, unwrought and wrought -	Tons	123	106	—13·7
Sugar refined - -	Cwts.	339	331	— 2·5
Woollen manufactures:—				
Cloths, coatings, &c.	Yds.	3,470	2,924	—15·7
Worsted stuffs -	,,	18,029	12,944	—28·2
Carpets & druggets	,,	1,137	1,006	—11·5

Our exports to Canada have greatly decreased since 1874. In that year they amounted to in value over eight millions eight hundred thousands pounds, whereas last year they were under six million pounds sterling, and in every description of our exports does one note a decrease except in refined sugar.

In woollen goods our exports in 1878 amounted in value to £1,099,000, whereas in 1874 they were £1,233,000, and this notwithstanding we sent them last year over one million and a-half more yards of this produce of our manufactories. This fact alone gives one some tangible idea of the late fall in prices. And it appears that our woollen manufacturers in Yorkshire at present fear that one result of the new tariff will be to lose them the power of selling at a profit in Canada, and already a deputation of woollen manufacturers of York shire have moved in the matter, and have sent a deputation respecting their industry to Sir Michael Hicks-Beach. They told him their markets were depressed, and this, they stated, had been in a great measure caused by the exclusion of their manufactures from Canada, which used formerly to be sent from Yorkshire, this being the result of the Canadian protective tariff; whilst he, in reply, informed them 'that he should consider very carefully what they had placed before him.' No doubt any British Ministry would be willing to do all in its power to assist our manufacturers in maintaining their export trade ; but in this particular instance, unless some great change is made in our commercial system, it is difficult to see in what way they can move. And the result will be to the Canadians generally that they will have to pay more for their woollen goods, and may, as they are letting in machinery free for worsted or cotton mills, start a few manufactories, which may or may not answer. Indeed, certain Canadians assert that they will, aided by their new tariff, be soon able to supply their home markets with cotton and woollen goods. To us it may mean the ruin of a few manufacturers, and might even cause the gradual depopulation of a few Yorkshire towns.

Nor may we yet have seen the worst of this re-arrangement of their tariffs in Canada, for it is rumoured the Americans are anxious to give the Canadians and take from them in return reciprocal duties, lower in both cases than our manufacturers will have to pay. At present it appears improbable that the Canadians would assent to this arrangement; still, it appears that the late Canadian Government wrested from the home Government the right of imposing differential duties, and therefore the Canadians have full power, if they see fit, to give the American an advantage over the British producer. It is an absurd anomaly that the Government of this country should, perhaps by this concession, have authorized the Queen's son-in-law to establish a customs union between Canada and the United States, and it almost makes one wish that we had first started 'free trade' by showing the world, as thirty years ago we might with great ease have done, how well we and our colonies flourished with a 'Free Trade Zollverein,' and got them thus one by one to follow our example, by placing on those nations who refused to give us free trade the disadvantage of a higher tariff. There can be no doubt that, with their numerous and high import duties, the Canadian Custom-house officials will have great difficulty in effectively guarding the frontier, particularly that bordering on the United States. In one class of goods which we send to Canada we seem to have always distanced the Americans —namely, in cotton goods; in fact, ten years back our exports, as compared to those from the United States, were as seven to one. But, if we congratulate ourselves on this fact, we must remember that—although I firmly believe English cotton goods are both cheaper and better than American—their merchants are probably more, to use a business expression, 'pushing,' and will leave no stone unturned to try and gain a larger share of the Canadian market. Their sugar refiners will, however, not be able, as they have lately done, to enjoy an undue advantage over eithe the Canadian or English manufacturers, owing to the Canadian tariff charging a duty *on the drawback or bounty*, as I have previously noticed.

Years have rolled by, still I remember a remark once made to me by an American merchant, which, although it amused me (as to my mind nothing is more quaint than a sudden contrast of ideas), did not fail at the same time to strike me with the American practical turn of mind. It was in midwinter. We were both standing on the Canadian side of the Falls of Niagara, looking on one of the most magnificent —I might almost say awe-inspiring—sights in the world : that mighty mass of water dashing from the heights above into a foaming abyss, whilst even the spray, as it separated from the huge volume of waters, appeared powerful enough to dash asunder the ice-bound rocks on either side of the Fall. My friend remarked to me, ' What a big waste of water power ! '

It appears that the interests of Canada require not so much increased mercantile transactions with the United States—who, having nearly all the produce Canada can sell in their own land in abundance, can never purchase largely from the Canadians—but to have larger reciprocal dealings with the United Kingdom. Nor do I mean by this arrangement one in which the interests of either country would be injured by a 'cute' diplomatist or a slily-arranged tariff, but one in which they both would have absolute free trade. Should this ever be the case, the Canadian would find that his money had greatly-increased purchasing power, and that he would purchase for his shilling in Canada a great deal more than he could for twenty-five cents in the United States.

We all know that the Canadians are a most loyal people; and though there are some in this country who despise loyalty, and who, whilst having a vague belief that perhaps our three estates of the realm are as good a form of Government as could be devised, and are peaceful, law-abiding subjects in this country, yet would not scruple to sell arms to the foes of their country in any part of the world if by so doing they could earn 'a few pieces of silver'—failing to believe in either patriotism or loyalty themselves, they doubt it in others. Yet Canada showed us last year the sentiment of some of her sons when it was a question if this country should not have to fight a powerful foe. I refer to the offers of aid that came across the sea to us in 1877 and 1878 from the great Dominion.

'These offers,' says the official report, 'some of personal service, others to raise battalions, bore the stamp of a thorough determination to give willing and material reinforcements to Her Majesty's troops. They were the spontaneous expressions of a loyal and a high-spirited people to throw in their lot as a very important factor in the destinies of Great Britain. These offers were as cordially received by the Imperial Government as they were loyally made, and should the occasion have arisen, no doubt but that the hardy and stalwart sons of Canada would have been found standing manfully shoulder to shoulder with their native-born brethren of "that old country" which they love so well.'

The number, I am informed, the Canadians offered as a first draft was 15,000 well-drilled and hardy soldiers.

It would be well, both for Canada and the mother

country, that the links which bind us together in danger should be equally strongly welded in time of peace and prosperity. That that day will arrive I hope, and I will finish this imperfect attempt to treat on the trade prospects of the 'old Dominion' by quoting this extract from one of Lord Dufferin's eloquent addresses :—

'In a world apart, secluded from all extraneous influences, nestling at the feet of her majestic mother, Canada dreams her dream and forebodes her destiny—a dream of ever-blooming harvests, multiplying towns and villages, and expanding pastures, of constitutional self-government, and a confederated empire, of page after page of honourable history added as her contribution to the annals of the mother country, and to the glories of the British race, of a perpetuation for all time upon this continent of that temperate and well-balanced system of monarchical government which combines in one mighty whole, as the eternal possession of all Englishmen, the brilliant history and traditions of the past with the freest and most untrammelled liberty of action in the future.'

CHAPTER VII.

AUSTRALIA AND NEW ZEALAND.

THIS magnificent continent of Australia for a long time lay almost absolutely neglected, and it is hardly a century ago since we commenced forming the first colony of the present group, or even apparently realised that these regions were integral parts of the British Empire.

Since then the increase of these colonies in material prosperity has been very great, and taking them as a whole, during the last two generations their actual increment in nearly every direction has been beyond all precedent.

It is doubtless an actual fact that the cause which first drew those crowds of settlers to the Australian shores was the discovery of gold, and undoubtedly but for that we should never have seen the giant strides these youthful offshoots from the old country have made in their forward march towards that greatness to which they may ultimately rise. For the present, the gold 'mania' seems to be over. Now gold mining is, comparatively speaking, as humdrum and perhaps, in many cases, a not more profitable calling than tin mining in Cornwall. True, we have lately heard of new 'finds' in Queensland and elsewhere in this continent, but it seems difficult to conceive that we shall again see the time when sailors deserted from their ships and clerks left their desks to go to the 'diggings.'

Now we find, not only the men themselves who came

out to dig for gold, but their children, engaged in countless other ways besides mining in adding to the wealth of each of these colonies; some, for instance, as squatters, owning their 20,000 head of sheep; others, as farmers, possessing the freehold of well-tilled districts—as large, if not quite as highly cultivated, as the extent of land which would bring an English squire his £10,000 a year in this country.

One can arrive at a slight idea of the vastness of Australia, and the probability that the farmers and agriculturists of the Western States of America may not be as able in the future as some people imagine to rule the markets of the world in agricultural produce, when I state that although there are at present in Australia 69,129,855 acres alienated, there still remains unalienated the enormous acreage of 1,917,367,745.

Australia rose in thirty years from a population of 214,000 to that of 2,000,000 or 834 per cent., whilst her trade increased in the same generation from less than £6,000,000 to over £63,000,000. If we look in any direction, we see not only the increase of her towns, but also the increase of her wheat-producing area; the immense head of live stock throughout her borders, including well nigh fifty-eight thousand sheep; the large addition to her railway system year by year, there being already 2,000 miles open, whilst the telegraphic system throughout the Australian continent nearly unites every inhabited portion of it with the rest of the world.

It appears that the annual revenues of the several Governments amounted to, in 1877, nearly £14,000,000, or about seven pounds for each inhabitant of this continent. One might, without minutely inquiring from what source this revenue was collected, be inclined to imagine that the taxation was heavy; on the contrary, it is much lighter than in this country. We must also take into account that the revenue in Australia has not only to pay that which we in England consider the legitimate charges on the consolidated revenue, but also the interest on the railways and the entire cost of education, police, gaols, and lunatic asylums.

The cause of the slight taxation in the several colonies to raise this, is that the large amount which accrues to all of them except New Zealand each year from land sales, is placed to revenue account. This item alone added to the income of New South Wales in 1877 about four millions sterling; whilst in 1875 the taxation per head of the inhabitants of the several Australian colonies only amounted to, in the case of New South Wales, £1 18s. 3d.; in South Australia, £1 12s. 10d. In Queensland it was, however, much higher, namely, £3 5s. 3d.; and in Victoria, £3 2s. 9d.

It seems to my mind a mistaken policy on the part of these Australian colonies to treat this sale of land as revenue: it ought to be treated as capital, and the amount annually received from such a source should be either capitalized or spent in making railways and roads, or for other public works required. These would bring in revenues in the future, and our Australian colonies might then be able to show to the world States in the Antipodes, where there was not only large untouched resources and personal freedom, but where a colonist might feel all he earned was his own; where, in fact, the land itself paid the major part of the expenses of the State, and taxation, direct or indirect, on the individual was reduced to a minimum.

In looking towards the Australian continent, one's thoughts first turn to New South Wales—the mother colony, as it is fond of being styled—not only on account of its being the oldest of this group, but also by reason of its being the only colony which we possess which has voluntarily followed our steps in adopting Free Trade.

NEW SOUTH WALES.

To the shores of New South Wales, on the 26th of January, 1788, more than ninety years ago, Captain Philip, R.N., with the 'first fleet,' as it has ever since been called, which consisted of one guardship, four storeships, and six transports, arrived at Botany Bay, and on that day hoisted the British ensign and read his commission as the first Governor. This first fleet appears to have contained about 1,030 souls, and was almost immediately followed by a second, which brought 1,025 males and 65 females. New South Wales, although not settled until 1788, was discovered in 1770 by Captain Cook, and its real commercial history begins with the 19th century. It once included the territory of the colonies of South Australia, Victoria, and Queensland, and, although the progress of settlement rendered it expedient to subdivide this extensive territory, the present reduced area is nearly equal to the united states of North and South Carolina, Tennessee, Mississippi, Alabama, Georgia, and Florida, and embraces 323,437 square miles, stretching in a south-westerly direction from 28° 10' south, to 37° 28' south, and the coast line measures over 800 miles, indented with many bays affording fine harbours, and it is its proud boast that its principal port—Port Jackson—could afford perfectly safe refuge to the fleets, armed as well as mercantile, of all nations, while its mountainous regions form its natural water shed, and it is drained by numerous streams of large and sufficient volume. Its natural divisions are its eastern seaboard, the central range of mountains, and its western plains; the first being very undulating, and possessing the richest soil, adapted to every description of cultivation. The central range abounds in minerals, more particularly coal, gold, lead, tin, and copper, and the extensive plains which form its interior are specially adapted to grazing, the grasses being very numerous and extremely succulent, and of sufficient extent for the feeding of millions of sheep and other cattle.

The climate is such that the European can readily adapt himself to it, and the colony compares favourably in vital statistics with most parts of the world of similarly various temperature.

In 1803, Tasmania was created a separate Government, and South Australia in 1836. In 1851, after several years' guidance under a superintendent, Victoria was separated, and, in 1859, Queensland reduced its area still further.

At the first numbering of the people there were found to be one thousand and thirty men, women, and children; and the table below* will show the increase of population in each decade from 1851 down to the year 1871, when the last census was returned.

At the close of the year 1877 the population was estimated at over six hundred and sixty thousand, and the total addition to the population during the ten years ended the 31st of December, 1876, was about

* Year.	Population.	Births.	Marriages.	Deaths.
1851 - - - - -	197,168	7,675	1,915	2,600
1861 - - - - -	358,278	14,681	3,222	5,343
1871 - - - - -	519,182	20,143	3,953	6,407

183,000 persons, of which number only fourteen thousand, or about seven and a half per cent., are shown to have been immigrants who arrived in the colony from the United Kingdom.

I have entered thus minutely into this question of population because the greatest want is a steady increase in this direction, chiefly of the agricultural classes, and enterprising men of the mechanical class, as well as servants. With the great and natural advantages possessed by its central position, vast area, resources, magnificent harbours, with coal and iron in abundance, it appears to me a great pity, looking at the depression existing in some of the branches of industry in the mother country, that those working men who suffer from want or insufficient means, and would here find an easy and comfortable subsistence, are not aided by *combined effort* to feed this and other colonies. We send no inconsiderable number of emigrants to Australia. Still, one cannot help regretting that the main stream goes to the United States—it seems nearer home, and in mere distance it is, but in other ways it is not, as an emigrant to get on in the States must change his nationality, and so sever all his ties with the 'old country,' and his sons may become bitter enemies of the country their father felt many pangs to leave. The more Englishmen that go to English colonies the greater *ought to be* the mutual increase of wealth both to the mother country and the lands they people.

Of course, at first, a newly-settled land has in proportion to its population a very large proportion of the producing class, and a small of the non-effective. With the growth of the community and the increase of family life, it is found that the proportion of non-effectives (a class consisting largely of infants) increases, and that the relative proportion of these classes more nearly resembles that of England than it was at first. There can be no doubt that colonial life is progressive, and any man who possesses perseverance and sobriety will rise, as the surrounding society does. Those who succeed in becoming the wealthier class of colonists—merchants, landowners, and sheep farmers— live very much as the same class do in England; and many men who, if they had remained in this country, would inevitably have died in a workhouse, are to be found in our colonies, owners of fine freehold estates of hundreds, and even thousands of acres well cultivated and stocked. A very eminent member of Her Majesty's present Government has stated that colonists were men who went abroad to get rich; came home to spend their money, and get made high sheriffs, as there are about eight million British colonists, and only forty of those ornamental, if not very useful, functionaries. That seems rather a flight of imagination. In any large migration of emigrants to a given colony, whether at their own unassisted expense, or aided by any fund for the purpose, great care has to be, of course, taken, not only to induce the right sort of colonists for the given field to emigrate, but not to suddenly overflood any given community beyond its actual wants. There is little fear of this at present, as Canada and Australia are a great deal more opened out than they were ten years ago, and wide fields for labour and the production of wealth lay open in their boundless territories.

Sir Richard MacDonnell, ex-Governor of South Australia, mentioned a case of this sort occurring, in a eech he delivered at the Royal Colonial Institute. In 1855, when this colony (of South Australia) only consisted of about 80,000 inhabitants, the land fund had proved most prolific, and the emigration agents in England sent out in one year 12,000 emigrants, of whom a third were women. If I remember rightly, it was shortly after the invention of that useful, but slightly fidgetting American invention—the sewing machine, so probably many of them were 'distressed needlewomen.' Sir R. MacDonnell said :—' Nothing could be more wholesome than good beef as diet for a working-man, and if suitable time were allowed he could get with advantage through a ton of it; but an attempt to force him to eat a stone weight of it at once might kill him. This was precisely what had occurred in South Australia. The great want of that and all new colonies was of course people—people settled on the land and working the land ; but when they were sent out in such numbers there was neither time nor opportunity to settle them. They might fancy, moreover, how much the difficulty of the position was augmented when he told them that of the above number no less than 4,004—for he had good reason to recollect the exact figures—were able-bodied single ladies. Now he questioned whether any other man than himself ever had previously such a number of single women thrust upon him. He saw that they sympathised with him, and he owned that he had never been so embarrassed. He did what he could for them—built them barracks, offered to pay their fare and all expenses to any employers willing to take them off his hands, for he was sorry to have to add that they were occasionally very unruly. Now, as women in a state of rebellion are not so easily dealt with as men, he might mention that, by a "happy thought," they were on one occasion reduced to obedience by the cooling effects of water from a fire engine.'

Victoria and the other Australian Colonies, however, came to the rescue of this perplexed governor, and took a large number of his fair charges off his hands, and doubtless many of these ladies are now both the mothers of sons and daughters married and out in the world, and also mistresses of happy homes—homes supplied with every comfort that money can procure.

The evidence of enterprise is most indubitable. In 1855 an Act was obtained by the Government which enabled them to purchase the railways and plant of a private company, and there were in 1877 six hundred and forty-three miles open for traffic. During the last ten years large sums have been spent on telegraphs, roads, improving harbours and rivers, and in erecting public buildings. The railways seem to pay fairly well, and in 1874 gave a return of 4 per cent.on the cost of construction. The colony is already well supplied with telegraph stations, there being over two hundred. Besides this, at least ten thousand miles of road are now open, communicating with every part of the country.

The central position of New South Wales, the fact of her being the oldest, richest, and most settled colony of Australasia, and the acknowledged superiority of her harbours, afford her many advantages over her competitors. She is not only the centre of the group, as well as of the islands in the South Pacific, but she is within easy reach, not only of the American continent, but also of Asia, and her situation could not, therefore, be better for purposes of trade and commerce.

About one-third of the whole of the Australasian inward and outward shipping trade is to New South Wales, and in the following tables the wealth-producing power of the colony is fully exemplified. She abounds in minerals. The gold-fields comprise an area of 13,656 square miles, and extend the whole length of the colony. At present larger fortunes are made out of sheep farming than gold mining. Sydney, the capital, is the centre of the coal basin ; the quality of the coal is of the best, and in the Eastern countries of Asia competes with English coal.*

The miner of Australia is far above the agricultural labourer of Europe in the scale of intelligence ; his wits are sharper and his life produces a stalwart form and a self-reliant character. He is not that picturesque being described in sensation novels, armed with bowie knife and revolver, with homicidal tendencies strongly developed, but as peaceable, well-disposed, and industrious as the average of his class in the oldest states in the world.

Copper, tin, silver, and lead are found disseminated in large quantities, and in several places coal, limestone,

* EXPORTS THE PRODUCE OF THE COLONY.

Note.—In this table the thousands are omitted. Thus, 16,358 stands for 16,358,000.

Year.	WOOL.		TALLOW.		GOLD.		COAL.	
	Quantity.	Value.	Quantity.	Value.	Quantity.	Value.	Quantity.	Value.
	lbs.	£	*cwts.*	£	*ozs.*	£	*tons.*	£
1853	16,358	999	90	134	548	1,781	51	81
1863	14,791	1,262	17	31	605	2,361	298	220
1873	31,606	2,201	66	106	665	2,590	773	529
1877	102,150	5,256	90	147	468	1,824	915	648

and iron are to be found in close proximity. Diamonds, opals, rubies, and other stones, have also been discovered in this colony.

There can be little doubt that much of the progress of this colony is due to the suitability of the climate and to all its surroundings for the production of wool. The only condition Government requires from a person taking up land is that he shall stock and turn it to a beneficial use. Here are to be found long, coarse-woolled sheep—the Lincoln, Leicester, and Cotswold, as well as Llamas and Angoras. Markets for wool have been established in Europe, in the United States, and in the parent country; and it is a well-known fact that many of the squatters have amassed enormous wealth, derived entirely from pastoral pursuits. It cannot be too clearly understood that the variety of the soil and climate of the colony enable it to produce in perfection every kind of wool which manufacturers can require; and, as an evidence of this, one hundred samples of New South Wales wool were shown in the Court assigned to that colony in the exhibition held last year in Paris.

The live stock has increased greatly, and in 1877 there were three hundred and twenty-eight thousand horses, two million seven hundred and forty-six thousand horned cattle, and about twenty-one million sheep. Snow is of very rare occurrence, and, excepting the danger of drought, it is a favourable climate for agriculture, which may be pursued under, as a rule, equally favourable conditions as in Europe.

During the last five years the sale of land has proceeded at such a rate that money has been poured into the Treasury faster than it could be spent, and there has consequently been a sensible accumulation. This surplus has therefore been chiefly caused by these land sales. Last year the acreage sold was nearly four millions. Of the whole of New South Wales they have already alienated over 27,235,162 acres, and have still remaining 171,764,838.

The day cannot be a far distant one when we shall import four times more from this colony even than the very large quantity of wool we took from them in 1877, which had doubled that which it was in the previous year, and was over one hundred and seven million pounds weight of that commodity. Pauperism does not exist to any extent, and it is only in cases of accident or intemperance, that poverty is met with.

One would imagine that this colony was well supplied with news, for it possesses no less than one hundred journals, or one to every six thousand of its inhabitants; and all the social, political, and religious institutions of European life are represented. Education is generally diffused, and is a department of the State. Of the whole colony it may generally and truly be affirmed that wages are high, and are reported to have been for the last ten years from 8s. to 12s. per day of eight hours; that living is uniformly cheap, clothes certainly are dearer than in England, whilst fresh beef averages about 6d. per lb., and mutton 4d. per lb.; and that work is abundant and not difficult to be obtained. The latest approved labour-saving appliances and tools are in use, and the manufacturers are able to compete in the supply of local requirements with those of Europe, and, what is more to the purpose, to hold their own.

One must not lose sight of the fact that New South Wales, notwithstanding the freedom of her tariff, has the great advantage in her home market over our manufacturers in not having to pay the cost of transit of goods, and already year by year is adding maufactory to manufactory and warehouse to warehouse —in fact, the probability is that in certain commodities it will be the utmost we shall do to hold our own, and may even find New South Wales a competitor with the old country in the markets of India, China, and Japan. But whether this colony in the future purchases from us as much as it now does in that class of goods which I may describe as the 'utilities of commerce,' or those goods which are more properly classed as luxuries, and those miscellaneous articles which can be purchased more cheaply in this country than they can be manufactured in Australia; it seems doubtless that in proportion as the wealth of New South Wales increases, so shall we, directly and indirectly, reap the advantages of it in this country. It might be a pleaasant fact at the present time for a Russian Minister, or should we continue being engaged in these interminable 'little wars' —might also be even for an English Finance Minister to state in his yearly budget that 'for the past year the revenue had exceeded the expenditure by over one million one hundred thousand pounds.' Such was the fact, however, in New South Wales in 1877 ; indeed, the surplus amounted to nearly one-fifth of their yearly income.

Nearly one-half the revenue accrues from the sale and rent of public lands, whilst of the produce of taxation five-sixths come from the consumption of tobacco and intoxicating liquors, and is, therefore, a voluntary contribution paid for luxuries. If these figures be compared with those appertaining *to our own great but heavily taxed country*, and *to those of the United States of America*, it will be seen what immense results have been obtained at the cost to the inhabitants themselves of a minimum of taxation.

There remains for me to touch upon one other subject only before closing, and that a satisfactory one. The colony of New South Wales levies import duty on few articles, and where they do so it is for the most part on luxuries, and the duty imposed cannot be justly stigmatised as heavy.

In a recent return issued in answer to a question in the House of Commons respecting the tariffs of the Colonies of Victoria and New South Wales, I cannot give a more concise idea of their respective length and complexity than by mentioning that whereas the former took twenty-four pages to describe, the latter required *but one*. Hardly any of our imports are taxed by this colony; the few that are appear to be so simply for the purpose of revenue.*

---

* *Certain import duties charged in the New South Wales tariff:—*

Soda Crystals................	20s	per	ton.
Galvanized iron	40s	,,	ton.
Nails	40s	,,	ton.
Iron wire	20s	,,	ton.
Paper.......................	1d	,,	lb.
Rope	40s	,,	ton.
Sacks.	1s	,,	dozen
Sugar.......................	5s	,,	cwt.
Tea.	3d	,,	lb.

Exports from United Kingdom to New South Wales:

	1874.	1878.
Cottons, entered by the yard......	12,899,400	25,014,000
Linens, entered by the yard......	2,697,400	4,506,700
Iron, wrought and unwrought, tons	38,383	56,903
Woollens, entered by the yard	5,513,560	7,495,800
Paper of all sorts, cwts.	31,633	60,910
Spirits, gallons.................	64,859	149,335
Hats of all sorts, dozens.	42,482	114,780

The social peculiarities of the inhabitants of New South Wales are like those of all small British communities, with most of their good and many of their weak points. Their legislators, as in most Australian colonies are chiefly engaged in either business or agricultural pursuits. Their total imports to the United Kingdom have shown an increase since 1874, when they slightly exceeded £3,000,000, having risen to £4,463,000 in 1878. Sheep and lambs' wool form the staple product we purchase, and reached the sum of nearly £3,300,000. Our exports are the chief manufactures of this country, and have displayed a marked increment both in volume and intrinsic value to this free trade State in the Antipodes (nearly the only increase in our exports we have to notice since 1874) whilst in that year New South Wales purchased from us goods valued at over £4,300,000, our exports to them had increased to £5,700,000 in 1878. The short table on the last page will give a fair idea of the increase of our trade.

In one or two items there is a slight decrease. Still, had our commerce increased with other countries as we here find it, we should not have heard so much, unfortunately, lately said regarding the depression of our trade. That both for the present and future our commerce will prosper for the advantage of both countries by this mutually fair and equal and not *one-sided interchange of commodities*, I firmly believe.

Of the off-shoots from the mother country, New South Wales has already become not the least vigorous, and gives promise of even a greater future—a future in which she will endeavour not the least worthily to carry out the proud motto of this group of lands, inhabited by our progressive race, the watchwords—

'Advance, Australia!'

VICTORIA.

Now, turning to that great offshoot from New South Wales, the Province of Victoria, to begin *ab initio*, we find that this territory was first discovered on the 18th of April, 1770.

Victoria borders on one side upon New South Wales, from which it is separated by a straight line from its south-easternmost point, Cape Howe, to the Murray, and thence as far as the 141st degree of east longitude, separating it from South Australia on the western side. It measures about three hundred miles from its northern boundary to the sea, and about five hundred and sixty miles in its greatest length from east to west. Its extent is estimated at about two thousand five hundred square miles less than the entire area of Great Britain. With the exception of the periods of hot winds, which occur somewhat frequently during the summer months, the climate is a pleasant one. The deficiency of water for a large portion of the year throughout almost the entire country is its great natural drawback.

On the 15th of January, 1802, Port Phillip Bay was discovered by Acting-Lieutenant John Murray, and about three months afterwards it was entered by Flinders. The first attempt to colonise the territory appears to have been made by Lieutenant-Colonel David Collins and party, consisting of about eight hundred individuals. The point chosen for settlement was, however, found so unfit that the expedition was withdrawn, some to Van Dieman's Land, and others to Sydney; and although several subsequent expeditions were sent out, it was not until 1834 that the first permanent settlement was founded by Mr. Edward Henty, of Launceston, at Portland Bay. In the year 1835, Mr

John Pascoe Fawkner fixed upon the Yarra locality, and to him is due the honour of founding the city of Melbourne, the magnificent metropolis of Victoria. From that moment Victoria made rapid strides, until in 1851, after several years' guidance under a superintendent, it was separated from New South Wales, in which it had hitherto been incorporated.

According to the latest computation the area of Victoria is 88,198 square miles, or 56,446,720 acres, 40,000,000 of which are available for pastoral or agricultural purposes. Though the country is generally level, there is one great range the highest peaks of which attain an elevation of more than six thousand feet. Victoria contains, in addition to its mineral wealth, fine soils suitable to growing wheat, barley, oats, potatoes, grapes, olives, figs, dates, sugar, millet, and tobacco, and in a few places cotton, rice, and the tea plant. One-third of the total area of the colony may be considered as occupied by gold-bearing rocks, and deposits of this rich mineral are found at various depths. As a timber-producing country, Victoria has many advantages; large vineyards have been planted, and, from the nature of the soil and climate, wine as well as oil can be easily produced. Sheep, cattle, and horses, together with poultry of every kind, breed prolifically as in a congenial home. Cereal crops are heavy: in some districts over thirty bushels an acre are said to be the average in a good year.

In 1836 the Government of New South Wales sent a magistrate to preside over the district. In 1851, when it was, as before stated, separated from New South Wales, its inhabitants numbered over ninety thousand. This progress continued with rapid strides, and reached in 1877 over eight hundred and sixty thousand individuals.

It is worthy of remark here that, according to the

experience of the last forty years, the mortality at all periods of life of both males and females is considerably lower in this colony than in England and Wales, and only amounted to 15·03 per 1,000 in 1877, and the mortality among children also is said to be very much lower.

Whilst giving some facts relating to the population of this country, it may be of interest to note that there were more marriages in 1877 than in any previous year, the tendency being for the women to marry younger and the men slightly older than in England. In a table contained in the last official report published with regard to Victoria, the ages of the parties married are stated, and I notice some curious inequalities. Thus a man between 50 and 55 is shown to have married a girl of 14. This marriage was solemnized according to the rites of the Bible Christian Church, the bridegroom being an Englishman, aged 54, and the bride a native of Victoria. One finds, as in this country, old people entering into the wedded state; thus a man between 75 and 80 married a woman between 50 and 55, and this record sets forth that a lady of 55 married a man of 30. I also notice that one child out of every 32 born in 1877 in Victoria was illegitimate.

From the official report, I also gather the following facts, and I had no idea till I read it that the proportion of men's deaths caused by accidents or from violent causes was so much greater than women's. How much greater must it be in Europe with our constant wars!

Males are much more subject to death from external causes than females. Of those who died from such causes in 1877, 649, or 76 per cent., belonged to the male, and 200, or 24 per cent., to the female sex.

Omitting fractions, it may be roughly stated that where 1 female dies a violent death in Victoria, 4 males die violent deaths; where 1 female dies of an accident, 4 males die of accidents; where 1 female is murdered, about 2 males are murdered; where 1 female commits suicide, 5 males do so; only one woman has been executed in the colony since its first settlement. In the 11 years ended with 1877 33 males were executed.

The only violent deaths which habitually affect females more than males are those resulting from burns and scalds. All other circumstances which occasion such deaths bear more hardly upon males than upon females.

Ninety-two persons took their own lives in 1877, and 100 in the previous year. Both these numbers are above the average. During the 10 years ended with 1876 the mean annual number of deaths by suicide was 82.

Hanging is the most common mode by which men commit suicide, cutting or stabbing the next, drowning and taking poison with almost equal frequency the next, shooting the next. Females most frequently take their lives by drowning, next so by taking poison, next by cutting or stabbing, next by hanging, and only once in 162 cases by shooting.

Notwithstanding its rapid increase, it would appear that at the present moment the population of the colony is very much below that which a country with such natural resources is capable of providing for, and it is, as in the case of New South Wales, therefore obvious that here again willing hands alone are wanting to grow food and provide for the wants of many millions in addition to the few thousands at present in the colony. The transition from England to Victoria no doubt is in many ways considerable, but it is still in not a few respects, old colonists urge, simply like a change from one part of this country to another. What Victoria requires are industrious and frugal agricultural labourers, small farmers, skilled workmen, and men with small capital for which they can find no proper or promising outlet elsewhere. I may here remark that one of the most striking evidences of the rapidity with which the farming interest is growing is to be found in the fact that all kinds of live stock, except sheep, are held at the present time in far the greatest proportion by persons not connected with what is known as the 'squatting' interest. There can be no doubt that at present the great exodus of emigrants is over, and the most Victoria and the other Australian colonies appear to be able to do is to attract a steady though diminished stream of colonists to their shores. A man must have a certain nomadic feeling to become a colonist, and if the taxation in Victoria becomes much higher than in New South Wales—if the necessaries of life, owing to this protective tariff, become much higher than in the mother colony—the very desire for a change that first brought the colonist to the Australian shores may cause him to migrate to New South Wales; for in a new country the inhabitants are not to such an extent, so to speak, rooted to the soil as in an old one.

This colony boasts of having amidst the Australian group the greatest extent of railways, of which there were open in 1877 931 miles; they have been constructed upon a gauge of 5ft. 3in., and are mostly in the hands of the Government. The facility of conveyance afforded by the construction of these railways and by the formation of macadamised roads and the erection of bridges is very creditable; and I notice there was at the end of 1877 nearly two hundred more miles in course of construction. Still, in considering this question of the rapid opening out of railway communication in a new colony, one is always obliged to ask the question—Are these lines in excess of the requirements of the country or not? They do not seem to be, however, more than the present wants of Victoria should require; and the passenger rate is not excessive, being from 1d. to 2d. a mile. Here, also, one finds the usual Anglo-Saxon thoroughness in the way in which there has been established throughout all the populated parts of this territory both postal and telegraphic communication.

The proceeds of sale of land in Victoria, although it amounted to three hundred and seventy-five thousand pounds in 1877, was barely two-thirds the revenue they received from this source in 1874. It is always a noticeable fact that when the squatters are making large profits out of their 'wool,' they immediately invest large sums in purchasing the land from the State: hence the 'large men' have already purchased whole counties; and already the Victorians are complaining that there is a prospect that should this continue none will remain of value for farmers to select, the principle being to let huge tracts to 'squatters,' whilst reserving to farmers or 'free selectors' the liberty to purchase any portion they please so rented. The squatters, as I before stated, have considered it their interest to keep the farmer out by purchasing the fee simple themselves at low rates; and already there is a great agitation concerning this question in the colony, and indeed a proposal has been suggested to tax freehold land over a certain area at a higher *pro rata* charge in order to make the large holders sell their land to smaller men. The land is sold by Government by auction, originally at an upset price of from £1 to £5 an acre for the country, and £1 to £10 for suburban land.

Victoria has already incurred—partly, I am aware, for the construction of her railways—a debt amounting at the end of 1877 to over seventeen millions sterling; her indebtedness was then at the rate of £19 5s. 5d. a head for each inhabitant, and is in that latter respect two pounds higher than the debt of New South Wales.

Whilst, on the one hand, there is latterly a sensible

diminution in the productiveness of the gold mines of Victoria, on the other hand I find the exportation of wool has increased four-fold since 1863. It has not taken many years for these colonies to transplant many of the same customs and institutions one finds in England, although in some particulars there is a somewhat marked divergence in the way they have carried them out.

Building Societies have been in existence in the colony for a long period, showing that thrift is not one of the attributes of an English-speaking community that has been lost by change of soil and circumstances.

Like New South Wales, education in Victoria is a department of the State, and the education is purely secular, no teacher being allowed to impart any other instruction. Education is compulsory between the ages of 6 and 15. For general subjects the education is free, a small charge being made for extra subjects. In 1874 there were one thousand one hundred and eleven State schools and six hundred and ten private schools.

The Government is modelled upon that of England; the Legislative Council consists of thirty members, representing six provinces, and the Legislative Assembly consists of seventy-five members. The members of the Council are elected for ten and of the Assembly for three years. There is no State Church in Victoria.

Notwithstanding the depression in the building and some other trades which seems for some time to have existed in Melbourne, wages remain high, and the colony, from its general circumstances and its peculiar position and condition, has advanced and cannot fail to advance further. In 1880 there is to be an Exhibition of the Arts, Industries, and Products of every Nation, in Melbourne; and there has been, as we are aware, in the autumn of 1879, an Exhibition at Sydney. The Government of

Victoria have passed an Act for the purpose, and have voted £100,000 for their Exhibition building. When it is borne in mind that until recently there has not been an International Exhibition held in the southern hemisphere, I cannot but look forward to the immense source of enlightenment such Exhibitions will be both to the people of the parent country as well as to foreign countries of the immense strides made by British colonies, which up to the present time is not fully understood or appreciated. Free traders have ridiculed the idea of Protectionists inviting people to send for exhibition goods which could not be bought, but the vote for the Melbourne Exhibition building has been obtained by a large majority; both Free-traders and Protectionists have combined to make it, what I believe it is certain to be, a success.

The number of live stock in Victoria in 1877 was over ten million sheep and one million one hundred and seventy thousand horned cattle; in both cases, however, only about half the number there is in New South Wales.

I have not room here to enter as fully as I should have wished into the financial position of this colony, nor of making comparisons with it and the mean population. The following, however, will give a succinct epitome of the revenue and expenditure, the former being slightly over four million seven hundred thousand pounds, the expenditure being about four hundred thousand pounds less. This is very satisfactory, but these returns, however, do not usually include loans raised and paid off. Their tariff is a very long one, and I will not weary my readers by a recapitulation of it, but consider it sufficient to note that the majority of goods, including most of our principal exports, are charged an *ad valorem* duty of about twenty per cent. I cannot refrain from giving the spirit of it by selecting from amongst the numerous articles taxed the item of matches, which articles, I believe, are sold in the United Kingdom for about 3½d. per dozen boxes :—

Matches and Vestas—
  Wooden Matches—
    For every gross of boxes containing in each box 100 matches or under .... 6d.
    For every gross of boxes containing in each box over 100 and not exceeding 200 matches 1s.
    And so on per gross of boxes for each additional 100 matches or part thereof.......... 6d. additional.

Wax Vestas—
    For every gross of metal boxes, not otherwise specified, containing in each box 100 vestas or under .... 1s. 3d.
    For every gross of metal boxes, not otherwise specified, containing in each box over 100 and not exceeding 200 vestas.............. 2s. 6d.
    And so on per gross of metal boxes for each additional 100 vestas or part thereof...... 1s. 3d. addl.

Not content with taxing the boxes, they actually have a duty on the paper in which they are enveloped !—

Wax Vestas (*Continued*).—
    For every gross of paper small round tin, or other boxes, containing in each box 100 vestas or under .... 1s.
    For every gross of paper small round tin, containing in each box over 100 and not exceeding 200 vestas..................... ...... 2s.
    And so on per gross of boxes for each additional 100 vestas or part thereof.......... 1s. additional.

There are two or three hundred articles in their tariff on which on exportation a drawback is allowed. The drawback regulations are most voluminous, and to describe all their rules shortly would be next to impossible. I will, however, endeavour to give a clear idea of some.

It appears that a merchant having goods to ship on

which he wishes to claim a drawback has first to apply to the Collector of Customs for a Custom-house officer to be sent to inspect the packing of them. He has at the same time to transmit a certain sum to defray the expenses of the services of the inspecting officer, which are charged at the rate of 1s. 2d. an hour. After sundry declarations have been signed by the exporter, stating that these said goods have already paid a duty and are bonâ fide imported foreign goods, the Custom-house inspector has to sign other documents to the same effect, and that he has duly seen them packed. They are then sealed and despatched in charge of a carrier, duly licensed under the custom laws, into the custom shed, and delivered to the custody of the export officer for shipment, or if not so forthwith removed, they must be deposited in some secure room approved by the Commissioner of Trade and Customs, under the lock of the Crown, until removal. In case of any irregularity or fraud being suspected, they can be again examined. Should the Collector of Customs desire it, any goods may be re-opened or re-examined after having been passed by the drawback officer, the unpacking or repacking to be conducted by or at the expense of the exporter. There are also clauses in this tariff act which give the Governor-General in Council power to make arrangements with the Governors of New South Wales or South Australia to admit goods free. Were this system in force—unless the authorities of Victoria were fortunate enough to have in their service not only the most upright, but at the same time the most keen-witted body of Custom-house officials in the world—I am almost inclined to think it would lead, to use a mild expression, to a great deal of 'confusion,' and to a larger loss than might be imagined to their Exchequer. To quote the Act: 'Where any person desires to take from Victoria into New South Wales or South Australia by land over the boundary between the said colonies any goods chargeable with duty on their importation into either of the said colonies, it shall be lawful for any officer in that behalf, appointed by the Governor in Council, to grant to such person a *permit* under the provisions of this Act. From and after the date and throughout the period on and during which such permits will entitle the holders thereof to import the goods mentioned therein into South Wales or South Australia respectively without payment of duty, permits of a like character granted by any duly appointed officer of New South Wales or South Australia respectively will entitle the holder thereof to bring into Victoria from New South Wales or South Australia, as the case may be, by land over the said boundary, without payment of duty, the goods specified on such permit.'

I cannot quit this short review of the trade of Victoria without a passing allusion to her 'gold fields.' These were first made a practicable use of in 1851. The first effect of their discovery is well described by Mr. Trollope. So great was the excitement that men of all classes— lawyers, medical men, clerks, and officers of the Government, as soon as they could free themselves from their engagements—marched off to the diggings. Emigrants poured in by their thousands from every part of the world. They were then literally ' gold fields '—tracts of alluvial soil in which the gold lay at depths of a few feet below the surface, and whence it would be extracted without any mining skill or costly machinery merely by the use of a common pickaxe, a shovel, a cradle, and a shallow tin dish. The ore then found was so abundant, that a party of diggers, usually consisting of three or four men, almost invariably succeeded in obtaining an ample renumeration for their labour. The work at this time was very heavy and they usually had no shelter but a tent. On the return of these diggers to Melbourne in the winter of 1851 there was certainly some rioting and debauchery, and the proverbially reckless digger who lit his pipe with a five-pound note, or presented one to the first lady he met to buy a bonnet, is said to have done so that Christmas at Melbourne. In a few years after their first discovery alluvial gold fields ceased to yield a remunerative amount of ore, and, therefore, were deserted, or taken possession of by the Chinese. Fortunately for Victoria at this time *gold mines* were discovered. To work these mines shafts have to be sunk, crushing machines and steam engines used; in fact, they required capital to work them, and gave work to a large number of skilled and unskilled labourers. The men engaged in this occupation have no particular hardships to endure, and are well paid, residing in comfortable towns and adjoining villages. One fact greatly to the credit of the Australian colonies, that without wishing to reflect on any country, I think ought to be noted. Unlike California at the time of the gold fever there—when judges were openly bribed and justice became a mockery, a result which led to the organisation of vigilance committees—nothing of the kind occurred here: the firm arm of the law alone punished offenders and maintained order, and justice was regularly administered. Of course at the first rush of an enormously increased population to Victoria, there was a certain amount of inconvenience. The town of Melbourne being full to overflowing, a 'canvas town' had to be erected in the vicinity, lacking, in some respects, in sufficient sanitary arrangements. Prices of agricultural produce rose to an abnormal extent; hay was even sold at £50, and in one instance as high as £70 a ton; and even at Melbourne the price was as high as £30. Gradually things assumed their natural level and returned to their normal groove, and the present gains in gold mining do not greatly (if at all) exceed the average profit in any other mining industry.

In this colony, with a climate one of the finest in the world, and admitting of the growth of all European and of many semi-tropical productions, industries of every form and kind may be carried on and flourish. The Protection which, however, exists in Victoria causes, there can be no doubt, a great deal of valuable labour to be diverted to some highly protected industry. This Protection has caused many of the ordinary necessaries of life to become dearer than they would otherwise be, and it must be remembered that the 10 and 20 per cent. ad valorem duty imposed on imported articles, such as boots and shoes, for instance, becomes to the supporter of family 50 and 100 per cent. Let us hope that this may be altered.

Just a few words in conclusion. We find the colonies of Victoria and New South Wales have practically the same natural advantages; the former, indeed, has this gain over the latter, that she has a larger and a more comparatively settled population and better railway communication. Now, I will quote, connected with these colonies, a fact from no musty document, but from 'The Annual Statement of Trade of the United Kingdom,' published in the middle of August, 1879, and that is this, that whereas our exports to New South Wales exceeded in 1878 those of 1874 by £1,400,000, they had decreased to Victoria in the latter of those five years by £1,100,000.*

* The following appeared in the "*Times*" of Dec 4th 1879:—
NEW SOUTH WALES.
SYDNEY, Nov. 6 (*via* San Francisco).—The New South Wales

What is the main cause of this falling off in our trade to Victoria ? I say, unhesitatingly, nothing but their protective tariff; and the question to be solved is, how to induce them to change it for a Free Trade interchange with Great Britain?

NEW ZEALAND.

The most remarkable feature connected with our original settlement of New Zealand is that, with the exception of South Australia, it was the only British possession which had been in a great measure established under the system advocated by that grand old colonist, Gibbon Wakefield. Mr. Wakefield's contention was that a colony ought to be in almost every essential a duplicate of the country by which it was established, with this difference, that everything that was good should be selected, and everything bad in the parent state be rejected. He also, to obviate the improvident and reckless distribution of the waste lands, which led to too great a dispersion of the inhabitants, advocated the abolishing of free grants of land, and the charging for it what is termed 'a sufficient price,' to be registered and vary with the circumstances of each case. The acquisition of land in New Zealand is now practically, however, within the reach of all emigrants.

New Zealand appears to have been discovered and first peopled by the Maoris, who still inhabit portions of it; but the time at which they first entered the island cannot, with any decision, be ascertained. From the similarity of their language it has been frequently held that they probably derived their origin from Malay.

Parliament was opened on the 28th ult. The Trades Union Congress was closed on the 13th ult., after passing resolutions against Asiatic immigration and favouring a policy of Protection.

Tasman, the navigator, who visited the island in 1642, first made it known to Europeans, and gave it the name it now bears. In 1769 Captain Cook arrived at the island, reaching its east coast on the 8th of October. He found the inhabitants very warlike, and, as is not unfrequently the case amongst the aborigines in many quarters of the globe, they employed women to carry the load which in European countries are usually carried by men. Their agriculture was limited to the sweet potato and the taro; and although the country appeared to abound in iron ore, its use was entirely unknown, even for warlike instruments. Cereals were not to be found, and the one all-absorbing idea of the natives was war, and cannibalism was their general practice. I do not here propose to attempt to enter into a dissertation as to the causes which have led to the reduction of the number of this race, but will simply here treat on the many endeavours (not in every case successful at first) to better the condition of the island and adapt it to the wants of a civilised people.

It appears that Europeans are not known to have resided in the island until the Rev. Samuel Marsden, Colonial Chaplain to the Government of New South Wales, visited it in 1814. From that moment, however, the colonization commenced, and this action was precipitated by the New Zealand Company, formed by Lord Durham in 1837. In 1839, that company commenced operations by despatching a preliminary expedition.

The population of the island in 1843, from the most reliable returns, appears to have been about thirteen thousand, whilst in 1877, according to the official statement, there were estimated to be 417,000 individuals in this colony.

The area of New Zealand is twice that of England and Wales, and is about 105,000 square miles. Of this extent of country two-thirds is available for agricultural and grazing. It is stated that in 1872 there were in New Zealand only four persons on each square mile of available land, while in England and Wales there were three hundred and eighty-nine.

New Zealand comprises three islands, the North and the South Island, and a smaller one called Stewart Island. The climate is peculiarly fitted to agricultural and pastoral pursuits, and it has also the great advantage of being remarkably free from drought, that great bane to agriculture in some parts of Australia. The form of Government is grafted on the English system, the executive power being a Governor appointed by Her Majesty's Home Government. There are two Chambers —the Legislative Council, consisting of forty-nine life members nominated by the Governor, and the House of Representatives, elected for five years, and consisting of about eighty members, four of whom are natives. The colony is divided into nine provinces, each with a superintendent and elective provincial council. It will also be observed that the colonists have preserved the parent system in that they have municipal bodies—Road Boards, Boards of Health, Town Councils, &c.

Emigration to New Zealand appears to progress most favourably. A larger proportion of the emigrants from Great Britain go to this colony than to any other in Australasia. Many of these emigrants have their outward expenses paid by the Government of the colony. This, of course, is a considerable charge on the colonial exchequer, which, however, showed a surplus of about one hundred thousand pounds in 1877; and while on the subject of public expenditure, I may mention that there are certain individuals in this country who take a very gloomy view of the future prospects of New Zealand, amongst others Mr. A. J. Wilson, who sums up his remarks on the subject in an article in *Fraser* by the following blunt assertion:—' The outlook for New Zealand is not bright, take it how we will.' He lays great stress on the drag the public debt must be on the resources of so young a colony, and that £20,000,000 is a large debt to have amassed in forty years. None can deny the general truth of this, and that it must act to some degree as an incubus on this colony is undeniable. It would, however, seem barely fair to roundly state, with regard to the accumulation of this debt, ' The colony,' in this respect, ' has not been content to rival Victoria, it has sought to rival Canada.' The debt in the aggregate, as given in the official returns, exceeds that of Victoria, I am aware, by about three and a half million pounds sterling; but in the case of New Zealand this includes *the debts of provincial governments,* which amounted in 1876 to about the difference between the debts of the Governments of New Zealand and Victoria. They were thus, practically, the same in amount, and we must recollect that in the case of New Zealand the debt has not been entirely voluntary expenditure on the part of the colonists, nearly one-third having been incurred in the wars caused by native disturbances. And it appears to me that a great field lays open for our capitalists in investing their money in this country to open out its undoubted resources. They would appear to have more undoubted security in lending money to men of their own religious faith and commercial principles than to Sultans and Khedives, nor need they fear not being repaid.

Another point which this writer maintains will cause that which he describes as the ' show of prosperity in

New Zealand to disappear,' is, that the value of the imports exceed the exports. This, he contends, can be done by England's trade, because we pay for our imports out of 'stored wealth' (and would appear to have been doing so for the last few years); however, I agree in this respect with the writer, that except under special circumstances the exports of a nation ought to be equal to the imports. Let us, however, examine the figures connected with the total trade of England and New Zealand in 1877, and see whether England could better afford to pay the difference out of her 'stored wealth' or New Zealand whilst progressing in the development of her great resources. In English trade last year the excess of imports over exports amounted to one-third the value of our imports, or over £123,287,000. In New Zealand's trade by the last returns in 1877 we find their total imports amounted to in value £6,973,418 and exports £6,327,472—a difference of about £600,000, or less than one-eleventh the total amount of their imports.

Whilst a man is improving and opening out a new estate he may be expected to have to expend certain sums out of capital which will not at first bring in any return; that has been the case with New Zealand. What increased acreage of ground under tillage or new manufacturing industry have we started to show for this large balance England has lately paid out of her 'stored wealth,' this £123,000,000 sent out of the country?—as far as I can see, practically speaking, none.

Now, to take the case of New Zealand; first to examine the facts concerning her agricultural interests, to which industry Mr. Wilson thus alludes:—
'According to the returns up to March of last year, about 2,400,000 acres were under cultivation, of which 91,000 acres were sown under wheat. This is a

small proportion, and, of course, precludes the colony from being able to export this grain ; indeed, it has to import, which is always an extravagant position for a young colony to assume.' It seems that this 91,000 acres was the return under wheat in 1875 ; it had increased to 142,000 acres in 1876, and to 244,000 in 1877—nearly three-fold in three years. There is also a slight increase to be noticed of the acreage under barley in the latter of those three years, and about 33,000 acres more under oats. To what he alludes in the latter part of the above-quoted statement,—that New Zealand has been unable to export grain, and has, on the contrary, to import,—I am at a loss to conjecture ; for whilst I find that since 1863 New Zealand has exported wheat, oats, and barley, in considerable quantities, I fail to discover any return of grain imported into that colony—a colony in which the soil is so fertile and the agriculture already brought to such a state of perfection that from 31 to 32 bushels of wheat per acre are not considered much over the average. Whilst New Zealand has been reclaiming her soil, her flocks have not been allowed to decrease, her exportation of wool being the third highest in the Australian group, and rose from over fifty-four millions pounds weight in 1875 to over sixty-four millions pounds weight in 1877. Besides which, New Zealand has great, but has yet very partially developed resources in gold, silver, and iron sand mines, also large coalfields, some portion of which have latterly been opened out.

When one glances at the items in the import side of the New Zealand trade, one finds that in the last four years £1,600,000 has been expended on railway materials. During this period there has been a large increase in railway mileage, which has risen from 209 miles in 1874 to 954 in 1877. I know that there are those who would draw scant consolation from this 'progress mania,' and simply enquire, do these railways pay half-yearly at the rate of five per cent.? for if not, they say the colony is going to ruin, and consider that for the next fifty to a hundred years it would have been much better for them to have contented themselves with roads. These roads, however, could not have been either constructed without a considerable outlay nor kept in repair without large assistance from the state. Again, in a sparsely-populated newly-settled country labour is valuable, and a man's time represents a great deal more value than it would to a farmer in Europe. It pays in more ways than one for a New Zealand farmer to put his goods on the line of railway and send them quickly to market, instead of having his waggons and waggoners crawling along a country road at about six miles an hour, besides having to waste time in crossing ferries. He gets his workmen, after delivering the goods at the railway station, back to his farm quickly, who certainly would appear to be employed at more productive labour there—in for instance, clearing some new land—than they would in dawdling along by a side of a waggon for a few days' tramp to market.

Railways also induce colonists to settle and open out large districts long before they would be touched were there only roads, and the taxes paid by these new colonists, direct and indirect, represent a larger amount to the state than the aid it has *at first* to give in the maintenance of these lines of railway, which means of locomotion add not only to the farmer's gains, but also to the wealth and comfort of the whole community.

The tariff charged by New Zealand, though lighter in comparison than we find in the case of Victoria, still is far from being a Free Trade one. Textiles of various description, cotton, woollen, linen, and silk, are charged an *ad valorem* duty of about ten per cent. In metals part are admitted free and part charged an *ad valorem* duty of about ten per cent.; on coals there is no import duty. Taking the tariff all round, it is about 11 per cent. *ad valorem* on the invoice price of the goods imported. Hitherto the manufacturing interest has not been large enough to cause this tax to have a prejudicial effect on our imports. When this interest increases, as it undoubtedly will, this may prove to be another market where we shall have great difficulty in selling our goods unless, ere then, a change is made in the import tariff. Out of their total imports for 1877, which amounted to nearly seven millions sterling, we sent to them goods to the value of over four millions one hundred thousand pounds, the Americans about two hundred and seventy thousand pounds, whilst from the French they purchased only to the value of eighteen hundred pounds. Their imports from this country had increased from the above figures last year, when their imports from this country increased by nearly £1,000,000, and they had transmitted to us exports of the increased value last year over 1877 of nearly £300,000. There is, in fact, transacted both to and from these shores and New Zealand a steady and I trust increasing trade in most of our staple industries and manufactures and in their raw products.

AUSTRALASIA.

I shall briefly touch on the remainder of the Australian Colonies. Queensland, which is the third largest in point of size, being 669,520 square miles, contains only 203,084 inhabitants, or under one to every three square miles, so that no one in that colony ought to feel, to use an American expression, 'crowded.' Stock has, however, increased here in even greater rapidity than it has in New South Wales, and in a few years hence the traveller will find princely properties where at present he would only meet with the black man or the kangaroo. There are many properties in Queensland in which nearly 200,000 sheep or a number of cattle of equal value are depastured. The farmer combines tillage with grazing with the best possible results. In proceeding to cultivate his newly-acquired farm, he finds that where the soil is richest it is most thickly covered with timber. The trees he cuts down a little above the roots and burns them; then, without any further preparation or any manuring, the seed is roughly put into the ground by the aid of a hoe, or some other instrument. In this way he obtains two crops annually for years. The stumps left in the ground rot out in a short time and are easily removed. Of course, there is a good deal of upland land without timber, and which must be broken with the plough. The first few years of a settler's life in this country are spent in toil—toil, however, with the prospect of ultimately succeeding and founding a home for himself, and his family after him.

Very recently gold fields have been discovered within the boundaries of Queensland, and have, as was the case in both Victoria and New South Wales, yielded largely at first; the area of this auriferous country now being worked cannot be much less than 4,000 square miles.

The country where the Palmer gold fields now are was unknown in 1873, it being nearly two hundred miles distant from the coast, and three hundred from the point which the nearest settlement had reached to. In a year large communities settled in it, a town soon sprung up, numbering 3,000 inhabitants, and thus an extent of land equal to England has been opened out as the squatter, farmer, tradesman, and mechanic soon followed in the wake of the miner. The country is said to be healthy, and at Brisbane, the capital, the climatè almost exactly resembles that of Madeira, whilst in the higher parts of the south of the colony the climate is more bracing Brisbane is a town in which the inhabitants are justly proud of their fine public buildings—the Parliament House, the Governor's Palace, and the various public offices, besides the noble bridge which is constructed across their river, exceeding in its span London Bridge. It also has every accommodation in the shape of wharfs, railways, docks, and warehouses for conducting a large and prosperous trade.

In this immense territory there still remains over 425,000,000 acres of land still unalienated.*

It appears that labour is considerably better paid than in this country, the lowest average wages being seven shillings a day; if hired by the year £40 with board and lodging. Even higher wages than this are generally

* The Hon. E. O. Macdevitt, ex-Attorney-General of Queensland, thus states the mode by which the land is either leased or alienated in Queensland:—' In remote unsettled districts the land is leased to the squatters in blocks of not less than 25 square miles for 21 years, *at a rent of* 5s. a square mile for the first seven years, 10s. for the second, and 15s. for the third. When land is aliened in fee, the quantity allowed to a single purchaser and the price he has to pay depend on the position of the district in which the land is situate. If near the capital or other large towns, the quantity is less and the price higher than for land in more remote districts. The Governor, by proclamation, determines the price and quantity; but he cannot restrict the quantities to *less than* 640 *acres*, nor increase it to more than 5,120 *acres*, nor can he fix a lower price than 5s. an acre, while the maximum is seldom over £1 an acre. The average price would be 10s. an acre. The purchase money is divided by ten, and may be paid by equal payments yearly for ten years, without interest. But for the emigrant of more moderate desires and restricted means there is an opportunity, under the Homestead Law, of acquiring a freehold at a nominal sum. The Homestead Law allows the settler up to 160 acres of land, at the rate of sixpence an acre for five years. If during that time the settler has made a home of it by residing on and cultivating a portion, he has it made over to him in fee free of rent and taxes for ever.

paid. Mechanics are paid 10s., 12s., and 15s. a day and meat is said to be so cheap that all the poorest labourers have abundance at each of their daily meals, and all the other substances of life are similarly within their reach—tea, bread, vegetables, and fruit. And in glancing at the statistics of the colony, I find there are over 124,000 males to 78,000 females, so that the latter should be highly esteemed in that far distant land.

In Queensland the tariff appears to more closely resemble the Colony of Victoria than that of New South Wales; it averages about 12½ per cent. *ad valorem*. The value of our exports to this colony seems to have fluctuated in rather a remarkable manner during the last few years. Thus we find it amounted to over £868,000 in 1874, rose in 1875 to 1,123,000, and fell again in 1876 to £893,000; in 1877 was £1,072,000, and in 1878 was £916,000—a falling-off of about £150,000.

Turning to South Australia—the greatest corn-producing district of the Australian continent—we find that there was grown in 1877 over nine million bushels of wheat alone. The great difficulty with which they have to contend is the occasional seasons of drought. Should this difficulty be overcome by the increased moisture caused by the planting of forests, and, if practicable, large irrigation works, one may, in the course of years, expect to see the amount under cultivation increase ten-fold, and the yearly average bushels per acre grown each year neither increase nor decrease greatly, but continue at a steady average.

Already our export trade to South Australia—the produce and manufacture of the United Kingdom (excluding bullion)—is considerable, when we take into account the population is little over nine hundred thousand, and amounted in value in 1878 to £2,376,707. Our exports from them were, in value, over £3,000,000, of which sum two million pounds were the receipts for their wool, and about half a million for their wheat. Neither with Western Australia or Tasmania do we as yet do a considerable trade, as will be seen from the note below. Their population is at present not a large one.*

* This table, which I have drawn up from the statistical returns published by our Government concerning these Colonies, will give a fair idea concerning their relative positions and aggregate importance with regard to the trade of the United Kingdom at the close of the year 1877. The *ad valorem* duty charged on imports is only approximate. The imports and exports in this table to and from the United Kingdom include bullion.

	Area, Sq. Miles.	Population, 1877.	Gross Amount Public Revenue.	Gross Amount Public Expenditure.
Australia :—			£	£
New South Wales ..	323,437	662,212	5,748,245	4,627,979
Victoria	88,198	860,787	4,723,877	4,358,096‡
South Australia	903,690	236,864	1,441,401	1,443,653
Western Australia ..	1,057,250	27,838	165,413	182,959
Tasmania	26,215	107,104	361,771	352,564
New Zealand	105,000	417,622	3,916,023	3,822,426
Queensland........	669,520	203,084	1,436,582	1,382,806‡
Total of Australia....	3,173,310	2,515,511	17,793,312	16,170,483

	Public Debt.	Total Imports from United Kingdom (including Bullion).	Total Exports to United Kingdom (including Bullion).	Average *ad valorem* tariff charged on our principal imports, as far as the same can be stated.
Australia :—	£	£	£	*per cent.*
New South Wales	11,724,419	6,471,780	6,018,926	- Free.
Victoria	17,018,913	8,300,411	6,574,848	- 20
South Australia ..	4,737,200	2,828,835	2,542,806	- 7½
Western Australia	161,000	156,993	208,030	- 7½
Tasmania	1,589,705	377,499	632,741	
New Zealand	20,691,111	4,115,544	5,321,499	- 11
Queensland	7,685,350	1,164,377	1,201,528	- 12½
Total of Australia	63,607,698	23,415,439	22,500,378	

Tasmania is a country full of the greatest interest, and has equal advantages in agriculture to any of the Australian Colonies, and superior to some of them. Its towns, and also the natural features of the country, more closely resemble England than does one find in any other part of the Australian continent, and it is said that 80 bushels of wheat, 60 of barley, 100 of oats, 16 tons of potatoes to the acre, have been constantly grown in this region. And in no respect does Tasmania excel than in the amazingly large crops of fruit which are grown there. It is said that you never seem to lose sight of orchards, and fruit and vegetable gardens are apparent at every cottage. Their tariff is stated not to be a high one, but our official returns do not give sufficient data to draw from them any average *ad valorem* duty charged on our principal exports. The exports from Tasmania in 1877 to the various countries, with the increase or decrease as compared with 1876, are shown below:—

	Value.	Increase.
	£	£
United Kingdom	632,741	82,991
Victoria	316,729	28,381
New South Wales	342,590	167,113
New Zealand	72,095	1,497
Queensland	21,608	1,140
South Australia	28,474	5,012
Mauritius	986	986
Other British Possessions	49	49
		Decrease.
Foreign States	1,703	1,177

Respecting this analysis of their exports, Mr. E. C. Nowell, writing from Hobart Town, in his report to the Colonial Secretary, draws the following deductions:—

These figures are worthy of careful attention. The first thing that strikes us is the enormous increase of the trade with New South Wales, amounting to 95·24 per cent. *in one year.* This increase is the largest which has occurred during the last ten years, but there has been a steady regular advance from £82,426 in 1869. The increase as regards the United Kingdom is 15·09, as regards South Australia 21·36 per cent.; while as regards Victoria it was only 9·85 per cent. Now, taking into consideration the fact that Victoria is, of all our customers, the nearest, and that we have the closest relations with her in matters of trade, it is but natural that we should look to her for the largest proportion of the increase. But instead of this, we find that other countries twice, six times, even fifty times as distant, have a larger rate of increase than herself! We can attribute this anomaly to one cause only—Protection.

In one respect the Australian Colonies seem deficient, and this is in properly combined arrangements for their joint defence. They have individually small but excellent forces, partly of regulars and partly of volunteers, besides having three or four guard ships. It would be well if they would combine and have several interchangeable colonial regiments kept by them jointly, and always up to the mark for any emergency. That may be a thing which we shall see in the future—certainly, not from apparent indications, at present. Now they seem to a measure but scattered, disjointed States, scattered mostly round the coast line of the Australian shores without any cohesion or unity. That they would be stronger in a military sense, richer in a mercantile one, if united, seems obvious. Were they ever so, Great Britain would indeed possess a sister 'dominion ' to that of Canada, and Australia would fulfil in a measure the prophetic lines of Campbell. ' Verses in a treatise on the question of our trade relations with the various countries of the world?' perhaps some critic may remark. To that I would reply, be the ideas given in poetry or in prose, any that tend to picture the future greatness of Australia *are to the point;*

and when we remember that their trade already is not only a very important factor in our trade, as will be seen by the table in Appendix No. 3, but also in that of the world at large, Australia's future may be a great one when many States in the European system have sunk below the horizon either through decay, or from being absorbed by some of their more powerful neighbours. Be that as it may, Australia may one day realize the destiny here shadowed forth :—

'Delightful land, in wildness e'en benign,
The glorious past is ours, the future thine!
As in a cradled Hercules we trace
The lines of empire in thine infant face.
What nations in thy wide horizon's span,
Shall teem on tracts untrodden yet by man;
What spacious cities with their spires shall gleam,
Where now the wild-dog* laps a lonely stream,
And all but brute and reptile life is dumb.
Land of the free! Thy kingdom is to come,
Of States, with laws from Gothic bondage burst
And creeds by angry discord unaccurst;
Of navies, hoisting their emblazoned flags
Where shipless seas now wash unbeaconed crags;
Of hosts reviewed in dazzling files and squares,
Their pennoned trumpets breathing native airs.
For minstrels thou shalt have of native fire,
And maids to sing the songs themselves inspire—
Our very speech methinks in after time
Shall catch th' Ionian blandness of thy clime;
And whilst the light and luxury of thy skies
Give brighter smiles to beauteous woman's eyes,
The arts, whose soul is love, shall all spontaneous rise.'

† The word 'panther' in the original has been changed to 'wild-dog,' as there are none of the former found as natural denizens of the Australian forests; and also the words 'chartered priesthoods' have been changed to 'angry discord' as being less likely to create 'discord' should this work have any clerical readers.

CHAPTER VIII.

SOUTH AFRICA AND HER COLONIES.

SPEAKING at the Royal Colonial Institute in 1876, Dr. Atherstone (fifty years of whose life had been spent at the Cape) remarked 'that he was not a little surprised at the profound ignorance which appeared to prevail in England on subjects connected with South Africa. He found there was a vague kind of notion that South Africa was a Kaffir-breeding island somewhere in the South Seas.' He attributed this in a measure to the disproportionate and unequal size of the maps used at the various schools in the United Kingdom, and said :—
'An uniform scale should be adopted ; but he found England represented as ten times as large as the whole of the South African Colonies (and these impressions, recollect, were made in childhood, when the brain is soft and impressionable, and retains them for life) ; whereas, in point of fact, the Cape Colonies were nearly ten times as large as all England, their area being 500,000 square miles, and that of England only 58,000. In fact, the only country in Europe of superior area was Russia. It might have been expected that their commerce, chiefly with Great Britain, amounting to some ten millions of exports and seven millions sterling of imports yearly, would have sufficed to correct these inadequate ideas about our vast possessions in South Africa.'

Nothing, however, brings vividly home to us at the present day all matters connected with the geography and resources of a country as a war does. And if our minds are not thoroughly 'saturated' with the affairs of South Africa, it is not from want of description of them. I shall, therefore, be very brief in my remarks concerning the Cape, and touch only on the leading facts concerning her resources. South Africa comprises four colonies—the Cape, Natal, the Orange Free State, and the Transvaal. In dealing with these colonies, I propose to do so separately in the order in which I have named them. The Cape of Good Hope was discovered in 1486, and colonised by the Dutch in 1652. Having been taken by the English and returned to the Dutch, it was finally retaken by the former in 1806, and since has continued a dependency of the British Crown. The early settlers had great privations to endure, but the indomitable pluck and perseverance of the Anglo-Saxon race prevailed over all difficulties.

The first English settlers arrived at the Cape of Good Hope in 1820, from which time practically the colony became an integral part of the Empire.

In 1806 the revenue was only £180,000, and had increased in 1877 to £2,931,692; whilst the expenditure in 1877 (for the year ending 30th of June) was £3,428,392.

Their chief articles of export are wool and minerals. The first named is the chief staple commodity, and 25,209,004 lbs. of it were exported in 1862. This gradually increased until, in 1874, it arrived at the immense quantity of 42,620,481.lbs, valued at about £3,000,000. In 1877, however, we find there was a falling of about 6,000,000lbs. Most of the wool which leaves the Cape starts from the town of Port Elizabeth, which town, owing to the expansion of this trade, has latterly greatly increased in size and importance, The flocks and herds of Natal and the Cape already exceed those of Canada by some eight million head. The principal articles exported from this colony are copper ore, ostrich feathers, hides, ivory, goat and sheep skins, gold, silver, and last, although by no means least, diamonds. The first diamond was discovered in the early part of the year 1867, and the principal diamond fields are situated in Griqualand West and the Orange Free State. In three years the number had increased to nearly 6,000, worth £153,460, and up to the end of 1876 over £12,000,000 worth have been found, which is at the rate of £2,000,000 a year, or, to bring it nearer home, £5,000 worth a day.

A word here concerning the 'black diamonds' of South Africa, as well as the white or yellow ones there. An ex-Governor of Natal—Lieut.-General Bisset, C.B.,—tells us the coal fields extend in that colony over an area of above 300 square miles, and, strange to say, 'they were discovered in the county of Newcastle, bringing forcibly to mind the old English saying;' and adds :—' I visited these black diamond fields, and saw seams quite twelve feet thick, with only a few feet of soil above this strata of coal; at other places layers of it run horizontally into mountains, so that there would be no necessity to go down into the bowels of the earth, as in England, to the great risk of human life; but it would be brought along its own plane, and run down into trucks on to the railway.'

Five million pounds has been voted to be spent in the construction of railways in the Cape Colony; and, prosperous as the past of the Cape has been, the inauguration of a system of railways throughout the country must aid materially in its progress, for there cannot be any doubt that the only two great drawbacks experienced have been the want of railways and even in a greater degree of a more numerous white population. The Cape Colony is said to be capable of maintaining at least ten persons to the square mile, whereas it is an established fact that the cases are very numerous where it is found that one settler has ten square miles to himself. There is said to be room for millions where there are not thousands in this land ; and it is to be hoped that, now this war is over, many more emigrants from the United Kingdom will seek a home in this splendid but overlooked South African territory. The soil in many parts consists of loam and clay, decomposed granite and gravel, and is consequently particularly adapted to the cultivation of wheat and other meals. The following table, which I cannot avoid compiling, will give the last returns of the average of land under cultivation and its produce in 1865 and in 1875 :

	Wheat.		Barley.		Oats.
	Land.	Produce.	Land.	Produce.	Land.
	acres.	bushels.	acres.	bushels.	acres.
1865 - -	202,257	1,389,769	34,569	308,318	99,609
*1875 - -	188,340	1,687,936	29,179	447,992	114,651

	Oats.	Maize.		Potatoes.	
	Produce	Land.	Produce.	Land.	Produce.
	bushels.	acres.	bushels.	acres.	bushels.
1865 - -	433,342	50,126	324,683	—	—
1875 - -	918,494	131,304	1,113,007	9,012	371,524

* These are the latest returns made at the Cape of their agricultural resources. There being no Consul General of that colony

In 1865 there were 226,610 horses, 692,514 horned cattle, 9,836,065 sheep and 78,666 pigs, and in 1875 there were 241,342 horses, 1,329,445 horned cattle, 11,279,743 sheep, and 132,373 pigs in the Cape of Good Hope. These figures of themselves bear witness to the immensely ncreasing prosperity of this colony. It possesses great advantages for agricultural purposes along the coast line; and in some of the river valleys there are splendid tracts of country capable of the highest degree of cultivation, the only serious drawback in the province being the great disproportion of white to black population.

The war which is just concluded, and to which our thoughts have been so keenly directed, and the wars which have preceded it, are apt to create very misleading impressions, and an antagonistic idea is often formed against South Africa as a field for colonisation and settlement; but certainly, so far as the country itself is concerned, nothing can be more fallacious. In most parts the soil is of a very prolific nature, and the country is interspersed with well-watered belts of forest lands, With respect to the war, let us hope that the occurrences which are now taking place will once and for all settle our supremacy, that in the time to come we may have a regiment of Zulus fighting for instead of against us. If this does come to pass, we must hope that we shall be able to depend upon and receive as good service from them as we have, in several instances, from the Ghoorkas and Sikhs.

The Cape Colonies now embrace a territory nearly as large as France and Germany together, and the total

---

in London, I called on the Emigration Agent, who showed me their last "Blue Book," by which it appears these returns are only made once in ten years, at the same time the Census is taken. Therefore, the next returns will be made in 1885.

T

population of the Cape in 1875 was 848,685. I find it reported that the Government appears to be fully alive to the importance of increasing the numbers of the white population, especially of the industrial and agricultural classes, and have framed a scheme for the free introduction and settlement of colonists. To the end of 1877 over 69,000,000 acres of Crown lands had been granted and sold, and in some districts land has been disposed of for one shilling an acre.

The Cape Colony, as a whole, affords every facility for pastoral and agricultural avocation; its natural grasses and plants give food to large flocks of animals of all kinds, and the majority of the products of the temperate and sub-tropical zones, including vines, may be most successfully and readily cultivated.

NATAL

Derives its name (Terra Natalis) from the fact of the discovery of the district by the Portuguese on the festival of the Nativity, or Christmas Day, 1497. It is situated in 30° south latitude about 800 miles from the Cape of Good Hope. It was ceded to the English Government in 1806, contains an area of 18,750 square miles, and the population in 1877 was 325,000. The land adjutting on the capital is almost bare of wood, but well adapted for the growth of maize and the other European cereals; and the other tracts supply large areas for pasturage, with timber trees of considerable size and serviceable quality.

In 1845, after for some time previously being an appanage of the Dutch, Natal was proclaimed a portion of the Cape of Good Hope, and in 1856 was made a separate colony. The rains fall during spring and summer, and are more copious than in the sister colony. The coast lands yield tea, cotton, rice, sugar, coffee, and arrowroot.

The colony is capable of providing for a very large European population, and it only requires railroads and transport to make it a very valuable country. Here, again, the Government are alive to one of their chief requirements, and have voted a sum of £1,000,000 to be used in the construction of railways.

The proportion of the black to the white population is larger than would seem advisable, and is nearly twenty to one.

THE ORANGE FREE STATE,

Which is an offshoot from the Cape Colony, does not enter into the system of the English colonies, as, although it adjoins them in South Africa, it is a Dutch settlement. I do not propose to discuss the wisdom of the policy of relinquishing this tract of country as we have done, but will simply state that it contains an area of about 70,000 square miles, with a population of one hundred thousand equally divided between the European and coloured races. Wheat and grain of all kinds can be raised to any extent; it abounds in mineral wealth, and there cannot be a doubt that under proper auspices it would have a great future before it.

THE TRANSVAAL.

This colony has been recently brought under the rule of the British Government. The question as to whether our annexation of this territory, and the acquisition of some 50,000 not particularly well-affected Dutch subjects, was good or bad policy—whether, in fact, we had or had not any choice in the matter—has been so fully discussed of late that I will not enter into it here, and simply take this fact as it stands. Like the Free State, it is situated on a higher plateau than the other English colonies, and embraces a healthy climate for Europeans. It is evidently destined to become one of the principal markets for British manufactures and commerce, and when it has been more developed will be a most valuable addition to our colonies. The area is said to be about one hundred and twenty thousand square miles, and to have a population of two hundred and ninety thousand, six parts of which are coloured, and there are only about five thousand English there. The revenue and expenditure is about seventy-two thousand pounds a year. There is an abundance of open and uncultivated land, which at the present time realizes one shilling per acre; but as the district increases in population the price of land must also naturally rise.

The great future of the Transvaal consists of its mineral wealth; and, so far as at present known, its mineral wealth consists of its recently discovered gold, besides copper, lead, cobalt, iron, plumbago, and coal, nickel lead, tin, silver, besides saltpetre and sulphur. The country is well watered and healthy, the soil rich, and its agricultural and grazing capabilities great.

The principal products are wool, corn, potatoes, maize, barley, oats, tobacco, cattle, sheep, and pigs; but it has a great drawback (which will no doubt shortly be rectified by a railway) in its distance from the nearest seaport—Natal. The import tariff charged by the Government of the Cape on our principal manufactures averages about 8 per cent. *ad valorem*. Natal has at present a separate tariff of its own—not, however, as high as that in the Cape.

SOUTH AFRICA AND HER COLONIES. 277

The following are some of the principal rates of import duty levied in Natal and the Cape of Good Hope:—

Cotton - - - -	Natal,	6 per cent.	- Cape,	10 per cent.	
Silk - - - - -	„	6 per cent.	- „	10 per cent.	
Woollen and Worsted -	„	6 per cent.	- „	10 per cent.	
Metals - - -	„	some free, others 6 per cent.	„	from 5 to 10 per cent.	
Oils - - - -	„	6 per cent. ad val.	„	6 to 10 per cent. ad val.	
Candles - - -	„	9/4 per cwt.	- „	18/8 per cwt.	
Salt - - - -	„	free - -	- „	3¼d. per cwt.	
Wheat - - - -	„	free - -	- „	8d. per 100lbs.	
Indian Corn - -	„	free - -	- „	8d. per 100lbs.	
Sugar - - - -	„	3/6 to 6/- per cent.	„	6/2 to 8/11½ per cent.	
Tea - - - - -	„	6d. per lb.	- „	7½d. per lb.	
Beer and Ale -	„	6d. to 1/-	- „	4 to 8.	
Spirits - - - -	„	6/3 - - -	- „	6/3 to 7/6.	
Wine - - - -	„	2/- to 4/-	- „	4/4 to 8/8.	

No doubt, when the federation of the colonies of South Africa, of which so much has lately been heard, has, so to speak, got into thorough working order, all the diverse tariffs will be assimilated.

In conclusion, I may remark that the commerce of the Cape and Natal, amounting to about £4,500,000 of their exports (excluding diamonds, of which product there are imperfect returns) and £7,000,000 of imports yearly, is chiefly with Great Britain. Although I am told that the Americans are rapidly gaining a larger share of trade at the Cape, her mineral resources are as unlimited as the country is extensive, and it only requires British enterprise and capital to develop the great agricultural wealth, and increase ten-fold both herds and the grain-producing districts, and to make her diamond fields the richest and the most productive in the world, and also to develope her gold fields and other sources of mineral wealth. Soon we shall look at news from the Cape received 'by telegraph,' printed in a few hours after its transmission, as a matter of course, and wonder that the days ever were when the tragic death in Zululand of the gallant grandnephew of the greatest 'captain' the world has ever seen, was not known in England till three weeks after it occurred.

CHAPTER IX.

BRITISH INDIA.

TIME was when—unless in time of war, or when some extraordinary event like the trial of Warren Hastings aroused the whole nation from its apathy—little interest was taken in India by any Englishmen except those who were intimate with directors of the H.E.I.C., or chanced to have relatives in that country.

That, however, is not the case now, and *in a sense* India is more brought home to us than it was fifty years ago. More of us have been to India; the distance is apparently shortened by the decreased time it takes to reach it, owing to the aid of steam and the "overland route"—which, by the way, is somewhat of a misnomer now that the whole distance is accomplished through the Suez Canal, by water. The telegraph now keeps us posted up with what is occurring in India, and we in London now learn what is happening in Afghanistan much quicker than, in 1842, people in Lahore could have received news respecting the avenging army under General Pollock. Our leading statesmen talk of India in their vacation speeches; two of the Queen's sons have lately visited the country; and if everything Indian was not brought home to us during their progresses, it certainly was not the fault of the English press.

To judge from some recent debates, the members of our two Houses of Legislature view it from different standpoints. One, for instance, takes a philanthropic view, and points out that it is our duty to improve the condition of the toiling masses whom we rule; while another regards it as an immense mart for cotton goods, and considers the increase of the Indian cotton mills as " truly alarming;" an ex-secretary to an Indian Finance Minister speaks of it as "the brightest jewel in the English crown;" and a fourth bluntly declares it to be "a gigantic burden."

An Indian debate now attracts more attention than it once did, and sometimes quite half as many members assemble to take part in or listen to a debate affecting the vital interest of about 191,000,000 of Her Majesty's subjects as would attend to discuss the alleged advantages of a suburban tramway. I except in this statement, of course, the occasions when a party vote may be expected to be taken during a discussion on Indian affairs.

We have little correct knowledge of the people of India, and they are equally ignorant of us. Our respective religious and social ideas are so widely different that it is hard, very hard, for us to acquire knowledge of each other. Before the Indian Mutiny, it was not at all uncommon for the English and natives to meet at one another's houses much more frequently than they do now; invitations were often accepted, and many pleasant hours were spent by the " Sahibs " at the Rajahs' houses, who used in turn to come and see their English friends; and to the good feeling thus generated may be attributed the fact that many lives of both our countrymen and women were preserved at the time of that disastrous outbreak.

All things are now, however, greatly changed. The competitive system has had a certain effect in severing the ties of the two races. A family does not send out its sons generation after generation, each inheriting from the last tastes and predilections suiting them for a life in the East. Men do not remain there, as they once did, for twenty and thirty years at a stretch ; and the old type of Anglo-Indian is rapidly dying out. In a certain sense, he may be said to have made room for better men—more scientific, and perhaps a great deal harder workers. But, both under the old *régime* and the new, probably no body of men fulfil their at times very difficult work with greater skill and with greater probity than our Indian civilians. It is impossible to step across the boundary between the parts of India directly under our rule and those ruled by their native princes without at once remarking the difference. In the former provinces the natives make no attempt to bribe European officials, as they know that their designs will be defeated and their bribes refused; whilst in the latter the native looks on a bribe as his sheet anchor.

The European Indian civil servants in our own territories have a vast amount of influence, which they would most gladly use in protecting the people, but they often remain so short a time at one station as to be hardly able to exactly estimate their requirements, or to be able to advise the central Government how to aid their material progress, being so closely confined to their office work. Besides which, the natives are a much more litigious race than those of most European countries. A great deal of the Indian civilian's time is spent in court, settling what in many cases may be tersely described as 'squabbles,' which might, one would imagine, be equally well settled by ' a punchayet,' or native court composed of headmen from a circle of say five adjoining villages, meeting once a week, and having the same kind of jurisdiction as our petty sessions have.

Perhaps in no judicial courts in the world has a magistrate to exercise more care and discretion in weighing evidence than in India. Sometimes it is complicated by there not only being two sides giving the most contradictory statement of facts imaginable, but a fresh body of witnesses arrive with a third and totally different story altogether! Still, from this chaos of discrepancies they generally sift out the truth, and we find that a comparatively small percentage of their decisions are reversed by the superior courts.

The tendency of the whole government of India is towards centralization. Everything done in every corner in the Empire has to be reported to the Lieutenant-Governor of each province, who in turn has to send a report to head-quarters. On this subject Mr. Monier Williams says: 'Half the time of a collector is now occupied in replying to the enquiries of inquisitive under-secretaries. Every post brings piles of official documents and demands for reports and written statistics on every conceivable subject ; while in return piles of foolscap find their way from the collectors' cutcherry into the pigeon-holes of the under-secretary's office. There these precious bundles of foolscap are forthwith entombed, and from these graves there is seldom any resurrection to the light of day. It is said that not long ago a collector in the North-West Provinces was requested to write a report on the habits of the *Gangetic porpoise* !'

Nothing appears to afford a greater subject of controversy at present than the state of the finances of India. It is apparent to all that, partly owing to the famine, there was a deficit in the years 1876-7 ; and whilst few take a very sanguine view of the state of Indian finance, others paint its condition in the most gloomy colours. Indeed, I saw in a magazine not long ago an article headed with the ominous words 'The bankruptcy of India' on its title-page. Personally, I do not agree with those who take this pessimist view of the situation, but I will not presume to sit in judgment on the diverse opinions held by the high Indian financial authorities. I will simply state facts, and leave those that read them to judge for themselves.

The gross amount of the public revenue of British India rose from £51,310,063 in 1875-6 to £58,969,301 in 1877-8. By far the most important source of revenue was land, with over twenty millions sterling; next came opium, £9,182,722; and salt, with £6,460,082; then followed stamps, £2,993,483; customs, £2,622,296; and excise, £2,457,075. Although land is the largest source of revenue, the falling-off in its productiveness was greater in 1876-7 and 1877-8 than it had been since 1869. That can be more than accounted for, as, owing to the famine in 1876-7, the land revenue of Madras had fallen off in the financial year ending 1877, by £1,300,000. On the other hand the revenue on opium had increased by about £700,000 since 1876. The Government of India divide their expenditure under two heads —ordinary, and 'on productive public works.' First, to take the former: In the financial years 1875-6 there was a *surplus* revenue over ordinary expenditure of over one million and a half sterling, whilst in 1876-7 there was a *deficiency* of over two millions sterling, and in 1877-8 again a deficiency of over three and a half millions.

In the decade of financial years ending 1876-7 there had been four instances of a deficiency, but for the whole period the public revenue and expenditure might be then said to have preserved an equilibrium, the surplus of revenue being about seven hundred thousand pounds. This equilibrium by last year's deficit has, however, been lost. Excluding payments in realization of revenue and capital outlay in productive public works, the principal heads of the expenditure in 1877-8 were— Army, £16,639,761 ; interest on debt, £5,028,318 ; public works (ordinary), £3,676,274 ; law and justice, £3,319,673; *loss by exchange on transactions with London*, £1,653,377 (this sum, although a very large one, is about half a million sterling *less* than in 1876-7) ; police, £2,158,237 ; and *famine relief*, £5,345,775. The greater part of this relief appears to have been paid for in the financial year ending 1878, as in 1876-7 the sum charged under this head slightly exceeded two millions sterling. From 1869 to 1873 there were, fortunately, no payments for famine relief. It must also be borne in mind that this famine relief has not only pressed heavily on India, and greatly increased the expenditure, but also in decreasing the annual income, especially the receipts from land, and has caused a heavy loss in the financial receipts from Mysore and parts of Madras during the years 1876-7 and 1877-8, which loss may now be hoped to have ceased, and the land revenue in 1878-9 to have again risen to its former level.

Mr. Hyndman ought to be credited with having made a *discovery ;* for in his article on Indian finance in the *Nineteenth Century,* speaking of the Punjab, which district he calls 'the Garden of India,' he says *the only thing* which prevents the people being more often brought within the grip of starvation and famine is *'the natural fertility of the soil and the abundant supply of water.'* The outlay on productive public works in 1878 was £4,791,052. This included irrigation works and railways, but not the erection or repair of civil or military buildings, which are now placed to ordinary expenditure. I know that some allege that irrigation works are not productive. They appear to me to be productive works. Some show themselves to be so immediately after their construction, by being used year by year to irrigate the crops; others, perhaps in a more favoured district, only come into play when they are required to save the crops from the effects of a drought. To give an example, a late member of the Indian Council has informed me that the effect of the Irrigation Works in a portion of the district adjoining the river Godavery, which were constructed under the orders and superintendence of Sir Arthur Cotton, was to treble the revenue in a few years, that the natives largely increased in wealth after their construction, and that the signs of this wealth were obviously apparent, as few of the peasants were seen at the date he referred to in that district without *gold bangles* on their arms.

In the district near Cawnpore, in which both wheat and barley are largely cultivated, the mode of irrigating the land is to carry the water over the country by a series of main channels provided by Government, from which the cultivator makes his own offset into a small pond, and distributes it over the crops by means of smaller conduits. This system of irrigation from the main channels he arranges and maintains at his own cost. The water is turned on the growing wheat, patch after patch, in a most skilful and careful manner.

Railways in India appear to have increased in popularity since their first introduction, as the natives became more accustomed to use them, as will be seen from the following table:—

State or Guaranteed Railways	1868. Miles. 3,961	1877. Miles. 6,029	1878. Miles. 6,044
No. of passengers conveyed..	15,056,502	29,799,019	32,206,570
Tons of goods	2,809,289	8,412,528	7,166,205
Gross receipts	£5,307,083	£10,655,308	£9,503,721
Gross expenses	2,792,647	4,584,613	4,501,693
Net earnings	2,514,386	6,070,695	5,002,028

It will be observed from the above that although the mileage has increased by only about one-third more than it was in 1868, the net earnings of the railways have increased two-fold. The falling-off in goods traffic in 1878 as compared with 1877 was caused by the decreased requirements in the transport of grain to the districts suffering from famine in the last named year. The passenger traffic has, however, on the other hand, increased. No one who has been in India can fail but be struck by the immense passenger traffic carried on the lines during the time of some native fair or festival. I chanced once to be at Benares during the 'Ramlela,' and have never in Europe seen such crowds as arrived, literally 'packed' in train after train. The amount received by railway companies in India from European passenger traffic, even including the movement of troops and the annual migration to Simla, is comparatively speaking small. The first-class carriages for Europeans are particularly roomy and comfortable, each carriage being supplied with a washing compartment—a great boon in such a hot climate. The carriages used by the natives seem to meet their requirements—there being also on most lines separate compartments for native ladies. The principal railway stations in India are built so that they could be readily strongly fortified. Around many of them I noticed well laid-out gardens full of the most variegated and luxuriant 'tropical' plants and flowers.

At one time it was said that should ever the British leave India they would leave no monument in the shape of any great public work to be a lasting memorial of their rule. That can hardly be alleged at present, since the vast network of railways have been spread over the land, besides the important irrigation works we have constructed. The former have been constructed in the most thorough manner, the roads being well laid, and the bridges and stations substantially built. Travelling in India is therefore now, comparatively speaking, as I previously remarked, comfortable, and in going on their smooth, well-laid lines one is not jolted to pieces as over some of the roughly laid ones in the Western States of America. For this we have to thank those English engineers, contractors, and foremen who first planned and executed these great lines, hundreds — I might almost say thousands—of whom lost their lives from fever, ague, and cholera, pushing these railways through the trackless and malarious jungle, rendered doubly noxious by the unavoidable disturbance of the soil.

When we remember that, according to Adam Smith, the rate of wages is in proportionate ratio to the risk which the work entails, these engineers ought to have been, and indeed were, well paid. When we also bring to mind the difficulties with respect to transit, and the then price of iron and railway materials generally, these lines were not dearly constructed. And it ought to be no matter for astonishment, as it appears to be with some critics (with railway materials and plant 50 per cent. cheaper, as it has been during the past three years, and increased facilities of transit, to bring these materials to the lines being constructed), that *narrow* gauge railways can now be less expensively built than were the *broad* gauge arterial lines at first constructed.

During the year 1877, it will be noticed by the table above, there were over thirty-two million travellers on the Indian lines. I have seen it stated, as a proof of the folly of 'burdening' India with railway communication, (which was alleged to be too costly even for most parts of the world), that the passenger fare charged by the East Indian Company's system was *con-*

siderably under one halfpenny a mile. That strikes me as a fact to be commended and not carped at. To quote from the official report respecting a portion of the Great Indian Peninsula Railway, opened in 1876, which gives a clear idea of the increased popularity by the reduction of railway fares:—' A considerable reduction of the fares and rates was accompanied by great increase in the receipts from both passenger and goods traffic, amounting together to £300,000. The bridge over the Jhelum, on the Punjab State Railway, was opened in September, 1876, when railway communication was opened between Lahore and Jhelum, a distance of 103 miles. The success of this line exceeded all anticipations, and the public demands far outgrew the traffic resources.' To quote another instance, 'the Rangoon and Irrawaddy (State) Railway was pushed on rapidly in 1876-7, and opened for traffic 1st May, 1877. It connects Rangoon and Prome, a distance of 163 miles, and its opening caused a very appreciable increase of population in the tracts through which it runs, attracting to its neighbourhood numbers of families from other districts.'

One feature alone which ought to commend railways in India to an economist is that Government officials, when they are ordered either to join or change their posts, can travel from one part of India and proceed to their work in a few days, instead of having to waste their time for weeks, and in some instances for months, in those abominable contrivances on wheels resembling bathing machines, and called Dâkgaries, or in the now nearly obsolete slowly travelling river boats, in which they were nearly bitten to death by mosquitoes, for the time lost in these pilgrimages by our officials could hardly be described as employed in productive labour.

These railways in India appear to pay, taking one

with another, about 3¾ per cent. on their capital, which is more than can be said of the railway systems of America, Russia, or Canada, whilst during 1877 and 1878 the earnings of the guaranteed lines have enabled them to pay them interest, without the aid of Government. In many districts during the late famine had there not been railway communication thousands of our Indian fellow-subjects must have perished of hunger.

I now propose to touch on the present import tariff, which has a certain importance to this country in the recent removal of the import duty charged on the coarser descriptions of grey cotton goods. It came into operation in April, 1879, and I append below* some of the

* Import duty charged by the Indian tariff of 1879, on several classes of goods—   Rate per cent.
COTTONS—   *ad valorem*.
    Grey Cotton piece goods, containing no higher
      yarn than 30s. .. .. Free.
    Piece goods, average .. .. 5 per cent.
    Cotton Twist, Nos. 33 to 70, average .. .. 3½ „
      „ Water, Nos. 21 to 50, „ .. .. 3½ „
Drugs .. .. .. (a decrease in duty)
Dyeing and colouring materials,   do.
Glass and glass ware .. ..   do.   5 „
Gums .. ..   do.
Ivory and ivory ware .. .. (slight increase)
Metals, wrought and unwrought—
    Brass .. .. average 5 „
    Copper .. .. „ 5 „
    Iron .. .. „ 1 „
    Lead .. .. „ 5 „
Paints .. .. „   „
Perfumery .. .. „   „
Shells .. .. „   „
Silk .. .. „   „
Articles made of silk .. .. .. „ 5 „
Spices .. .. „   „
Sug ir .. .. „   „
Tea .. .. „   „
Umbrellas .. .. „   „

In this tariff there has been a reduction of duties on coarse cotton goods, a slight increase in the rates charged for lead and ivory—why ivory, it is difficult to imagine, as the manufacture of ivory ware is a great industry in India. Probably some Chinese mandarin has viewed its increased manufacture as 'truly alarming.'

duties charged. It will be seen that they are, comparatively speaking, lighter than nearly any other large colony or dependency of Great Britain, except New South Wales. Each succeeding Indian tariff has decreased the duties since 1871, when the duties charged on most goods imported were as high as 7½ per cent. *ad valorem*.

Mr. Briggs, in his speech advocating the entire repeal of the cotton duties, does not appear to have hit the right nail on the head when he stated that nobody objected to them but the Indian officials, who, he said invested their money in protected manufactories, and thus, although debarred from receiving presents from natives, levied a tax on both Englishmen and natives. I happen to know many Indian civil servants. I have never yet met one who had a share in a cotton mill. Indian civil servants are much more likely to start a co-operative store to try and make their reduced salaries (owing to the depreciation of silver) go as far as possible. They have neither the capital nor the inclination to ' run cotton mills.'

The men who are really interested in the retention of this duty are the rich native landowners, and, amongst other powerful classes of rich natives, the 'Zemindars of Bengal,' who have many of them great wealth, partly owing to the greatly enhanced value of their property, for which increment they have to pay no additional rent to the Government, owing to the amount having been finally settled by the act of ' perpetual ' settlement made in 1793, when Lord Cornwallis was Governor-General.

These wealthy natives, under the title of the ' British Indian Association,' last summer memorialized Lord Lytton and urged that the cotton duties were not protective. Lord Lytton, in replying to these mill-owning Zemindars, who are one of the most important and favoured groups of the Indian community, remarked 'that there was no class of Her Majesty's Indian subjects which, in proportion to its collective wealth and social advantages, bore so small a share of the public burdens;' and he noted with 'disappointment and surprise' that whilst deprecating forms of taxation which fall mainly on their own class, 'they have not shrunk from advocating the forms of taxation which fall almost exclusively on the main body of the poor.' These remarks would apply with equal force to the salt tax. Still there is no doubt they are very lightly taxed, and it appears very difficult, though our Indian Finance Ministers seem to have made some progress in that direction, to get the just quota of taxation from the rich natives, and they will probably, as heretofore, be always lightly taxed. It may be asked why was this particular moment chosen to remit the duty on cotton, when it is urged by many that the finances of India are in an embarrassed condition? Mr. E. Stanhope tells us 'that as it had been discovered what duties had a directly protective action, they could not be abolished too soon. Trade was in jeopardy, and it would not do to wait until it was destroyed.'

Happy omen! An English Government has actually moved before the times, and not after them. It needed a famine in Ireland to awaken us to the necessity of abolishing the corn laws, and not until the occurrence of the Isandula 'disaster' could our Government be persuaded to lend a helping hand towards the establishment of a direct telegraphic cable with South Africa, though Mr. Donald Currie and others had for years past frequently pointed out the incalculable advantages of such a means of communication. It is an encouraging sign that we are now looking to the interests of our trade before we lose it altogether, and that we have not determined to emulate the Irish gentleman 'who was most particular how he spent his money when he had not got any.'

Many persons still living may call to recollection the fact of our having not always been generous in our dealings with Indian manufacturers. At one time, at Dacca, there was manufactured the most excellent muslin, finer than any at present made, so that countless yards in breadth could be passed through an ordinary gold ring. We placed the *moderate* duty of about 70 per cent. *ad valorem* on the importation of this muslin into England, which duty was not removed till the year 1840, on the report of a select committee of the House of Commons, on which, I believe, Sir James Hogg sat as chairman.

Whilst on the subject of the Indian cotton trade no one in this country can help noticing without satisfaction that a bill has been proposed in the Indian Council by a Mr. Soraljee regulating the grinding, the almost unceasing toil, of the factory workers in Bombay. It will be a 'Factory Act' for Bombay, and it has been endorsed by the local government of that province. It provides that the mills shall be open from six a.m. to six p.m. for six days out of seven, that women shall work no more than ten hours a day, and young persons no more than nine, allowing in each case an hour for meals. When we remember the statement recently made by Lord Shaftesbury in the House of Lords respecting the fearful oppression to which he stated the workers in Indian mills were subjected, it must be admitted that Mr. Soraljee's measure cannot be passed a moment too soon.

His Lordship said :—'Children—female children, too, of the tenderest years—are worked 11 or 13 hours a day for seven consecutive days, for the Sunday is rarely observed except for the purpose of cleaning the machinery, in a temperature of from 90 to 95 degrees Fahrenheit, with one interval of 15 minutes for rest.

Women within a month of confinement, and less than that afterwards, are oppressed after the same fashion. Why, my lords, what more do you require? The whole evidence of 1833 rises up as a witness against them. Creed and colour, latitude and longitude, make no difference in the essential nature of man. No climate can enable infants to do the work of adults or turn suffering women into mere steam engines. But it is not thought enough, and I must go further and adduce more than adequate proof for the necessity of this motion. The late Miss Carpenter, a lady well known for her talents and large sympathies, says after her fourth journey to India :—

'The Bombay Factory Commission, which sat in the spring of last year, brought before the public facts of an appalling kind, which showed that, unless legal protection were given to factory operatives and their children, an amount of labour might be exacted from them, often in hot and ill-ventilated workrooms, which must be very injurious both to themselves and to their children, while these last would grow up without any education.'

Factory labour, be it in the east or west, is never at the best of times a healthy occupation. Still the mortality amongst the native factory hands, either young or old, does not appear to exceed in any marked degree any other class of the native community. Mr. Caird, whilst in India as a member of the late Famine Commission, in a recently published article, gives us some particulars respecting Indian manufactories, and in describing his stay at Bombay remarks—

I visited a cotton mill in the suburbs, the native owner of which was anxious to deprecate any advantage of cheap labour being in his favour compared with our cotton spinners at home. 'It takes one thousand two hundred people here to do what five hundred can with you, but then they are so idle.' He took us to see their houses—huts placed in flat ground under the shade of great trees. They are such as one would suppose would breed fever—but the people are said to be very healthy—wide, low houses, the roofs covered with broad leaves down to within two feet of the ground, no window, and a low door through which any grown person must almost creep. But the thickly-thatched roof and the absence of windows keep out the sun, and the people take their food generally out of doors. The little naked children looked quite healthy. In the mills the people seemed to carry on the work much as with us. The hours of work are from six to six, with an hour at midday for meals and rest. The monthly wages are for a girl or boy 10s., a woman 16s., and a man 32s. English machinery cheap labour, native cotton, but coal 40s. a ton. The Indian cotton has 15 per cent. of size in it, the English much more, according to my Indian friend. Besides supplying the local demand there is an export of twist and yarn, valued at £400,000, which goes chiefly to China.'

In examining our export trade I find that cotton goods head the list, then our manufactures of iron, which are lightly taxed. The quantity of machinery sent to India I find greatly fluctuates, and is naturally regulated to a great extent by the demands of the railway companies. During 1878 we exported to India less by over £2,100,000 of goods, the produce and manufacture of the United Kingdom, than in the previous year. A survey of the relative volume of our trade to India in the past two years seems worthy of a passing notice. Our Eastern trade already shows a favourable reaction from this state of things.

PRINCIPAL ARTICLES EXPORTED TO INDIA.
QUANTITIES.

	1877.	1878.	Increase or Decrease per cent.
Beer and ale barrels	141,270	99,813	—29·3
Coals, &c. tons	895,963	682,233	—23·9
Cotton yarn lbs.	38,865,925	35,778,900	— 7·9
,, piece goods- yds.	1,446,500,796	1,295,474,600	— 10·4
Metals :—			
Iron, unwrought and wrought - tons	241,782	219,916	— 9·1
Copper, unwrought and wrought - cwts.	227,068	226,344	— 0·3
Woollen manufactures :—			
Cloths, coatings, &c. yds.	2,372,498	1,884,500	—20·6
Worsted stuffs - ,,	2,418,360	2,584,800	— 6·9

This reduction may be in some measure accounted for by the poverty of the inhabitants, in many districts caused by the effects of the late famine.

In 1878 we appear to have exported over twenty-four and a half millions sterling of our produce, or eight millions in excess of our outward trade to the United States.

Whilst mentioning America, I am reminded that ice, which is an absolute necessity to make an Indian summer at all endurable to a European, is principally exported from that country to India. A hundred years ago the transmission of ice from America to India would have been an impossibility. Great Britain has taken on the average for the last few years about half the total exports from India, China coming next in the list, chiefly through the trade in opium.

In analyzing the imports to British India, one notices that the trade with France is gradually decreasing, there being little or no demand for the 'luxuries' supplied by the French except by a comparatively few rich natives, who are able to adorn their houses with gilt-framed mirrors and ormolu clocks, and their persons with silks, satins, and velvets overlaid with gold lace. But not only is France incapable of developing largely her outward trade to India, but on account of her almost prohibitory duties on coffee, tea, and other articles of import *from* India, this branch of trade has gradually diminished.

It will give an idea of the extent of the British mercantile marine, which practically possesses a monopoly of the carrying trade with India, when I state that out of a total of over 2,800,000 tons register of shipping that was cleared from this Eastern Empire in 1878

2,200,000 tons were British ships; of the remainder, over 300,000 tons were British Indian native craft.

The Indian and Italian interchange is, however, of some importance, and as the latter country possesses the nearest Mediterranean ports in Europe to India, may increase to still larger proportions in the future, and the American, German, and French flags are also fairly well represented in the Indian seas.

Since 1874 the quantity of raw cotton we receive from India has considerably decreased; in that year it was over 3,600,000 cwts.; whilst last year it was not one half, or only 1,433,000 cwts. One reason for this is, that its recent reduction in price has made it more difficult to compete with the American cotton, which also has the advantage in the greater length of fibre; besides which, Indian cotton is said not to come as 'clean' as that which we receive from other sources of supply (from all of which combined we purchased $5\frac{1}{2}$ per cent. less last year than in 1877). It is probable that the development of native industry in the manufacture of cotton fabrics has also necessitated the withdrawal for home use of the raw material which might have been otherwise sent to a European market. In Bengal, for instance, for the last few years cotton has not been cultivated so much for an article of external commerce as for home consumption, the agricultural classes preferring, it is said, strong, home-made spun cloth to the less durable machine-made European cotton piece goods procurable in the bazaars. Notwithstanding this, the foreign prints and cloth are gradually, in certain descriptions, driving native cotton goods out of the market.

Latterly a great deal of land in India previously devoted to the cultivation of cotton has been put under grain, and I notice a marked increase in the amount of wheat imported from India up to the year 1877. In 1878, however, there was a falling-off in their exports to us of that produce. That fact, I am aware, can be readily accounted for, as being, I need hardly remark, the year succeeding the drought and consequent famine in many districts; therefore grain would not be so largely sent out of the country, being to a greater extent than usual required for home consumption. There appears every prospect that our supply of grain from India will increase yearly, but I will defer my remarks on Indian wheat till later, in touching on the future prospects of our external food supply.

The cultivation of tea has been steadily increasing, and the consumption of Indian tea in England has increased from 9 million ℔s. in 1868 to twenty-eight million ℔s. in 1876, and to over thirty-five million ℔s. in 1878. It is now grown not only in the Assam district at Hazairbagh, in Bengal, but on the pleasant slopes of the Neilgherries, in Madras, the plantations of which district have increased from 38 in 1875-6 to 44 in 1876-7, and also in the Kangra valley, beneath the shadow of the mighty Himalayas. I remember going over a tea plantation in that district in 1870, and it was most interesting to see the squat little tea bushes ranged in rows, the particularly clean buildings where the drying, pressing, and packing of the leaves were carried on, and to remember that all this trouble would have for its result the 'cheering but not inebriating' of a large portion of Her Majesty's subjects in the United Kingdom.

Tea-planters, I found, at that time looked on tea principally as an article 'of export,' and preferred champagne. However, since those days I hear there are fewer European supervisors of the tea plantations, and more is left to the management of natives, who receive much less remuneration. As a rule, I understand nearly all the tea plantations of India are paying fair dividends. From tea to sugar is an easy transition. An allusion to the sugar trade always reminds me of the anecdote respecting Lord Chatham, who grandiloquently commenced a speech in the House — 'Sugar, sir!' His audience had the temerity to laugh, until his awful frown reduced them to silence.

Our importation of that commodity which Mr. Lowe once poetically described as 'the charm of childhood and the solace of old age' has increased three-fold from our Indian Empire since 1873, and it reached nearly nine hundred thousand cwt. in 1877, but there was a marked falling-off in 1878 owing to a failure in that crop. In no part of the world, except China, are they more conservative of old customs, than in India. In 1870, when on a tour through Bengal, I went with a friend to be for two or three days the guest of Mr. J——, an English planter at Bohea, who had an estate of about forty thousand acres. His house was a curious one for a tropical climate, being built like a castle, and had been thus constructed just after the mutiny. The morning after our arrival Mr. J—— drove us in his dog-cart over his estate to see the sugar cane just then being cut, and also his indigo works. The general appearance of the country struck me as being most prim, as the fields were all square, and there were no demarcations between them other than the roads or footpaths. This rectangular shape of the fields and absence of hedges and ditches saved disputes as to the extent of boundaries, as he made all his tenants keep their paths quite straight. Before he had adopted that system he told me there were endless disputes, sometimes even carried into the law courts.

This being one of the first places I had visited 'up country' in India, in common with all other Europeans I found the female workers in the fields, or those walking along the roads, turned their backs on us as we drove past. This is meant, I was told, from no sense of rudeness, but is simply the native idea of modesty, and if you turned round after passing them you generally noticed that curiosity had made them do the same. Amongst other things we saw, in one of his villages, were some natives crushing sugar cane. They were doing this in the most primitive fashion, having a hollow trunk of a tree as a receptacle for the cane, their mode of pressing the sugar out being by pushing round a heavy log of wood above it. In this manner for hundreds of years had the sugar been extracted. Mr. J—— informed us that he had tried to make them use a sugar-cane crushing machine, but they objected to doing so. If you give a native a wheelbarrow it is not uncommon to see him carrying it, containing its load, on his head; as, being accustomed to carry weights in that manner, he is said to find that the easiest way.

The natives all appeared to like Mr. J—— and look up to him as a friend. When they were ill they came to him for medicine, and he had acquired a great reputation amongst them for curing snake bites, as he had been successful in one or two instances where the individual bitten had been instantly brought to him. He told us one could hardly credit the yearly number of deaths caused by snake bites in India, and that on his estate alone five or six died every year from that cause. As a rule, he said, the most venomous snakes in India were distinguishable by their having flat heads, and from the bite of several descriptions he believed there was no cure yet discovered, and that death was certain.

I find that in the year 1875 the enormous number of over twenty-one thousand individuals were killed in India by wild beasts and venomous snakes; in both 1876 and 1877, the number killed was between nineteen and twenty thousand; of that number in the first-named year *over seventeen thousand* met their death from venomous snake bites. The much-talked-of tiger was only a 'man-eater' to the extent of eight hundred and twenty-eight, whilst wolves destroyed over a thousand individuals in India during that year.

The Government paid in rewards for the destruction of these animals and reptiles during the same year £12,001, for which sum were destroyed over seventeen hundred tigers, five thousand six hundred wolves, and two hundred and seventy thousand one hundred and eighty-four snakes.

By a recent Order in Council, the natives of India have been admitted to a large number of minor civil appointments. Whether it is a step in the right direction, and whether ultimately they will be allowed to fill the highest offices in India, it is difficult to say. From that which I could gather whilst in India, the majority of the natives appear to prefer seeking justice in any case of importance before a European judge in preference to one of their own race. Still, although the more intelligent natives are quite willing to allow that they enjoy greater benefits under our rule than they would under any other, English statesmen who rule the natives of India from Downing-street and try to treat them and the wild tribes adjoining their country as if they were Europeans, must not lose sight of the fact that, unfortunately, nothing really rules a native of India but *fear*. Our hold in India is simply as 'the paramount power.' This, in my humble experience, is the unfortunate but the true state of the case; and there are thousands of the unthinking lower orders of India who would rather be badly governed by their own chiefs than well ruled by us. There is much to be urged on the score of economy in having native instead of European officials in many more of the grades in the civil service than at present; whether it would work well in practice is a totally different question. India is a country full of interest. How much could be said on that institution of India, 'caste,' which interweaves their whole religious and social polity! And while there can be no doubt that the institutions of a country have a marked influence on its commercial relations, I consider that in looking at the question of our trade relations with India, we have to take the institutions of the country as we find them; and, therefore, till they are changed—which fact anyone treating on our trade prospects in the future may note—discussion on them is useless.

There is one thing 'caste' neither in the east nor in the west will ever prevent a man doing, and that is *making the best bargain he possibly can*; and there is also a feature in Indian retail traffic perhaps not peculiar to India— one may find the same thing in either Paris or London, though perhaps not to the same extent --and that is this: the seller does not dispose of his goods so much to their 'natural value,' as Adam Smith calls it, but to the value that he imagines the purchaser is rich enough to pay. Amongst the hundred transactions which daily enforce this fact on all residents in India, a friend of mine gave me this instance:—He, having received promotion and an increased salary, had taken his servants from the old station where he had been previously residing to Lucknow, and amongst others an individual who did the work of an English 'house steward.' He noticed, on his arrival at Lucknow, that although his living was exactly the same as before in all respects, his bills were greatly increased, and sent for his 'house steward' to explain. The reason assigned was this: 'Oh, great Sahib, Allah has ordained that as thy riches increase so shall thy expenditure.'

The number of European and native troops that we maintain in India does not appear at all excessive when we consider that for a country populated by over 190,000,000 nhabitants we have only 65,000 European and 125,000 native soldiers; this is the proportion of troops we maintain in the territory under the direct administration of the Indian Government. But we find the proportion of soldiers and 'armed followers' vastly greater in the native states, in which the number is 315,000 in a population of about fifty millions. I write the words 'armed followers,' for with the exception of the greater proportion of the troops of Scindia and Holkar, and a certain proportion of fairly drilled forces of other Princes, the constituent parts of these armies may best be described by the word 'irregular.' Still, they form an unnecessarily large body of troops, which in case of an insurrection might seriously add to our difficulties, nor could we always rely that, however loyal the chief or his ministers might be to our 'raj,' on the reliability of their troops. Bearing in mind that we guarantee these feudatory rulers from both foreign invasion and internal rebellion, and receive three quarters of a million sterling out of their total revenues of about sixteen millions for doing so, there can be no doubt that they possess a dangerously large force to be allowed by us to be kept in the midst of our Indian Empire.

These large forces kept up by these native princes necessarily impoverish the people, and greatly hinder the productiveness of their countries; and it seems a pity that the large amount of money which is wasted on senseless military show and needless armaments is not more usefully employed. Whilst in India, amongst other reviews which I saw was that of the troops of the Maharaja of Kasmir before the late Sir Henry Durand. They were a fine body of men as far as physique went, and were dressed in divers uniforms of various periods, some being clothed in old British uniform coatees, whilst the 'war paint' of others was of an Oriental type. The marching past, which was done in slow time, was more grotesque than military. At that time a large proportion of the Maharaja's troops were armed with the old flint and steel musket, with powder horns attached to their belts; and during the review, through one of these powder horns having accidentally caught fire, many others became ignited, and about half a battalion literally managed to blow themselves up! The Maharaja of Kasmir is a prince of great intelligence, and is distinguished from the other native rulers of India by his fondness for literature. He appears to be on good terms with the English, and I never spent a pleasanter six months in my life than in his dominions. The physical characteristics of Kasmir are almost the same as the adjoining country of Afghanistan, and no one who has not visited these regions can form a conception of the immense difficulties one has to surmount in traversing the wild passes of these regions, many of them taking three and four days to climb over— this even with all the facilities of a peaceful march and all the transport of one's belongings easily arranged, as from twenty to thirty coolies or porters are provided by the head man of each village to carry your tents, baggage, and other belongings, to the next. The rope bridges which one often finds thrown across the rivers take some time to become accustomed to, if indeed one ever does. The only one of the kind I have ever seen in this country is that which crosses the Dee near Abergeldie.

Whilst in Kasmir I heard that the Maharaja pays a tribute of twenty Kasmir shawls yearly to Her Majesty the Queen. I will not vouch for the accuracy of this fact, or the number, but I recollect going to see their manufacture. They are made by men in their cottages, one shawl of the finer description taking years to embroider, and are, when completed, to my mind barely worth the immense amount of labour bestowed. 'The fashion' for them, and therefore the demand, seems to have much fallen off since the Franco-Prussian War.

Many of the native princes whose territories have been absorbed in our own have no possessions beyond the immediate vicinity of their palaces; they are in many instances allowed large pensions by the British Government, and live surrounded by countless followers in a sort of semi-state, possessing armed retainers in numbers sufficient to form a guard of honour; whilst in other respects their position is similar to that of a wealthy English nobleman. I remember whilst at Benares going to see the Maharaja of that town, who spoke English perfectly, and was evidently pleased with a present he had then recently received from the Duke of Edinburgh. Like many of the native princes he was a very good shot, and, as many of his position in India are, a very keen sportsman.

The famine of 1876-7 did much to tax the powers of the Government. As it is now fortunately a thing of the past, I shall only refer to it in a few words. During the famine, Government did much to facilitate the traffic, and on *only* one occasion was there any interference with private trade, namely, when 30,000 tons of grain were bought by the Madras Government at the commencement of the famine and carried into the interior. Some idea of the vastness of the distress may be gathered from the fact that at one time no less than 1,050,000 persons in the Madras district, and 266,000 in Bombay, were receiving relief. The difficulty of finding productive labour for such large numbers was great, more especially as they were dispersed over large districts. Still, in Bombay 90 per cent. were employed on useful works under professional engineers, in Mysore 47 per cent., and in Madras 11 per cent. The report, however, adds: 'It is not intended to be implied that the relief works managed by revenue officers were absolutely useless or wholly unsupervised, but much of the road work was not of lasting value, while its cost was from twice to twenty times that of the ordinary rates; whereas, on the other hand, some of the irrigation and railway works executed under professional supervision, which will be of permanent use in improving the country and averting future famines, were executed at only from 20 to 80 per cent. above the ordinary rates.'

It has been alleged that one of the causes of famine in India was the small margin of profit allowed to the cultivator of the soil—that the Government charge him, in fact, too highly for rent. I am informed by those who have been lately in India that that is not borne out by facts. Naturally a famine will destroy any calculation; still, an Indian ryot has as good if not better chances of profit than an English farmer has.

In 1840 a general settlement was effected, fixing the amount to be paid by each village for thirty years, and a similar course was adopted in the Punjab. In 1874 and 1875 there was a revision of these settlements made, mostly for a tenure of thirty years, thus giving the cultivator fixity of tenure and of rent.

This assessment appears to have been made on about two-thirds of the yearly value—that is, the surplus remaining after deducting expenses of cultivation, profits of stock, and wages of labour. This has been *reduced* to one-half in the revised settlements recently made.

In Bombay the whole country is surveyed and mapped, and the fields distinguished by permanent boundary marks. When fixed, the rate charged here was, as I previously noticed, one-half the yearly rental, but owing to the improvement of the land is probably now not more than a *fourth to an eighth* in the districts not recently settled.

In the thirty years' revision only public improvements, and a general change of prices, but not improvements effected by the ryots themselves, are considered as grounds for enhancing the assessment. The ryot's tenure is permanent, provided he pays the assessment.*

---

* See *Statesman's Year-book.*

Mr. Caird points out, in his articles 'In India, the Land and People,' that the Sikhs are a superior race, intelligent and outspoken, and that to throughly develope the productiveness of the Punjab a great impetus would be given if some energetic European agriculturists were planted amongst them, and were farming this fine soil simply for profit, and using the means that capital and wider knowledge would command.

But he also contends that the *low wages*, and comparatively speaking *low rent*, and the great number of people seeking land, would probably lead to a safer mode of making money—namely, *by purchasing the zemindar's rights.* Farm servants are paid by being given two good meals a day, coarse clothing costing probably from 8s. to 10s., and 2s. a month, in cash. 'The farm labourers' have given them for the morning meal usually corn cakes, with a pot of buttermilk, and the evening meal of the same kind of cakes, hot, with boiled pulse or greens. They eat on an average 2 lbs. of flour and 4 oz. of pulse per day. A ploughman, working hard on his own land from morning to night, will eat 3 lbs. of flour. The cakes are

There can appear no doubt that the depreciation of silver, which forms such a heavy item of loss yearly to the Indian exchequer, can be most wisely counteracted, not by Government loans, but by the development of the export trade of India—not only to these shores, but also to the world at large. Mr. Jacob Bright, in his speech delivered this summer, calls India 'a gigantic burden.' It is difficult to see in what way he could prove that contention, except that probably during the time the inhabitants were starving they did not purchase a sufficient quantity of his constituents' 'grey shirtings.' He may probably, however, allude to the present Afghan war, which, be its outcome what it may—and as I write these lines our troops are entering the city of Cabul— has at any rate been a 'burden' on the Indian, not the

usually of wheat and barley mixed, or maize or millet. The grain is ground by the women of the house in hand-mills of stone. The rent in some instances for land in the Punjab, including the Government assessment and local cesses, amounts to 3s. an acre. There are three modes of irrigation in the Punjab, that *of wells*, canal irrigation and inundation irrigation, and about one-fifth of the land through which the canals pass is supplied with water. The people may alter this fifth from year to year, so as in five years to bring the whole of their land in irrigation in turn. The inundation irrigation does not extend beyond the river basin. It makes the summer crops safe in most years, and if it continues late helps also the winter crops.

It is so easy to acquire the zemindar's right at a few years' purchase of the Government assessment, and the land can then be so readily sublet at a profit, that there is no advantage to be gained by entering into speculative farming. The Englishman embarking his capital in the purchase of land as a zemindar, and letting it on the native plan of a share of the produce, which he would then have an interest in bringing up to the highest point by liberal outlay as a landlord, might thus get a capital return for his money, whilst largely benefiting the people. *He could impose his own terms to prevent too great subdivision and its consequent certain poverty*, and could betake himself to the hills in hot weather. There is no reason why these fertile plains under such management should not display the same smiling picture of comfort and well-directed industry which gladdens the eye of the traveller through the plains of Lombardy, where the owner and the cultivator participate in the cost of improvement, and share in the produce.

English, exchequer, and in that respect differs from the 'Zulu war.' We must all hope that the outcome of this second expedition will be to *thoroughly complete* the object in view, namely, to give India a strong and easily defensible northern frontier, and to have quiet and peace on that border for many years.

No admirer of our present system of trade ought to object to India; for one thing this 'gigantic burden' has done for England has been this: that by yearly sending us, not only large sums for the purchase of our products, but also bullion for the pay and pensions of our Indian officials, interest for her railways and debt, besides large remittances from English men residing in that country as merchants and planters, not omitting some received as rents by our countrymen who are Indian land and house holders—one thing this combined accretion of wealth has done is this : to help us to maintain our Free Import system of trade, and partly to aid us in paying the United States for the grain we import from her shores.

CHAPTER X.

STRAITS SETTLEMENTS—HONG KONG, CHINA, JAPAN.

IN my short survey of the position of our trade with the Straits, China, and Japan, I purpose following the same route I chanced to take when sailing from Calcutta in the Glenartney, one of Messrs. Jardine—Matheson's opium steamers bound for Hong Kong. She was a well-found vessel, in charge of a very good staff of officers; nor did I find that the opium on board had, as far as my experience went, a soporific effect. Talking of soporifics reminds me of an amusing incident that occurred whilst we were in the Bay of Bengal. The passengers during that part of the voyage preferred sleeping on the roofs of the saloons, owing to the intense heat in that latitude. We all, therefore, had our bedding brought up, and I found the berth not altogether uncomfortable, though I shared my particular saloon top with an English clergyman, two Jewish rabbis, and a young German merchant. At the mouth of the bay we got into some rather heavy sea, and on one occasion, the ship having given a heavier lurch than usual, a wave breaking over us swept us all off our roof on to the deck. When we had severally recovered ourselves, the two rabbis commenced using very guttural and hoarse expressions in Arabic, which, as I am ignorant of that language, I cannot interpret, and the English clergyman made use of some strong phrases not to be found in the Thirty-nine Articles. Next morning, however, the latter came to me saying that he trusted he had uttered nothing in the excitement of the moment that he ought not to have done. The question was embarrassing, but I consoled him by saying that if he had given vent to any expressions of surprise, they at any rate seemed to come from the heart.

During my different voyages in the Pacific and other seas, I often noted, as a fact agreeable to an Englishman who takes an interest in the welfare of his country, that of the vessels one meets on the ocean, at least three out of every five carry the British ensign—a fact that can easily be accounted for when we consider the large number of ocean-going vessels owned in this country.*

Our first stop before entering the Straits of Malacca was at Penang, whence we sailed for Singapore. If I remember rightly, this part of the world was brought into great prominence at the time of the general election of 1874. Mr. Disraeli, in a speech delivered at

* A return has just been issued by the Board of Trade which exhibits the growth of our mercantile marine and of our foreign trade during the past forty years. In 1840 the British ships engaged in the foreign trade of the United Kingdom measured 6,490,485 tons; in 1878 they measured 35,291,483 tons: the British tonnage in the foreign trade of the United Kingdom has thus been multiplied more than five and a half times. The foreign ships in 1840 measured 2,949,182 tons; and in 1878 they measured 16,303,596 tons: showing about the same growth. But in 1840 the British steam tonnage was only 603,048; in 1878 it was 25,441,200 tons; or about fifty times greater. The foreign steam tonnage rose from 128,507 tons to 5,115,514. It will be seen that it is in steamers the principal British growth has been. Of the whole British tonnage entered and cleared in the foreign trade, whether in cargo or ballast, in 1878, five-sevenths consisted of steamers, whereas less than one-third of the foreign tonnage consisted of steamers. Now one steamer is equal, according to ordinary calculation, to three sailers; consequently, the real British superiority is very much greater than the figures just given show. If we confine our attention to vessels with cargoes, the facts are precisely similar. The British steamers with cargoes entered and cleared at ports of the United Kingdom in 1878 measured 22,124,501 tons, the foreign only 4,272 599 tons. Of foreign steamers the Germans were by far the most numerous, their tonnage being 957,316 tons, against 130,699 American, 477,204 French, and 808,898 tons Dutch.

Aylesbury that year, having stated certain facts relative to the then position of affairs in the Straits of Malacca, Mr. Gladstone, commenting on it when speaking at Woolwich, repeated the following lines :—

'The farmers at Aylesbury gathered to dine,
And they ate their prime beef and they drank their old wine;
With the wine there was beer, with the beer there was 'bacca,
The liquors went round, and the banquet was crowned
With some thundering news from the Straits of Malacca.'

To this the Earl of Beaconsfield (then Mr. Disraeli), in a speech at Newport Pagnell, made the following rejoinder :—' Gentlemen, I thought to myself when I read that composition how advantageous it is to give up one's days and nights to the study of Homer.

But to return to the consideration of these Straits —an important though small dependency which want of space will prevent my referring to in a more than passing manner —I may remark that nothing can exceed the extreme beauty of the scenery of this portion of the globe as seen from the sea, and one is struck, even after having just left British India, with the variety and luxuriance of the tropical vegetation growing along the coast. In no part of the world are the fruits of so varied a description, and notable, amongst others, that most delicious of all fruits, the mangustan, which has been described as resembling in its flavour a mixture of the peach and the strawberry. Some of their fruits, however, though pleasant to the palate, have even when first plucked a most offensive smell ; and this is especially the case with the durian, which strongly reminded me, on first making its acquaintance, of a tumbler of full-flavoured mineral water. A story is told, but I will not vouch for the accuracy of it, that Lord Elgin, on his return from his mission to China in 1858, whilst being entertained at a banquet given in his honour by the Governor of the Straits Settlement, one of these durians was offered to him. The Governor told him this fruit was highly esteemed in the Straits, and asked his Lordship what he thought of it. Lord Elgin looked at it rather dubiously, and replied, " Indeed! but hasn't this one been kept rather too long?"

The town of Penang struck me as particularly well looked after, the roads and public buildings having the appearance of having been originally well made and built, and of being carefully inspected and repaired every year.

Amongst other inhabitants of the Penang district, there are a large number of Indian coolies, who are employed mostly on the farms as agricultural labourers. Their lot is said at one time to have been a hard one. It is to be remembered that a European proprietor of an estate in the tropics is, as a rule, unlike the proprietor of an estate in England in this respect, that he does not regard his estate as a life investment of his money, but anticipates making large profits with as little outlay and delay as possible, in order that he may return home and live on the capital he hopes to make out of the property, the money for the purchase or opening of which has generally been borrowed. Under these circumstances, it is of the greatest importance to estate owners to keep down all expenditure not absolutely necessary, and the coolie, whose wages form one of the principal items of disbursement, is, therefore, hardly likely to receive more than his agreement obliges ; and, indeed, I regret to say that experience has proved that one of the objects of establishing special protection in his behalf is to insure his getting even that. An 'Indian immigration ordinance' has, therefore, been enacted for this purpose, which came into force in 1878, and which

STRAITS SETTLEMENTS. 313

provides for the appointment of an official who is styled a 'Protector' to look after the interests of these East Indian colonists.

The interests of the Chinese workers in this colony have also been latterly more carefully guarded, and immigrant Chinese arriving now in the Settlement have their engagements explained to them, and receive their advances in presence of the Protector, who gives them every assistance and information they require. Chinese emigrating from the Settlement receive like protection, assistance, and information. The effect of this useful measure has been to put an end to the associations that had previously existed for the crimping of Chinese, or their engagement under false pretences, to labour in the Dutch Settlements in Sumatra; as well as to close all unauthorised depôts for their detention while awaiting shipment. These depôts were dark, secluded and unwholesome dens, in which the immigrants were kept entirely at the mercy of the crimp or cooly-broker.

No one can help approving of the almost 'paternal; care we are here taking of those helpless individuals of different nationalities whom chance has brought under our jurisdiction in the Straits Settlements. But there is another feature connected with our rule in the Straits which one cannot note with the same satisfaction, and that is the trouble we are already reported to have been put to, and the possible greater danger we may have to meet in the future, which is caused by the secret societies there established.

The Mahomedan red flag and white flag societies are also very troublesome, especially in Province Wellesley. All the secret societies are on the increase, and their influence is extremely mischievous, as well as, at times, dangerous to the peace of the community. They not only augment and encourage crime, but, in some cases, by largely bribing, in others by fiercely intimidating witnesses and by producing false evidence, prevent the police from successfully prosecuting in cases of crime in which any of their members have been implicated. The red flag and white flag societies endeavour to magnify the most trivial insult offered by a member of the one society to a member of the other into a serious crime, and waste the time of the police and magistrates by bringing numbers of false witnesses into court to corroborate their exaggerated complaints ; at other times these trivial insults lead to disturbances between the two societies, and frequently to serious affrays.

In passing onwards down the Straits to Singapore it was curious to pass several sailing vessels having on board, to my ideas, rather an unusual living cargo ; which consisted of thousands of green parrots and other bright-plumaged birds, which were perched on crossbars attached to the masts, and all destined, as I was informed, for the Indian market

The principal products we take from the Straits are tin, spices, sago, cutch, and gambier—gambier contains from 40 to 50 per cent. of pure tannin, and hence it has been of late years largely imported into Europe to be used for the purposes of dying and tanning—and a small though increasing quantity of untanned hides. Our chief export is cotton goods—in fact, this class of materials amounts to more than half our total outward trade, and last year, although showing a slight falling-off, nearly reached one million sterling out of a total of £1,775,000. There is no import duty charged on either cotton, linen, silk, wool, iron, or coals.

It will be seen from the following table that Great

Britain and the British Colonies are the main foreign sources from which Singapore purchases the various descriptions of merchandise she may require. Singapore, where the residence of the Governor is situated, is a town of some importance. I need hardly remark that it is the principal emporium in the Straits. Its future appeared to me to be but faintly shadowed forth by the past; and that it will become a greater and more important possession of Great Britain than at present there appears every probability.

The following table shows the value of the imports to and exports from Singapore in the year 1877, as compared with 1876 :—

IMPORTS from—

	1877.	1876.
	$	$
United Kingdom	13,217,940	10,252,234
British Colonies	16,999,848	17,055,094
Foreign Countries	19,109,529	18,158,642

EXPORTS to—

	$	$
United Kingdom	7,975,402	6,719,787
British Colonies	7,881,996	8,991,175
Foreign Countries	25,571,009	24,903,821

On leaving the Straits I went to China, and trust that should any who may read these pages pursue the same route, they may not be caught in a 'cyclone,' which may be well described as an aggravated form of a tempest, as it was my lot to be. Should, however, that be their fate, it would considerably add to their security if the majority of the crew were not Lascars; for a poorer specimen of humanity in a storm it never was my lot to meet. The most of them, in the case I have alluded to, crept under hen coops or hid below, and left the officers, Chinese sailors, the European stewards, and passengers to work the ship and shorten sail.

Arrived at the British colony of Hong Kong, I was greatly struck with the appearance of that flourishing settlement, its substantially built houses, handsome public buildings. and splendid praya or parade, facing a huge land-locked bay, large enough to float all the fleets of the world in. This port possesses very ample dock accommodation, and has lately had its defensive fortifications strengthened and improved. Behind the praya the town appears to climb street above street on to the sides of the hill, which forms a background to the whole, and is named 'Victoria Peak.' In fact, it looked in many respects like a prosperous English seaport transported into the East.

Hong Kong is a colony whose revenue has hitherto always on the average exceeded its expenditure. This, as far as I am aware, cannot be said of any other dependency of the British Empire; and Governor Sir A. E. Kennedy, K.C.M.G., in one of his late reports to the Earl of Carnarvon, was able to state under the heading of the 'Public Debt,' 'There is none.' Nor has this satisfactory state of things been the result of a high import tariff, for every species of goods, not excepting wines, spirits, and cigars, are admitted *free of duty* to Hong Kong. The aggregate trade with this colony and Great Britain in 1878 was about £4,200,000.

The tonnage of British vessels entered and cleared in Hong Kong in 1870 was 1,649,250, and in 1876 (the last returns published) 3,150,952. Our total inward and outward shipping trade to British North America (including the Dominion of Canada, Prince Edward Island, British Columbia, Vancouver's Island, and Newfoundland), whilst it was 4,929,601 tons in the former year, in the latter it amounted to 3,980,567 tons, or only about 800,000 tons in excess of the tonnage of our ships entered and cleared at this prosperous British colony of Hong Kong.

CHINA.

It would be impossible, even had I the power, in a work of this size, to attempt to treat exhaustively, or even give a concise summary, of all the varied customs and institutions in the Chinese Empire; but I may perhaps be permitted shortly to touch on several of the incidents of their commerce which affect Great Britain, and to make some passing allusion to certain facts connected with the agricultural system of this the oldest existing empire in the world.

I chanced to visit both Canton and Shanghai during my stay in China. These 'treaty ports' are of great importance both to this country, to America, Germany, and France, and any other powers who have commercial dealings with China. They are, however, as far as the European and American settlements are concerned, used simply as depôts for the receipt and transmission of goods, though it may be noted that there is a considerable amount of manufacture of silk and ivory ware in the native town of Canton.

'A Quarterly Reviewer' has well and truly said China is a storehouse of men and means; its outer door has scarcely yet been opened.

China is still an Empire *per se*, a country which

hitherto, notwithstanding all the endeavours we and other powers have made to open it out, has practically remained to the rest of the world a closed market.

Should that barrier which the Chinese mandarins and other authorities have hitherto maintained be relaxed, it would be difficult to estimate the important changes which might ensue, and the greater relative importance the Chinese interchange might create in the trade of the British Empire and the whole world. No portion of our dominions at present derives such a large direct revenue from the trade it has succeeded in creating with China as British India. I allude to the opium traffic, the production of which in our Eastern Empire is mostly for the Chinese market. From the revenue derived from opium alone the Indian Exchequer received in 1878 over nine millions sterling. Many have asked, will this trade be a permanent one or not? On such a subject there is a great diversity of opinion. Some of those who are the most dogmatic, and who state their opinion as if they considered it to be indisputable one way or the other, appear to me to base their views on the slightest amount of enquiry into the subject, and having had one or two facts placed before them concerning this trade, to jump immediately to whatever conclusions those facts seem to lead them to. On this subject personally it seems to me impossible for any one residing in England to have either the means or the power of forming a fair judgment. That there has been an increase of native-grown opium in China of late years is indisputable. Whether it will oust Indian opium from the market or merely create an increased demand for that drug, I leave time to decide, and shall merely give here a few extracts from Mr. Nicholson's report from Pekin respecting the opium trade in China. He states:—

Of late years the cultivation of native opium has been increasing to such an extent as to afford some ground for the fears which are entertained of the Indian drug being supplanted in the market.

The ports most affected by this new commodity are Newchwang, Tientsin, and Chefoo in the north, and Hankow on the Yangtze, which draw supplies from Central Manchuria, South-Eastern Mongolia, Shensi, Shantung, and Szechuen provinces respectively Edicts have from time to time been issued prohibiting the cultivation of opium, but they have been in most cases ignored, the only result being an increase in the price of the article, consequent on the necessity of the producer 'silencing' the officials; on this point the Acting Statistical Secretary of the Imperial Maritime Customs at Shanghai reports, in 1876, as follows:—

'That the Imperial Government viewed, with extreme dissatisfaction and alarm, the continually increasing consumption of opium, and would willingly have made the heaviest sacrifices to secure its restriction, is undoubted, but the policy it adopted to gain this end was ill-advised and based upon erroneous principles. The importation of foreign opium having been legalised by express Treaty stipulations, the only policy open to the Government was to accept as an established fact, however much it deplores its use, and leave the desired abatement in its consumption to be effected by the gradual working of moral influences. By developing the poppy cultivation and simultaneously increasing the import duty upon the foreign drug, the Government would divert to its own use a considerable portion of the revenue now derived from this source from India.'

He also mentions that it is difficult to estimate exactly the duty charged on the native-grown opium, but that its consumption has increased in the Canton district forty per cent. more than it was ten years ago, and adds:

The native cultivation has not as yet materially affected the supply from India, but authorities on the subject do not doubt that before long the effects will become apparent. They also consider that the growth of the native drug may so far have only increased the consumption; but as supply outstrips the newly-created demand, it must finally decrease the sale of the imported article, unless the value of the latter is greatly reduced, which can be effected by a reduction of the high duty charged in India It appears from the statistics that at some ports the importation of Indian opium has fallen off considerably, in some it has received a momentary mpulse owing to local drought, while in others it has obtained an increase.

In the north of China, the cultivation of the poppy requires the utmost care and the richest soil. In the southern and central provinces the soil is rich and fertile, the most suitable ground for the poppy being the terraced hill-sides, where it cannot be so easily injured by the effect of the heavy rains which fall at certain seasons of the year. It is sown in November and blossoms in early April, thus leaving the fields free for a summer crop. The price paid for the foreign drug is still much higher in China than that given for the home-grown one ; the former being said to be at present more esteemed. Mr. Nicholson sums up his remarks on this subject in the following statements : --

1. That within the last few years the production of native opium has increased and is increasing.

2. That the poppy is cultivated in spite of prohibitory Government edicts, and in most cases with the connivance of the authorities.

3. That the cultivation is likely to be still further extended, owing to the large profits which can be made.

4. That the native can easily undersell the foreign drug in the market.

5. That the chief, and apparently the sole, advantage possessed by the Indian over the native article lies in its superior quality.

Out of the total export trade of the produce and manufacture of the United Kingdom with China, including Hongkong and Macâo, according to our Board of Trade returns, amounting in 1878 to over £6,600,000, nearly four millions sterling consisted of our cotton goods ; and it ought to be a special consolation to certain of our narrow-minded politicians, who appear to view with disfavour anything connected with our Eastern trade, that amongst his other virtues John Chinaman appears to have a partiality for being buried in a covering composed of a certain mixture of cotton and size imported from this country.

Of our two great imports from China, tea and silk, notwithstanding the increased volume of late years received in this country from India, our dealers bought of the former product 154 million lbs. in 1878, as against 127 millions five years before. Mr. William Gow Gregor, in a recent work on China, gives some very minute and interesting information respecting the production and manufacture of the different descriptions of Chinese tea for home and foreign consumption, to which I would refer any one interested in this subject, merely noticing what he states respecting green teas, as an idea has often been prevalent that they were manufactured by being placed on sheets of copper, and were therefore injurious. Whilst in China I was informed that such was not the case, and that the following was the manner in which green tea is prepared:—The leaves of the tea-plant are placed in iron pans as soon as they are plucked, to undergo, for two or three minutes only, the action of heat over a charcoal fire. They are then rubbed together for a short time, after which they are again exposed to the action of fire. The process of firing the leaves a second time is continued, not for two or three minutes only, as in the first instance, but for two or three hours. To the care of each person engaged in the firing department of a green-tea factory, a bundle of leaves, weighing eight or ten catties, is entrusted ; and while the leaves are being fired a second time, they are kept constantly stirred by hand. In the case of fine tea, the leaves are constantly fanned during the first hour of the second time of firing, so as to preserve their green colour. When the leaves have undergone this process, they are

Y

packed and sold to the proprietors of tea hongs. By them the leaves are again exposed to the action of heat for the space of half-an-hour. They are then cleansed by the usual methods of sifting, picking, and winnowing.

Our purchase of Chinese silk has exceeded, on the average, over three million pounds sterling for the last three years, and appears to have increased considerably since 1874. Their exportation of this fabric to Europe is of the greatest antiquity, and it is said that the silken stuffs of China were exposed for sale in all the marts of Greece B.C. 325. Nor does the manufacture of silk in Europe date earlier than the sixth century of the Christian era. Mr. Gow Gregor mentions that its first introduction into this quarter of the globe was brought about in the following way :—

'For several centuries after the introduction of silk as an article of sale into Greece and Italy, it was regarded by some Europeans as a species of down gathered from the leaves of trees, and by others as a very delicate skin of wool or cotton. From the language which he employs in his Georgics (ii. 121), Virgil evidently imagined that the Chinese (Seres) carded the silk from leaves ; for he writes—

'Velleraque ut foliis depectant tenuia Seres.'

At the commencement of the sixth century, however, all such conjectures were set aside by more correct information from China. Two Nestorian monks, belonging to Persia, having travelled to China, regarded it as a duty to make themselves well acquainted, during their stay in that country, with the natural history of the silkworm, and to learn how silk was manufactured by the Chinese. When they were in possession of this knowledge, they returned at once to Europe, and, on their arrival at Constantinople, immediately laid the

CHINA. 323

results of their investigations before the Emperor Justinian. Fully alive to the great commercial advantages which would accrue from the manufacture of silk, the Emperor persuaded the monks to return to China, to obtain, if possible, a collection of silkworms' eggs. They had little or no difficulty in collecting them, and they packed them in hollow bamboo tubes, for safe conveyance to Constantinople. The eggs thus introduced to Europe were, it is said, hatched by the heat of a manure heap. The larvæ were fed upon the leaves of the mulberry tree, and the silkworms multiplied so rapidly in the land of their adoption, that they were to be found, before many years had elapsed, in great numbers throughout the southern countries of Europe.'

Space will prevent my treating at all fully on the great care the Chinese take in the rearing and breeding of their silkworms and the great importance of this industry in China, whole towns being devoted to the rearing of the silkworms and the manufacture of silken textures. Suffice to say that they attribute great importance to the fact of the temperature in which the worms are kept being uniform. This they ascertain, not by means of a thermometer, but by the sensations produced on the naked body of the person in charge, who divests himself of his clothes, enters the chamber where the worms are kept, and, should he find the air cool or damp, gains additional heat by means of a Chinese stove. Thunder is considered to have a detrimental effect on these insects, as it 'frightens them,' and great care is taken that the mulberry leaves which are given them are fresh, but at the same time not damp. The houses in which they are kept are wide and clean, are preserved from all noxious smells, and are mostly surrounded by mulberry tree plantations. There are two departments in the north of

China—Kushing and Hoochow—where the cultivation of the mulberry tree is almost universal, and both are celebrated silk-producing districts. The silk-weaving machines used in China are still, to our mind, of a somewhat primitive description. 'A draw boy' sits above the frame, and with great regularity pulls the strings or cords by which he can bring down the necessary warp threads preparatory to the movement of the shuttle; and it is probable that it will be many years, if ever, before the excellent contrivance of M. Jacquart will supersede the draw loom used and the draw boy engaged in this industry. As all are aware, the manufacture of porcelain is a very important branch of Chinese industry, and I was somewhat surprised to find, in looking at our import returns of this commodity, how small was the actual amount we really import from China, which slightly exceeded £21,000 in 1878, so that doubtless a large amount of the china we see ornamenting our English houses, 'artistically' hung in my lady's drawing-room or boudoir, or placed on constructions resembling dark-coloured Mediæval kitchen dressers, must be made elsewhere.

Of the eighteen provinces of China, the most famous for the quality of its plastic clays used in manufacture of pottery is Kiang-si. The town of Kin-tee-ching has been for centuries the most famous centre in China for the potters' art. Should one arrive here at dusk, he is reminded in some respects of the lurid glare thrown from the furnaces of districts engaged in the same manufacture in Staffordshire. This town is said to contain as many inhabitants at present as Birmingham. At one time it was probably even more populous, but it was unfortunately captured by the insurgents in the Taiping rebellion, during which troublous period, extending principally from 1847 to 1858, the fairest portions of China were devastated. The rebels behaved to the inhabitants of this town with the greatest cruelty, massacreing them by thousands, sparing neither age, sex, nor condition, but destroying without mercy all they came across, whether aged, young, or infirm—in fact, treating Kin-tee-ching in this respect in the same *thorough* manner that one reads the Israelites did the inhabitants of the Philistine cities they captured. It was also at this time partially destroyed by fire ; the Imperial manufactory of pottery here situated was burnt. This manufactory is dated from an early epoch, having been originally erected by imperial decree about the year 1366.

These works were of great importance, and a high Government functionary placed in charge of them ; and doubtless they have, Phœnix-like, long ere this risen from the ashes and are in full working order again. Besides the Government works there are innumerable potteries owned by private individuals. In the Government factory the workers were divided into five classes, named respectively 'fire,' 'water,' 'wood,' 'metal,' and earth. These were again subdivided into no less than twenty-two different heads, including, amongst others, those employed in the various methods of shaping, carving, and painting the pottery. It may not be altogether uninteresting for those who take an interest in either old or modern china to give a description of how the clay is prepared in that country for the ' potter's wheel.'

The clay is of two descriptions—Kao-lin and Pe-tun-se—and it is detached in pieces of various sizes from the mines or quarries from which it is dug by means of pickaxes, and then carried to the pounding mills. It is then placed in large mortars, with several of which each mill is furnished. It is thoroughly crushed by means of pestles kept in regular motion by water-wheels. The plastic earth, having sufficiently undergone the process of pounding, is now carried in baskets to a neighbouring pond, into which it is thrown, so that it may become well mixed with the water. The mixture thus formed is permitted to remain undisturbed for some time, and the heavier portions of the pulverised matter sink to the bottom. On the surface of the pond a liquid of cream-like appearance is eventually found. This is drawn off and poured into another basin, where it is well stirred by the feet of labourers, who walk to and fro in the basin. The heavier particles of the pulverized clay, which sank to the bottom of the first basin, are conveyed back to the pounding mill to be reduced to a finer powder. After this they are brought back to the pond, and the process is repeated. Meanwhile, the cream-like liquid which was poured into the second basin is, after its thorough agitation, allowed to remain undisturbed for some time. When all the fine matter has sunk to the bottom the water is drawn off, and the pe-tun-tse or kao-lin clay is removed, and formed by means of moulds into bricks.

The bricks are afterwards reduced to a powder, and having been carefully washed in spring water, the two clays are mixed and formed into a paste, which is kneaded sometimes by men and sometimes by buffaloes, and is then ready for the potters' hands. In the painting of porcelain there is a great division of labour. One artist draws the design, another paints landscapes, a third rivers, a fourth trees, a fifth butterflies, a sixth birds, and a seventh human figures and buildings.

If I mistake not, our old friend the willow-pattern plate has all these artists' 'specialities' on its surface; therefore a plate painted in Kin-tee-ching has to pass through all these hands before being completed. Whether the result is much better than the cheap printed copies we see in this country I leave connoisseurs to judge.

The artists use an oil for the purpose of giving smoothness to their work, and have a perfect knowledge of the pigments which are best suited to undergo the action of fire. Gum water is also occasionally used for the purpose of retaining the colours used ; for thick painting clear water is held in much estimation.

The colours are fixed in ovens; the larger class of vessels in one called Om-fo or dark fire, and the smaller in Ming-fo, or bright fire.

In China lands are all freehold, and are held by families under the Sovereign on the payment of a certain annual tax. These taxes are collected and paid to the Imperial Exchequer by the district rulers, who give a receipt to the landowner; should, however, the crop be destroyed by inundation or the ravages of insects, the land tax is according to law not to be exacted, and the mandarins are punished should they, under such circumstances, enforce payment. When the farmers have been deprived of their crops by inundation, the representatives of the provincial government are authorized to advance money to them to purchase seeds, on the condition of repayment at an expiration of ten years; and yet some of our legislators in this country speak of China as if it were a country inhabited by a race of savages.

With regard to the transfer of property in China, all land is carefully registered at the office of the district ruler, and no transfer can be made without his knowledge. The apparent wish is to retain the property as far as practicable in the same family. Therefore, an intending seller must first offer it to his father or his next of kin. Should all the members of the family be indisposed or unable to purchase the estate, it is then offered to others. The auctioneer makes known to likely purchasers that the sale will take place, by means of handbills, public advertisements being disliked by the Chinese in disposing of their properties.

The following is the translation of a handbill of the sale of a house: —

'Tsay Yow-yan has a large family residence for sale. It is situate in the street called Tai-shap-poo, and looks towards the north. The frontage of the house is seven halls or rooms in extent, and the back part of the residence is eleven halls or chambers in extent. The back door looks upon the Cham-loo street or lane. In the centre of the house there is a handsome altar. There is a hall for the reception of male visitors, and one for the reception of female visitors. There are also a great many rooms, sitting and sleeping. The materials of which the house is built are of the strongest and most durable nature. The price required for the property is the ordinary market price. Any person who may have a desire to purchase the property can, by bearing a copy of this advertisement in his hand, and being accompanied by the middleman, inspect the property, and treat with regard to the price.

Sixth month of seventh year of Tung-chee.'

The notice also usually sets forth that it is to be sold with the full consent of the family.

The farms in the northern and central provinces are as a rule divided into small fields of one or two acres, separated from one another by low, narrow embankments. With such a teeming population as China possesses, the thorough cultivation of the land is of the greatest importance; little space is therefore wasted in hedges, the roads are narrow, mostly only tracks, and comparatively few horses are kept, as they would consume too much food. One mode of locomotion (where they have not the rivers and canals so widely dispersed throughout this country) is by means of wheelbarrows drawn by men; nor is it an uncommon sight to see a farmer's wife going to market sitting on one.

The amount of land under cultivation is said to be little short of six millions of English acres.

The farmer's year is solemnly inaugurated in China, and spring ushered in by a festival. No farmer is supposed to begin to plough till such ceremonies have been performed. These rites are not only undertaken by the governors and administrators of the various provinces, but also by the Emperor himself in person, at his capital at Pekin. After certain religious ceremonies have been gone through, the Emperor and high Government officials repair to Government lands adjoining the Temple for the purpose of ploughing nine furrows each, and having been severally presented with a whip, they are escorted to a plough to which a buffalo is yoked; when the word is given by the master of the ceremonies, the ploughs are set in motion. At the head of each buffalo, to direct its course, a peasant is placed, who is permitted to wear on this occasion the colour of distinction in China—namely, yellow, his jacket being of that hue. Behind each of these illustrious ploughmen walk three or four officers of the civil service, whose duty it is to sow at each step seeds of grain into the newly-made furrows. Whilst this is going on a band of youths attired in gay costumes sing pæans to the god of agriculture. There are also present on the scene a large body of graduates, corresponding to our Bachelors of Arts. The proceedings terminate by the holding of an official levee.

This ceremony doubtless seems excessively strange to our own preconceived ideas, nor is it applicable to this age or this country. Still we ought not lightly to accuse the Chinese of want of civilisation for continuing it. Of course, when compared with the majestic simplicity and utility of our own official ceremonies, it will not hold water. For example, let us for a moment contemplate how our Lord Mayor of London, the chief citizen of the greatest commercial city of the world, inaugurates his coming into office, and sets the whole mercantile community an example of economy, good taste, and commercial industry, by parading the streets of London in a gilt carriage drawn by six horses, attended by 'men in armour,' elephants, brass bands, and flags!

When this great festival has inaugurated the agricultural year, the first duty of the Chinese farmers is to follow the good example set by their rulers, and put their own hands to the plough.

Care is taken that the land is not allowed to lie fallow. With the view of superintending farmers and agricultural labourers in their operations, an agricultural board is established in almost every village throughout the empire. This board is presided over by three or four aged agriculturists, upon each of whom the eighth degree of rank is conferred. This board insists upon each farmer cultivating his lands to the fullest extent, and sowing and reaping in due season. A farmer who is negligent in these respects is taken, at the suggestion of the board, into the presence of the magistrate to receive a flogging. The number of stripes is in proportion to the quantity of land which he has left uncultivated. Nor is the law confined to renters. There is a decree which enjoins all landed proprietors to see that their estates are kept in high cultivation; and the penalty inflicted for a breach of this law is an entire confiscation of the neglected property to the Crown. Farming in Great Britain and in China involve very different outlays. In Great Britain it is impossible for a man without capital to enter upon a farm. In many of the provinces of China, however, the reverse is the case, as a Chinese farm—I speak more particularly of the south of China—is without stock. The Government authorities frequently receive petitions from poor farmers asking to be appointed tenants of the public lands, as the Government sometimes appoints men who are acquainted with husbandry to farm its estates. Like their masters, the agricultural labourers are very industrious. As in some parts of England, women are employed as well as men.

Notwithstanding all this care, there is at times, as we have been lately only too well aware of, great scarcity of food in China. Then merchants are encouraged to import from other countries, and rice merchants who have imported grain from Saigon in sufficient quantities to reduce its price in Canton have been known to receive from the Emperor degrees of rank for their meritorious conduct. The Chinese have never had to abolish any 'corn laws,' for never, as far as I am able to trace, from the very earliest epochs have they ever had any duty charged on the importation of grain. To protect their grain from the ravages of weevils, to which China, like India, is much exposed, Chinese farmers adopt the following expedient :—Carbon being, as we are aware, destructive to animal life, and the husks of rice when reduced to ashes yielding carbon, the farmers mix this freely with the rice, and by this simple process place it beyond the reach of destructive insects of all kinds.

As I have already occupied more space than I had intended in touching on some of the points connected with the trade and agriculture of this vast empire, I will not make any attempt to describe its great and varied shipping interests, its system of irrigation, or the habits of the large population who reside in floating towns on its rivers. When I steamed up to Canton in a recently-constructed

American steamer, some portion of our route from Hong Kong reminding me of the scenery in the Western Highlands of Scotland, and passed these quaint, slowly-moving junks, their curiously-shaped boats of various descriptions moored together and forming streets in the water, their gaily-painted flower-boats covered with bright pennons, the latter being, in fact, floating hotels or restaurants, there seemed as many different descriptions of boats flitting about as there are carriages and conveyances in 'the season' in Regent Street. Ferry boats take the place of omnibuses cargo boats lumbered and got into everybody's way, just as carts often do—light tanka boats, with one or two passengers, and deftly worked by a single oar astern, cut in and out like hansoms. There were also larger boats for the conveyance of passengers on longer journeys, whilst private carriages were represented by gorgeously-painted mandarin junks, or the more sombre but equally useful 'Hong' boats belonging to the foreign merchants. One of the most curious description of sights in boat life in China to see—which, however, it was not my fortune to view—was the boats which carry the fishing cormorants, which Mr. Oliphant describes as 'solemnly perched in successive rows on stages projecting from the sides. They looked like a number of gentlemen in black on the platform at a meeting of a grave and serious character.' Having gazed on these varied craft, and then looked at the matter-of-fact steamer I was on, it brought the Old and the New World into very close juxtaposition, and afforded much room for reflecion.

How different are their customs in many respects from our own! White, instead of black, is the colour used for mourning. The prow of the vessel is considered the place of honour, instead of the stern, as with us.

Their mode of writing is from right to left; and also, when warm they fan themselves behind, and not, as we do, in front; lastly, their great dislike to change, lately instanced by their discontinuing the short line of railway laid at Shanghai. But it is needless to multiply instances of such facts; they are well known and have been well described.

It may not be uninteresting to note here the history of this short-lived line. It appears that certain British merchants in Shanghai obtained permission from the Government to make a road. They accordingly first decided to lay a tramway, and then, bolder counsels prevailing, a railway, which, whilst it continued, was not an unpaying concern. The Governor of Nankin, Shun-pao-Shen, made them a very fair offer for the purchase of this line, and having bought it, had it, to many people's astonishment, taken up and removed to Formosa, where it was considered by the Chinese authorities not to be able to regenerate the country—to be, in fact, out of harm's way.

The Chinese mandarins' arguments against railways—from, to my mind, *mistaken* ideas of political economy—doubtless are these:—Let the foreigners once make railways, it will break down all the institutions of this country, destroy our influence, and may lead to the loss of our independence as a nation. We have not the money to make them ourselves, and should the foreigner do so, he will drain the resources of our country in the interest we shall have to pay him for them. What gain has this western civilization been to the Japanese? They have thrown off their national dress and customs, and imitated more or less successfully those of other races. They despise anything native, and look with admiration on everything foreign. They have thrown aside their old weapons, and have purchased the man-destroying armaments of civilized communities. The result is they are very quarrelsome, and want to pick quarrels with their neighbours; and we fail to see that railways, post-offices, telegraphs, 'tall hats,' or the use of champagne and brandy, have made the great mass of the Japanese happier or more contented, or has the use of opium made our people in any way better or more 'civilized.' We as a nation, these mandarins also contend, desire nothing we have not got. Our Government is conducted on a system which surpervises all classes of the community, from the greatest to the humblest individual in it, whilst we duly protect all classes by a strict enforcement of our criminal code. Education is wide-spread throughout our Empire, and the humblest can rise to the highest position, next to the Emperor himself, if he only displays talent and application of sufficient merit entitling him to do so, for even in our village schools our text books indoctrinate this maxim (to quote a translation of the first few lines of one entitled 'Youthful Learning')—

'All things in the world may be considered unworthy of consideration, only, and except, the study of literature, which is ennobling, and through which you may rise to the highest position in the service of the State.'

To revert, however, to the subject I commenced with, viz., railways, the Chinese authorities appear to feel that they would also injure the trade of that numerous class now engaged in the water carriage of goods, and there might also arise some difficulties in the feeling aroused against them, if their route chanced to be through the cemeteries, which are there held in higher esteem even than among western nations. Such difficulties and others have, however, been surmounted in other states, and there can be no doubt, despite the prejudice at present against their use, that when the day comes for the general development of railway communication in China it will add to the material prosperity of that empire.

On quitting my reference to this important Empire, with its teeming population, I will make my way once more to the docks of the prosperous treaty port of Shanghai, where I spent many pleasant hours, for the English and other merchants in the East manage in their leisure hours not only to enjoy themselves in such sports as shooting, horse racing, and boat racing, but in such social amusements as theatres and balls, though at the latter there is a large proportion of the male sex; and when I was there about eight years ago Shanghai boasted of three or four companies of well-drilled and equipped volunteers ready to do their duty if required.

At the docks I witnessed the departure of a large vessel crowded with Chinese coolies bound for America, where they go for a few years to make some dollars, though but few of them ever look on that country as anything but a temporary place to sojourn in; and even should they die there leaving sufficient funds, have their bodies brought home to China to be buried amidst their ancestors, who are held in great reverence by all Chinamen, 'ancestral worship' forming, in fact, an important part of their religious system. Having seen them off, I will therefore take ship on a P. and O. steamer bound for Japan, making but slight mention of the magnificent scenery one passes in traversing the inland sea, lest I should by so doing be tempted from my subject.

JAPAN.

The first port at which we stopped was the treaty port of Nagasaki, 450 miles from Shanghai, an important settlement, which transacts a total volume of trade of between three and four million dollars yearly. Its principal exports are coal, dried fish, and camphor, it being very conveniently situated to receive the products of several important coal fields in the vicinity.

It has at present several valuable appliances for the repair of ships and the assistance of navigation, and possesses also telegraphic communication with the surrounding country. It is a favourite station of our Chinese squadron, it being considered healthy, and also being a most secure and commodious natural harbour, with the island of Pappenberg guarding its entrance, beyond which formerly foreign ships were not allowed to penetrate. This island has an unenviable notoriety in the historical annals of Japan, as down its precipitous sides hundreds of Christians were hurled during the fierce persecutions which had for their object the utter extermination of all who professed that creed.

Probably no history of the conversion of large numbers of any race to Christianity is more fraught with interest than the rapid conversion made by the zeal, attainments, and energy of the sainted Xavier of thousands of Japanese converts. His biographers record hundreds of miraculous conversions, and he is even said to have restored a girl to life under circumstances which utterly confounded his enemies. I cannot here, however, dwell on his history, nor is this the place for me to dilate on the early struggle for the mastery in this land between the Spaniards and Portuguese settlers; how ultimately, it is said, owing, in a measure, to the intrigues of the Jesuits against the power of the Tycoon, they were finally expelled Japan; how their expulsion and persecutions were said to have been also partly brought about by the jealousy of the time-serving Dutch, who aided the Japanese in driving these settlers from their shores and persecuting the converts; how in reward for these services the Dutch were permitted to have a factory on the Island of Decima adjoining Nagasaki, where they were allowed, under the most stringent restrictions, to trade with the inhabitants, being kept in a species of quarantine, and having to submit to every species of restraint and humiliation that the Japanese authorities saw fit to make them suffer—living, in fact, an existence to which life in a penal settlement must have been preferable; all these facts are matter of history, and cannot be treated of here.

In 1613, King James I. sent out Captain Saris to Japan, who, through the instrumentality of William Adams, an Englishman in the employ of Ogosho-Sama —then Emperor of Japan—was enabled to arrange a favourable treaty, and we established a factory at Firando in consequence. Owing, however, to the bitter animosity of the Dutch, and the unscrupulous means they are said to have resorted to to obstruct our trade, as well as to our merchants' apparent ignorance of the resources and demands of the country, the factory was closed, and the enterprise ultimately abandoned; and it was not until Aug. 3, 1858, when Lord Elgin, on board the Furious, steamed into the harbour of Nagasaki, that we can have been said to have made the first real step towards any commercial intercourse with this country. He there found the sole traders in Japan were the Dutch and Russian merchants, and that the trade they conducted was subject to every description of hindering and irritating check imaginable. What do we find now? These hindrances have been mostly removed; and of the foreign shipping entered and cleared at Nagasaki in 1877—in all, 143,000 tons, 92,000 were

English, 8,000 were Russian, and there is no return of any Dutch vessel having entered that port; whilst of the 181 adult European and American residents in Nagasaki, 83 were British, who (excluding the Chinese merchants) were the proprietors of four out of thirteen firms transacting business at Nagasaki.

No one who has visited the porcelain and pottery warehouses in Nagasaki could fail to be struck with the beauty of the lacquered ware, and especially the eggshell china, most of which is made in the provinces of Fizen and Satsuma. Whilst we seem perfectly flooded at present with Japanese china in this country, it is my impression that I have seen much better specimens of their art in this respect at Nagasaki and also at Yedo.

I need hardly say that it would seem to me of more general interest to give some extracts of Lord Elgin's historical voyage to Yedo in 1858 than my own unimportant journey there, for much connected with the former may already have faded from our recollections. It has always struck me as a curious thing that people who never care to describe the hundred and one things of interest they daily see when on shore, always immediately begin keeping diaries when they are at sea, and duly chronicle what they eat, and how many porpoises and ships they may chance to meet.

Lord Elgin having left Nagasaki, and having escaped the effects of a storm in which a large Dutch vessel was wrecked, steamed on to Simonda, with the intention of presenting to the Tycoon at Yedo the yacht sent by Her Majesty to him, Mr. Lawrence Oliphant, private secretary to Lord Elgin, thus describes the event :—

'The day following our arrival at Simonda, Lord Elgin received a visit from the Governor. He had learnt that we proposed going up the Bay of Yedo, and his object now was to exert all his powers of persuasion to induce Lord Elgin to forego this intention. He brought a large suite on board with him, all of whom seemed to appreciate an English luncheon. I was rather startled to hear one of them refuse curacoa, and ask for Maraschino instead. The Governor himself was a man of a most jovial temperament; he indulged in constant chuckles, and rather reminded me of Mr. Weller, senior. He seemed to consider everything a capital joke —even Lord Elgin's positive refusal to comply with his request to hand over the yacht at Simonda and remain at that place. He used every possible argument to carry his point, but without avail. He said he dreaded the consequences to himself, and chuckled. Still more did he dread the consequences to us, and chuckled again; and when at last he found that we were neither to be frightened or cajoled, he seemed perfectly contented, and proceeded to wrap up in square pieces of paper any articles of food which particularly struck his fancy, which he carried in the folds of his shirt, saying as he did so that he had a number of children at home of an age to appreciate the culinary curiosities of foreign parts. Many of his suite seemed to have families too, for they followed his example. I rather think one attempted to carry away some strawberry jam in his bosom or in the sleeve of his coat, which was made full and baggy for the purpose. These square pieces of paper are not used exclusively for wrapping up food in: upon them inquisitive Japanese take notes, and in them they blow their noses. It is a mark of politeness to carry away a quantity of food from a dinner table; so much so that a very civil guest sometimes brings a servant and a basket to carry away those remnants which a careful English housekeeper would appreciate at luncheon next day.

'We got under weigh from Simonda at daylight on the morning of the 12th August, and with a fair wind proceeded rapidly up the Bay, passing on our left a mountain-range about 6,000 feet in height. The shores now begin to close in, and at the Straits of Uraga, which we reached in about five hours from Simonda, they are not above ten miles apart. At this point the scenery was very pretty: wooded hills rise from the water's edge, sloping gently back here and there, deeply furrowed with a charming glen, in which cottages with steep-thatched roofs and overhanging eaves are snugly ensconced. The western shore resembles some parts of the coast of the Isle of Wight. The town of Uraga itself is the most important-looking place on the coast. It is considered a sort of barrier to Yedo, and even country craft would stop here to give an account of themselves. Two boat-loads of two-sworded officials pushed off in haste as we steamed up, and by gesticulations and gestures of entreaty invited us to stop ; but we passed on, utterly indifferent to their signals, and as we left them far behind we could still discern them trudging hopelessly after us, in the vain attempt to overtake a steamer of 400 horse-power going at full speed. We could scarcely believe our eyes when, at anchor the same night, we observed these identical boats pull alongside, they having never relinquished the pursuit.

'Meantime we steamed steadily on through waters traversed for the first time by Commodore Terry's squadron a few years ago, and consequently but little surveyed. Passing the Terry and Webster islands, prettily wooded and of a picturesque form, we came within sight of the Russian squadron, anchored at Kanawangwa, at about mid-day. Lord Elgin, instead of stopping at Kanawangwa, determined to adopt the unprecedented course of sailing straight up to the capital, believing that if the achievement were feasible, it would not only save valuable time, but that the presence of our ships there would produce a most salutary effect upon the Government, and in all probability tend to facilitate our negotiations.

'Our unexpected appearance must have somewhat astonished our Muscovite friends, more especially as we passed on at full speed up the bay, where no western ship had ever before ventured. Up to this point the western shore under which we had been coasting was uniformly high and broken with projecting promontories ; now, however, it sinks to a level with the waters of the bay.

'The water now becomes shallow and the channel somewhat intricate. We were just doubting whether the undertaking was practicable, when we saw in the distance some large square-rigged ships of a tonnage which satisfied us that their anchorage would do for us, but for a moment we felt bitterly disappointed at the discovery of European-built ships, betokening, as we supposed, the presence of some foreign flag more enterprising than our own It was only when we approached nearer that we perceived that these western-looking craft were in reality Japanese, and observed the white flag with the red ball floating from the peak of a dapper little steamer and marking it "Imperial."

'Gradually behind these vessels the island forts, and then the houses of the city of Yedo, rose into view. Gently, with two leads going, we crept up to the long-desired haven, closely followed by the Retribution and yacht, and by two o'clock the same afternoon, after a most prosperous passage from Simonda, we anchored not far from the Japanese fleet, at a distance of about three miles from the shore, and five from the capital of the empire.'

A few days after the arrival above described at Yedo, Lord Elgin and his suite went on shore, and were most comfortably housed and hospitably entertained by the Japanese authorities, and a treaty was ultimately concluded between Lord Elgin and certain Japanese commissioners who had been appointed on behalf of their respective countries. By it certain ports were opened to British commerce, and an import tariff was arranged, in which cottons, woollens, machinery, silk, lead, tin, and coals were to be charged an *ad valorem* five per cent. duty ; all other articles twenty per cent, except intoxicating liquors, which were to be charged a thirty-five per cent. duty.

At this date the Mikado was the spiritual governor of Japan, the Tycoon the temporal administrator or ruler ; but both of them were of such exalted and lofty positions that they virtually led the lives of State prisoners shut up in their own castles, in magnificent but at the same time dreary state.

The Tycoon was rarely, if ever, seen by the vulgar gaze, except, as Mr. Oliphant remarks, that it was the practice then in Japan (and it may thence have extended to other countries) for the Sovereign to do certain things ' Nayboen,' as it is there called—that is to say, in a recognised incognito.

It was a cruel satire to present a yacht to this unhappy potentate, who could rarely leave the exterior walls of his palace : one might as well request the Pope's acceptance of a wife.

The yacht was, however, handed over to the Tycoon's Government with due solemnity, and for the first time in Japanese history a salute was fired by native gunners in honour of a foreign flag. It being the then custom in Japan that the Tycoon's death should be kept secret for six weeks until his successor was firmly seated on the throne—at this very time, although it was unknown in the country, the Tycoon was actually dead, and had been privately buried.

Lord Elgin's quiet determination and the dignified tact with which he arranged this treaty must have been in marked contrast to the subservience of the Dutch Resident:—

In order to appreciate the pitch to which the Dutch carried at that time their compliance with the humiliating code of Court etiquette forced upon them by the Japanese Government, it is worth while glancing at the account which we have received from the veracious Kæmpfer of the ceremonies of the audience at Jeddo between the Resident of the Dutch factory and the temporal Emperor:—

'As soon as the Resident entered the hall of audience,' says the old German physician, 'they cried out "Holanda, captain," which was the signal for him to draw near and make his obeisances; accordingly he *crawled* on his hands and knees to a place shown him, between the presents ranged in due order on one side, and the place where the Emperor sat on the other; and there kneeling, he bowed his forehead quite down to the ground, and so crawled backwards like a crab without uttering a single word. So mean and short a thing is the audience we have with this mighty monarch.'

This was the form of the audience of ceremony; but now let us see what took place on the next occasion, when his Japanese Majesty condescended to unbend. After the members of the Dutch mission had, to use the words of the same writer, crept into the audience chamber, the Emperor sat himself on our right behind the lattices, as near as he possibly could. Then he ordered us to take off our 'cappa,' or cloak, being our garment of ceremony, then to stand upright, that he might have a full view of us again, to walk, to stand still, to compliment each other, to dance, to jump, to play the drunkard, to speak broken Japanese, to read Dutch, to paint, to sing, to put our cloaks on and off. Meanwhile we obeyed the Emperor's commands in the best manner we could. I joined to my dance a love song in High German. In this manner, and with numerous other such apish tricks, we must suffer ourselves to contribute to the Emperor's and the Court's diversion.'

Times have greatly changed since then. The great Tycoon's power has been overthrown, and the authority of the office of the Mikado has once again, after its representatives have endured six or seven centuries of enforced abeyance at Kioto, become paramount.

Till the restoration, as it is called in Japan, the Daimios levied the tax or rent which was paid for the land over a considerable part of the country. This tax varied considerably in some provinces, four-tenths of the produce of the soil being exacted by the over-lord and six-tenths left to the cultivator. But at that time the theory that the Mikado was the sole lord paramount of the soil was again started, and ultimately brought into practice, and all the land of Japan was again vested in the head of the State, the four hundred and fifty-nine nobles receiving, in lieu of their land, pensions, which were also granted to the 'samurai,' or two-sworded class, who were originally peasant farmers, cultivating their own lands, but who had gradually become a class who held the *de facto* position of governors of the country.

These two classes were granted pensions calculated at one-tenth of their previous incomes, and amounted in number to no less than three hundred and eighteen thousand four hundred and twenty-eight.

Whether there has been a breach of faith or not it is not for foreigners to enquire, but the fact remains that the Government, finding they experienced great difficulty in providing funds to pay these pensions, decided to reduce them, and in 1876 determined on a compulsory commutation of the pensions. The payment of the commuted capital is to commence in five years, and to extend, at the convenience of the Government, over a period of twenty-five years; so that in thirty years at latest this charge will entirely disappear from the budget. Mr.

Mounsey, writing from the British Embassy in Japan, states that the large incomes are those most affected by this scheme. For instance, instead of an hereditary annual income of 70,000 yen, a pensioner of the first class will only be entitled to a capital sum of 350,000 yen, payable in the course of thirty years, and will, meanwhile, only receive interest at 5 per cent. on that sum, viz., 17,500 yen, or one-quarter of his former income. The small incomes are, on the other hand, treated less harshly. A 100 yen pensioner will retain two-thirds of what he formerly enjoyed, and the very numerous class below him—302,350—will suffer still less loss from the new measure.

Until quite recently a man's wealth and income in Japan was calculated in rice, and it was adopted nearly universally as a medium for the payment of salaries, wages, and taxes. It was at one time decided that this system should be thoroughly reformed, and a metallic currency should be universally adopted. One year's experience, however, of the inconvenience of this sudden change has sufficed to show that for the present it is advisable still to receive a certain portion of the land tax, as heretofore, in rice.

This product of the field is held in the highest honour, and there are, doubtless, still many Japanese who are at a loss to understand how life can be sustained or the affairs of a State carried on without it; and as there is still in Japan—and is there not in countries nearer home, and nominally more civilized?—a certain amount of superstition, they attribute to this plant the pre-eminent virtue of keeping away evil spirits, and ropes made of rice straw are stretched across the portals of the shrines of one of their chief religious sects, the 'Shintos,' as a protection against these ghostly enemies. Rice has been from the earliest ages in Japanese history one of their great staple products of agricultural industry, but until recently there has been no appreciable quantity of it exported to foreign climes. This was owing to the fact that at one time, and even at the epoch immediately following the conclusion of the treaty I have previously referred to, its exportation was prohibited owing to the fear that the drain of rice from this country might cause a famine. This restriction has, however, since been removed, and a certain quantity was imported last year to Great Britain, slightly exceeding two hundred thousand cwt. It is stated to be a most profitable grain to cultivate, more so than any other. Given the *proper supply of water*, a man can cultivate ten and a half acres of rice land, whereas he would only cultivate one acre of other arable land. It is, of course, at present still the food principally of the richer and higher orders of Japanese, but its use amongst the entire people is greatly extending, and with the quantity of waste land in Japan, which is simply enormous, no doubt the day is not far distant when its cultivation will be greatly extended. The Government have lately been importing seed from Java, as the rice from that market has hitherto commanded the highest price in Europe,

Previous to the partial opening of Japan to foreign commerce, wholesale trading, in almost all its branches, amongst the natives of the country, seems to have been in the hands of 'toyas,' or guilds. Guilds were close corporations, exacting high fees for the privilege of membership; possessing, apparently, the power of crushing all individual and independent trading; and having fixed rules for the transaction of business, the violation of which was often punished by the expulsion of the offending member. They were not co-operative associations, aiming at the development of trade by the employment of their united capital. Their tendency was, on the contrary, restrictive, inasmuch as the business transactions of each member were limited by the extent of his own individual resources. The most important of them were naturally the rice guilds, and they seem to have given rise to a great deal of the same sort of gambling speculation that is carried on in our European Stock Exchanges and Bourses.

These were similar in many respects to our own guilds, or corporations of traders in the Middle Ages. Repeated attempts have been made to revive them; but though the Government have been able to restrain this system within the letter of the law, the spirit of it still largely pervades the minds of all the trading classes in this country. The Government of Japan may be said to be the only body at present capable of exporting rice to any extent, as few Japanese merchants have the capital required to embark in competition with them in a foreign trade in this product. There appears to be little doubt but that it can be profitably exported to Europe, though *a great deal of care* is required in the storage and ventilation, in order that it may arrive in good condition.

In looking at this country, one must bear in mind that it has, with almost incredible rapidity, changed its system in accordance with western ideas of civilisation, and that these new customs and institutions have not slowly grown on the habits of the nation, as has been the case in most of the European States. Nor has this sudden transition, taken as a whole, had ill effects, for it must be recollected that the reform of the entire administration of that country, the creation of an army and navy, the adoption of an uniform system of taxation, which involved the abolition of no less than

2,000 petty dues and imports, the introduction of railways and telegraphs, the establishment of lighthouses and post offices, the issue of a new currency, the extension of public instruction, and the initiation of a new code of civil and criminal jurisprudence, have all taken place within the last few years. The total debt incurred in bringing about these changes by the Government of the restoration was, up to 1877, £9,250,000, but, to judge from the reports of their Finance Minister in that year, the various items of their expenditure appear to me to have been brought into a thoroughly satisfactory condition.

The Mikado's Government consists of a Prime Minister, assisted by two vice-Prime Ministers, and all the effective heads of the ten great administrative departments, and a senate composed of from twenty to thirty members, which is presided over by a prince of the blood. It is the duty of the latter body to elaborate all new reforms, but it cannot initiate them without the consent of the Government. There is, besides, a deliberative and consultative assembly consisting of local officials, which has only, however, once met since its formation—namely, in the year 1875.

To show the care and forethought with which some of the taxes are imposed, I may instance one which may not be uninteresting to those connected with medical science in this country, as this is a tax imposed on *patent medicines*.

Mr. Mounsey states that a tax was imposed in January, 1877, on druggists' licences. It does not affect the drugs and medicines used and prescribed by the medical profession, and its object is to restrict the sale of medical compounds partaking of the character of quack medicines, in which, as well as in the charms against every description of disease and misfortune sold at every temple, the Japanese seem to have great confidence. To obtain permission to make and sell these medicines, a minute description in writing of the nature and effect of each must be sent to the Ministry of the Interior, and heavy penalties are attached to their unauthorized sale and manufacture. A licence for the manufacture of one such medicine costs 8s. per annum. A druggist's licence for their sale costs 1s. per medicine; those of itinerant and other vendors 1s. for all sorts of these medicines. The latter licences are valid for five years.

As another example, I may mention that a shooting licence of £2 has been recently imposed, which has to be uniformly paid by both native and foreign sportsmen, the latter, however, *now* being confined to shooting within the treaty limits, about 25 miles radius, in most cases round the open ports. The Japanese authorities have contended that their recent somewhat arbitrary measure compelling their nobles and 'samurai' class to receive *nolens volens* a capitalized sum in lieu of their pensions, had for its object the lightening of the burdens on land, the lessening of which has been the tendency of their late financial legislation.

On turning to the returns of our trade with Japan in 1878, it appears that our imports have increased, whilst our exports have actually doubled in the last five years, their total value being in 1874 slightly over £1,200,000, and in 1878 2,600,000. It is also a noteworthy fact that the first signs of a slight increment in the cotton manufacturing industry of this country has been lately shown by larger demands from China and Japan. Whilst referring to this important industry, I will give here a short resumé of the general bearings of the Chinese and Japanese tariffs.

The tariffs at present in force in both these countries are of a much less onerous description than those levied by many communities nearer our own doors, who boast a higher standard of civilization. The tariff between this country and China was settled at Shanghai in the year 1858, in pursuance (Article XXVI.) of the Treaty of Tien-tsin of the same year, and the general principle upon which it was based appears to have been the imposition of specific duties of import and export calculated in an *ad valorem* rate of five per cent. In the case of imports this principle was adhered to very strictly. In exports, however, it appears, owing to the fact that the duty at that time levied was less than five per cent., not to have been in all cases consistently acted on.

It is said that the French Minister, shortly after our treaty was concluded, anxious to obtain what he considered equivalent advantages for France, requested an interview with the Imperial commissioners. On this being granted, he requested that the duty on wine imported into China might be reduced. The Chinese commissioner, concealing with his native self-possession his opinion of the needlessness of the request, replied, 'We charge no import on wine at the treaty ports, but if transported into the interior it will be charged a transit duty at the rate of two and a half per cent. *ad valorem*. With regard to opium, the import duty then settled was 30 taels per pecul, the importer only to sell at the port. It was to be carried into the interior by Chinese only as Chinese property; nor were the provisions permitting foreigners to proceed into the interior with passports for the purpose of trading allowed to extend to opium.

The last Convention between Great Britain, France, the United States, the Netherlands, and Japan, modifying the tariff of import and export duties, was settled in 1866, and appears to have been arranged on a similar basis to the Chinese import tariff I have previously referred to—namely, the admission of certain specified goods free and the charging on certain others of a duty approximating to five per cent. *ad valorem*. The Japanese have export duties on a large proportion of their products, but none of them appear to be of a prohibitive nature, and they have, as I previously remarked, relaxed the restriction on the exportation of rice.

Having examined the incidence of *our commercial tariffs* with China and Japan, it may not be considered out of place to notice a fact which we ought not to overlook in connection with our present trade with these two Empires—namely, that there unfortunately appears to be a subject of dispute betwixt them, which may possibly end in war I allude to their present dispute concerning the Loochoo Islands. It appears that Loochoo is the chief of a group of thirty-six islands in the North Pacific Ocean, about 250 miles from the southern extremity of Japan, and about 350 miles from the coast of China. Intercourse between the principal islands of the group and Japan has existed since A.D. 1451, and an Embassy was sent from them to the Court of Taikô-Sama in 1580. After that date trade relations seem to have become frequent betwen them and Satsuma, and vessels came annually to Kagoshima, the capital of that Province, laden with presents for its Prince. In the beginning of the 17th century the Loochooans stopped all communication with Japan, in order to curry favour with the rulers of China. Thereupon (A.D 1609) the Prince of Satsuma, with the consent of the then reigning Shôgun, invaded the islands, took their King prisoner, and confined him for three years at Kagoshima. From this date the Kingdom of Loochoo became subject to the Princes of Satsuma, and through them to the Shôguns. The homage exacted by the latter consisted in the submission of the Kings of Loochoo to re-investiture on the accession of each Shôgun, and fifteen Embassies, principally undertaken for this purpose, are mentioned in Japanese annals as having come to Yedo between 1611 and 1850. Similar homage has been at different times paid by the Kings of Loochoo to the Court of Pekin. It would seem, therefore, that China has often disputed the right of Japan to absolute authority over these islands ; and till quite recently, I am informed, the inhabitants paid a small tribute, not only to Japan, but also to China. No one can form an exact estimate of what the result might be should such a war arise.

Some might imagine, and with a certain amount of probability, that the conflict, should it take place, would be mainly a naval one. The Japanese navy appears to have consisted at the end of June, 1878, of one ironclad frigate, two ironclad corvettes, two wooden corvettes, and several smaller vessels.

It is difficult to estimate the exact strength of the Chinese modern navy, as they are said to have built one or two ships on the lines of European vessels in their own dockyards. They also possess about six ironclad gunboats, built in this country. They have no doubt greater resources than their opponents, both in men and money, and possess numbers of well-tried, true, and skilful sailors.

The Chinese soldier, well led and properly disciplined, is by no means to be despised. He has those two great attributes for a soldier, endurance and obedience, and is not deficient in personal courage; though I am aware that in several encounters which the troops of the Celestial Empire have had with our own, if our opponents have not actually run away, they have at any rate eminently displayed that quality for which a Chinaman ever prays—an eager desire for longevity. But these Chinese braves have also shown on many occasions great pluck and determination, and all English officers who have served with them during the final suppression of the Tai-ping rebellion speak highly in their praise.

The Japanese army is said to consist of about 80,000 men, well drilled and equipped, and a number of Japanese officers and sub-officers have in recent years been instructed by French military men at Yokohama. There has, doubtless, been a complete change in their military system since 1858, at which date bows and arrows had not been entirely laid aside in Japan, and the casing of armour composed of shells, which made a warrior when fully equipped resemble a huge tortoise, was still worn. Mr. Oliphant at that time writes:—' Perhaps, however, the most singular arm which the Japanese employ in the battlefield is the war fan. This is a paper fan of a larger size than usual, the ribs of which are made of iron, so that if fatigued by a violent personal encounter a warrior sits down for a moment to rest and cool himself, and if unexpectedly attacked, he immediately hits his enemy. I endeavoured to obtain one of these, but they were only made to order, and were not completed when we left Jeddo.'

The pattern on the fan is the national emblem—a red sun on a black ground, but the process of fanning oneself with an iron-ribbed fan cannot be cooling. Ladies in Spain, if report speaks truly, are said to be able to use their fans for another, in its way not a less dangerous, purpose—that is, to flash secret signals to their admirers, and by means of these weapons to elude the vigilance of the enemy—their duennas. All the Japanese carry fans which they use as a screen from the sun; or at times to make notes on.

The administration of justice in Japan is said to be most satisfactorily conducted. I cannot refrain from giving a decision of the Mikado, the spiritual head of the Sinto religion, as I think it is well worthy of imitation by our ecclesiastical courts in this country.

A dispute having arisen amongst the votaries of the Sinto religion as to the colour of the devil—one party maintaining that he was black, another that he was red, a third that he was white, and a fourth that he was green—the Mikado, on being appealed to to decide this vexed question, judiciously ruled that he could assume all four colours at will.

I much regret that space and the nature of this work forbid me to enter at all fully into any of my own personal recollections of Japan, and that I am therefore unable to do more than allude to some of my experiences during my stay at Yedo, in many ways one of the most interesting cities of the world. Whilst there my friends and myself stayed at the hotel—a huge, rather dreary-looking building much resembling a barrack, the manager of which was a negro American citizen, who, though very obliging, did everything with that air of condescending familiarity affected by his race, which at times was very amusing. Like all visitors to the country, I was greatly struck by the thoroughness of the Japanese workmanship, and the particularly business-like manner in which all transactions in their bazaars are conducted; although in that latter respect the Chinese are not at all behind their neighbours.

The Government—the reason for which I could never discover, as the people did not appear unfriendly—provided us with a couple of troopers to trot about with us whenever we went out for a drive. During such excursions, as well as when travelling through various parts of the country which I was able to visit, I found the roads fairly good, and the scenery a beautiful alternation of hills and dales, varied by abundance of timber, which much reminded me of Devonshire. There were no lack of rest-houses along the various roads I chanced to travel. These particularly neat and clean buildings had, as a rule, little tables set out in front of them, temptingly placed in the cool shade, on which fair damsels placed fruit or tea for the traveller. The Japanese young women, while single, spare no pains to improve their looks, colouring their lips and cheeks and arranging their hair and quiet, becoming dress, with every attention to effect; but when they become married, they blacken their teeth and pull out their eye-brows, in order, it is said, to render themselves unattractive. I was told, however, that there were certain handmaidens attached to each Japanese gentleman's establishment who do *not* seem to find it needful to thus disfigure themselves.

Near Yedo there are several very good 'tea houses,' where, however, tea is by no means the only beverage consumed, and equal latitude in that respect is allowed us in an English so-called 'coffee room,' to one of which we on one occasion went down by river to dine with a Japanese friend. These institutions are to Yedo much what the hotels on the banks of the Thames are to London. On arriving at our destination we were duly shown into a room, which was divided from the adjoining one, as is almost universally the custom in Japan, by paper screens running on slides and moveable at pleasure. During dinner we all sat on the floor, which was matted, as is almost invariably the case, with scrupulously clean straw wadded mats, every mat being for this purpose precisely the same size—six feet three inches long by three feet two inches wide. Our dinner was served in little lacquered dishes, and in lieu of a knife and fork one had to make the best use one could of two little chop sticks—a substitution which it is difficult to appreciate, though some people contend that it indicates a higher degree of refinement, since not only do you have your dishes cut up at a side table, but even have the contents divided into such minute portions that the diner has not the needless trouble of *cutting up* the portion on his plate for himself. On my right sat a young lady, who, although eating very little except a few sweetmeats, occasionally took two or three whiffs of a pipe, which, between all the courses, was smoked by each of the male guests as well as by the fair sex.

But I shall, however, if I dwell more on my reminiscences, be accused by some critic of digressing from my subject, although the customs of a people have an indirect bearing on their commercial transactions, as ignorance of them may lead to blunders in transmitting goods not suitable to the requirements of the inhabitants, thus entailing on both consignor and the consignee annoyance and loss.

In examining our Board of Trade returns for the last fifteen years, it is satisfactory to notice that the aggregate volume of our trade with this country seems to have gradually increased, nor does there appear any reason for doubting from present appearances that it will cease to do so in future.

In Japan there is a universal desire for the acquisition of every species of knowledge; its inhabitants are apparently a race like the Athenians of old, constantly desiring to obtain informtion respecting 'some new thing,' and they pride themselves in acquiring with great facility foreign languages and foreign ideas—a tendency which cannot fail to have in the main a good effect on a nation.

I cannot say farewell to Japan and conclude this part of my subject without taking, as I did when leaving Yedo, one last glance at their great volcanic mountain—Fusi-yama, 'the matchless mountain,' whose snow-clad summit forms a background in my mind's eye to the pleasant days I spent in that most interesting country. This mountain, so remarkable for its grandeur, is frequently ascended by Japanese pilgrims as an act of devotion, and is inhabited by a sect of priests called Gemmiboos, whose daughters, according to Kæmpfer, are remarkable for their beauty. The origin of the pilgrimage is traced to the time when Sintoo, the founder of the religion of that name, took up his residence in the mountain, and his spirit is supposed to have influence to bestow various blessings. The ascent is usually only undertaken by Japanese of the middle and lower classes, whilst the pilgrims wear a distinctive dress made of a white cotton material, which is stamped with various mystic characters by the Bonzes or priests, who during the season occupy the small temples round the crater for this purpose, it being 14,177 feet above the level of the sea. July and August are the months when it is considered sufficiently clear of snow to permit of its ascent. Fusi-yama forms a subject, as we are well aware, on almost every piece of lacquer work and china executed by Japanese artists. Its ascent was said to take three days, but doubtless many enterprising English travellers could accomplish it in less. I will thus conclude this part of my subject, and this review of some of the leading incidents of our commercial intercourse with foreign nations and our colonies, in which I have endeavoured to point out not only the present condition of our trade, but also to show where its due outflow was checked and hindered by protective tariffs.

CHAPTER XI.

OUR EXTERNAL FOOD SUPPLIES.

GREAT BRITAIN is at present in the somewhat startling position of only being able to grow food to supply the wants of little more than half its inhabitants. The value of our food importations in 1878 was £165,032,000, or forty-four per cent. of the value of the total importations to this country in that year. Of this large sum £92,466,000 was for articles of food *which can be or are produced in the United Kingdom*, and £57,082,000 for those which cannot, or are not usually produced within these shores. In whatever way one looks at these general facts connected with our food supplies, they seem to me of extreme gravity. True, it is quite evident that there is no lack either in the will or the power of other nations to produce all the food we may need for the support of our population, and equally so that we have both the means and the desire to manufacture more than sufficient goods wherewith to make payment for the supplies they send; but the ever-increasing divergence which I have previously noticed between the amount of our purchases and our sales cannot continue growing to an indefinite extent. Whatever may be our accumulations of wealth at home, they will not suffice to ward off a scarcity of food, if those who have it to give to us will not take the produce of our labour and capital in exchange; and viewed in this aspect the problem seems difficult of solution.

When Adam Smith wrote the 'Wealth of Nations'

England was in a far different position in this respect. We were not only able to supply in ordinary years the inhabitants of these isles with home-grown alimentary substances, but even to export grain. But, to come down to more recent times and to notice the great difference in the total values of the food imports for the two years 1857, £64,000,000, and 1877, £181,000,000 (which periods most fairly compare with each other from the similarity in the price of wheat ruling in those years), the whole situation appears to be well worthy of the closest consideration. However slight the importance, and with whatever easy flow of trite axioms political economists may attempt to account for it, this country is now much more dependent upon foreign sources of food supply than it was some years ago, and as our population grows the extent of this dependence increases at a more and more rapid rate, and thus two great questions press upon us for solution : first, can we always rely upon these foreign sources, in the event, for instance, of war? and secondly, can we afford to continue to pay for food at the rate we now do without impoverishment? I have no desire to exaggerate the difficulties of the situation. It may be that a cycle of good harvests will relieve us from the pressure of excessive expenditure brought about in some degree by bad crops, although one is not, unfortunately, given good accounts of our this year's crops, and a bad harvest is said to entail on this country a loss of thirty million pounds sterling. *

And now, in proceeding to examine in what our imports of food consisted in 1878, it may be well to carefully con the following concise table of the value of some of the principal articles of food imported in the two years:—

* See Appendix 4.

Note.—In this table the thousands are omitted. Thus, 83 stands for 83,000.

	1877.	1878.	Increase.	Decrease.
	£	£	£	£
Living animals - - -	6,012	7,454	1,442	—
Bacon - - - - - -	5,732	6,695	963	—
Hams - - - - - -	1,156	1,915	759	—
Beef - - - - - - -	1,686	1,753	67	—
Pork - - - - - - -	608	656	48	—
Meat, unenumerated -	1,823	1,740	- - -	83
Fish - - - - - - -	1,640	1,541	- - -	99
Butter - - - - - -	9,543	9,940	397	—
Lard - - - - - - -	1,472	1,786	314	—
Cheese - - - - - -	4,771	4,939	168	—
Eggs - - - - - - -	2,473	2,511	38	—
Potatoes - - - - -	2,348	2,396	48	—
Rice - - - - - - -	3,490	3,192	- - -	298
Sago and other farinaceous substances - -	766	845	79	—
Wheat and Wheat Flour	40,623	34,187	- - -	6,436
Indian corn - - - -	9,871	12,589	2,718	—
Barley - - - - - -	5,396	5,545	149	—
Total - - - -	£99,410	99,684	274	—

In this table it will be noticed each enumerated class of imported food competes with our own produce, except rice, sago, and Indian corn. Besides those mentioned in the above table, we also import poultry and game, hops, fruit (of this class alone over two millions' worth), and also beer, ale, and yeast.

Having ascertained the principal articles of food we imported from foreign producers, the next thing to be enquired into is what proportion came from each country.* To begin with the 'staff of life,' which heads the list in point of value, it will be noticed there was a considerable diminution in value—not so great, however, in

* See Appendix 4.

quantity. This is to be accounted for, as the average price of wheat in 1877 was 56s. 9d. per quarter and 46s. 5d. last year, when there was a corresponding fall more or less marked in the price of commodities generally; so that we only purchased eight per cent. less quantity of wheat, but paid nineteen per cent. less for it. Looking first at 1877, we find we imported during that year 54,250,000 cwts. of wheat. Some 44,750,000 cwts. came from fifteen different foreign countries. 9,500,000 cwts. came from our own possessions; of this nine and a half millions, some six millions came from India, and three and a half millions from the Colonies. It is to be observed that of the total wheat required by these two islands in 1877, only about one-ninth came from India, and only about one-seventeenth of the whole was furnished by the Colonies. We were supplied with our imported cereals from eighteen different sources, viz., Australasia, India, Canada, and fifteen foreign countries. In 1878 wheat was imported to the extent of 49,800,000 cwts., being a decrease of 4,300,000 cwts. Of the total quantity, America supplied 29,900,000 cwts., or about three fifths; Russia and Germany 14,100,000 cwts; and our own possessions, viz., India, Australia, and British North America, 5,800,000 cwts. So that it will be noticed that this decrease was mainly from our own Colonies, from which source we purchased 3,200,000 cwts. less in 1878 than in the previous year.

This is a fact to be deplored when one bears in mind that travellers in Canada, Australia, and South Africa see one common thing, and all tell the same regarding it, and that is this, unlimited food-producing resources belonging to the English race lying waste. It must also be borne in mind that India is at present one of the largest wheat-producing countries in the world, second only to the United States, which latter country produced during each of the past two years 45,000,000 quarters, whilst in India, Russia, and France there are grown 30,000,000 to 35,000,000 quarters of wheat per annum. Respecting the superior quality of a large extent of the Indian grain, I will speak later on.

Next in importance in point of value comes the butter we imported—' that curiously-constructed preparation composed of strange fats.' Of this compound we have to thank free import trade for the introduction to our shores in 1878 from France of over three millions' worth, from Holland two and a half millions', and from Denmark one and a half millions'. From our Colonies we only purchased to the value of three hundred thousand pounds, which came chiefly from British North America and the Channel Islands.

Of living animals imported we find a marked increase, which numerically amounted to over ten per cent., or 1,095,282 and 1,201,498 respectively in 1877 and 1878—of these in the latter year, of horned cattle, 68,000 came from America and 53,000 from Denmark.

Sheep and lambs were mostly sent to us by the Germans and Dutch; the former exported to Great Britain over four hundred and forty thousand, and the latter two hundred and fifty thousand. Holland is credited with sending us the largest number of swine, and the quantity of bacon and hams brought to these islands from abroad in 1878 was unexampled, the increased quantity from the previous year being 51 per cent., whilst, owing to the prices having been unusually low, the value was only 25 per cent. in excess of 1877.

A sudden lowering of value in a commodity such as bacon is rarely an appreciable gain in diminution of price to the consumer, the greater portion of this profit being divided between the middle man and shopkeeper. From the United States we also purchased Indian corn valued at ten millions and cheese at over three—one million sterling of the latter product being sent us by the Dutch.

I have entered thus minutely into the dry details of the sources from whence several of the principal importations of the different descriptions of alimentary substances into this country are drawn, as the countries on whom we are dependent for food at the present time is not in my opinion a matter of such complete indifference to us as some would try to make us believe; and it is to be noticed that out of our total importation of these products from the whole world, including not only those to which I have previously alluded, but also sugar, wine, tea, coffee, and maize, nearly one-third, or about fifty-two million pounds in value, came from the United States, to which country our total exports have fallen off since 1874 by 48 per cent., and amounted in 1878 to only the comparatively small sum of fourteen and a half million pounds sterling. In looking at a question of this importance, it is well not to confine ourselves to one year only; therefore, in referring back and looking at the general position of our import trade for the last three years, we find that in the year 1876 our principal imports of food amounted in value to eighty-eight million pounds, or about eleven millions less than last year. We find that in that year, as at present, the United States stood far before any other country in the value of our food imports from them; they were £36,000,000. France came next with £18,000,000; British India, £13,000,000; China, £11,000,000; Germany, £10,000,000; the West Indies and Holland each £9,000,000; Russia, £7,000,000;

Turkey, £6,000,000, and British North America, £5,000,000. America took even a more marked lead in 1877 in this respect than in 1876. To quote one instance of our imports from them, namely, wheat—whilst it amounted in value to over £10,000,000 in 1876, it exceeded £13,000,000 in 1877. The countries I have previously mentioned supplied us with nearly four-fifths of the contributions to our necessities of the whole world.

Germany and Holland are, to a great extent, not the real sources of supply, but only the countries through which the rivers and railways of the Continent pass supplies to our shores; and it is probable that some portion of our receipts from the United States are really the produce of Canada shipped from Portland during the month when the navigation of the St. Lawrence is closed.

Turkey, too, gets the credit of much Austrian produce, which finds its way down the Danube. China, on the other hand, sends to the extent of perhaps a million by way of Hong Kong. Pursuing another mode of division, and collecting together those which come from our own Indian and Colonial possessions, we shall find about 31 million pounds, *or one-fifth of the whole*, to come from places which own our sway; this proportion being nearly equally divided between India and the Colonies, both together, however, falling short of that which the United States alone sends us.

Turning for a moment to statistics of British produce and manufacture which we exported to these nine countries previously alluded to, we find in 1876 a total of 120 millions, *or four millions less* than we took from them of alimentary substances, to say nothing of all the raw material and manufactured articles which we also purchased.

Having thus examined the sources from which our extraneous food supply comes, it may not be without interest to consider whether in future years, notwithstanding the decreased importation in 1878, we could not receive a larger proportion of the imported food from our Colonies, and so make this country not so entirely dependent for her food supply on foreign powers. I grant that this importation of food, as of all commodities, to this country is simply a question of supply and demand; but, presuming such a thing to be possible, are we right in placing ourselves in the position that the price of grain might be greatly increased in this country by a 'ring' of Yankee corn merchants? But, putting that perhaps improbable case aside, it would tend to lower the price of wheat were there more large sources of supply ready and able to supply us with grain, and would remove the contingency of a heavy rise in price, in the event of the contingency occurring of there being a bad harvest the same year in both England and the United States: it would tend to modify that which would be the result, namely, a large increment in the price of wheat.

I am far from saying, do not let us purchase food from extraneous sources. The fact stands that, be the reason what it may, we are obliged to do so, and we are of necessity the greatest purchasers of alimentary substances in the world.

Take wheat as an instance of this. Our average annual importation of wheat into the United Kingdom is eleven million quarters, and the approximate annual demand for wheat in the market of the world is from twenty to twenty-five million quarters. One fact we must not lose sight of—*there are nations who depend much more on their sale of raw produce, including food, to us, than*

England does in losing her sale of iron or cotton goods to them, amidst her wide-world trade. Therefore, I contend if they make so large a profit out of this country, let us either receive fair and reciprocal terms from them, or direct our trade to other quarters of the globe where we can sell what we produce and receive their produce in return. That is an opinion of more Englishmen than perhaps some of our legislators may imagine.

Without further comment, I will touch on the prospects of some of the colonies and dependencies of Great Britain, and the probabilities there are of their increasing their supply of food to this country. In doing so I shall refer solely to grain, as the question of both the imports of living animals and dead meat from such colonies as Canada, the Cape, and Australia, is not whether they have superabundant stock of animal food to send—this they all, doubtless, possess—but whether science can suggest a system by which they can be brought to this country without deterioration, and enable them to be sold at a price that would leave the vendors a margin of profit ; and already Canada seems to have surmounted this difficulty.

Amongst the dependencies of Great Britain there is none that would reap greater advantages by an increase in their export of wheat to our shores than would India. I understand that the cultivation of wheat is greatly increasing over the North-west Provinces, Oude, the Punjab, and Bengal, the Government having apparently done all in their power to improve the cultivation of it, and have established in different parts of India model farms. In the Central Provinces the Nâghur model farm had a very successful year (1876), and did much to demonstrate to the cultivating community the advantage of improved modes of culture for the ordinary crops of the country. For wheat cultivation the results obtained from manuring and irrigation are such that the produce of an acre of white-eared wheat amounted to 2,200 lbs. instead of about 410, and the value would be over £6, the cost of cultivation being not more than £1.

There can be no doubt that any effort made by our Government, whether by giving agricultural prizes for farms judged to have excelled in the cultivation of the superior descriptions of wheat, or by any other kindred means, cannot fail to have a beneficial effect.

Dr. Forbes Watson, in his report on Indian wheat, published last summer, states that after an examination of samples from nearly every district of India he has found descriptions of white soft wheat equal to the finest Australian or Californian wheat, and white hard wheat equal to the best that comes from Russia. He, however, adds :—

> 'It must be, however, kept in mind that a considerable number of the samples sent from India were far superior to any Indian wheat usually seen in the London market, and that without more local information than we now possess it is not possible to decide whether these fine varieties could at present be forthcoming in quantities sufficient for the development of an important trade. (On this point the Government are at present collecting statistical facts.) Be this, however, as it may, one result is clearly apparent from the mere inspection of the samples, and that is that the cultivation of the finest wheat cannot be considered as anything exceptional, but that it is spread over a considerable portion of the country. If samples like those mentioned in the valuations as being equal to the finest Australian or Californian had only been sent from a few places, their occurrence might have been explained as due to unusually favourable conditions which do not apply to the country at large. But samples of equal or only slightly inferior value were sent from district after district. It is not from one nor half-a-dozen places that the best samples were received, but probably from more than 100 different localities. More than 60 districts sent one or more samples of soft white wheat reported as

superior to No. 1, and valued at from 44s. to 48s. (The average price of English wheat was at that time 38s. a quarter, and it is on that standard of price he has based his deductions.) These 60 districts include the greater portion of Behar, the North-west Provinces, Oude, and the Central Provinces ; and it is probable that but for the weevilled condition in which most of their samples were received, the same might have been said of the Punjab and Sind. In addition, perhaps a dozen more districts in Bengal, Bombay, and Berar may be counted, which, though not producing soft white of a similarly high character, yet grow a hard white wheat equal to the finest wheat of the same kind grown anywhere. Mr. Watson mentions that a gentleman of great practical experience in the milling of wheat was particularly struck with the fine hard wheat, which he thinks is not sufficiently appreciated in this market; and he refers to some experiments undertaken some time ago, at his instance, with flour produced from the hard St. Petersburg wheat, which yielded per sack of 280 lbs. 110 four-pound loaves of fine bread, whereas the best English wheat yields only 90 to 92 loaves. Some of the Indian samples of hard wheat are even finer than the best hard St. Petersburg or Kubanka wheat. The provinces above mentioned include the whole of the wheat-growing area proper in India.

'In competing in the wheat market of the world, India would chiefly have to contend with the produce of Russia and the United States, and in both countries the area for the production of fine full grown winter wheat is comparatively restricted. Spring wheat forms a very large proportion of the Russian supply, as the greater part of the country is too cold for the growth of winter wheat ; in the United States, likewise, the climate of Minnesota, Iowa, and the other States, on the Canadian border, in which the cultivation of wheat has been recently so rapidly extending, is only adapted for the growth of spring wheat. This wheat, which is mostly red, is not only inferior in quality to a good winter wheat, but it produces also a much lighter crop, not more than 12 to 15 bushels per acre. Thus, however much the cultivation may extend in these parts, it is not likely to affect the supply of the finest varieties, such as are grown in some of the older States or in California.

'The true policy for India, therefore, appears to consist in taking advantage of her climatic position, and cultivating for export only the finest varieties, in which the competition of Russia and the Far West in America is not likely to be as severe as in the case of the common varieties. Such a policy receives additional recommendation from the fact that the price of the finer varieties is always better kept up, and suffers less in a falling market than that of the common wheat. The higher priced wheat will likewise support better the necessarily high charges of transport and freight.'

The question both of price in India and cost of transit enters largely into our calculations when considering the probabilities of an increased trade in wheat from India to England; and having heard it stated that wheat could be grown in a good year in the North-west Provinces of India for from 14s. to 16s. a quarter, I wrote to a friend of practical experience on the subject, asking him some questions respecting the prospects of the Indian trade in wheat, its price in India, and the cost of transit. He replied as follows:—

'As regards wheat, it is really very difficult to say what it costs to raise, as it is nearly, if not all, grown by natives, and they don't tell much. But, for whatever a personal opinion is worth, I do not think it could be done at 16s. Freight is a very uncertain element in the cost; within the last two years freight in wheat from Calcutta to London has been as high as 57s. 6d. and as low as 5s., but I should say that 30s. would be a fair average. The landing charges are about 2s. per quarter. Two years ago we had a good deal of Indian wheat. The grain is of pretty good quality, but it is rather hard and gritty, and can only be used by a miller when mixed with soft grain. It is worth 5s. to 6s. a quarter less than Californian wheat, and there is never a very "free market" for it.'

Mr. Forbes Watson on this question of price states that it averages per quarter from 9 to 14 rupees in India, and also calculates that the charge for the transit from the Punjab to England viâ Calcutta is from 22s. 6d. to 27s. 2d. per quarter, according as the distance by rail from which the wheat has to be sent is nearer or farther from that port, but anticipates that a saving of 8s. a quarter will be effected when the Indus Valley Railway is completed in the transmission of grain to England from the Punjab viâ Kurrachee, instead of from Calcutta, and already, except the bridge at Sukkui, that line is nearly constructed and will be opened shortly. This saving in cost of transit may be expected to make the whole difference between a profitable and a losing trade—in fact, between a trade of the largest dimensions and hardly any trade at all.

The completion of this Indus Valley Railway is thus calculated to bring about a complete revolution in the wheat trade of India, which is likely to assume in the Punjab a magnitude considerably greater than that which it is likely to attain in the districts from which the wheat is at present exported. With regard to the state in which the Indian wheat arrives in this country, the three principal causes which at present tend to depreciate Indian wheat are—the mixtures of different varieties of wheat, red and white, in the same consignment; secondly, the admixture of other grain, such as barley, grain, rape, or linseed; and also the presence of foreign matter, such as chaff, earth, lumps of clay, and dirt of every description.

These existing causes are easily removable with care, and the Indian ryot and grain merchant would soon find this care to well repay them, as Mr. Watson tells us that his valuer found many samples of Indian wheat which would have been worth 4s. or 5s. a quarter more in the English market if they had been clean.

Excellent seed can be found in almost every wheat-growing district, and all that is required is that the foreign matter should be removed before the grain is exported by the introduction of comparatively simple and cheap screening and winnowing machinery. No doubt, if steam threshing machinery came to be extensively adopted in India, the benefit derived from its use would be considerable. In view, however, of the great cost and general unsuitability of such machines to the Indian system of farming, it is impossible to entertain the hope that they could ever be adopted for general use in India. But it cannot be doubted that in some of the principal exporting districts such machines might be used with the greatest advantage. It may be mentioned that since the introduction of steam threshing machinery into Russia, and quite recently into Egypt, there has resulted a considerable improvement of the quality of the wheat sent from these countries.

The hard white Indian wheat to which I previously referred as equal, if not better, to the best Kubanka wheat (which is considered the best wheat of this class) is specially suited to the manufacture of macaroni, which is so important an industry in Genoa, Naples, and other places in Italy, and being in great demand there, the price is much higher than that quoted in London. The difference in favour of Italy may sometimes amount to as much as 5s. a quarter; moreover, the shipping charges from India to Italy are less than those to England.

The Indian wheat has been often much used in England to mix with our own, and to dry it after a wet season in this country. Objections have been made that some classes of hard Indian wheat were not suitable to be ground by the machinery in our flour mills, but by the recent improvements in the milling machinery that difficulty has been got over, and grindstones are now replaced by crushing cylinders, and the previous injury to the former by hard wheat is thus avoided.

Specimens of two new systems of this machinery were shown at the Paris Exhibition.

I have in a previous part of this work referred to the immense districts capable of growing corn at present lying waste in Canada and the Cape. Touching the former country, Lord Beaconsfield mentioned in his speech delivered at Aylesbury, Sept. 19, 1879, that 'since the surrender of the Hudson Bay Company, Canada has become an illimitable wilderness of fertile land;' and again remarks, respecting the competition of our own agriculturists with those residing in the United States, 'that it is a singular circumstance that at this moment the greatest apprehension is felt in the United States that they cannot compete with Canada. The taxation in America is so high, the rates of wages are so high, that it is impossible, according to some of the best American authorities, that they can any longer continue to successfully compete with Canada. If we are to be fed by Canada, it is at least satisfactory that we shall be fed by our fellow-subjects;' and again tells his audience, with regard to the large supply of grain now coming from the United States, that circumstances are of so transitory a nature 'that the very place of competition is doubtful, and when you hear that Canada expects completely and successfully to beat the United States from the European markets, it is wise for us not to take any precipitate steps,' and that it was difficult to estimate the exact result of the 200 millions of acres now lying waste in Canada being gradually brought into cultivation.

On this subject of our new corn fields in the North-West, Mr. T. T. Vernon Smith, in an article in the *Nineteenth Century* of last July, remarks, after having described the new American corn fields in Northern Minnesota:—

'So much for the American side: enormous as the influx of immigrants and the development of Northern Minnesota have been, it is nothing to what is now going on in Manitobah across the Canadian boundary. This rush could only take place on the opening of navigation, but as soon as the season opened, it was estimated that the influx of immigration added about 400 persons per day to the population of the province. In 1876, the total sales of land to 807 settlers were 153,535 acres; in 1877, the sales to 2,283 applicants amounted to 400,423 acres; and to the 31st of October, 1877, the total land sales in the province from its commencement amounted to 1,392,368 acres to 8,648 applicants. In April of 1878 the Emerson Land Office alone disposed of 52,960 acres, and in the first week of May 30,400 acres were appropriated. Emerson is on the American boundary immediately north of the line, and about seventy miles south of Winnepeg, which is the principal land office for the Dominion. From the influx of population and the rate of sales just referred to, it appears that about 3,000,000 acres of wheat land were allotted last year to actual settlers in this province of Canada alone, and when the rail communication is complete the rush of immigration and the rapid breaking up of the land into cultivation bid fair to be something beyond all previous experience.'

The immigrants to these new corn fields are not the poverty-stricken offscourings of Europe, but prosperous farmers from the older States and Settlements, from Canada, and especially from the best parts of Ontario— from, in fact, rich and fertile districts. Many of the new settlers in Manitobah have indeed sold their old farms in the older cultivated provinces of the dominion for from 25 to 30 dollars per acre, and having gained a large profit over their original price by these sales, are again acting as pioneers to reclaim this wilderness and bring it into cultivation, with the almost certainty before them of increasing their wealth and doubling the value of their new purchases in two or three years. To give an example of the profits which accrue to a fortunate farmer in these regions, bearing, however, in mind that this is a case of exceptionally good fortune:—

A Mr. Dalrymple is quoted in the *St. Paul Pioneer Press* as having had in 1877 8,000 acres under wheat, which yielded him all round 25 bushels to the acre, or over 200,000 bushels. His total outlay for seed, cultivation, harvesting, and threshing was under £2 per acre, leaving him a margin of over £3, or £24,000 on his 8,000 acres. Last year he had 12,000 acres under cultivation, and all in wheat. This was in Minnesota; but north of the Canadian line they got a much larger yield than this, and in twenty-seven miles along the Assiniboine River in 1877 over 400,000 bushels were harvested that averaged considerably over 30 bushels to the acre. In the North-western provinces of Canada wheat often produces 40 and 50 bushels to the acre, while in South Minnesota 20 bushels is the average crop, in Wisconsin only 14, in Pennsylvania and Ohio 15.

Want of space will compel me to forbear touching on the facilities of water transit, which can be utilized in this favoured region with a comparatively speaking small outlay, or of the railway communication already made and in process of construction to open it out; suffice to say, the two rivers Saskatchewan drain what is specially known as the fertile belt, containing no less than 90,000,000 acres of fine wheat land. These, together with the large Nelson river issuing from the north-east angle of Lake Winnepeg—a lake destined to be the future 'Black Sea' of Canada—which discharges its surplus waters into Hudson's Bay, form a vast and comprehensive water system available for steam navigation to 4,000 miles of their distance into Hudson's Bay. The outlet of Nelson River forms a fine natural and safe harbour, averaging one mile in width, with great depth of water.

'Port Nelson, although situated in 938° of west longitude, in the very heart of the continent, *is eighty miles nearer to Liverpool than New York is.* For four certainly, probably for five, months in the year it is as clear of ice as any other of the North Atlantic ports. There is no question about its accessibility for ordinary ocean steamers from June to October, and it only remains to be proved whether these same vessels cannot force their way up the great Nelson River, and load their cargoes directly at the mouth of the Saskatchewan, the Red River, or the Winnepeg, in the very centre and heart of this great wheat-field of the North-west, where 200,000, 000 acres now await the advent of the farmer to be rapidly brought into cultivation.

'At the present rate of immigration and the rapid reclamation of this easily cultivated land, it is by no means unlikely that within the next two years 2,000,000 acres of this prairie will be under wheat cultivation, and this probably will be doubled within five years from the present time. This means an addition to the wheat products of the world of 100,000,000 bushels, which may be increased almost indefinitely.'

From the 11th of Sep., 1877, to the 11th of May, 1878, the total exports of cereals from the whole American continent to these shores did not exceed 100,000,000 bushels. It is not at all improbable that the annual production in the course of a few years in the wheat fields of the Winnepeg watershed may be equal to our above-named total supply of bread stuffs from America. Well might the late Hon. William Seward, whilst Prime Minister of the United States, write thus his impressions of Canada (that region nearly equalling in size all Europe, which even many of us have looked on as the fag-end of America, a waste bit of the world) :—' Hitherto, in common with most of my countrymen, as I suppose, I have thought Canada a mere strip lying north of the United States, easily detached from the parent State, but incapable of sustaining itself, and therefore ultimately, nay right soon, to be taken on by the Federal Union, without materially changing or affecting its own development. I have dropped the opinion as a national conceit. I see in British North America, stretching as it does across the continent from the Atlantic to the Pacific, in its wheat-fields of the West, its invaluable fisheries, and its mineral wealth, a region grand enough for the seat of a great empire.'

In turning to Australia and her wheat-growing districts, I am reminded by my previous reference to the Paris Exhibition that our colonial show of cereals there gained high commendation. Indeed, in his report to Sir Michael Hicks-Beach respecting the colonial exhibits in Paris in 1878, H.R.H. the Prince of Wales, as President of the Royal Commission, after treating of the zeal and energy displayed by the local commissions appointed in the several colonies, and noting that the sum voted in aid of the work by the various legislatures and crown colonies amounted to £80,000, proceeded to touch on each colony in detail, and remarked that the goods sent for exhibition by the Canadian and Australian colonies were so numerous that some difficulty was experienced in finding room for them, and that those of Canada surpassed any previous display of the products and manufactures of British America. In spite of the unsettled condition of affairs at the Cape, the South African exhibitors displayed samples of almost every product in that country. Australia and New Zealand had advanced with great strides from the previous exhibition in Paris, and New South Wales, the oldest Australian colony, gained a grand prix for wool, whilst South Australia (the granary of Australia—a land which also furnishes to the mother country some of the finest descriptions of grain) received the highest award for her magnificent collection of wheat, and a gold medal for flour. The report also stated that amongst the smaller colonies, the Straits Settlements, for the first time since their establishment as a colonial government, made an interesting representative collection, and concluded by saying—' Considering the number of exhibitors were more limited, the colonies have carried away a greater proportion of medals than the mother country;' and expressed the warm interest with which his Royal Highness would continue to regard every proposal tending to knit more closely the colonies with each other and the Empire at large.

CHAPTER XII.

A FREE TRADE ZOLLVEREIN.

IN concluding this review of the course of our interchange with certain foreign countries and the colonies, it is a matter of satisfaction to be able to note the fact that the trade of this country has once more shown its wonted elasticity, and has given grounds for the hope that we may see many of our most important industries again busily engaged in adding to the wealth and general prosperity of the nation. But, as I previously remarked, we must look at a question of this sort not as one glances at a daily newspaper, nor as one considers a passing event, but in the quiet, earnest, and thoughtful way in which a subject of such importance ought to be approached; and it is worthy of note that even in our current literature we see complaints that the Premier, when lately addressing the world from the heart of the Metropolis, did not entirely confine his remarks to the Cabul massacre, the Turkish system of rule in Asia, or the Zulu war, but first directed his auditors' attention to the 'prosaic subject of trade.' Lord Beaconsfield told us that he believed that this revival of trade was likely to prove permanent, and that we had at length seen our way out of the long period of depression through which it has been passing.

I wish I could *entirely* concur with such a satisfactory conclusion, and with the fact stated by such an eminent authority. There can be no doubt that we are shortly about to see what is commonly described as a 'revival of trade;' but with all deference I doubt its 'permanence,' even giving that expression its usually applied limited sense.

It would be well to enquire, whence comes this revival of trade? It must be answered, mainly from the great source of our external food supply—the United States of America. They have received, and probably will receive, larger amounts of our bullion in exchange for their wheat. That cause is, doubtless, a legitimate source of demand for our goods; but the question we have to enquire into is this: is this demand a permanent one? Can we, under existing circumstances, always suppose the United States will be a steady and sure market for our manufactured commodities? For the last two years, unfortunately, we have had bad harvests: they have had good ones; they have bought back their bonds, and our bullion is at present being poured back into the States. They are at present seeking to develope the undoubted resources of their great continent, and have come to the greatest market in the world for supplying their wants. Hence we are opening our mines and manufactories, and they are doing the same.

But let us try quietly to examine this. Can we, when trade flows back into its usual groove, beat the manufacturers of the United States when we have to pay a tax of from 60 to 100 per cent. on the commodities we send to their shores?

I am aware we have other open markets for our goods, and do not wish to doubt the fact that our manufacturers and merchants will hold their own in them with any nation in the world. Nor do I wish to allude to the chance of our having this year less money than usual circulating amongst the greatest interest in this country, namely, the agricultural. That state of things may next year be reversed, and all must hope such may be the case.

The other day a work entitled 'Free Trade and English Commerce,' and bearing the 'cachet' of the words 'Cobden Club' on its cover, was shown to me : in it the author seems to inculcate the following sublime doctrine —'Let us have an extensive foreign trade, to consist wholly of imports.' He also takes some pride in pointing out that he is carrying out the advice given by the immortal Mr. Pickwick in shouting with the 'biggest crowd,' for he finds the majority of writers favour his views of the question. Had he lived in Charles II.'s time he might have given an equally conclusive argument for the divine right of kings; but without attempting to weary my readers by recapitulating where I disagree with M. Mongredien, I will point out where I entirely agree. He says :—

'But let us glance at another contingency. At present, the United States and the Dominion of Canada form two separate and distinct governments. Accordingly, each is hedged round by *chevaux de frise* of tariffs, and their commercial intercourse is checked and hampered by impost duties and restrictions having for avowed object the protection of their respective populations and the increase of their prosperity. According to the protectionist theory, each nation is benefited by these arrangements, and would be injured by their removal. Very good; but let us suppose that political changes were to bring about the admission of Canada into the Union, and a fusion of the two dominions into one federal republic, what would happen with regard to the fiscal regulations which are now declared to be essential to the prosperity of both populations ? Would they be persevered in ? It is not likely; it would be an unexampled anomaly that one part of a republic should be debarred from free commercial intercourse with the other parts. Consequently, the principle of free trade which now governs the commercial relations of the different states of the Union among themselves would be extended to Canada, and the results of unrestricted commercial intercourse between the two dominions, now so carefully guarded against, would have to be faced. It is pretty evident to us that those results would be found, not only not to justify protectionist apprehensions, but indicative of largely increased prosperity to all.'

In this quotation it will be noticed he points out that 'it would be an unexampled anomaly that one part of a republic should be debarred from free commercial intercourse with the other parts.' It seems strange that if those are the views of Mr. Cobden's disciples, they have never stirred hand or finger to prevent this *glaring anomaly* in the British Empire. Why should Canada, if she were joined to the United States, enjoy all those advantages of free trade which it is now left to chance or to the 'magic of patience' to permit her to possess under the rule of the British Government? Let members of the Cobden Club, in attempting to prove their argument, knock off 11 per cent. from imports and add 11 per cent. on exports as they like. It appears to me that the only way to give permanence to the trade of this country is to ensure for ourselves a sufficient supply of open markets such as we at present find India and China are, where our products can always find a free mart, and not the occasional overflow of a few 'preventive markets.'

The question that ought to attract our most urgent attention is this: have we, under existing circumstances, an export trade of such a character as to justify our yearly increased purchases from abroad, bearing in mind that that yearly increment is greatly more marked in our demands for foreign food than for raw produce for manufacture, and that we are sending realized capital out of this country to pay for the alimentary substances we are importing?

Whilst on the subject of our importation of foreign agricultural products, it may not be uninteresting to notice the advice Mr. Gladstone has lately given our farmers in one of his speeches delivered in November, 1879, in Mid Lothian. Having pointed out the operation of certain economic laws, and stated a fact which it appears difficult to doubt—that it would be inexpedient to cut up the land of this country into the multitude of small holdings held in France—he then proceeds to add:

'I cannot help having this belief—that our destiny is to have other means of meeting the difficulties in which we may be placed; that a great deal more attention will have to be given than heretofore even by the agriculturists of England, and perhaps even in Scotland, to the production of fruits, vegetables, and flowers, of all that variety of objects which are sure to find a market in a rich and wealthy country like this, but which have hitherto been confined almost exclusively to farming production. You know that in Scotland, in Aberdeenshire, as I am told also in Perthshire, a great example of this kind has been set in the cultivation of strawberries over hundreds of acres at once.'

Now, I will not presume to pre-suppose the extreme case that this advice was carried out literally, and that the United Kingdom was at some future date to present throughout its length and breadth the Arcadian beauties of a flower and strawberry garden, or that this charming ideal was marred by the Earl of Beaconsfield's 'chemicals,' but will simply refer to certain other economic laws apparently here lost sight of. I mean the laws which enjoin that it is an undoubted advantage to a country to supply food for the greatest possible number of its inhabitants. And in doing so I will acknowledge the undoubted fact that whatever our agriculturists find pays best, that will they grow. As I previously noticed, more than half the population of this country are dependent on a foreign food supply. Let us now examine what would be the result even presuming that emigration kept down the existing ratio of the increase of our population; and in order to consider this question thoroughly, I must refer my readers, not to a periodical of the present day, but to a very cleverly-written book at the time of the potato famine in Ireland. At that time there appeared a work by Mr. Newenham entitled 'Inquiry into the Population of Ireland,' in which the author remarks, that 'the average quantity of land requisite for the support of an individual who subsists on animal food, and uses bread only as a supplementary article, will maintain *four* people who subsist wholly on bread, or *twelve* who subsist wholly on potatoes.' I have no means of comparing the relative extent of land required to support an individual on potatoes or one on strawberries or flowers, nor will I presume to decide whether it is to our advantage to go against the doctrines of the economic law I previously referred to. It is, however, abundantly apparent that as we gradually cease to become a grain-growing country, and increase our cattle and flocks, strawberry beds, and flower gardens, by so much do we gradually become a nation day by day, and year by year, more dependent on a foreign food supply.

Some thirty years ago, as we are all aware, our manufacturers started a theory apparently very sound in principle, but which has not been found to be realized in practice, that if England showed the world the advantages of free trade, all the nations of the earth would follow her example and become free traders; and as we have the advantages of cheap iron and coal, besides possessing machinery capable of doing the work of fifty millions of slaves, that we should permanently hold the position of being the workshop of the world.

For a long time it appeared they were right. English trade increased immensely, and certain nations were even induced to lower their tariffs. Thence it came to be an axiom, to appear to controvert which would draw down on one very hard names even at the present day, that the sole reason of our success was the system then inaugurated and no credit was given to the great inventions of modern days, of which, if we were not in all cases the originators, we were at any rate the first who took large advantage of. I allude to the inventions by which trade has been greatly increased and facilitated, such as railways, steamers, telegraphs and an improved and cheapened postal system. But now it would appear that foreign countries are about to accept the good and reject the evil, pour all descriptions of goods into England, and put on prohibitory duties against our exports. But I have heard it said that, notwithstanding these duties, we are selling nearly as great a quantity as we were in 1873, and that it is merely the price that has diminished; but that fact in itself amounts to *a real retrogression*, allowing for the *increase* of population which must have occurred in the interval. A report has been presented to the Secretary of the Board of Trade, and a very elaborate table compiled, which shows the relative fall in price and the quantity in volume exported from this country in 1873 and 1877 very clearly. I will give three striking examples and the general total. The table is headed:

Statement of the Quantity and Value of the Exports of the under mentioned articles in 1873, with the average prices at which they were exported; of the quantity of the same articles exported in 1877, and the values they would exhibit at the average prices of 1873; and of the actual values declared in 1877:—

In this table thousands (000) omitted, thus, 785 stands for 785,000.

ARTICLES.	Quantities of Articles Exported in 1873.	Quantities of Articles Exported in 1877.	Declared Values of Articles Exported in 1873.	Computed Values of Articles Exported in 1877 at the Prices of 1873.	Declared Values of Articles Exported in 1877.
Coals, Cinders	Tons. 12,617	Tons. 15,420	£ 13,118	£ 16,113	£ 7,844
Cotton Yarn	lbs. 214,778	lbs. 227,651	£ 15,895	£ 16,846	£ 12,192
Metals, Iron for Railroads of all sorts	785	498	£ 10,418	£ 6,611	£ 3,868
General Total .. £			192,453	191,530	147,801

An examination of the above table does not convey a satisfactory impression to my mind, and it would seem a poor consolation to reflect that had the prices realized been as high as in 1873, we should have received over forty-three millions sterling more for them, for it appears that the fall in price of our goods has greatly exceeded the decrease in the cost of their prodction, and as a rule where we have even maintained the same volume of our trade it has been in raw produce sold, if not absolutely at a loss, at a sum which barely covered working expenses; the principal effect of this exportation of raw produce being that the foreigner became better able to successfully compete with our manufacturer. That he can compete more successfully than he once did there is not a shadow of a doubt; we have shown him how to do so at our exhibitions; we have sold him our machinery, sent out skilled workmen to instruct his artificers in the various details of each trade, and we were till recently actually selling him iron and coals at a minimum profit.*

One reason that has contributed in a great measure to the fact that although the volume of our trade had not fallen to a very appreciable extent from what it was five years previously, whilst we received forty-three millions sterling less, is that our manufacturers had indirectly to pay a large proportion of the high import duties charged by the Governments of our foreign and colonial purchasers.

But it may with justice be enquired, what do you suggest to obviate this? To this question I would reply —I have no dogma to lay down, no special nostrum, no wonder-working panacea of my own to proclaim, no startling discovery to announce. I simply say—Let us have absolute *Free Trade;* if we cannot have it with *all the world at once,* at least with as many countries as possible, and I contend that we shall obtain this, not by the motive power hitherto tried without success, namely, 'a good example,' but by the more powerful influence of self-interest.

Let us endeavour to open out fresh fields for our commerce, not by wars, but by developing our colonial resources by well-directed emigration, and if needful by furthering this not only with our private but even our public capital. Such money, if judiciously expended, would realize a more certain and higher interest than either a Suez Canal investment or a Bolivian (State) Loan.

It is a matter for regret that the great markets for our international commerce are so few in number. It will

* For the greater portion of the years 1876-9 coals were actually sold at a loss in many of the Lancashire coal pits. From this state of affairs I am glad to notice a reaction has already set in.

C C

be noticed that considerably more than one half of our total commerce is carried on with six countries, namely, the United States, France, British India, Germany, Australia, and Russia. It is also to be observed that not only are the most important markets for our international commerce few in number, but that *the bulk* of our export trade consists in two great articles only, namely, a certain description of *textile fabrics* and *iron*. We must, therefore, extend more largely our manufacturing industries, and not consider the cotton and iron industries as the only two sheet anchors of our commercial prosperity; and even although it may cost a great deal in the first instance to divert capital from its present use and turn our attention to other industries, we must endeavour not only to confine our energies to the spinning of cotton, flax, and wool, but see whether the manufacture of silk—once so prosperous at Coventry and Spitalfields—cannot be revived, by the higher technical education of our workers, and the production of designs of greater taste, and also to the increased manufacture of leather goods and glass, the production of these three classes I have just named being our province as much as that of any other nation of the world. No one can deny that one reason that these trades are not increasing in their proper ratio is that many of the largest states of the world absolutely prohibit their exportation from Great Britain by the high duties imposed on them by their tariffs. Still, we ought in England to manufacture more of the ten to eleven millions worth of the silk we import from France; and it would seem our interest, so to speak, not to place all our eggs in one basket, more particularly when we leave that basket in the power of any foreign nation to upset, by imposing high import duties on two great industries, so as virtually to debar their sale in its markets. What we require is fixity of tenure for our manufacturing interest; for though I am aware that term is usually applied to the holding of land, it applies with equal force to the manufacturer. What farmer would work his farm with confidence and thoroughly develop the resources of it, if the question whether he held it from one year to another was to be left to the uncertain decision of those whose views from time to time he had no power of gauging?

In the same way our manufacturers have no fixity of tenure. They may be able, as in some instance they appear to have succeeded in doing at present, by improved machinery, cheapness of labour, and indefatigable industry, to pay the duty charged on their produce by a certain State, and yet obtain a certain margin of profit; but when suddenly this State raises its import duties 15 per cent., the manufacturer perhaps finds himself with a large stock on his hands and no available market, and he may, from the reason above stated, fail, should a large proportion of those engaged in this trade do the same. This particular branch of industry is then mentioned in a casual way in the *Times* as being 'depressed,' and yet none is allowed to doubt the wisdom of the system that *permits*, nay, almost gives a *premium* to the foreigner to exclude our manufactured goods and hinder our export trade, and at the same time protect his own manufactures. If, as I before remarked, either this ruined manufacturer or any of his hundreds of workmen thrown out of employment dare to doubt the wisdom of this system, they are told by our modern political economists that their loss is a gain to the consumer. Still, many amongst us enquire, why should we, after acquiring a supremacy in an industry, be suddenly shut out of it by prohibitive duties? Why should we submit to be deprived of that which is really the most important advantage of Free Trade? Is there either justice or reason in passively submitting to such a deprivation? Amongst the large and increasing number of those holding the first rank from their public positions in this country, who have entertained doubts as to the reality of our present so-called 'Free Trade'—men whose position gives them a right to speak of facts as they are, not mere theorists—I will quote Mr. Richard Moon, who last February, at the general meeting of the largest railway company in England —the London and North Western—said, in alluding to the then depressed state of the country, which he believed was unprecedented :—' We are buying an enormous quantity of foreign food ; probably nearly two-thirds of the population are fed on foreign food, and we wanted but could not get a free exchange of our commodities for these foreign goods. They heard, too, a great deal about free trade, and there was free trade for the foreigner in this country, but there was no free trade for the English people.'

But granting this, is there any lever we can bring to bear to alter this condition of things? In the first place, we must bear in mind that we are the largest importing nation in the world. I grant that our imports principally consist of articles of food, and those in a raw state to be used in manufacture. Still, not including sugar, condiments, or stimulants, or any description of food, we imported in 1877 80 millions of goods wholly or partially manufactured. Now the question arises : Have we at present any lever to keep the markets of the world open for our manufactures? And whilst giving due attention to the opinions of those who hold that any change from our present system would be inexpedient, it will be well to examine the opinions of others who fail to see any chance of our obtaining Free Trade, except through the stepping-stone of Reciprocity. The latter argue as follows: When we at present ask a foreign nation to repeal a duty, such as that on plate and sheet glass, the reply immediately is— 'What duty in England would you repeal as an equivalent for giving up that duty?' A reply to that question would be not difficult. Let this country elect to place a uniform rate of duty on certain manufactured articles, such as glass and silk and leather, and a countervailing duty on sugar equal to the bonus paid by foreign nations, and in each case to strive to counterbalance as nearly as possible the gain a foreign merchant has at present in importing these goods into England over an English merchant importing them abroad (the duties to be imposed, *not for the protection* of our manufactures in the home market, but as a means to the ultimate *extension of our export trade*), let it consent to leave all other articles of food as at present, and place no tax on any species of raw produce *unless we found that we could obtain a supply sufficient* to our demand, and *at an equal price* from countries which gave us Free Trade; *for instance* such products as raw wool, sawn timber, hides, and partially manufactured leather. *Then*, but *not till then*, let a small nominal duty be placed on them, which would act as an additional lever to gain the desired object of universal free trade, which we first seem to have tried to obtain by giving all we had to give for an 'idea,' instead of gradually but surely gaining our object by a mutual removal of restrictive tariffs. There can be no doubt that no change such as is here indicated ought to be even considered in this country, unless it became abundantly apparent that we were gradually becoming year by year less able to find export markets for our manufactured products; but it may be noted that one advantage of an import duty, however nominal, on the manufactured products of Protectionist States, would be this:—We should then be in a position to offer to our colonies an exemption from this increased rate of duties on their giving us a reciprocal reduction. We are debarred by no 'most favoured nation' stipulation in any treaty of commerce at present existing from giving this advantage to the British possessions except in the case of Belgium. In respect to foreign countries, several of these treaties will soon cease; and I am of opinion, after having carefully perused them, that with regard to the remainder it is in our power to terminate them should we see it our interest to do so, giving each of them twelve months' notice (except in the case of two countries where the tariff is a low one, namely, China and Turkey), and, as we make new treaties, to give free trade for free trade, or protection for protection.* Were we able, by so doing, to offer to our Colonial possessions an advantage of this description over the Protectionist States of the world, I believe that one by one we should find that their 'self-interest' would induce them to join and form our great British Empire into a Free Trade Zollverein, resembling the States of the American Republic in its internal freedom of commerce. Ours would be a by far greater one in commercial importance than that of either the United States or the United German Bund, and few States in the world could afford to find themselves placed at a disadvantage with the trade of the 'United British Empire.' In such a Zollverein the same

* See Appendix on "Commercial Treaties."

duty would have to be imposed on certain specified articles of commerce. Nor do I believe the result would be *a permanent increase* of price to the consumer. We should manufacture more of the goods at home we now buy abroad, but the competition amongst our own manufacturers would keep prices down, whilst we should have the Cape and Australia competing in the sale of wool, and Canada supplying us with more hides and sawn timber

The trade to India and Australia and Canada would increase both in imports and exports; there would be greater competition amongst shipowners to trade to ports to which they had not to send their vessels one way 'in ballast.' This competition would cause the rate at which goods were carried *to be reduced*, and by the exact amount of this reduction would it give to our colonists the advantage. Again, though doubtless it would be easier to obtain Free Trade with the Colonies had we some advantage in the shape of lower duties to offer them, it appears to me that, in any case, the many and undoubted advantages which would result from having a Free Trade system throughout the British Empire have been quite overlooked.

I do not, however, lay claim for this roughly-sketched scheme that it is the only way to attain the desired end, namely, free trade; but in support of it, it may be pointed out that, after all, *the sole great advantage of ' trade,' put what adjective you choose before it, is the mutual interchange of commodities*, and the more divergent the products, the greater the advantage to be gained by their exchange. Thus a whole street full of spectacle makers would not to any appreciable extent add to one another's wealth, however free their trade was. So freedom of commerce between two agricultural states is not of as great advantage as between an agricultural and manufacturing community. Hence the advantage that would accrue from a Free Trade Zollverein of the Empire, for I have yet to learn that we have not natural advantages to produce or manufacture every article of importance we mutually require as well and as cheaply in Great Britain, British India, Canada, Australia, and the Cape, Hong Kong, the Straits Settlements, the West Indies, the Mauritius, and the other British possessions, as in any other part of the world.

I acknowledge that *at present* our colonies could not supply us with the *quantity* of wheat and raw cotton we require, and that we should under any circumstances, as far as one can at present see, have to purchase a large proportion of our wines from foreign nations. We are apparently at the present time not purchasing as much of that product as heretofore, our importation of wine having been sixteen per cent. less in 1878 than in the previous year. Such being the case, is it not possible, in an Empire which practically contains every want and need of man, to frame a tariff which shall be of equal and mutual advantage to the mother country and the Colonies?

Mr. Thomas Brassey, in an article in the *Nineteenth Century*, writes:—' Mr. Gladstone, in his contribution to the *North American Review* entitled "Kin Beyond Sea," has rightly said that "the commercial supremacy of the world must ultimately pass from the United Kingdom to the United States. The territory at their command is, in comparison with the narrow one of the United Kingdom, unlimited, and it possesses every natural advantage." To that I would ask, have we not other kin beyond sea besides those thus alluded to?—have we not "kin" in territories more unlimited, with equal, and in some cases superior, natural advantages than we find in the United States—" kin " who own the same allegiance to the same throne that we do, whose increase in wealth, especially in Australia, has been latterly in even more rapid ratio than that which our American cousins can boast of? Let the day arrive when Greater Britain is united in a commercial union, then our commercial supremacy will be assured to the mutual advantage of both the British Colonies and the mother country.'

Writing more than a generation ago, when these colonies were in their infancy, and no indications were manifested of the prospective growth on which we may now venture to rely, Mr. Porter opened the Chapter on Colonies in his 'Progress of the Nations' with these glowing words : —

'If called upon to declare what circumstance in the condition of England which, more than all other things, makes her the envy of surrounding nations, it would be to her colonial possessions that we must attribute that feeling. In the eyes of foreigners, those possessions are at once the evidence of our power, and the surest indicant of its increase.'

It is estimated that in about 21 years the population of Canada, Australasia, and the Cape will be some fifteen millions, about equal to that which the United Kingdom contained at the date of Waterloo.

Professor Fawcett, in his work on 'Free Trade and Protection,' allows that the cost of the transit of wheat falls on the importing nation, and says the effect of reducing from 6s. to 3s. of a quarter of wheat from New York to Liverpool would be, to quote his remarks, as follows :—
' If, therefore, this cost is reduced, the price of American wheat in England must be reduced by nearly an equivalent amount.' But in the question of carriage, which in such a bulky article as grain is an important factor, the advantage that must accrue to the 'consumer'

by purchasing his food from a free-trading instead of a protectionist State is even more marked. Again to take the United States as an example, we purchase from them in bulk and value nearly four times the amount they buy of us; and under the present system that ratio is more likely to increase in favour of the Americans than to diminish; for we must not lose sight of the fact that, notwithstanding the present increased demands for certain of our iron goods from the United States, *whilst their present tariff exists* (which exacts an import duty or fine of from fifty to one hundred per cent. on that product), our manufacturers will sooner or later be beaten in the American market, when their own iron works and foundries are again fully working. As stands to reason, a large number of our ships going to America to bring back cargoes of wheat have to make their outward voyage in ballast, and the shipowner has to recoup himself for this by charging higher freights for the grain he carries to England. This additional charge, as Mr. Fawcett acknowledges, falls on the consumer of the United States grain. Had we *absolute* free trade with the state or states from whom we obtain our principal food supply, we should only have to pay the rate the shipowner would expect to receive for his expenses and profits *on one journey*.

Those who argue that there is no drawing back from our present system, no other way to gain the desired end of universal free trade but a 'good example,' that however important any industry may be to a district in this country—nay, more, even if its destruction is a matter of national importance, that we are to place, as I previously remarked, its continuance entirely at the mercy of the good nature of any foreign state with whom we have large dealings, to submit it to the discriminating justice of a Spanish Cortes, or the irreproachable wisdom and uprightness of the rulers of some South American Republic, should remember that if we are only true to this all-sufficient 'good example' system, we ought to let the grass grow in the streets of Manchester and Birmingham sooner than budge an inch from it. Nothing must be done to make the other nations of the earth free-traders, no other mode of obtaining the desired end, that is, absolute freedom in the interchange of the products and labour of the different nations of the earth, is to be tolerated. Popular opinion has been led by the hard-and-fast rule so unceasingly repeated to it. Let the tariffs of every nation be not only protective, but prohibitive, and whether we find any permanent fields of employment for our labour or not, we must unswervingly maintain our present system.

No doubt some of the arguments of those who uphold this doctrine are entitled to, and they doubtless receive, serious consideration. There is one line of argument, however, which I cannot bring myself to believe is a right one, and that is their mode of taking the present position of the trade of England with one nation, proving that it would be difficult or inconvenient to make any change in our system with this particular State, and then, taking a series of States, each in detail, and saying as the one first-named has an undue advantage in a very marked degree, it would not be our interest to make a change with a country where the injury is less. They never, in fact, look on our trade relations as a whole, but first they cast their eyes invariably on the United States, and, oblivious that it would, perhaps, require a less lever than some imagine to change a system contrary to the direct interests of three-fifths of the inhabitants of the United States and the entire population of these isles, they decide that no change can be made in our present system. This Sir Louis Mallet has done in his recent pamphlet on Reciprocity. Having concluded his review on our American trade, and given *his estimate* of the goods we might tax, he proceeds to discuss the question with regard to France, and says:—' But France, it will be said, which sends us every year a value of £16,000,000 in silks and woollens, shoes, gloves, and " articles de Paris," and other finished manufactures—surely here at least we can do to others as we do not wish them to do to us. No doubt we could; but to retaliate on a country which, as a rule, taxes our imports about 20 per cent. or less, while we leave untouched a country like the United States, which taxes them double, may be good or bad policy, but it is not reciprocity.' From this he proceeds to say that it would be inexpedient to tax the products of Belgium, Holland, and Switzerland, because their import tariffs are less than France, and so on in succession, or, as he puts it, *ex uno disce omnes*.

Another argument which Sir Louis Mallet lays apparently greater stress on, and which he gives a table to prove, is that we have too much instead of too little reciprocity, and he bases this on the fact that we received more custom duties from the Americans and French in 1876-7 than we paid them. He omits to notice *the value* of the goods on which these dues were received—that whilst the seventy-seven million sterling of produce sent from the United States to these shores were only taxed at about eight per cent., the import dues charged on the 16 million of our exports, as he remarks, ' can hardly be put higher than *thirty per cent.*' Nor does it appear to strike him that the decreased sum we paid in the French Custom House was owing to the French duties checking, if not absolutely prohibiting, our imports. If the object

of his system is for us to pay little import dues because
we import very little, we shall, probably, have this sorry
consolation in the case of our trade with the German
Empire this year; but Sir Louis Mallet is entirely
mistaken when he describes this state of things as
'reciprocity.'

But, whilst in this pamphlet Sir Louis Mallet appears
to be at a loss to discover what 'Reciprocity' is, he
seems however on other occasions not only to be cogni-
sant of what it means, but to have actually suggested the
advisability of its being carried out in practice. It must
be granted, however, that he was not then addressing
theorists, but giving evidence before practical men. (I
allude to the gentlemen appointed as the select committee on the wine duties.) In the minutes of the evidence
taken before this committee, I find Sir Louis Mallet
made the following reply, in answer to a question by the
Chairman:—

'Personally, I entertain a strong opinion that if the cheap wines
could be introduced at a lower rate of duty, there would be a largely
increased consumption, and in the long run an increased revenue ;
but it is an opinion, and it would be an experiment, and therefore
it may very well be argued that unless other advantages could be
derived from such a scale of duties, it would not be worth while to
incur that possible risk. And therefore, in considering the wine
duties, I always think that it is most important, in making up one's
mind as to the rate of duty, that very distinct reference should be
had to the prospects which any such reductions might afford us of
enlarged commercial relations with the wine-growing countries.
We all know that those enlarged commercial relations can only
really be brought about by two methods. The mere reduction of
duty is itself important, and would extend, no doubt, our commercial relations if it increased our importations; *but that of itself is
only one-half the story.* It is not adequate of itself, and if in the
countries in favour of whose produce those reductions were made,
we find that the condition of their fiscal legislation, or their commercial legislation, *is such as to exclude our trade*, it appears to me
that it is most important to ascertain how far any reduction of our

wine duties *might be made the means of obtaining certain reductions of those foreign tariffs.* For my own part I should be disposed, under present circumstances, considering the peculiar position of our wine duties, *to make that an essential condition of any change in our wine duties.* It is obvious that if a foreign country prohibits our manufactures, and prohibits our produce, it is perfectly useless for us to reduce our wine duties. *If they do not take our goods we cannot take theirs.* So that it really is a very essential part of the question, in deciding the amount of duty, *to ascertain how far any reductions should be accompanied by corresponding improvements of the tariffs of the countries from which the wine would come.*'

'*If they do not take our goods we cannot take theirs,*' says Sir Louis Mallet, whilst M. Augustus Mongredien maintains '*that the increased excess of our imports over our exports is a sign of our wealth.*' In that statement he appears to me correct to this extent, it is a sign of our *possessing* large stores of realized wealth, such as, for instance, American bonds, but it is also a sign that we are *spending* our wealth, and not, as every progressive State should, *adding* to it. For were this dogma a correct one, a bad harvest would be a gain to this country, instead of being an undoubted loss. As I understand Free Trade, or at least the system Adam Smith advocated under that name, it is the mutual and reciprocal interchange of those commodities for which each nation on the earth has the greatest natural or acquired facilities of production and of manufacture. Now, was Mr. Gladstone advocating Free Trade or Protection when he said to the *farmers* of Mid-Lothian, ' Bring reciprocity into play, and then, if the reciprocity doctors are right, the Americans will knock off all their protective duties, and the American farmer, instead of producing, as he does now, under a disadvantage—a heavy disadvantage—by having to pay protective prices for everything that constitutes his farming stock, will have all his tools, implements, manures, and everything else purchased *in the free and open market of the world* at free trade prices, and he will be able to produce his corn and compete with you a great deal cheaper than he does now.' Strange language for a Free Trader! If I mistake not, 'the free and open market' of the world in this case would practically apply to the 'free and open market' of this, to use Mr. Gladstone's designation, 'small little island.' The American would purchase his plough cheaper, and we our corn; we should each gain by this exchange, and if reciprocity would do this, it would indeed give us Free Trade.

Again, a writer in an article in 1879 in *Macmillan* incidentally remarked that our present system is like 'a new revelation,' in fact, that it has made some amongst us think this nation 'the chosen of heaven.' Do we want to shut ourselves within our own borders? and if so, who will then feed us? If not, what on earth are we to do? I confess questions like these puzzle me much. It does not appear whether the writer included by the words 'our own borders' England, Great Britain, or the more extended 'borders' of the British Empire. At one time—not so long ago—these words would only have conveyed the idea of the limit of one English county; and we can scarcely have forgotten that the word 'borders' had a very limited sense both in Italy and Germany before the formation of the Italian Kingdom and the German Empire; nor can it have faded from the recollection of all English travellers the annoyance the interminable inspection of luggage at the various Custom Houses in these countries subjected them to.

The only 'borders' that the gradual extension of a Free Trade Zollverein (inaugurated, if possible, by the majority of States forming the British Empire) would hope ultimately to enclose would be every civilized State in the world, although there may be reasons that might render it inexpedient for a country to give a free trade import tariff to a nation giving free trade, or, in the contrary case, a relatively higher one; it appears to me an unfair description to designate this a policy of 'retaliation;' and those who argue thus appear to hold a certain Trades Unionists' fallacy.

Let me put the case thus :—A master goldsmith has two workmen in his shop: one executes his work both skilfully and quickly, and the goldsmith makes large profits by the sale of his highly finished workmanship; the other is slower and less skilful—would it be called a policy of 'retaliation' if the goldsmith gave the former higher wages than the latter? In like manner, would not the country gain more by having dealings with a Free Trade instead of a Protectionist State; and, therefore, should we not be justified in giving the former certain advantages to induce them to be free traders?

The great question, therefore, resolves itself into this: how are we to induce the British Colonies and the nations of the earth to become free traders? for at present, with the exception of New South Wales, there is not a single colony that can be so described. Certain Crown Colonies, such as Ceylon, Hong Kong, and the Straits Settlements, have had free trade tariffs allotted to them. So that after thirty years' trial of our present system this 'chosen nation of heaven' has only been able to induce one State (viz., New South Wales) to voluntarily follow its good example. It would be a better example if we could show the foreign nations the whole British Empire formed into a Free Trade Union, and one more likely to make them become free traders.

Now, to avoid any mistaken view of my suggestions, I am perfectly aware of the bearings of our old colonial system, and also conversant with the objections that have been urged against it, nor do I at all wish to see that system renewed. It appears beyond doubt that at some future date we shall have to discuss whether we may not have to treat a British colony or a foreign country according as it chose to enrol itself in the one class or the other as being free trading or protectionist, whilst giving to all the option to permit them to import goods to us under a free trade tariff if they *at any time* choose to give us like advantages.

The *sole* motive power to induce the Legislatures of the different colonies to become free traders would be the discovery that it was for their own individual interests to be so. So it must be clearly understood that every word I here write, pointing out the advantages of a free trade system in contradistinction to a free import trade system between ourselves and our colonies, *applies with equal force to all the nations of the earth.* I do not lay claim to any originality in this idea. Adam Smith pointed out the advantages of free trade between the British possessions. In Vol. II. of his 'Wealth of Nations'* we find the following :—

'The most perfect freedom of trade is permitted between the British colonies in America and the West Indies. These colonies are now become so populous and thriving that each of them finds in some of the others a great and extensive market for every part of its produce. All of them taken together make a *great internal market* for the produce of one another;' and again he advocates the advantages which the encouragement of this system would give to the empire.

* Vol. II., page 486, Edition 1828.

'The freedom of interior commerce, the effect of the uniformity of the system of taxation, is perhaps one of the principal causes of the prosperity of Great Britain, every great country being necessarily the best and most extensive market for the greater part of the production of its own industry. If the same freedom in consequence of the same uniformity could be extended to Ireland and the Plantations, both the grandeur of the state and the prosperity of every part of the empire would probably be still greater than at present.' And it would seem to me difficult to controvert the following argument :—

'If it be found practicable to unite the whole British Empire for commercial relations, why keep them apart? for what more logical reason should they be dissevered than Wales or Ireland? Why not have tolls taken on the border of every county in Great Britain to protect the interior trade of each county?' Our colonies and dependencies have lately shown that in case of war not only are they aware that they must necessarily be affected by any danger which might threaten the British nation, but both India and Canada have shown they were ready to aid us with troops for general service. Why, if our interests are thus united in case of war, should they not be equally so in time of peace, and consistently with our mutual interests throw as much of the trade of both mother country and colonies in each other's hands as possible? It would be as much for the interests of the colonies to gain a larger proportion of our trade than they have at present as it would be for the interests of the mother country. Never will the trade increase greatly on either hand till equally free reciprocal trade is established all over the Empire, trade as free as it is from Kent to Lancashire.

Not only would these advantages accrue to the British

Colonies, but to any free trade nation. Thus the trade of the British Empire and of those nations that joined the Free Trade Union would be as an open market where all could buy what they pleased, or sell what they could, without any undue restriction of tax or impost.

To sum up these suggestions, the mode which would seem the only practical one for us to arrive at the desired goal, namely, *universal free trade*, I submit the following propositions:—

1. That for the purposes of trade the *whole Empire* ought to be *as one nation*. 2. That the loss of that trade to a nation with a protective tariff would be virtually the loss of the free trade with the British Empire, that is to say, with *one-third of the trading community of the world*. 3. That if other foreign nations joined the Free Trade Union, as they probably would, the loss to a protective nation of their outlet for trade would be *even greater*. 4. That the only force required to make the nations free traders is to make it their *interest to be so*.

What do we find to be the relative importance of our trade to the British Colonies and dependencies as compared with the rest of the world? In 1878 it appears to have been nearly one-fourth of our total imports, and one-third of our exports. The total volume of our trade with British possessions was about 150 millions sterling: 52 millions of this, we find, was our trade with India; 42 millions with Australia; about 17 millions with Canada; whilst with South Africa our commerce was to the value of 10, and Hong Kong 4 millions sterling. This gives, I am well aware, but a bare outline of the vast and ever-increasing commercial relations of this country and her colonies. How great they are, and how deeply rooted in our national existence, perhaps it would be difficult to realise. That there

is in these colonies a vast amount of friendly sentiment
towards the old country and loyalty to the Crown we are all
aware, and that there is here a deep feeling of sympathy
towards the Colonies is beyond doubt. But that either
we perfectly understand them or that they understand
us appears very doubtful; we have no means of acquiring
any information of their real prospects and in what
manner our mutual interests might both be equally
advanced, except, perhaps, from an occasional newspaper
report, a book of travels—often a mixture of facts and
fiction—and the Governor's report in a Blue Book, the
latter crammed full of 'facts,' though sometimes of a
dreary but perfectly useless description, such as the number
of tombstones erected in a given number of years, and their
average cost reduced to decimals, together with the
average height and width of the sign-posts in his Excellency's Colonial Governorship, and how many of them
per cent. per annum on the average are blown down.

It has often struck the writer of this work—and I
believe I am not singular in that respect—that if it were
practicable it would be well if there was some consultative
body in this country either in the form of a colonial
council or some other institution kindred to our present
Indian Council, to give, if required, advice and assistance to either the Colonial or Foreign Secretary of
State on matters connected with the colonies. To lightly
sketch some suggestions on this subject, the number
of such a council might be about twenty members, one-fourth of whom could be appointed by the Government
to represent the Crown Colonies, their duties being
those of a Parliamentary Committee sitting *en permenance*,
to investigate and report to the home and colonial
authorities on any question affecting our colonial possessions either with regard to their military resources,

their agriculture, their requirements as to emigrants, and the advantages they could offer them. The question of a greater union in our trade interests and a general tariff might be brought before their notice in order to report on the subject to the Imperial and Colonial Parliaments. That their opinion on this important topic would result in unanimity is more, I fear, than one can at present expect; but that its outcome might be to cause some other colonies besides New South Wales to give us reciprocal terms in our trade is, I trust, not beyond the bounds of possibility, more particularly if in the mutual interchange of a free trade tariff England did not come empty-handed—but could give her Colonies a *quid pro quo*.

Nor can I altogether ignore an idea which many would wish to see realized, an idea I grant Utopian at present, but if ever realized, one which would not fail to have important and I believe very beneficial effects on both Great Britain and her colonies, and that is the representation of every part of the Empire in the Imperial Parliament. We should then, were this ever carried out, by unanimous consent form ourselves into a mighty Bund circling the world, with commerce flowing and returning from Great Britain and every British possession, giving increased vitality to every part, as the blood gives life by flowing through the whole human system, for trade is the lifeblood of an Anglo-Saxon community, and railways are its arteries.

But whether with this federation of the separate States owing allegiance to the British Crown, or whether before that day arrives, I trust that the time may not be far distant when we shall as an Empire be able to show the world that which we have often read of, often heard speeches made respecting, but never yet actually realized, and that is *real free trade*. As Mr. Donald Currie remarked in a speech at the United Service Institution on the resources of the Colonies:—' Time will develope this problem, and I hope unite us more and more. A common sympathy and loyalty, a thorough union in feeling and of interest will be developed, and some day in joint and cohesive, or even Federal linking, the British Empire will exhibit the solid strength of an organized force and power such as the world has not yet seen.'

This country possesses an enormous amount of *vis inertiæ*. Once we have firmly made up our minds to take a certain line, whether we find it right or wrong we stick to it on principle. But the time may arrive when we shall have to make up our minds whether our commercial system exists for the good of England or England exists to prove the correctness of the theories of certain political economists. Any one who presumes to enquire into the present condition of our trade is immediately designated as an individual imbued with the 'old, old superstition of the balance of trade!' Even at this risk I must clearly state my humble opinion that no nation, however wealthy, can go on indefinitely increasing its imports year by year whilst its exports are decreasing in inverse ratio.

Professor Fawcett seems the favourite authority whom all writers on this question seem to rely on, and they almost invariably quote this passage from his last work: —' Suppose,' says England to France, 'you give me fifteen sacks of wheat for each ton of iron that I send you, then we shall each gain five sacks of wheat in every transaction; for if you manufacture the ton of iron yourself, it would cost you as much as twenty sacks of wheat, whereas you only have to give me fifteen sacks. On the other hand, I should only be able to get ten sacks of wheat for a ton of iron, if I sold the iron in my own country. We therefore each of us obtain a profit upon the transaction, which is represented in value by five sacks of wheat.'

Professor Fawcett, in this supposed transaction, takes for granted that which is unfortunately contrary to fact, namely, that each country permits the free importation of corn and iron without any import duty. The Frenchman truly gains the five sacks of wheat, but the Englishman only gains the proportion of the five sacks which is not deducted from his profits by the French Custom-house authorities in the shape of import dues *for permission to sell his manufactured iron*. Professor Fawcett has wisely chosen our iron trade with France to illustrate this proposition, as this happens to be the least taxed manufactured commodity in their import tariff. Thin sheet iron is, however, charged 4s. a cwt. and steel wire 8s. 2d. a cwt. import dues.

If, instead of the present equal system by which letters posted to England from France, or to France from England, are charged precisely the same, an arrangement having been come to by both countries, we had decided that so long as letters would be received cheaply from France, say for the present sum—2½d., it mattered nothing what we paid to write to that country for each letter, and the present charge for an equivalent weight of letter was 4d. on our sending it to France, the total cost of a French and English merchant exchanging letters would then be 6½d., instead of under the present well-arranged system 5d. Even acknowledging that the increased postage would have to come out of Frenchmen's pockets, which I consider is contrary to the actual fact, can our free import traders allege that it is any direct advantage to us that a nation with whom we

have commercial relations should have to pay more than
the actual cost of carriage for the receipt of their letters?
If we have carefully and judiciously made reciprocal
arrangements with the French in the comparatively
small matter of the receipt of letters to and from our respective shores, why, may I enquire, cannot we find statesmen in this country to take equal care of our commercial
interests?

Others of Professor Fawcett's followers have decided
that the cause of the recent depression of trade for
several years past was the 'undue extension' of manufacture. That is assuredly a remarkable change of front,
when we call to mind that when the paper manufacturers
protested to Lord Palmerston that the French treaty
would ruin their paper trade, they were told to increase
their production and cheapen their manufacture. They
did so; and this advice was universally followed. English
labour was diverted from the plough, and from the
natural flow of colonization—the opening out of the
boundless resources of our colonies. It was publicly
proclaimed that the mission of the Anglo-Saxon race
was to spin cotton goods, and to manufacture cheap
cutlery for the whole world. And now they actually turn
round on our manufacturers for having too literally
followed their advice, and say : Illimitable expansion has
become a creed; we have built too many factories,
opened up too many mines, erected too many blast
furnaces, built too many ships.

One also finds ' extravagance' set down in an article
in *Macmillan* by Mr. Ryder as one of the causes of the present lack of prosperity in some branches of England's
commerce. We are told that London is too big, that
large as it is it does not appear to be entirely a workshop, forgetting that London occupies in England's trade

the same position as the 'office' and the 'warehouse' does in a manufactory. Respecting this alleged extravagance, which is laid to the doors of our merchants and manufacturers, I believe it to be in a great measure the outcome of the present system, which causes by its very uncertainty sudden periods of prosperous trade, or the reverse. If the manufacturer felt that foreign nations dare not put on arbitrarily protective tariffs from the certainty that by so doing they would be excluded from the Free Trade Zollverein, he would feel confident of always having a *steady* demand for his produce. This *confidence* would not only conduce to his striving to attain excellence in his manufactures, knowing that his sale of them would be permanent, but also would conduce to *cheapness*, as the very fact of this confidence would multiply competition amongst the manufacturers of the countries who had a free trade interchange. This steady, regular flow of trade would, besides, have, of course, a great tendency to prevent periods of inflation and depression in trade.

The position of our trade at present is very much like a stream that has been dammed up when suddenly the pressure becoming great it bursts, and the waters, surmounting the barriers, rush from their artificial restraint. So do our exports during times of inflation. The stream afterwards resumes its natural level, and a fresh dam is constructed as we find higher protective duties are now placed on our exports.* And again, like this stream our commerce becomes restricted and forced back, or, as we call it, depressed. Better would it seem to encourage some system by which, as far as one could see, there would not only be *a steady* but also an *increasing* volume of imports and exports to and from this country,

* See Appendices 1 and 2, German and Canadian tariffs.

and by which our manufacturers would have some guarantee for fixity of tenure in their honourable industries. Nor should we then hear so much said about the manufacturer starting his 'coach' and the miner drinking his 'champagne' when trade was more than ordinarily prosperous. The writer quoted above is especially vehement in his strictures on the Stock Exchange, which appears to have been in his mind partly the cause of destroying our commercial activity. Be that as it may, how can its members be considered more blame-worthy than those who employ them?

One thing which I believe has had a far more detrimental effect on our trade of late years than those above referred to has been the number of hopeless 'strikes' which the trades unions have forced the workmen into undertaking. It is simply striving against fate to attempt to maintain a rate of wages higher than the market price of the produce manufactured will warrant. In fact, as a general rule, it might almost be said that there is an axiom which, if carried out, would have saved this country many millions sterling and the workmen much needless privation, and that is, don't 'strike' on a falling market; and it almost appears that the unionists opposition to the giving a man the right to exercise and receive a reward for his superior skill, is a mistaken policy. Mr. Brassey, in the article previously referred to, reminds one of Tuigot's famous preamble to the edict of 1776, by which Louis the Sixteenth suppressed the guilds and monopolies established by Colbert, and the freedom of labour was asserted in these memorable words :—

'When God created man, a being with many' wants, and compelled to labour for his livelihood, he gave to every individual the right to labour; *and that right is his most sacred possession.* We consider that it is the first duty which justice requires us to discharge, to set free our subjects from all restrictions imposed on that indefeasible right of man—restrictions which deprive industry of the incentives derived from emulation, and render talents useless.'

The report of the recent French Commission on the condition of the working classes concludes with a similar declaration.

There has been in use in the Durham and West Cumberland coal trade, and amongst the iron miners and blast furnacemen of Cleveland, a system for regulating the rate of wages which has certain great advantages. I allude to the mechanical determination of the rate of wages by 'sliding scales.' Under this arrangement, according to the rise or fall in price of the commodity on which the labour is expended, so is the rate of that labour remunerated. This appears a fair and just basis by which the rate of wages should be regulated, for it seems incontrovertible that the employé should receive his fair share of the prosperity or the reverse of the work in which he is engaged. The great difficulty is the basis on which this sliding scale is framed, for none can doubt that in any arrangement of this description great care must be exercised that the interests of both the employer and the employé should be equally jealously guarded. This method cannot lay claim to be a scientific or even an exact system in determining the value of labour, but it is a rough-and-ready mode of so doing, based usually upon the experience of trades for many years. It has its disadvantages, chief of which is its want of flexibility, there being, as we are aware, from time to time, changes in the costs of production of many articles other than that of the price of labour merely, and these naturally affect the price the employer can afford to pay for that labour. In the coal trade the cost of labour—or rather, I should say, *the proportionate cost of labour*—remains tolerably constant. One of the most eminent coal owners in the Wigan district stated, for instance, at the time of the Coal Commission, that the cost of hewing in that district was one-fifth of the total cost of bringing coal to the pit's mouth. One advantage this system undoubtedly has when carried out is, that it prevents strikes, whilst combinations amongst the employers or the employed are not interfered with.*

---

* The following is an American view of the British workman, extracted from the *British Trade Journal* November, 1879:—

'Thus far the British working man would seem to have believed that the British manufacturer sought a reduction of his wages in mere hostility to labour, not being capable, it would appear, to look beyond the narrow circle of his own interest to the broader fact that the manufacturer has sacrificed much already for British pride, and, to his honour be it noted, for the interest of the workman, in running his establishment *often at a loss rather than cease manufacturing altogether.*

'*A few years more of strikes and disorganization in England, and it may be doubted whether any compromise between the employers and the employés will restore to that country her manufacturing supremacy.* As capital will not remain idle, nor permanently in unprofitable investments, it may be expected that English capitalists will seek new fields for investment, *such as the transfer of the cotton manufacture to India,* which may be said to have already begun.

'There can scarcely be a doubt that within the next five years 500,000 of English working men will emigrate. Indeed, should the spirit of emigration once seize the English mind, there can be no reasonable limit set to the hegira. That the greater number of these emigrants will seek "work and bread" in the United States may be fairly assumed. We (in the United States) have, therefore, more interest in those people than even their own Government: they are Englishmen to-day, in ten years they will be American citizens. That they are as good material in physique, in pluck, and as working men as Europe has ever driven hither is undeniable, and if they will only rise up to the height of their new and more favourable surroundings, *leave their trade unions and strikes behind them, as well as their ruined manufactures,* and fall into the ranks of the American working men proper, they will be a strength and an addition to our country.'

But, if I may suggest it, is not it time for the followers of Mr. Cobden, who have posed before the world as the great reformers of commercial systems, to leave off abusing those who suggest a method of arriving at Free Trade, not exactly coinciding with their own preconceived notions, who advocate, for instance, reciprocity, that is, *equal advantages in commercial interchange* as a stepping-stone to the desired end? Is it not time to cast away their defensive armour of vituperation, and to show us how they intend to preserve our mutual interchange of commodities with foreign nations? For we all agree in this, that it cannot fail to have a detrimental effect on English commerce, that Italy in 1878 *revised* her tariff, and that Germany and Canada have this year passed Protectionist tariffs. The question that it might be equally useful to this country that they should discuss, is not to sneeringly enquire what is Reciprocity, but in what manner can we continue to have regular outlets for our commerce?

There are also a certain number, particularly in the sister isle, who appear to consider the primary cause of any distress in this country, whether in the agricultural or manufacturing interests, is caused by their old enemies, 'the landlord and rent.' They consider the former as a class apart—as having no interests with the rest of the nation. These views appear inconsistent with the actual facts of the case.

Let us, then, closely examine the question, and see what rent really is. Rent, I take it, is nothing after all but the interest one man receives from another for the loan of his possessions of whatever description. This rent falls or rises according to the surplus of profit these possessions give in a series of years to the borrower, and in this respect the agricultural and manufacturing trades are not divergent interests, but are inseparably bound up in one another's prosperity or the reverse; they are, in fact, but *one trade* containing two classes. To begin *ab initio*, supposing two brothers were to start for Australia from this country, the one deciding to become a manufacturer, the other turning his attention to agriculture. Both of them work hard and prosper— the former is able to build a large cotton mill, and the latter, having built a farm house, cleared and drained a certain portion of his land, constructed farm buildings, and fenced in large cattle runs, finds that soon after he has completely settled in his new home a small town springs up in his vicinity. As this town prospers, so does he in having an available and easily come-at-able market for his goods. The market value of his farm then increases. The town is also the gainer by the fact of having at its doors the food products it requires. Should this town decay for any reason, his farm would also decrease in value. Should, however, any increased facilities and cheapness of locomotion be obtained by this town—such as, for instance, the construction of a railway, and enable farmers at a greater distance to compete with his produce, the price of his dairy and other stock, and also the market value of his farm, would fall, unless the demands of the town increased in proportion to the increased supply of food. This is the exact case in point at present as between the English and American farmers, the latter of whom enjoy increased facilities and cheapness of transit. Let us further suppose that after a time both of these men desire to retire from their respective avocations, and live at Melbourne. They advertise their properties and obtain tenants, the one receiving £1,000 a year for the rent of the mill, and the other £1,000 a year for the rent of the farm. These captious critics would not grudge the millowner the rent of his manufactory, but would object to the *rent* received by the owner of the farm. That the agricultural interests of this country are not the cause of the condition of our trade for the past few years, although they have been amongst the chief sufferers by it, is abundantly shown from the following fact, that wheat during the winter of 1878-9 was 15s. a quarter lower than it was in the previous winter. The fact yet is that the land in this country has to bear directly and indirectly probably more than its fair share of taxation. Should any change be made in our import tariffs, I need hardly say that it is apparent that under no circumstances that one can foresee will it be our policy to revert to taxation on the importation of grain. Now this would be, on the face of it, an injustice to the agricultural trade of this country. As Mr. Hunter Rodwell, Q.C., in his pamphlet on Reciprocity considered with a view to its effects on the agricultural interest, justly remarks:—

'The experiment of doing away with protection was first made not upon the least, but upon the most important body in the country, the experiences of it are too well known by the sufferers;' and again he says:—

'The greatest and most important industry in this great country has for thirty years struggled against the keenest competition; the last rag of protection having been rudely torn away to gratify some sentimental crotchet of Mr. Robert Lowe, by whose whim some millions of money have been lost to the Exchequer.' He also contends that it would be unfair to impose duties on the manufactured produce of foreign nations should an equally reciprocal tariff be denied to the bread stuffs and cattle of the United Kingdom. He starts on the assumption that the farmer would have to pay increased prices for his purchases, from a mouse trap to a steam cultivator. Now, I maintain an increased duty on manufactures *in this country* would not permanently increase prices, for we are a nation who could manufacture if we chose all we required for home consumption—we could, in fact, double our manufactories. Competition at home would bring down prices to even below their present level; but as regards grain and cattle, from the natural limits of Great Britain we are practically unable to increase our food supply to meet our present and probable future wants; therefore, with an import duty their price would inevitably become dearer. The farmer would not have permanently to pay a fraction more for his plough or the labourer for his smock frock, though there might be a slight rise in some commodities at first. Prices, however, in manufactured goods in this country would find their *natural level within a year* after any change in our tariff. Middlesborough, Stockton, Darlington, West Hartlepool, Birmingham, and Staffordshire generally would, in their competition one with the other, soon beat prices down. But even granting that no rise in prices were to occur, the manufacturing interest have a marked advantage in this country over the agricultural in respect to the amount of taxation levied on the latter, 'land' in England being doubly taxed in proportion to any other species of property, 'land' has mostly to support the Church, pay for the roads, build asylums, workhouses, prisons, &c. It would, therefore, be but justice to the agricultural interest, presuming we were forced into making any change in our fiscal system, that half *the amount of the increased custom receipts* caused by any revision in our import tariff should be taken off *the direct taxation on land*. By that amount could the landowner reduce his rent and thus enable the farmer to compete with success with produce grown in less highly taxed countries.

Mr. Gladstone gave, last November, the following consolation to the farmers of Great Britain, and said if they found their products undersold by the farmers of the Western States of America, their case was no worse than the farmers in the Eastern territories of the United States. He failed to notice that in the American continent, as within the borders of the United Kingdom, there is absolute free trade, and that each portion of the United States adds to the wealth and prosperity of the 'Union;' that the movement of wealth and population from one side of the United States to the other makes no more material difference to the aggregate wealth of that republic than any temporary displacement of wealth from one English county to another would make to the general material prosperity of the United Kingdom.

Like nearly every Englishman of the present day, I am strongly adverse to protective tariffs *per se*. If we cannot, by any other means, obtain Free Trade, we shall have, however, to revert to that step we jumped over in our eager desire to obtain the desired end. We shall have to revert to the step we left out, namely, ' Reciprocity,' and bear in mind that if an English merchant buys a bale of cotton from an American it is not to prove a theory, but because he deems it is for his self-interest so to do. As with an individual, so it is with a nation—and we shall have some day or other to decide whether we can always give foreign nations the power to exclude our goods they now possess.

The keystone to the arch of our future greatness is

to my mind a federation of the whole British Empire linked together in commercial, social, and political interests. Whether such a result will ever be consummated or not is what the future alone can decide. Mr. Kerry Nicholls, speaking on this point during a discussion at the Royal Colonial Institute, after describing England's colonial possessions as bidding fair to outrival the mother country in population and greatness, said :—

'Although the colonies were called dependencies of the Crown, it must be conceded that there was very little spirit of dependence amongst the colonists themselves. Responsible government, the sentiment of nationality which had sprung up with it, and other causes, had taught them to know their political and material strength and importance ; and whilst he believed they would hail with readiness, nay even with pride, any form of Imperial federation in which their interests would be fairly represented, he was sure they would stand firmly aloof from any scheme of Imperial federation in which they could not enjoy relatively the same privilege with ourselves. The colonists, mindful of the important position they had acquired for themselves in the world, would be apt to look upon Imperial federation in a very matter-of-fact way. They would say, *cui bono ?* and if arguing the point with the mother country they might justly add, " You gave birth to us, you nursed us when in our swaddling clothes, you sent us to school in our own parliaments to learn how to govern ourselves, and now that we have attained our majority and are likely to cut a big figure in the world, you talk about Imperial federation, and ask us to enter into a bond of eternal fellowship." Recognising, as we must, the great political and commercial eminence to which the colonies had attained, it seemed clear to his mind that any form of Imperial federation must be based upon measures of equality, and assimilated as near as possible to our present constitution and form of government. In other words, if we invited the colonies to enter into an Imperial federation, we must meet them as near as circumstances would allow upon an equal footing, and extend to them relatively the same constitutional privileges with ourselves. We could not at this late stage say to the colonies, "You shall do this," nor could the colonies say to us, "You shall do the other." There must be an equal, voluntary, and conjoint action on the part of the mother country and the colonies, and community of commercial interest in time of peace, and a firm and united action in time of war, must form the principal links in the great bond of union.' If that day should ever arrive, England would not have to feel grateful to the inhabitants of the United States for occasionally purchasing some of her iron, on which product they only levy a duty of from sixty to one hundred per cent.

It is not at present the privilege of any one party of the State to strive to see us united to our colonies in at any rate community of interest, and it appears to me that were we all bound together as an Empire in a Free Trade compact, commercially speaking our 'community of interest' would be complete. About the middle of last February, at a banquet given by the Reform Club to the Earl of Dufferin, Earl Granville said*—'Now, may I say one word with regard to our relations with our colonies ? The noble Marquis near me (Lord Hartington), I thought expressed admirably well at Edinburgh the other day, the Liberal policy

* From the *Observer*, February 23, 1879.

with regard to our colonies when he said that the connection was not one of mere obligation, but it must rest upon a community of interest and feeling. I believe there is not one of us here who would consent, even if the attempt were possible, to enforce with restraints any connection between ourselves and the great self-governing dependencies of Her Majesty.'

Judging from the speeches one sees reported, I think I am not wrong in saying that in that speech Earl Granville expressed equally the sentiments of the Conservative party. Nearly every Englishman takes a deep interest in the colonies, and one cannot fail to be aware that the feeling of the colonists is, as a rule, equally at one with the mother country. Were we drawn together with our colonies in the bonds of a Free Trade union, it would conduce not only to cement the British Empire, to give both to them and to us commercial prosperity, but to more firmly unite us in mutuality of interests and hopes, and to increase in this country the sentiments so well expressed by the Earl of Dufferin. On the occasion just referred to he said :—' Your presence here to-night under such auspices as these is a proof, and as such it will be taken in Canada, of the interest, of the affection, of the good-will felt by some ot the most distinguished and influential public men in England in the future destinies not only of Canada, but of every other colony of Great Britain.'

I will now bring this work to a conclusion, with the hope that whether my readers are able to agree with my arguments or not, I have not wearied them in the discussion of this necessarily rather dry subject. I must also wish to disclaim any such intention as that which Professor Fawcett attributes to those who advocate an enquiry into our system of trade. I neither wish by any suggestion here submitted to retaliate on the Americans, or to injure the French; and in this work my only wish is, that whatever our statesmen decide will tend to preserve a steady, continuous, and increasing flow in the trade of this country, and also in that of the mighty and wide-spread Empire over which Her Majesty reigns.

APPENDICES.

APPENDIX I.

GERMAN TARIFF (PAST AND PRESENT).

(Which came in full force January 1st, 1880).

Table shewing the present and past Import Duties charged in the Empire of Germany, on the principal Articles of Produce or Manufacture of the United Kingdom, viz., Cotton, Hardware, Leather, Linen, Machinery, Metals, Oil, Silk, and Wool,

[The duty, when not otherwise stated, is per 100 kilog. 1 Reichsmark of 100 pfennige=1 shilling].

Description of Articles.	(Duties.) Present (1880) Mk. pf.	Past. Mk. pf.
I COTTON GOODS—		
(a) Cotton, raw, carded, combed, and dyed	..	..
(b) Cotton wadding	1 50	,,
(c) Cotton yarn, unmixed or mixed with linen, silk, wool, or other vegetable or animal material—		
1. Single twist, raw, up to No. 17 English	12 00	
From No. 17 to 45	18 00	
From No. 45 to 60	24 00	12 00
From No. 60 to 79	30 00	
Above No. 79	36 00	
2. Double twist, raw, up to No. 17	15 00	
From No. 17 to 45	21 00	
From No. 45 to 60	27 00	12 00
From No. 60 to 79	33 00	
Above No. 79	39 00	
3. Single or double twist, bleached or dyed, up to No. 17 English	24 00	
From No. 17 to 45	30 00	
From No. 45 to 60	36 00	24 00
From No. 60 to 79	42 00	
Above No. 79	48 00	
4. Treble or more twist, raw, bleached, or dyed	48 00	
5. Twisted sewing thread	70 00	36 00
6. Wicks, not woven	24 00	
(d) Goods of cotton alone, or with metal threads, without mixture of silk or wool—		
1. Raw close textures, except velvets; tulle raw, not patterned	80 00	60 00
2. Bleached, close-woven, dressed, except velvets	100 00	
3. All close-woven textures not included under Nos. 2 and 6; raw open textures, with the exception of window curtains, hosiery, fringes, and button goods; also twist, combined with metal thread	120 00	96 00
4. Window curtains	230 00	

APPENDIX I.—*Continued.*

Description of Articles.	Duties Present (1880) Mk. pf.	Past. Mk. pf.
5. Jaconet, muslin, tulle, marley, gauze, not comprised in 1, 3, and 4..	200 00	156 00
6. Lace and embroidery	250 00	
Cotton fishing nets ..	12 00	3 00
Very coarse textures, made from cotton waste, &c...	10 00	
Emery cloth, and raw cotton cloth for manufacture of emery cloth	Free	Free
II. HARDWARE—		
(a) Goods wholly or in part made with precious metals, pearls, &c., and watches; gold and silver leaf ..	600 00	300 00
(b) 1. Wares wholly or in parts of amber, celluloid ivory, agate, jet, lava, meerschaum, mother-of-pearl and tortoise shell; of base metal, gilt or silvered, or dipped in gold and silver; teeth, in combination with wires or tubes of platinum, &c...	..	..
2. Fine fancy and small wares	200 00	..
III. LEATHER—		
(a) Leather, undyed; Russian leather, dyed; parchment, &c.	18 00	12 00
(b) Sole leather, Belgian and Danish glove kid, Morocco and dyed lacquered leather, not under (a)	36 00	30 00
Note—Half dressed kid, tanned but undyed goat and Sheep kid..	3 00	..
(c) Coarse saddler's, shoemaker's, strapmakers' goods, and other coarse leather stuffs	50 00	24 00
(d) Fine leather goods, Cordova, Morocco, Belgian, and Danish leather, fine shoes, &c..	70 00	42 00
Note to (c) and (d)—Coarse shoemaker's wares of grey packing or sailcloth; wares of oilcloth, &c., will be treated as fine leather wares.		
(e) Gloves ..	100 00	80 00
IV LINEN AND JUTE—		
(a) Yarn not named under (b)—		
1. Up to No. 5 English..	3 00	
2. Over No. 5 English, and up to No. 8	5 00	
3. „ 8 „ „ 20	6 00	3 00
4. „ 20 „ „ 35	9 00	
5. „ 35 ..	12 00	
Note to (a)—Jute, Manilla hemp, and cocoa fibre, raw, washed, broken or heckled	Free	..
(b) Dyed, printed, bleached yarns—		
1. To 20 English..	12 00	
2. 20 to 35 ditto ..	15 00	10 00
3. Over 35 ditto ..	20 00	
(c) Thread of every kind	36 00	24 00
(d) Ropemakers' wares, unbleached; bleached ropes, cables, cord, girths, bands, and hose; coarse undyed carpets of Manilla hemp, cocoa, jute, and similar fibres	6 00	3 00

APPENDIX I.—*Continued.* 427

Description of Articles.	Duties. Present (1880) Mk. pf.	Past. Mk. pf.
(e) Linen, diaper, ticking, undyed, not printed or bleached—		
1. Up to 16 threads in warp and weft together, in a square of 4 centimetres	6 00	
2. Up to 40 threads in warp and weft, on a square of 4 centimetres; fine and dyed carpets of Manilla hemp, cocoa, jute, and other fibres	12 00	24 00
3. 41 to 80 threads ditto ditto; also ropemakers' wares dyed and bleached, except goods under (d)	24 00	
4. 81 to 120 threads ditto ditto	36 00	
5. With more than 120 threads ditto	60 00	
(f) Linen, diaper, ticking, dyed, printed, bleached; also woven with dyed, printed, and bleached yarns—		
1. Up to 120 threads in woof and weft, in a square of 4 centimetres	60 00	
2. With more than 120 threads ditto	120 00	
(g) Damask of all kinds, tablecloths, bed linen, and towelling, and linen jackets	60 00	60 00
(h) Ribands, edging, fringes, gauze, woven corner cloths, cord, embroidery, hosiery, yarns, and other wares, in combination with metal threads	100 00	
(i) Thread lace	600 00	240 00
V MACHINERY AND INSTRUMENTS—		
(a) Instruments, irrespective of the material of which they are made—		
Musical	30 00	12 00
Astronomical, surgical, mathematical	Free	Free
(b) Machinery—		
(1.) Locomotives, traction engines, locomobiles	8 00	,,
(2.) Others, chiefly of wood	3 00	,,
,, of cast iron	3 00	,,
,, of wrought iron	5 00	,,
,, of other metals	8 00	8 00
Cards and card mountings	36 00	36 00
Boilers and engines for ships built in Germany	Free	Free
Note to (b)—		
1 and 2. Steam engines and boilers to be used in ship-building	,,	,,
(c) Carriages and sleighs—		
1. Railway carriages—		
(a.) Unfitted	6 per cent. ad val.	6 per cent
(b.) Others	10 p.c. ad val.	10 p.c.
2. Other carriages and sleighs ..Each..	150 00	150 00
3. Sea and river boats	Free	Free
VI. METALS:—(IRON, LEAD, TIN)—		
Iron and manufactures of iron—		
(a.) Pig, scrap, and all other kinds not under No. 1	1 00	Free

APPENDIX I.—*Continued.*

Description of Articles.	Duties. Present (1880) Mk. pf.	Past. Mk. pf.
(*b.*) Iron for the purpose of being wrought (welded iron and steel, fused iron and steel), in bars, tires, ploughshares, angle and corner iron, rails, bolts, chairs and sleepers	2 50	,,
Note to 6 (*b*)—		
1. Ingots of iron still containing slag, raw rails, ingots	1 50	,,
2. Wrought iron in bars, for the manufacture of cards by permission and under control	0 50	,,
(*c.*) Wrought iron slabs and plate—		
1. Raw	3 00	,,
2. Polished, varnished, japanned, coppered, tinned (white plate), zinked or leaded	5 00	,,
(*d.*) Wire, also coppered, tinned, zinked, leaded, polished, or varnished	3 00	,,
(*e*) Ironware—		
1. Quite coarse—		
(α) Of cast iron	2 50	. ,,
(β) Iron, rough, wrought as parts of machines, bridges, and parts of same, anchors, chains, and wire ropes, iron axles, wheels and spokes, buffers, cannon tubes, anvils screw-drivers, nails, hammers springs, skids, horse shoes, windlass, &c.	3 00	,,
(γ) Tubes rolled and drawn of wrought iron	5 00	,,
2. Coarse—		
(α) Otherwise not named, and combined with wood..	6 00	,,
(β) Ground, varnished, coppered, tinned, zinked, leaded, or enamelled, but not polished or japanned ; also skates, hammers, axes, choppers, locks, knives, scythes, &c.. ..	10 00	,,
(γ) Files, sword-blades, planing-irons, chisels, cloth-shearers, saws, gimblets, &c.	15 00	,,
Note to (*e*) 2—		
Chains and wire ropes, for towing...	Free	,,
3. Fine—		
(α) Fine cast-iron, light ornament do., polished do., artificial do. ; also of wrought iron..		
(β) Of wrought iron, polished or japanned ; knives, scissors, needles for knitting and crotchet, and all the above ; also in combination with wood and other materials, so far as not comprised in No. 20	24 00	24 00

APPENDIX I.—*Continued.*

Description of Articles.	Duties. Present (1880) Mk. pf.	Past. Mk. pf.
(γ) Needles, pens, watch-works, &c.; and fowling-pieces and guns	60 00	60 00
VII. OIL—		
(a) Oil not designated elsewhere, and grease—		
1. All sorts of oils in flasks or jars	20 00	5 00
2. Table oil, such as olive, poppy, sesame, &c., in oil	8 00	3 00
3. Olive oil in casks, methylated	Free	
4. Other liquid oil in casks	4 00	3 00
Palm and cocoa-nut oil	2 00	Free
(b) Lees, not liquid from oil manufacture; also unground	Free	,,
(c) 1. Fatty substances; pig's and goose lard	10 00	,,
2. Stearine, palmitine, paraffin, spermaceti, wax..	8 00	3 00
Blubber and train oil	3 00	3 00
Other animal fat	2 90	Free
VIII. SILK AND SILK GOODS—		
(a) Silk Cocoons; silk grege or spun, combed and waste	Free	,,
Floss silk, spun, undyed	,,	,,
(b) Silk wadding	24 00	24 00
(c) Silk and floss ditto, dyed; raw silk thread and laces	36 00	24 00
(d) Silk thread, dyed or not dyed	100 00	24 00
(e) Stuffs manufactured out of silk or floss silk	600 00	240 00
(f) All silk or floss silk goods not specified in preceding class	300 00	180 00
1. Coarse stuffs of waste yarns, like grey packing, and for use as cleaning cloths	10 00	..
IX. WOOL AND WOOLLENS (inclusive of animals hair not elsewhere specified) with goods manufactured therefrom—		
(a) Wools, raw, dyed; also hair, raw, curled, dyed and curled	Free	Free
(b) Combed wool	2 00	,,
(c) Yarn; also with other materials except cotton—		
1. Of cattle hair and wadding..	3 00	..
2. Of hard combed yarn, *e.g.*, Genappe mohair and alpaca—		
(α) Single, undyed, or dyed, double undyed	3 00	3 00
(β) Double dyed, treble dyed, or undyed..	24 00	24 00
3. Other yarns—		
(α) Raw, single	8 00	3 00
(β) Doubled..	10 00	3 00
(γ) Bleached or dyed, single	12 00	3 00
(δ) Doubled or more..	24 00	24 00
(d) Woollen goods, also in combination with cotton, linen, or metal threads—		
1. Selvage	Free	Free
2. Coarse unprinted undyed felt	3 00	,,
3. Carpets containing dyed or undyed yarn of animal hair	24 00	60 00

APPENDIX. I—*Continued*.

Description of Articles.	Duties Present (1880). Mk. pf.	Past. Mk. pf.
4. Unprinted felts, so far as not being in No. 2; unprinted felt and hosiery goods; carpets, also printed, of wool or other animal hair, except hair of oxen, or cows, or horses; also in combination with vegetable fibres and other fibres ..	100 00	120 00
5. Wares of cloth or woollen stuff, so far as they do not come under No. 7	135 00	to 150 00
6. Printed wares, in so far as they are not carpets, trimming, and button wares, plush, and yarns in conjunction with metal threads	150 00	
7. Lace, net, and embroidery, as well as shawls of three or four colours	300 00	180 00
8. Woven shawls of five or more colours ..	450 00	..

The total value of cotton goods exported in 1878 to Germany was £3,897,174; hardware, £189,779; leather, £472,651; linen, £1,197,251 machinery, £904,902; iron, wrought and unwrought, £1,485,656; oil, £500,682; silk, £308,267; wool and woollen, £4,212,572.

The German, Austrian, and Hungarian Governments are in negotiations to establish a Customs union, and it is said that the exact terms will be finally fixed at a conference to be held this year (1880). The outcome of this, it is expected, will result in very satisfactory provisions for mutual commercial intercourse between the merchants of the German and Austrian Empires.

APPENDIX II.

THE PRESENT AND PAST CANADIAN TARIFFS AND THE TRADE OF GREAT BRITAIN AND AMERICA TO THAT COUNTRY.

Statement showing the Quantity or Value of certain of the Principal Articles imported into the Dominion of Canada from Great Britain and the United States, also the Rates of Duty payable thereon under the Old and New Tariffs respectively.

Articles.	Imported in 1878 from Great Britain.	Imported in 1878 from United States.	Former Rates of Duty, per cent.	Present Rates of Duty, per cent. 1880.
Agricul. Implements dols.	9,752	132,053	17½ ad val.	25 ad val.
Animals ,,	3,084	338,015	10 ,,	20 ,,
Books, printed periodicals, pamphlets, bound, &c. ....dols.	370,069	451,436	5 ,,	6 cents per lb.
British copyright works, reprints of dols.	—	3,550	12½ ,,	{ 6 cents per lb. & 12½
Brass, manufactures of ,,	22,351	64,915	17½ ,,	30 ad val.
Rice ....lbs.	5,483,447	950,692	1 cent per lb.	1 cent per lb.
Coal, anthracite.....tons	2,582	404,389	Free	50 c. per ton
,, bituminous ... ,,	124,614	331,323	,,	,, ,,
Copper, old and scrap, in pigs, bars, rods, bolts, &c. dols.	76,338	24,195	,,	10 ad val.
,, seamless drawn tubing	1,648	5,728	17½ ad val.	,, ,,
,, other manufactures of	8,637	15,884	,, ,,	30 ad val.
Cotton, manufac. of, viz. : Grey or unbleached, and bleached sheetings, drills, ducks, cotton or Canton flannels, not stained, painted, or printed .. yds. dols.	5,372,893 431,807	7,398,741 536,793	,, ,, ,, ,,	{ 1 cent per sq.yd.and 15 ad val.
Fruit, dried .... { lbs. dols.	3,872,863 166,018	6,127,404 261,430 }	,, ,,	1 cent per lb.
oranges........ ,,	121,899	-112,315	10 ,,	20 ad val.
Fur, manufactures of ,,	129,187	67,892	17½ ,,	25 ,,
Glass, certain manufactures of ....dols.	117,544	408,443	,, ,,	20 ,,
Indiarubber, manufactures of..............dols.	56,078	192,261	,, ,,	25 ,,
Iron, and manufactures of, viz. :* Pig iron ....tons	26,174	3,913	Free	2 dols. per ton
Bars, rolled or hammered, flats, rounds, squares, &c. ....dols.	1,436,328	224,165	5 ad val.	17½ ad val.
Sugar, above 14 D.S. { lbs. dols.	47,611,106 2,530,445	40,897,269 2,484,372	{ 1 cent per lb. and 25 ad val.	1 cent per lb. and 35 ad val.
,, equal to No. 9 and not above 14 D.S. .... { lbs. dols.	5,596,962 243,026	4,039,498 207,509	{ ¾ cent per lb. and 25 ad val.	¾ cent per lb. and 30 ad val.
Tea, green and Japan { lbs. dols.	1,254,154 250,955	4,144,872 1,006,633 }	6 cents per lb.	3 c. per lb. and 10 ad val.
,, black .... { lbs. dols.	3,426,536 788,905	1,666,094 411,381 }	5 cents per lb.	2 c. per lb. and 10 ad val.
Woollen manufactures, viz.: Shawls, blankets, &c. dols.	1,433,358	113,374	17½ ad val.	{ 7½ c. per lb. & 20 ad val.

* For rails the increase of duty is from nil to 15 per cent. ad val. Tin plates, from 5 to 10 per cent. ad val.

APPENDIX III.

BRITISH EXPORT TRADE TO AUSTRALIA.

Principal articles exported from the United Kingdom to Australia.

VALUES.

	1877.	1878.	Increase or Decrease.
	£	£	*per cent.*
Apparel and haberdashery.	2,603,945	2,760,067	+ 6·0
Beer and ale - - -	487,585	453,080	− 7·1
Books, printed - -	347,821	312,878	−10·0
Cotton, piece goods -	1,442,890	1,503,555	+ 4·2
„ other manufactures.	450,413	514,521	+14·2
Hardware and cutlery -	545,008	607,408	+11·4
Hats of all sorts - -	408,974	429,629	+ 5·0
Leather wrought :—			
Boots and shoes - -	631,757	576,140	− 8·8
Linen piece goods - -	382,582	430,989	+12·6
Machinery and mill work	610,729	693,491	+13·5
Metals :—			
Iron, unwrought and wrought.	3,174,968	2,946,216	− 7·2
Paper - - - -	451,764	501,587	+11.0
Silk manufactures :—			
Mixed and unmixed -	364,321	399,616	+ 9·7
Spirits, British - -	195,523	215,819	+10·4
Woollen manufactures :—			
Cloths, coatings, &c. -	527,567	532,585	+ 0·9
Worsted stuffs - -	646,594	651,201	+ 0·7
Carpets and druggets	135,125	165,843	+22·7
All other articles - -	5,878,152	5,878,580	—
Total value - -	19,285,718	19,573,205	+ 1·5

†This table shows the value of the principal articles we exported to Australia in 1877 and 1878. A slight increase will be noticed of about £300,000, which was owing to our increased exports to New Zealand and New South Wales, Queensland and Victoria showing reduced value in the exports sent from their shores.

APPENDIX IV.

SOURCES OF OUR FOOD SUPPLY.

TABLE showing principal Articles of Food imported into the United Kingdom in 1878, distinguishing, as far as possible, those from India, the Colonies, and Foreign Countries.

LIVING ANIMALS.

Nature of Food.	India.	Colonies.	Foreign.	Countries not Specified.[1]	TOTAL.
Live Animals		62,349	1,138,499	537	1,201,385 Number.
Meat and Fish		41,467	6,903,730	50,330	6,995,527 cwts.
Grain, Meal and Flour	1,804,680	7,676,179	121,474,471	336,835	131,292,165 ,,
Rice	5,780,935		292,282	35,803	6,109,020 ,,
Butter, Cheese, and Potatoes		862,799	11,612,805	35,610	12,511,214 ,,
Total cwts.	7,585,615	8,580,445	140,283,288	458,578	156,907,926 cwts.
Tea, lbs.	35,420,059		169,015,462	437,378	204,872,899 lbs.
Coffee, cwts.	171,672	591,211	502,340	4,453	1,269,676 cwts.
Sugar, cwts.	298,141	4,763,722	14,081,547	52,476	19,195,886 ,,
Cocoa, lbs		10,711,141	7,162,869	1,104,611	18,978,621 lbs.
Total in cwts. lbs.	777,063 59	14,918,423 63	30,314,087 91	194,599 85	40,452,293 32

BRITISH AND AMERICAN CROPS.

In the *Times* of Nov. 3rd, 1879, appears an article on the crops of 1879, some portions of which cannot fail to be of permanent interest to those interested in the agricultural position of this country.

It appears that for a lengthy period up to 1871 the standard average for the United Kingdom was 29½ bushels per acre for land under wheat, but an excess of inferior harvests in the series of subsequent years down to 1879 is estimated to have lowered the mean yield by three bushels per acre, the last five years having averaged only 24 bushels, or 5½ below the standard.

The average yield of the United Kingdom, calculated on a period of many years, being, as I previously remarked, 29½ bushels per acre, yielding an average of 11,278,400 quarters, for the present year the average per acre cannot be taken at more than 18 bushels an acre, making the total 6,846,000 quarters—that is, about three-fifths of the average. This may be put as the destruction of two-fifths of the wheat harvest alone, not to speak of other losses suffered by the agriculturists this year, some of them considerable.

But from this very small total—small indeed compared with the rather indifferent series of harvests we have had lately—large deductions have to be made. As much as 855,750 quarters of it have to be reserved for seed—a reduction of only 7½ per cent. on an average crop, but of 12½ per cent., or one-eighth, on the crop of this year. This reduces the total for consumption to 5,900,000 quarters. But from this are to be made various large deductions. The greater part of the wheat is so small, shrunk, and light that it cannot enter into competion with foreign wheat.

It may not be without interest to notice the proportion in which wheat is grown in the different districts within these isles. Taking the average yields and the distribution of the wheat area together, it appears that nearly half the total wheat produce of the United Kingdom is, on an average, grown in ten English counties—namely, Lincolnshire, Yorkshire, Norfolk, Essex, Suffolk, Cambridgeshire, Devonshire, Hampshire, Sussex, and Kent. Nearly one-fourth of our wheat crop is grown in three counties—namely, Lincolnshire, Yorkshire, and Norfolk; and) considerably more than a fourth in four counties, including Essex. Lincolnshire, which heads the list of wheat-bearing provinces with a *maximum* crop of over 1,000,000 quarters, reaps and thrashes over a fourth more wheat than all Scotland and Ireland together. Each one of 12 English counties exceeds Scotland in the amount of its wheat produce; Suffolk grows nearly as much wheat as Ireland does; and Wiltshire and the whole of the Principality send about equal quantities of wheat to market. In looking at the general production of wheat in this country for the last 14 years, the annexed table will give to any one, even cursorily looking at it, a clearer and more definite idea of the years when this crop has been above or below the average than any lengthily drawn-out verbal statement:—

APPENDIX IV.—*Continued.* 435

ESTIMATED WHEAT PRODUCTION OF THE UNITED KINGDOM.

Year.	Acres.	Assumed Yield per Acre.	Bushels.	Available for consumption after deducting seed. Quarters.
1866	3,661,000	Under average	27	11,440,000
1867	3,640,000	Much under average	25	10,390,000
1868	3,951,000	Much over average	34	15,790,000
1869	3,982,000	Under average	27	12,490,000
1870	3,773,000	Over average	32	14,100,000
1871	3,831,000	Under average	27	11,970,000
1872	3,840,000	Much under average	23	10,110,000
1873	3,670,000	Much under average	25	10,550,000
1874	3,833,000	Over average	31	13,700,000
1875	3,514,000	Much under average	23	9,124,000
1876	3,124,000	Under average	27	9,665,000
1877	3,321,000	Much under average	22	9,432,000
1878	3,382,000	Over average	30	11,825,000
1879	3,056,000	Much under average	18	5,990,000
Average of 14 years	3,612,000	Mean of 14 years	26¼	11,134,000
Standard produce	3,612,000	22 bushels per acre		12,053,000

It will be seen from the above that the over-average yields were 34 bushels in 1868, 32 bushels in 1870, 31 bushels in 1874, and 30 bushels (barely exceeding an average) in 1878. The lightest yield in the series until the present year was 22 bushels in 1877, while 1875 gave only a bushel more. For 1879 our enquiries led us to the unprecedented and pitiful yield of only 18 bushels, net. We also find that the *progressive falling off in production is remarkable.* For the first five years of the series of 14 the average number of acres of wheat in the United Kingdom was 3,801,400; in the last five years the average has been only 3,279,400 acres, a decrease of nearly 14 per cent.; and whereas we produced in the first five years on the average about 12,800,000 quarters, in the last this had decreased to about 9,200,000 quarters, or no less than 28 per cent.: the produce of 1879 is reckoned at only 5,990,000 quarters.

In the next tabular statement are arranged side by side the estimated home production and the imports with the exports deducted; the two together making the total amount of wheat available for consumption in each of the 13 years 1866 to 1878:—

ESTIMATED CONSUMPTION AND HOME AND FOREIGN SUPPLY OF WHEAT FOR THE UNITED KINGDOM.

Harvest year, Sept. 1 to August 31.	Home produce available for consumption. Qrs.	Imports of wheat and flour, deducting exports. Qrs.	Total available for consumption. Qrs.	Average price of British wheat for 12 months July 1 to June 30.
1866-7	11,444,000	7,600,000	19,040,000	58s. 0d.
1867-8	10,390,000	9,010,000	19,400,000	69s. 3d.
1868-9	15,790,000	7,880,000	23,670,000	51s. 8d.
1869-70	12,490,000	9,580,000	22,070,000	45s. 11d.
1870-1	14,100,000	7,950,000	22,050,000	53s. 5d.
1871-2	11,970,000	9,320,000	21,290,000	55s. 3d.
1872-3	10,110,000	11,720,000	21,830,000	57s. 1d.
1873-4	10,550,000	11,230,000	21,780,000	61s. 3d.

APPENDIX IV.—*Continued.*

Harvest year, Sept. 1 to August 31.	Home produce available for consumption. Qrs.	Imports of wheat and flour, deducting exports. Qrs.	Total available for consumption. Qrs.	Average price of British wheat for 12 months July 1 to June 30.
1874-5	13,700,000	11,640,000	25,340,000	46s. 4d.
1875-6	9,124,000	13,940,000	23,064,000	46s. 3d.
1876-7	9,665,000	12,156,000	21,821,000	55s. 3d.
1877-8	9,432,000	14,508,000	21,940,000	54s. 0d.
1878-9	11,825,000	14,417,000	26,242,000	41s. 10d.
1879-80	5,990,000	18,309,000	24,000,000 ?	— —
Mean of 13 Years	11,583,000	10,842,000	22,425,000	53s. 6d.

I previously noticed the falling off of 28 per cent. in our internal product of wheat. The mean of 13 years ending 1878-9 shows an annual home production of 11,583,000 qrs., and imports 10,842,000 qrs., making the total mean consumption of wheat 22,425,000 qrs. While our home production has fallen off 28 per cent. comparing the first five with the last five years (in 14 years ending 1879), the imports have hugely increased. In the first five years we imported on an average 8,404,000 qrs., but in the last five years (ending 1878-9) the quantity averaged 13,332,000 qrs. per annum, or an increase of over 58 per cent. In the last two years we imported 14,508,000 and 14,417,000 qrs. respectively.

The quantity for consumption according to this estimate has varied from 19,000,000 qrs. up to more than 26,000,000 qrs., the mean of 13 years being 22,425,000 qrs. For the first five years it averaged 21,246,000 qrs.; for the last five years, 23,681,000 qrs. per annum. Assuming that our population will need 24,000,000 qrs. of wheat in the harvest year September 1, 1879, to August 31, 1880, we must import, according to this calculation, 18,000,000 qrs. in that time, or about 3½ million quarters more than arrived at our ports last year or in the year before. This would be purchasing from abroad three times as much wheat as we at home have available of this cereal during the present year.

If the farmers make 48s. 9d. per quarter by the present year's crop, it will realize no more than £5 9s. 8d. an acre, and for the last five years the crops have only averaged £7 6s. 1d per acre. Be the reason what it may, this country is becoming year by year more dependent on her external supply of food. Our interest is to see that that supply comes from as many sources as possible. Our external wheat supply cost us £35,000,000 last year; but, as the *Times* truly points out in a leading article, 'in the press of more lively matter (a Zulu war ?) it passed almost unobserved.'

With regard to the Canadian wheat, Mr. J.W. Taylor, United States Consul at Winnepeg during the last 13 years, and with previous experience in various parts of America, confirms the generally entertained opinion that the quality of the wheat improves as the northern limit of its cultivation is approached, and declares that the spring wheats grown in Manitobah will always bring five to ten cents a bushel more tnan those raised 200 miles south.

And now, with regard to price, Mr. Dalrymple and other large farmers who keep accounts and carefully calculate expenses, are satisfied that they can profitably grow wheat at from eight to nine dollars an acre (32s. to 36s.)

Now for the expenses of transit. Taking as fairly representative Mr. Dalyrmple's payments, we have 15 cents per bushel for railway carriage over 254 miles from Casselton to Duluth on Lake Superior. Although this would be considered a low freight in England, I am aware of wheat being carried in this country upwards of 500 miles for this moderate cost. At Duluth 1½ per cent. goes for elevator charges, warehousing, and winnowing, which probably causes a shrinkage of about half per cent., but which ensures the wheat being graded as No. 1 hard spring. Freight from Duluth to Montreal or New York will absorb, say, 15 cents, while the ocean transport will cost 18 cents, and marine insurance and commission on sale may be set down at 3 cents. For variation in transport charges and other contingencies throw in 12½ cents. The bushel of wheat delivered in the British port will thus be delivered at 1 dol. 10 c.—4s. 5d. per bushel, or 35s. 4d. per quarter. At this moderate price a profit accrues to grower, railway companies, shippers, and all concerned.

These figures, setting forth the cost of a bushel of wheat grown in Minnesota, Dakota, or Manitobah, and forwarded to Great Britain, are subjoined in tabular form:—

	Cents.
Cost of growing	45
Transit to Duluth or other entrepot	15
Elevator charges	1½
Transit to seaboard	15
Ocean freight	18
Marine insurance and commission	3
Contingencies for enhanced freight, &c.	12½
	110—4s. 5d.

Satisfactory as such figures are to the British consumer, they are not very encouraging to the British wheat grower. For his fuller berried wheat, richer in starch, but poorer in gluten, he certainly gets 3s. or 4s. per quarter more than can be had for the foreign spring wheat. But £2 or even two guineas a quarter, which is all that English wheat can be calculated to make on an average of years, cannot, under present conditions, remunerate the English agriculturist.

APPENDIX V.

TREATIES OF COMMERCE AND NAVIGATION BETWEEN GREAT BRITAIN AND FOREIGN POWERS.

In the summer of 1879 there were no less than 63 treaties of commerce and navigation in force between this country and foreign Powers. After having carefully examined these treaties, it appears that nearly all of them are applicable to the British 'dominions and possessions. With Borneo, however, the treaty is applicable to the British dominions in Europe and Asia only.' With France, the Netherlands, China, and Japan these treaties do *not apply to the British Colonies;* with Belgium a clause is inserted to the following effect :—

Import Duties.

Articles the produce or manufacture of Belgium shall not be subject in the British Colonies to other or higher duties than those which may be imposed *upon similar articles of British origin.* (Article XV.)

With the exception of this State I have named we appear to have bound ourselves by treaty stipulation with regard to the course of our trade relating with the British Colonies to the following extent only :—

Commerce and Navigation.

Her Majesty the Queen of the United Kingdom of Great Britain and Ireland engages further that the inhabitants of the Republic of Bolivia shall have the like liberty of commerce and navigation stipulated for in the preceding Article in all her dominions situated out of Europe to the full extent in which the same is permitted at present, *or shall be permitted hereafter, to any other nation.* (Article III.)

With regard to the 'most favoured nation treatment' of our commercial interchange, that appears, as far as I can see, to be stipulated in every treaty—in some *with certain reservations.* Several of these clauses in these treaties run as follows :—

SUBJECTS, COMMERCE AND NAVIGATION, FAVOURS, PRIVILEGES, AND IMMUNITIES.

It being the intention of the two High Contracting Parties to bind themselves by the two preceding Articles to treat each other on the footing of the most favoured nation, it is hereby agreed between them that any favour, privilege, or immunity whatever, in matters of commerce and navigation, which either Contracting Party has actually granted or may hereafter grant, to the subjects or citizens of any other State, shall be extended to the subjects or citizens of the other High Contracting Party gratuitously, if the concession in favour of that other nation shall have been gratuitous, or in return for a compensation as nearly as possible of proportionate value and effect, to be adjusted by mutual agreement, if the concession shall have been conditional. (Article IV.)

Import Duties. Produce and Manufactures.

No higher or other duties shall be imposed on the importation into the territories of Her Britannic Majesty of any articles of the growth, produce, or manufacture of the Equator, and no higher or other duties shall be imposed on the importation into the territories of the Equator of any articles af the growth, produce, or manufacture of Her Britannic Majesty's dominions, than are or shall be payable on the like articles, being the growth, produce, or manufacture of any other foreign country. (Article V.)

Treaties. When Terminable.

All these treaties of commerce appear to be terminable at the option of either of the High Contracting Parties, on giving notice, such notice is in no case required to exceed twelve months except in the case of the Chinese and Turkish treaties, the next break in the former treaty being in 1888, and in the latter in 1882.

APPENDIX VI.

PROVISIONAL COMMERCIAL AGREEMENT BETWEEN THE BRITISH AND FRENCH GOVERNMENTS.

The British and French Governments have agreed to prolong for a period of *six months* the Conventional Acts in force between Great Britain and France, which would have terminated on the 31st December, 1879. To quote this declaration signed at Paris, October 10th, 1879 :—

The Government of Her Britannic Majesty and the Government of the French Republic, foreseeing the case in which the commercial and maritime relations between Great Britain and France should not have been settled by fresh arrangements before the 31st December, 1879, the period at which the existing Commercial Treaties and Conventions are to expire, and wishing to secure for the manufacturers and merchants of both countries a sufficient delay to conclude the operations in course of execution,—

Have agreed to prolong, for a period of six months before their definite termination, the Conventional Acts in force between Great Britain and France.

Considering, besides, that, according to the terms of the Law passed in France on the 4th August last, which confers on the Government of the Republic the power of prolonging the Commercial Treaties and Conventions, the duration of their prolongation cannot exceed six months from the pro mulgation of the new General Customs Tariff submitted to the approbato n of the French Chambers,—

The High Contracting Parties agree that the stipulated delay of six months shall commence from the day either anterior or posterior to the 1st January, 1880, on which the new General Customs Tariff shall have been promulgated.

The benefit of the prolongation shall apply to the Conventional Acts enumerated hereafter, that is to say :—

1. Treaty of Commerce of the 23rd January, 1860.
2. Additional Article of the 25th February, 1860.
3. Second Additional Article of the 27th June, 1860.
4. First Supplementary Convention of the 12th October, 1860.
5. Second Supplementary Convention of the 16th November, 1860.
6. Treaty of Commerce and Navigation of the 23rd July, 1873.
7. Supplementary Convention of the 24th January, 1874.
8. Declaration of the 24th January, 1874.

In witness, whereof, the Undersigned, acting in the name of their respective Governments, have drawn up the present Declaration, and have affixed thereto the seal of their arms.

Done in duplicate, at Paris, the 10th day of October, 1879.

(L.S.) F. O. ADAMS.
(L.S.) WADDINGTON.

So our merchants and statesmen have to wait till next summer for the decision of the French Republic.

APPENDIX VII.

THE OPIUM TRADE TO CHINA.

It may not be uninteresting to notice that which Mr. Gardner, British Consul at Chefoo, reports on this subject—

"The question of the morality of the opium trade seems to be exciting much attention at home, and as influential persons have expressed opinions on the subject founded, I conceive, on misinformation and misconception, a few facts may not be out of place.

"Opium smokers are of three classes—1st, occasional smokers; 2nd, habitual smokers, who smoke in moderation but have not got a craving; 3rd, habitual smokers, who smoke in excess and have the craving. When it is said of a Chinaman that he smokes opium, it is meant that he belongs to the third class, just as with us the expression a man drinks means he drinks too much. Sir Thomas Wade is stated to have estimated the number of opium smokers to be 5 per cent. of the adult population. If this estimate includes the first and second class, I should say it was too low; if it refers only to the third class, I should say it was too high.

"The average amount of foreign opium consumed in China is about 12,000,000 lbs. per annum; probably 5,000,000 more of native opium is produced. In smoking, only a portion of the opium is consumed; the ash is reprepared, and yields 50 per cent. of opium. It is this ash that enables the opinm saloon to sell opium at apparently cost price, the ash paying for the light, attendance, house rent, and profit. Deducting the unconsumed opium, few moderate smokers consume more than 1¼ lbs. a year, while occasional smokers do not consume more than an ounce or so. The most immoderate smoker does not consume more than 4 lbs. I think it would be about correct to reckon ¼ lb. as the average annual consumption of all classes of smokers. This would make the smokers half the adult population. This result accords with the estimate given me by a native gentleman, who, in his official position as district magistrate, in various parts of China, had caused returns to be given him by the heads of clans and elders of villages, and was therefore in a peculiarly favourable position to form an estimate It also accords with the estimate of the late Mr. Taintor, Statistical Secretary of the Foreign Inspectorate.

"It is difficult to bring an indictment against half a nation; and the question arises, if opium smoking is the great evil it is represented, how is it, that after so many years no inherited ill effects are visible."

Then he proceeds to point out that it has a beneficial effect in one respect in so much as it gives the population a comparative immunity from diseases of the bronchial tubes and lungs; and he also states that large numbers told him their first motive for smoking opium was to check the spitting of blood to which they had become subject.

"In the end of 1865," he adds, " being attacked with a severe fever which left me so weak that I gave up hopes of recovery, I felt justified in trying upon myself the experiment of moderate opium smoking.

"The following were the results:—

1. Temptation to excess greater than in the case of alcohol.
2. Excessive diminution of the memory.
3. Utter indifference to cares and anxieties.
4. I only had one opium vision, and that was after ten hours' hard smoking without intermission; the vision was of a pleasurable kind: the curtains of my couch extended, and I fancied I saw 'The Tempest' acted by real ' Anelo ' and ' Prosperos.'
5. A few months' excessive smoking produced the cravings of opiomania.
6. That the physical difficulty in breaking off the habit is greater, and the moral difficulty less in opiomania than in dipsomania.

"The argument that those who use a commodity as a medicine and harmless luxury shall not be deprived of it because weaker brethren abuse it is stronger in the case of opium than in that of alcohol. No one is maddened by smoking opium to crimes of violence, nor does the habit of smoking increase the criminal returns or swell the number of prison inmates.

"The abolition of the monopoly in India would swell rather than diminish the consumption in China. The attempt to prohibit the importation of the foreign drug, or to raise a prohibitive tax on it, would, with regard to an article so easy to smuggle, be followed by a state of affairs like that existing before 1840.

"The real remedy for the excess of opium smoking lies in the development of the resources of the country, whereby the people would be enriched sufficiently to inhabit healthy houses and partake of wholesome food, in which case the abuse of opium would die out in China, as the abuse of laudanum has died out in Lincolnshire after the draining of the fens."

There is said to be a very much larger demand for many descriptions of foreign goods such as lamps, cutlery, &c., springing up in China. One reason that has hitherto checked one branch of trade Mr. Gardner notices; painting this cause, however, one can hardly doubt, in unduly dark colours.

"Other adverse influences have tended to check our trade. Foremost among these, is the depreciation in the value of silver, commencing after the Franco-German war of 1870. After the payment of the war indemnity, China was flooded with silver from Germany, and since then the enormous out-turns of the Nevada mines have run down the price of silver. Our manufacturers have felt the effect of this very severely, and the American manufacturers have been placed at a great advantage. To counteract these disadvantages, Manchester hit upon the desperate remedy of heavily sizing its textiles; I say nothing of the morality of the practice, but there is a Chinese proverb that 'the conjuror does not deceive the man who beats the gong for him,' and the attempt to sell glue as cloth to a people as skilled as the Chinese are in the arts of putting iron filings and cactus leaves in tea, and water in silk, was certainly injudicious. The consequence is, our textiles have got a bad name in the country; the demand for them is yearly decreasing, and their place is being supplied by American manufacures.

APPENDIX VII.—*Continued.*

"American drills, though 40 per cent. dearer, are driving English drills out of the market. Last year the imports to this port, (Chefoo) were respectively—

	Pieces.
English drills	14,673
American ,,	58,108
English sheetings	871
American ,,	59,943

"JAPANESE FOREIGN LOAN.

Sir H. Parkes, H.B.M. Minister in Japan, states in his last published report:—The statement of the national liabilities this year (1878) shows that Japan has kept faith with her foreign creditors, the interest on her foreign debt and the sum requisite for the payment of the amount of capital redeemable during the year having been duly provided. The sum total of this debt is now £2,524,814, being a reduction of £154,989 since last year. There is no reason to doubt that care will be taken to ensure punctual payment future on this account until the entire extinction of this debt in 1895."

In fact, some nations of the East could give others in the West a good example in commercial integrity and also in proving the promise of their Government to be a " bond."

APPENDIX VIII.

BRITISH BOARD OF TRADE RETURNS.

The full Board of Trade Returns for 1879 are not published till next August (1880), namely, the "Annual Statement of the Trade of the United Kingdom with Foreign Countries and British Possessions;" and "The Statistical Abstract."—"Last year" in this volume refers to 1878, the *last year* of which the returns are now published. Looking at the accounts relating to the Trade and Navigation of the United Kingdom, published for each month of 1879, I find that in the one for November (published 9th December, 1879), the total declared value of the exports for November was £17,051,955, against £15,961,669 in November, 1878, and £16,753,364 in November, 1877. The total value of the exports for the past eleven months of the year was £174,916,052, against £178,143,305 in 1878, and £182,811,576 in 1877.

The total value of the imports for November was £34,343,388, against £25,684,557 in November, 1878, and £31,849,648 in November, 1877. The total value of the imports during the past eleven months was £326,806,185, against £338,982,932 in 1878, and £361,045,053 in 1877.

It will be seen that for these eleven months both our exports and imports were of less value than those of 1878. And, also, that during the month of November the value of our imports exceeded that of exports by more than two to one. Our exports for November, 1879, exceeded those of November, 1878, by about one million sterling, and our imports were nearly nine millions' sterling in excess.

Turning to the relative value of the price paid for our exports and imports, we find that in 1879 we sold our goods at a less rate than in November, 1878, whilst the price paid for our imports was considerably higher. The million sterling of goods exported from these shores, in excess of 1878, was mainly owing to our increased supply of iron to the United States.

Turning to our textile manufactures, we find the value of our exportation of cotton goods, in November, 1879, to have been slightly in excess of that in November, 1878. A marked falling off of this manufactured product is to be noticed to Germany, counterbalanced by an increase to China, Hong Kong, and Japan. Neither in linen nor woollen goods did we export to the same value as in the same month in the previous year. British North America showing a marked falling off in her demand for woollen goods.

The traffic returns of many of our principal lines have for the last few months improved, those showing the greatest increase in their goods traffic being lines like the "London and North-Western" and "Midland," chiefly affected by our increased exportation of iron, and also by our increased importation of grain from America, to be distributed throughout the length and breadth of the United Kingdom. This work being of a non-political character, no reference can be here made as to the probable revenue returns of the United Kingdom for the current year.

NOTE.—Although the Canadian Militia and Defence Act authorizes the formation of a Marine Militia, no force of this description has hitherto been enrolled in the Dominion. On page 354, 21st line from the top, read "is allowed as" instead of "is allowed us."

www.ingramcontent.com/pod-product-compliance
Lightning Source LLC
Chambersburg PA
CBHW022135300426
44115CB00006B/199